BORDERLAND LIVES
IN NORTHERN SOUTH ASIA

Edited by
David N. Gellner

With an afterword by
Willem van Schendel

Orient BlackSwan

ORIENT BLACKSWAN PRIVATE LIMITED

Registered Office
3-6-752 Himayatnagar, Hyderabad 500 029 (A.P.), India
Email: centraloffice@orientblackswan.com

Other Offices
Bangalore, Bhopal, Chennai, Ernakulam, Guwahati, Hyderabad,
Jaipur, Kolkata, Lucknow, Mumbai, New Delhi, Noida, Patna

Borderland Lives in Northern South Asia
© 2013 by Duke University Press. Reprinted by permission.

First published in India by
Orient Blackswan Private Limited 2014

ISBN 978 81 250 5423 8

Printed in India at
Yash Printographics
Noida

Published by
Orient Blackswan Private Limited
1/24 Asaf Ali Road
New Delhi 110 002
Email: delhi@orientblackswan.com

For sale only in India, Pakistan, Nepal, Bhutan, Bangladesh, Sri Lanka and
the Maldives

CONTENTS

PREFACE

The papers collected in this volume were first presented at the British Association of South Asian Studies (BASAS) annual conference in Edinburgh on 31 March 2009. This could not have happened without the support of the British Academy through a grant from its Area Panel for South Asia; I am grateful for its support and encouragement of young 'peridoctoral' scholars. I would also like to thank BASAS for helping us to invite Willem van Schendel to come as the panel discussant and the British Embassy Kathmandu, which enabled the journalist Prashant Jha's participation. Their comments and presentations greatly enriched our discussions.

Chapters 5 and 10 have appeared previously and are republished with permission (from *Contemporary South Asia,* Taylor and Francis, and *Modern Asian Studies,* Cambridge University Press, respectively). The maps were drawn (except where otherwise attributed) by Bill Nelson.

In this volume double quotation marks are used to indicate a citation from an identifiable source, whether written or oral (even when pseudonyms have been used). Single quotation marks are used for everything else (talking about words, scare quotes, etc.). We have also adopted the convention that when discussing the state as an idea or a nation-state the word 'state' remains uncapitalized, but when mentioning the various States of the Indian Union (Uttar Pradesh, Arunachal Pradesh, etc.), it is capitalized.

Northern South Asia's Diverse Borders, from Kachchh to Mizoram

The human being is the connecting creature who must always separate
and cannot connect without separating. . . . And the human being is
likewise the bordering creature who has no border.
—Simmel, "Bridge and Door" ([1909] 1994: 10)

This book proposes a new subregion: Northern South Asia.[1] The locations of
the book's detailed case studies are strung out along India's mainly mountainous northern borders that enclose this subregion. The authors address three
bodies of literature that have rarely been brought into conjunction before:
(1) new writings, largely (but not only) by anthropologists, that focus on how
ordinary people interact with, engage with, and experience the state in South
Asia (e.g., Fuller and Bénéï 2001); (2) recent work invigorated by a renewed
awareness of the dynamic relationship between upland and lowland peoples
or, as James C. Scott (2009) would have it, between people of the state and
people fleeing the state; and (3) work on borderlands, a topic that is old enough
to have spawned a whole subdiscipline in North America and to a lesser extent
in Europe, but which, as a focus of sustained academic investigation, is new
for South Asianists. Thus we are fortunate to have Willem van Schendel as the
author of the afterword to this volume, as he has done more than anyone to
demonstrate the fruitfulness of the academic study of borders in South Asia.
His publications are used and debated at numerous places in the pages that
follow.

The conjunction of these three themes puts both the state and its borders under the spotlight and undermines the unthinking methodological nationalism (so common in academia and policy circles) that takes the nation-state as the natural context and container for all social and political processes. In this volume neither the existence of borders nor their exact positioning nor what they imply for the movement of people, animals, or goods is taken for granted. As will be seen, these matters are also very far from being taken for granted by the people whose lives they affect, as we attempt to describe here. In interaction with the representatives of the states concerned and with other people they encounter on either side, Northern South Asians both produce and suffer from that most paradoxical of human creations: borders.

Studying the State, Studying Its Borders:
Radcliffe-Brown, Scott, Anderson, and Beyond

In 1940—a very different era—A. R. Radcliffe-Brown, one of the founding figures of British social anthropology, denounced the idea of the state as "a fiction of the philosophers."[2] Anthropologists should have nothing to do with it, he wrote, and should restrict themselves to studying government and politics. In an influential article, often cited as initiating a new turn in the anthropological study of the state, the historical sociologist Philip Abrams suggested that students of the modern state should follow Radcliffe-Brown's lead and dispense entirely with 'the state' as a category of analysis. Rather they should study the "*idea* of the state." Abrams argued that students of politics should no more be obliged to 'believe in' the state and accept its reality than sociologists of religion are called on to believe in the system of gods or spiritual beings whose existence they are studying and about which they are attempting to give a coherent account (Abrams 1988: 79–80).[3] There was some irony in Abrams's invocation of Radcliffe-Brown, since his theoretical standpoint, general aims, and style of argument were all very different from Radcliffe-Brown's starchy high-colonial positivism. Radcliffe-Brown wished to banish all talk of the state from serious empirical study; Abrams wished to put talk of the state at the heart of his analysis. Despite this, Radcliffe-Brown's insistence on the unreality of the state has gone on to be endorsed by anthropologists (e.g., Gupta 1995: 398n63) who are even further than Abrams was from Radcliffe-Brown's theoretical premises: functionalism comes full circle to Foucault, one might say.

Today ethnographers everywhere are increasingly forced to think about the state because it intrudes, far more forcibly than it did seventy years ago, on the lives of the people they study (Trouillot 2001). People themselves are no longer content to view the state as a necessary evil. Increasingly they make demands of it and expect it to act positively to improve their lives. In the study of South Asia this has led to what might appear, at first glance, to be two contrasting trends: on the one hand, the study of the 'everyday state,' how people actually interact with the state and what they expect from it (e.g., Gupta 1995; Fuller and Bénéï 2001; Tarlo 2003; Corbridge et al. 2005), and, on the other, following Abrams's call, studies of the *idea* of the state, the 'state effect,' as it has been called (e.g., Khilnani 1997; Spencer 2007; cf. Hansen and Stepputat 2001). In fact, of course, the two kinds of study necessarily overlap: ordinary people must have ideas about the state in order to interact with it, and any worthwhile ethnographic investigation must engage with both practices and ideas. When people's expectations of what their state can and should do for them are frustrated, there is fuel for all kinds of movement and protest. Under certain circumstances this is transformed into the aspiration to acquire a state (or federal unit, i.e., State) of one's own (as with the Nagas described in chapter 7).

Alongside people's understandable desires to influence the state or control it, there is also a long tradition—to which Scott (2009) has recently resensitized us in *The Art of Not Being Governed*—of evading the state and adopting ways of living that enable survival beyond its reach. Scott focused on highland areas as zones of resistance to state domination, particularly in Southeast Asia. Following Van Schendel (2002a), Scott refers to the whole upland area of Southeast Asia, stretching up to Tibet and including the eastern Himalayas, as 'Zomia,' a historical and cultural region that is either rendered invisible or carved up artificially by the usual area studies geographical divisions into East Asia, Southeast Asia, and South Asia. (On Zomia and area studies, see further Farrelly in chapter 8, this volume.)

Scott has a (perhaps unrecognized) distinguished forerunner in his namesake, the novelist Sir Walter Scott. Walter Scott was fascinated by the historical sociology of highland-lowland relationships in Scotland. He was very far from being the early nineteenth-century combination of *Braveheart* with Mills and Boon of popular stereotype; he was in fact a nuanced and sophisticated observer of Scottish history and society (Kidd 1993: 256–67), capable of seeing both sides and multiple points of view—as indeed should strike any reader of *Rob Roy*. One of the epigrams chosen as a chapter heading in *Rob*

Roy is taken from the poet Thomas Gray's "The Alliance of Education and Government: A Fragment" (1748):

> An iron race the mountain cliffs maintain,
> Foes to the gentler genius of the plain . . .
> Who, while their rocky ramparts round they see,
> The rough abode of want and liberty,
> As lawless force from confidence will grow,
> Insult the plenty of the vales below.[4]

"The rough abode of want and liberty": James Scott could have taken that as the motto of his Zomian highlands.

James Scott explicitly excludes most of the Himalayas from his discussion (perhaps because the Himalayas were home to small states themselves). But there are good arguments for extending his mode of argument westward, since these mountainous areas have also provided a home to plenty of refugees from the state. Much of the behavior of Himalayan peoples in Nepal can be interpreted within Scott's 'state-evading' paradigm. As Shneiderman (2010) points out, such state-evading strategies are still a deep part of the habitus of many people in the Himalayas, even today. In that sense 'Zomia thinking,' contrary to what Scott himself sometimes seems to suggest, is, as argued by Farrelly in chapter 8, far from wholly superseded.[5] Though this collection does not venture that far west, there would surely be mileage in extending the argument into Pakistan and Afghanistan as well. Furthermore, as Piliavsky points out in chapter 1, such state-evading behavior was formerly as salient *within* the borders of the state, associated with its internal borders (in the Indian case, marking police jurisdictions); today the inheritors of these evasive strategies have become so embroiled with the state that its borderlines determine the main outlines of their social organization.

There is a much longer tradition of thinking about borders within human geography than within anthropology, but both disciplines have converged on approaches that see borders as constructed through the action of states and individuals, a process that some have named territorialization. Borderland studies have tended to be dominated by North American and European examples.[6] Since the international (and indeed current internal) borders of South Asia are so new, much can be learned of a general and comparative nature by focusing on them. For a start, as Van Schendel has pointed out, a critical focus on borderlands is a highly effective way to escape from the often stultifying methodological nationalism of much conventional historical and social scientific work on South Asia.[7] This methodological nationalism takes for granted national units that have in many cases existed only for a very short time, leading to considerable distortions of the historical record and great lacunae in what is studied. Instead borders, states, and the people who inhabit all need to be taken as processes, not givens, and the manner in which they are produced and made to appear as given needs to be studied critically and, so far as humanly possible, dispassionately.

In order to understand this process of territorialization, it is necessary to look at the history of neighboring peoples and states side by side and in interaction with each other (all the interactions, namely, of people and state, people and people, and state and state, on both sides of the dividing line). The creation of the new nations of South Asia has had far-reaching effects on ordinary people's lives. This includes enormous suffering, not usually acknowledged in dominant narratives, of people who have found themselves near to these militarily enforced and unaccustomed lines on the map (see, especially, chapters 2, 5, 6, 9, and 10).[8] Evans shows in chapter 5 how listening to the narratives of the ordinary borderland people caught up in the tragedy of expulsions from southern Bhutan allows one to comprehend the seemingly completely incompatible accounts of the Bhutanese state and the refugee leaders in Nepal.

Following Scott, it is worth stressing that one key variable in determining how people experience and create borders is whether the terrain is in the highlands (meaning that the population is generally sparse) or the lowlands (where the population is usually dense and frequently culturally and linguistically continuous across frontiers). A second key variable is the way people imagine the border: whether as hard (modern) or soft (premodern). With all due caution about the distinction and in full recognition that these are ideal types—models, if you will—that will necessarily not correspond in every particular to the complexities of actual contemporary or historical cases, with due allowance for all this, there is a key difference in the conceptualization of borders between the premodern and the modern periods. Many have quoted Curzon's (1907) forthright statement: "The idea of a demarcated frontier is in itself an essentially modern conception, and finds little or no place in the ancient world."

Benedict Anderson (1991: chapter 10) has famously analyzed the emergence of the modern notion of territory in terms of the census and the map, and Mathur (chapter 3, this volume) applies these ideas to the India-China (Tibet) border. Thongchai Winichakul's work (1994) on the history of maps and nationalism in Thailand, earlier versions of which were heavily used by Anderson, also posits a radical difference in the ways borders and the nation came to be understood once King Rama V established a mapping school in Bangkok in 1882 and modern ideas of mapping were adopted. A telling example of the clash between modernizing ideas of borders and those subject to them holding very different ideas is given by Peter Robb (1997: 263–64). In 1881 a British colonial official in Assam led a punitive expedition against a village beyond the border because one of its members had committed a murder of someone living on the British side; the villagers all fled, so the soldiers burned the village; neighboring villagers, impressed, came forward and offered tribute to the British, but the official refused to accept it, on the grounds that the villagers were not British subjects, being on the other side of the border. What the villagers made of this strange refusal is apparently not recorded.

Boundaries in a broader sense—whether cultural, religious, linguistic, social, political, or various combinations—have always been there in South Asia; the barriers they place between different categories of people and the ways they are transgressed or ignored have long been the stuff of South Asian history and anthropology. The challenge, then, is to be as critical and constructivist about national and internal borders as anthropologists have learned to be about ethnic and other social boundaries, at least since the time of Barth's (1969) seminal intervention on ethnicity in Pakistan. Mitchell (1991) recommends that studies of the state should problematize the state-society boundary; this is even more necessary for the understanding of border regions, where it may appear that there is a sharp distinction between state personnel and everyone else (see Joshi, chapter 7, and Farrelly, chapter 8, this volume). These state personnel, and their view of their world, must also be a part of any understanding of the situation on the ground, as stressed in several of the contributions to this volume (chapters 1, 3, 4, 6, and 6).[9]

Northern South Asia and Its Margins

Nepal, Sri Lanka, Bhutan, and Bangladesh face many challenges, and they are not all the same. However, all four countries must confront one big problem that can be summed up in a single word: India. India's size, power, military strength, and latterly global economic success, all combine to make the smaller countries in the region feel that it has simply inherited the mantle of the former colonial power and adopts a paternalistic, not to say patronizing and sometimes overbearing, attitude to its neighbors. What is incontestable is that India inherited a colonial and indeed premodern set of borders along its northwestern, northern, and northeastern frontiers. They are 'premodern' in the sense that in practice—whatever the spurious precision of the lines drawn or claimed in treaties and maps—they are fuzzy and contested, and also because in many places along the borders the local populations have strong ties across them and often carry on daily life in disregard or even (in the past) in ignorance of them.

If we focus on the region rather than the borders, the area that concerns us here may be called 'Northern South Asia.' This regional expression was invented by Hiroshi Ishii, Katsuo Nawa, and myself,[10] when we were editing two volumes at the Tokyo University of Foreign Studies in 2004 (Ishii et al. 2007a, 2007b); there were contributions that ranged from Gujarat and Rajasthan in the west to Bengal and Orissa in the east, taking in many parts of Nepal. We argued that there were interesting cultural commonalities across the region so named, despite its division into different nation-states.

Northern South Asia is in fact a region crisscrossed by international borders, as the maps in this book demonstrate. Apart from the Nepal-China (Tibet) and Bhutan-China (Tibet) borders, they are all borders with India. It is India's international borders that present the most interesting and challenging variety—challenging both to the state and the scholar. Van Schendel (2007) has usefully distinguished three categories of border issues that today plague India and its northern neighbors: McMahonian (i.e., those between India and China, resulting from the McMahon line of 1914), Radcliffean (dating from Partition in 1947, i.e., those between India and Pakistan and India and Bangladesh), and Kashmirian (i.e., disputes thrown up by the merging of the approximately five hundred princely states into India, of which Kashmir was simply the largest and most intractable). All three types of dispute have led to violence that politicians have struggled to control.

Premodern states, such as China in the nineteenth century, frequently resisted attempts by colonial powers to establish unambiguous borders.[11] Stiller (1976: 217–27) has described how the Gorkhali state in the early nineteenth century initially resisted the British East India Company's attempt to fix the borders, and how Prime Minister Bhimsen Thapa eventually came to understand and use the British notion of an unambiguous dividing line to Nepal's advantage.[12] China, although it now accepts the idea of clearly demarcated borders, refuses to accept the McMahon line, both in the west and the east. For this reason, and because of intractable problems in Kashmir, in most of the west and northwest India's frontiers are heavily militarized and movement across the border is highly restricted or impossible.[13] Notoriously families have been split in two and have not met for decades, with travel difficult and only occasionally permitted. In chapter 2 Radhika Gupta describes the situation in Kargil, where a strong Shi'a Muslim identity, looking to Iran for religious leadership, is combined with Indian patriotism, strong identification with the Indian state, and deep hurt at suspicions of their loyalty. A similarly militarized situation exists in the northeast, where China claims parts of Arunachal Pradesh. The Indian border with Burma, though equally militarily sensitive, is not closed in the same way; access for nonlocals is strictly controlled, but locals can move across it at will. The Indian army is supposed to control movement, but the ability of insurgents to move freely to and fro across the border is a factor the army on the ground has to deal with on a daily basis.[14]

Where India's border with Nepal is concerned, there is a completely different situation: an open border, a border that for many purposes is not what we think of as a border at all. People move freely across it, and it corresponds to no geographical, linguistic, religious, or cultural dividing line (Gaige [1975] 2009; Hausner 2007a). Indian rupees and Indian mobile phones work just fine on the Nepalese side of the border. In April 2008, at a time when the border was declared 'sealed' for the Nepalese Constituent Assembly elections, I saw children walk from the Indian district of West Champaran into the Nepalese district of Parsa and then back into India on their way to school. A single large-bellied Indian policeman manned the border, and the crossing was closed to vehicular traffic, including bicycles. But he permitted people on foot to wander over to the other side at will.[15]

That India regards the Nepal-India and Bhutan-India borders as qualitatively different from its borders with Pakistan and Bangladesh is shown by the fact that the former two are policed by its SSB (Sashastra Seema Bal), whereas the latter are guarded by the BSF (Border Security Force, or Seema Suraksa Bal in Hindi).[16] Despite the fact that the names are easy to confuse, they are two independent organizations. The SSB was founded in 1963 to win the hearts and minds of people in the northeast and Himalayas following the India-China war of 1962 and was entrusted with the guarding of borders in 2001 and 2004.[17] The BSF was set up in 1965 specifically in order to guard

India's borders with Pakistan, subsequently also being used for antiterrorist operations in Kashmir.[18]

Though it was once as open as the Nepal-India border, the situation on the India-Bhutan border would seem to be evolving toward a 'hard' border of the kind aimed at for contemporary Pakistan and Bangladesh. Access today is strictly controlled by the Bhutanese army. Refugees sometimes cross the border surreptitiously to visit their relatives in Bhutan, but it is an exchange fraught with danger on both sides (see Evans, chapter 5).

The India-Bangladesh Borderlands:
The Anomalous *Chhitmahals*

Between these two extremes—highly militarized exclusion zones and borders that are not borders—lies the India-Bangladesh border. In parts it is effectively like the India-Nepal border, porous and ignored for many everyday purposes. Yet in other places the Indian and Bangladeshi states are an ever greater presence, with India having built a fence to keep Bangladeshis out on over half of the total 4,200-kilometer length (the longest border India has with any other country; see figure Intro.1).

The Bangladesh-India border also presents us with the intriguing and— for those who live in them—highly problematic phenomenon of *chhitmahals*. These are islands of territory belonging to one country surrounded by the territory of the other. There are in fact 123 Indian enclaves inside Bangladesh and seventy-four Bangladeshi enclaves inside India (Van Schendel 2002b). They are a leftover of the indirectly ruled princely state of Cooch Behar (which had pockets inside Mughal territory) and, vice versa, of Mughal territory that lay inside Cooch Behar (now Bangladeshi enclaves in India). There is also a popular myth (repeated in Sunday supplements in the Indian press) that these enclaves were created by the two rulers of the respective territories, who used to gamble villages with each other over football matches. There do not seem to be historical grounds for this story, but it is clearly still in circulation as it was repeated to me in January 2009 in Kathmandu.

Van Schendel has argued cogently that if we are to study the state effect, if we wish to understand Partition and what followed from it, we need to take seriously the experiences and history of the people whose lives were turned upside down by the creation of new international borders where none had existed before. Without moving, without being consulted, many found

FIGURE INTRO.1. Looking north along the India-Bangladesh border in South Tripura district, Tripura, with Bangladesh on the left, behind the barbed-wire fence, 2011. Photograph courtesy of W. van Schendel.

themselves, from one day to the next, being turned into citizens of new states and separated from relatives and neighbors in completely unexpected and unprecedented ways. Where the border runs along a river, the same thing can still happen overnight during the monsoon: people wake up to find that the river—the border—has changed its course.

As a Bangladesh specialist, Van Schendel had to confront the fact that almost all the districts of Bangladesh, bar a couple of central districts, were and are border districts. The entire frontier of what is Bangladesh today and was East Pakistan in 1947 was created ex nihilo from areas that had never before been international or even major regional frontiers. Van Schendel demolishes the myth that the border demarcated Hindu (on the Indian side) from Muslim (on the Bangladeshi) side; this was true for just 26 percent of its length. For the rest of it there were either Muslims on both sides, Hindus on both sides, non-Hindus on one or other or both sides, and so on (Van Schendel 2005a: ch. 3). This sheer complexity means that one could write as many as a dozen histories and anthropologies of the Bangladesh-India border (just two are included here, chapters 9 and 10).

Jason Cons (chapter 9) has studied in one of the larger chhitmahals, Dahagram, home to sixteen thousand Bangladeshis, where the contrast is the expected one, that is, it is largely between Muslims inside the Dahagram enclave and Hindus outside it. There the local experience has indeed been of harassment by Indians—both by locals who rustle their goats and by the Indian Border Security Force—and attachment to Bangladesh. For years the people of Dahagram have fought for a regularized crossing point so that they can enter Bangladesh freely. At night they are effectively locked in their enclave. In a formal sense, their situation is better than that of most other enclaves, since at least they know (since 1992) that during the daylight hours they may cross the 85-meter corridor to 'mainland' Bangladesh (Van Schendel 2002b: 139). In Dahagram Bangladeshi identity is strongly asserted, unlike in other enclaves where 'statelessness' has become a kind of positively asserted identity for some (139). However, in the smaller enclaves people also often manage to hold citizenship of the surrounding country, so in that sense their situation may be more livable than that of the Dahagram residents.

Summing up, Van Schendel (2002b: 141) concludes, "Although they appear as 'foreign' bodies within the nation's territory, each nation is able by means of its own enclaves to penetrate the other's territory. This interpenetration has led the two nations to dance to the same tune, locked in a slow tango from which they have been unable to extricate themselves." The India-Bangladesh border was produced in a hurry by people with no knowledge of the conditions on the ground. Attempts to make it behave like a modern 'hard' border are undermined not only by the existence of chhitmahals but by siltation, shifting of rivers, and adverse possession (see Cons, chapter 9). As Jalais shows in chapter 10, people on the ground have taken it into their own hands to tidy up the process of nation building, harassing Muslims on the Indian side and Hindus on the East Pakistan/Bangladesh side, until they are induced to leave.

A Sketch of the Premodern State

In order to understand this seemingly anomalous situation of the chhitmahals we need to step back and put a little more substance into the contrast between premodern and modern states. Anthropologists such as Geertz (1980), with his sketch of the theater state, and Tambiah ([1977] 1985), with his theory of the galactic polity, have built on classic accounts (e.g., Heine-Geldern 1942) in writing about the monarchical states of South and Southeast Asia. The key points about such polities were that (1) people were in scarce supply and land was generally plentiful (land without people was useless), and (2) power radiated out from the center; there was no conception that the ruler's command could or should be equally authoritative at all points of his realm. A third point followed from these: boundaries were fluid and messy. Sovereignties overlapped. It seems to have been in the interests of both rulers and ruled to encourage a situation in which the map was pockmarked with alternating and often multiple lines of allegiance.[19]

It is true that sometimes the state produced straight lines and even walls; one thinks of the Great Wall of China and Hadrian's wall. But the extent to which these were 'hard' boundaries should not be exaggerated; often they functioned more like glorified lookout posts. China's Great Wall did not stop the Mongols. In general, lines drawn on the ground were foreign to the premodern polity. Even where nature appeared to draw a clear boundary, with a sea, a broad river, or the foothills of a mountain range, people frequently moved across it with impunity.

The consequence for border areas before the rise of the modern state is that they simultaneously have multiple allegiances and none. If people are mobile (i.e., they are pastoralists, swidden agriculturalists, or foragers), they simply run away from rulers and are impossible to pin down. They may interact with the state, they may imitate the state, they may have deep-rooted and long-standing economic ties to the state, they may even raid or seek to dominate nearby settled agricultural areas (Wouters 2011), but they cannot, taken as a whole, be controlled or enslaved by it. As Scott (2009) has emphasized, where the terrain favors it, there are large areas that remain beyond the effective control of the state.

The essential contrast is between (relatively) mobile uplanders and the rice cultivators of the more densely populated lowlands. The latter leave their fields only to escape the most severe tyranny. Because rice ripens at the same time (unlike the staples of upland peoples), the representatives of the state need only turn up at harvest time to collect tribute. Those who grow the crop have no alternative but to accept the legitimacy of the demand and pay up. As a strategy of resistance to the state, rice agriculturalists do not have the option of flight and must instead cultivate social and cultural impenetrability, often thickly camouflaged as deference.[20] Geertz (1980) has described this well in his description of the highly ritualized nineteenth-century Balinese state. The Balinese peasants' cross-cutting social ties were so complex that the rulers had little chance of controlling village society effectively and had to try to persuade them through sheer ritual and symbolic impressiveness to hand over tribute and participate in state rituals. In such a society people had rights, but there was absolutely no idea that everyone had the same rights; rights, owned by specified groups, were handed down and validated by tradition.

Thus throughout Asia there was a contrast between urban civilization and the wild people beyond. In South Asia the wild areas and people were known as *jangali* (of the 'jungle' or wilderness) and could be found wherever there were hills and forests. The British called them 'tribes,' a terminology inherited, deepened, and turned into the basis of political classification and action by the postcolonial Indian state.[21] The most heavily tribal parts of India are now the heartland of Maoist/Naxalite action, the so-called red belt from Nepal in the north to Andhra in the south ('Pashupati to Tirupati')—an internal Other par excellence. Piliavsky in chapter 1 reminds us of modern fantasy novels that associate borderlands with ghouls, witchcraft, and danger; these same associations are made with borderlands in South and Southeast Asia today, building on old stereotypes.

Historically most of the Himalayan foothills of Nepal fit the mobile uplands pattern, even where people were rice cultivators in part. People moved all the time. There have been continual waves of migration into and along the Himalayas, and we can assume this must have been so even in prehistoric times. Within historic times the dominant trend has been for migration to be in a northwest to southeast direction along the Himalayan foothills. Thus the Khas people, who are mentioned in textual sources (the *Mahabharata*, among others) as inhabiting Kashmir, are to be found as the 'indigenous' and majority group in western Nepal today. The predominant eastward direction can be explained by the greater rainfall and greater fertility of the land the farther east one goes (Whelpton 2005: 13). As the Khas moved southeast along the Himalayan foothills they encountered peoples speaking Tibeto-Burman languages who were already settled in the area we now call the Nepalese middle hills (having arrived centuries earlier either from the north or the east). In addition to the overall macro west-to-east migratory trend, there have been plenty of local eddies and countercurrents, as the mapping work by Dolfuss et al. (2001) on forms of plows demonstrates. Furthermore, as mentioned in note 5, many Tharus, used to shifting agriculture in the Tarai plains, have moved long distances east to west along the Tarai over the past fifty to one hundred years in search of new land to settle. The end result of all these movements is a pattern of ethnic settlement that is thoroughly mixed, not to say Balkanized (P. Sharma 2008).

It is worth noting at this point that, in this tribal pattern based on shifting agriculture, repeated movement is taken for granted. Rootedness to a place since time immemorial is not particularly valued. This puts traditional tribal values completely at odds with the modern ideology of indigenism and indigenous rights, which shares with modern nation-states what Malkki (1997: 61) calls 'sedentarist metaphysics,' that is, the assumption that there is and must be an inalienable and primordial link between a people/culture and a particular place.[22]

In general the ideals of the modern state invert those of the theater state. In most modern cases people are plentiful, and it is land that has become scarce. Power is supposed to be exercised equally and impartially at every point in the state's sovereign domain without exception. (One recalls Prime Minister Margaret Thatcher stating in 1979 that Ulster was as British as Finchley, her suburban constituency in outer London—though the very fact that she needed to say it out loud demonstrated the highly contested nature of the claim.) Officially all citizens are equal and should be treated equally. The state takes on duties toward all its citizens. Ideally boundaries should be clear, straight, unambiguous, and certainly not contain all kinds of enclaves, which by their nature are anomalous. In this nationalist conception, movement of people across these clear lines should be controlled by the state. People should have unambiguous affiliations and loyalties, with associated citizenship rights, to one or other of the two states, but not both. Borders are then essential "to the creation and maintenance of the nation and the state," as Donnan and Wilson (1999: 5) point out. Many of the cases discussed in this book demonstrate ethnographically how it is that, paradoxically, borders—those areas often thought of as most peripheral—are central to the nation.

The British in India believed in the straight lines and unambiguous allegiances of the modern model, as we have seen already. Winichakul (1994: ch. 4) documents the misunderstandings that resulted when they tried to established what they thought of as commonsense and straightforward boundaries between their territory in Burma and that of the Kingdom of Siam in the mid-nineteenth century. However, both there and on the northern land frontiers of their subcontinental colony they were forced, as Robb (1997: 250) points out, to accept "many ambiguous edges. . . . There were layers of uncertainty here not only because of British policy-disagreements, but from political volatilities in regions where there were few proto-states to be conquered, and little sense of fixed property." Internally, as Robb also notes, the British allowed "a panoply of exceptions" to the notion of a single state ruled by a single uniform law, of which one example would be the India-Bangladesh enclaves discussed earlier. The extraordinary thing is that at no stage were these enclaves ever 'tidied up' by the obvious solution of simply exchanging them. Immediately following independence, while the two states dithered, the inhabitants of the surrounding areas often took it upon themselves to do the tidying up and indulged in what is now called, using the macabre euphemism that the former Yugoslavia has given the world, 'ethnic cleansing,' driving out Muslim inhabitants of Pakistani enclaves within India, while leaving the Hindu inhabitants in place (Van Schendel 2002b: 131; Jalais, chapter 10, this volume).

The Nepal-India Border Today: A Leftover of History?

In contrast to the India-Bangladesh border, with its increasing militarization and anomalous enclaves, the Indian border with the Nepalese Tarai is far more relaxed, though here too alleged Indian land grabs, water diversions, and border police incursions are the occasion for outraged newspaper comment and political protests in Kathmandu.[23] For many ordinary purposes, however, for the people who live there, the border hardly appears to exist at all. People move to and fro on a daily basis to work and regularly shop or go to school on the other side. They are used to handling two different currencies. The language is the same on both sides. People read the same newspapers and listen to the same radio stations on both sides of the border. Some districts have Muslims as the largest single group on the Nepalese side, as on the Indian side (Rautahat, Parsa, Kapilvastu, Banke); another five Nepalese districts bordering Bihar (Saptari, Siraha, Dhanusha, Mahottari, and Sarlahi) form a contiguous bloc where Yadavs are the single biggest group, just as they are over the border.[24] At the same time, in large parts of many Tarai districts there are local majorities of hill people (Pahadi), encouraged to settle by the Nepalese state after the eradication of malaria in the 1950s, and some Tarai districts, such as Morang (at least in its northern part) and Jhapa in the east and Chitwan in the center, have an overall majority of hill people, with significant consequences for local politics.[25]

Such invisibility of the border does not apply to most long-distance travelers, however. Most Nepali hill people traveling to India do not have the choice of taking an alternative route. Thus the movement of nonlocal people, unlike that of those who live in the border region and possess local knowledge and connections, is subject to control and intimidation, though often as much by freelance gatekeepers as by the official agents of the state (though the two categories may work together, of course). This is vividly described by Hausner and Sharma in chapter 5 on the rituals of border crossing. Hill people making the journey for work to India (and it is usually for work, more rarely for pilgrimage or other leisure purposes) must travel through the main checkpoints. There they are subject to routine harassment and forced to take buses and rickshaws on the other side by bullying touts. Women are subject to special surveillance: they may be stopped by NGOs, like Maiti Nepal, who try to test whether they are being trafficked or not by inquiring about the identity of the men they are traveling with.

Whereas people—at least local people—may go to and fro without let or hindrance, the movement of goods, at least goods in any quantity, is supposed to be subject to strict state control. There is therefore enormous scope for smuggling and corruption (see Mathur, chapter 3, this volume). Subsidized petrol, kerosene, and fertilizer from Nepal are smuggled in vast quantities over the border to India, costing the Nepalese state enormous sums. Vehicles go in both directions and are given new number plates on arrival in the other country.

In spite of this large-scale subversion of the state, state controls on the movement of goods are highly significant. It is tempting to say that the border between India and Nepal is not a border, but in fact the existence of two different states does make multiple differences to everyday life. It is worthwhile for Nepalis to cross to India to buy manufactured goods and foodstuffs, which are cheaper there. Likewise for many years Indians traveled to Nepal to buy Chinese goods that used to be unavailable in India. When the two states clash, there are severe consequences for the movement of goods. This happened in 1989, during what Nepal called an Indian blockade and India saw as a hiatus in negotiations of the Trade and Transit Treaty caused by Nepali intransigence. India closed all but two of the permitted border-crossing points (see map 5.1), and supplies of petrol and kerosene in Kathmandu quickly ran out. The consequent protests in Kathmandu were part of what led to the revolution or people's movement of 1990 there.

The existence of two separate states also has serious consequences for politics. It was clear at the time of the election in Nepal in April 2008 that those on the Nepalese side were fully engaged; they queued for hours in the sun to cast their vote. People just over the border on the Indian side were indifferent; they had their own member of the legislative assembly in Patna and member of Parliament in Delhi. They were simply waiting for the election to be over so that business would pick up again. There are, moreover, increasing numbers of armed police from both states positioned at regular intervals along the border to check on the illegal movement of goods or 'terrorists' (Shrestha 2011).

Physically the Tarai region looks like India, and indeed it is culturally and linguistically continuous with neighboring areas on the Indian side of the border. The violent demonstrations and clashes in the Nepalese Tarai in January 2007 and January 2008 were viewed in Kathmandu as instigated by India and as threatening national unity.[26] What the riots in fact indicated was that the Madheshis (people of Indian descent and culture in the Tarai) wished to be a part of Nepal's process of state restructuring and would no longer accept being left out. The center (Kathmandu) was no longer viewed with fear, and Madheshis were determined to seize the moment to overthrow a state system that in their eyes was no better than a form of colonial domination.[27] For their part hill Nepalis can never be persuaded to see the Tarai as the Madheshis do, much as the Sinhalese in Sri Lanka will never sympathize with the situation of Tamils. Both hill Nepalis and Sinhalese can be described by that hackneyed phrase 'a majority with a minority complex,' that is, a majority in their own country liable to behave with all the insensitivity and indignant aggression of an oppressed minority toward their own minority that is identified with the majority in the next-door big neighbor.

A Four-Part Model of State-People Relations at the Border

The arguments I have been making can be summarized in a four-part model of state-people relations at the border, as shown in table Intro.1. This attempts to capture some of the key differences between different types of borders and different responses to power in modern and premodern situations in Northern South Asia. What is proposed is a rough-and-ready typology, put forward in full awareness of the limits of such typologizing. The case studies in this volume support the conventional wisdom (found equally in contemporary anthropology and in human geography) that borders need to be understood as social and historical processes (Paasi 1999); any attempt to forge a 'border theory' without simultaneously theorizing the state and society is neither

TABLE INTRO.1 State-people-border configurations in Northern South Asia

Population	Premodern	Modern
Thin	People move or run away, state cannot extract much; no real borders, rather: fluid borderlands (relatively state-free spaces)	Army presence ensures frontiers; people either (i) display patriotism as a counterbalance to cultural affinities across the border, or (ii) are caught between insurgents and the state
Dense	Cultural and social complexity (high levels of ritual and tradition) provides some protection from oppressive rule	State rules by day, mafias etc. by night; there is often high penetration of state apparatus by local interests

attainable nor desirable (Paasi 2011; cf. Piliavsky's skeptical stance toward 'borderland theory' in chapter 1, this volume). Thus the model is not advanced as a total explanation, nor does it aspire to be such, but it is put forward in the belief that it has heuristic value as a point of departure for detailed investigations of particular places and interactions. All descriptions are, explicitly or implicitly, comparative. To describe a border as 'soft' is to contrast it to borders that are 'hard.' It is surely better therefore to reflect on the concepts we use and to attempt some degree of conceptual clarity.

A processual and historical approach presumes that actual social and political interactions are made up of complex mixtures of assumptions and expectations. Little is gained and considerable confusion is engendered by pulling apart social and political practices and sticking labels such as 'modern,' 'feudal,' 'backward,' or 'forward' on the parts. Thus the oppositions that underlie table Intro.1 are relative and contextual. What counts as modern in one era will appear as traditional in another. As discussed earlier, the colonial period saw the very beginnings of modern ideas about fixed borders; from today's perspective, the actual practice of those times was highly traditional, and the colonial state was often content to dramatize power, in practice allowing large areas of relatively state-free space to remain on the frontier (which they called a buffer zone).

Another target of the processual approach is another favorite trope of modernism: the frequently posited boundary between 'state' and 'society.' However, at the level of *ideas* of the state, the state-society distinction remains powerful. Ethnographic study reveals that many people in South Asia see themselves as part of groups deserving of special attention from the state, while others, even today, show a surprising ability to resist the ideas and pressures of modernist governmentality.

One key variable concerns the differences in both capacity and aspiration between modern and premodern states. Premodern states, as Scott has emphasized, are interested in controlling people in order to maximize revenue. The people, on the other hand, will either adopt state-fleeing or state-adapting strategies (and sometimes a mixture of the two). In the premodern situation there are only pockets of dense population where, typically, a single premodern state will be based. Power radiates out from such centers; where exactly it ends cannot be, and does not need to be, specified precisely. Ambiguity may be an advantage to all sides. At the center, people adopt strategies of deference and humility but above all give a high value to ritual, to cultural complexity, and to traditions as guarantors of rights. These act as some kind of protection from the oppression and arbitrariness of rulers.[28]

In the modern situation, even in areas of relatively low population, there are much higher levels of population generally. The state now has the technology to control people way beyond the dreams of premodern states.[29] Nonetheless there are strict limits to what the state can ensure. Where the population is relatively thin, the army can dominate and local people are likely to identify with the state (as described by Gupta in chapter 2, Mathur in chapter 3, and Mishra in chapter 6; it was also a strategy adopted by some Lhotshampas of Bhutan, described by Evans in chapter 5). Alternatively, where ethnically based insurgent groups are well entrenched and can easily operate across the international border, the population may have no option but to identify with them and will be caught between these groups and the state. Farrelly describes a variant of this situation for northern Burma (Myanmar) in chapter 8, as does Joshi for Nagaland in chapter 7; this is part of the situation described by Evans in chapter 5 as well. Where the borderland population is dense, on the other hand, we have a situation like the Nepal-India border, where the state is present but also in competition with many small armed and illegal groups. These groups may be politically motivated or driven more simply by greed (and the precise mix, not to mention perceptions of the mix, may fluctuate over time and by context).

The chapters in this book illustrate, for a variety of Northern South Asian cases, the two right-hand boxes of table Intro.1. Chapters 1, 4, 6, 7, 9, and 10 may be taken to illustrate the dense population options, and chapters 2, 3, 5, and 8 the more sparse variant—though the interpretation of the Naga and Bhutanese cases might well be contested. Even though all these cases lie, grosso modo, within the two 'modern' quadrants, there remain plenty of features of contemporary social practice—habits of avoiding the state or engaging with it ritualistically—that can be understood only with reference to the two 'premodern' quadrants. Past 'state effects' live on in the present, despite the fact that the technology of the state has now changed beyond recognition.

The boundary between the state and society more generally, as all the chapters here show, is no more clear-cut and easy to discern in everyday life than the border between two states. State models have effects, and the idea of the state is a powerful one; how the state operates at its borders is the outcome of a complex historical dance and interaction between people(s) and state representatives (who are sometimes deeply embedded in local networks themselves, sometimes not). The case studies assembled here demonstrate border situations scattered along the arc of India's northern borders, but at all of them, even at the Nepal-India border, there is, as Van Schendel argues in the afterword, anxiety, contestation, and fractiousness.[30] There is also, I would add, no easy consensus among scholars on how to interpret this anxiety and contestation, and I have not attempted to impose consensus on the contributions to this volume.

Nonetheless, placing these diverse case studies and the different state contexts side by side is, I hope and believe, instructive. If there are important methodological lessons to be derived from ethnographic approaches to these questions, of the kind attempted in this book, they are (1) that the interpretation of life at borders cannot be deduced from state classifications or nationalist ideologies, (2) that borderlands are highly variable and need to be studied from the bottom up, taking into account multiple points of view, and (3) that therefore the study of local politics is too important to be left to political scientists, legal scholars, or diplomats.[31]

NOTES TO INTRODUCTION

1. The history of the term is examined below. For helpful comments on earlier versions of this introduction, I would like to thank D. P. Martinez, W. van Schendel, J. Whelpton, S. Subedi, R. Guha, J. Sharma, A. Piliavsky, R. Gupta, S. L. Hausner, J. Cons, and two anonymous reviewers for Duke University Press. I would also like to thank Kanti Bajpai for advice. None of them should be held even remotely responsible for what I have written.

2. "The State . . . does not exist in the phenomenal world; it is a fiction of the philosophers. What does exist is an organization, i.e. a collection of individual human beings connected by a complex system of relations. . . . There is no such thing as the power of the State; there are only, in reality, powers of individuals—kings, prime ministers, magistrates, policemen, party bosses, and voters" (Radcliffe-Brown 1940: xxiii).

3. One may compare Shaw and Stewart's (1994) recommendation that anthropologists should eschew the attempt to find syncretism and restrict themselves to studying discourses of syncretism (and antisyncretism).

4. For Gray's poem, see Thomas Gray Archive, www.thomasgray.org.uk; for Walter Scott's use of it, Scott (1998: 295). I have followed Scott's slight misreading ('Who, while' for 'And while'). For a critique of simplistic views of the highland-lowland divide in Scotland, see Pittock (2001: 14–18).

5. See Campbell (1997) on the way in which the Tamangs, who live both north of and all around the Kathmandu Valley, view themselves as 'people in between,' outside state schemes on either side (Tibetan Buddhist to the north, Indianizing and Hindu to the south). See Krauskopff (2003) on the Tharus' attempts to evade the state by migrating to the far west of Nepal.

6. For example, Martínez 1994; Wilson and Donnan 1998a. See the website of the Association of Borderland Studies (absborderlands.org) and their newsletter, La Frontera. There are also various regional associations for the study of borders, most recently the Asian Borderlands Research Network (asianborderlands.net). For useful overviews of the literature, see Baud and Van Schendel 1997; Newman 2006a, 2006b; Donnan and Wilson 1999; Wilson and Donnan 2012a. Wastl-Walter (2011) and Wilson and Donnan (2012b) are two useful collections that survey the emerging global field of borderland studies. Heyman (1994) is a critique of the woolly and ethnographically unfocused way borders and boundary crossing are often invoked in some influential anthropological theorizing.

7. Van Schendel 2005a: 366; afterword, this volume. On methodological nationalism more generally, see Ammelina et al. (2012), and on methodological nationalism within anthropology, Gellner (2012).

8. That there may be a particularly gendered aspect to this suffering is suggested by Banerjee (2001) and Banerjee and Basu Ray Chaudhury (2011).

9. Heyman (1995) argues exactly this point for the U.S.-Mexico border.

10. As far as I know, we invented the term, but of course it is possible that we were unconsciously recycling a nomenclature that one of us had encountered elsewhere. After drafting these lines, I found that Kanak Dixit and others used the term 'North Southasia' in 2009 to cover the area from Uttar Pradesh to Afghanistan (Himal 2009).

11. See Maxwell (1970) on the history of India's northern frontiers. The British wished to use the Chinese to limit Russian expansion southward, but "the Chinese shied away from most British attempts to settle common boundaries with them" (20).

12. This did not prevent there being plenty of ambiguities and frontier disputes between the Company and Nepal in practice. Michael (2007, 2009) records the frustrations of late eighteenth- and early nineteenth-century officials of the East India Company. On the ground, tenurial relationships could be multiplex, land moved in and out of cultivation, and cultivators moved around according to the political situation, with the result that the officials could never be sure where the frontier between Company territory and the Gorkhas' land was.

13. Jayal (2013: ch. 3) describes the difficulties of those who do manage to get across to India as refugees from Pakistan and their struggles to achieve Indian citizenship and the benefits that brings with it (access to BPL—Below Poverty Line—ration card, etc.).

14. See Baruah 2009; chapters 6–8, this volume.

15. For an incident at the Hungary-Romania border illustrating how permeable it is for local people, even when officials of the state maintain that it is sealed, see Donnan and Wilson (2010: 10).

16. Yet a third force, the Indo-Tibet Border Police Force, guards the India-Tibet/China border from Ladakh in the west to Arunachal in the east (see itbpolice.nic.in). The border with Myanmar is guarded by the Assam Rifles, who come under the army; replacing them with the BSF, who come under the Home Ministry, has been mooted, and resisted, in recent times.

17. See Government of India, Ministry of Home Affairs, accessed 11 August 2012, www.ssb.nic.in, under 'about us' and 'history,' accessed 11 August 2012.

18. See the BSF website, accessed 11 August 2012, bsf.nic.in.

19. Berti and Tarabout (2009) is a collection that seeks to establish that the notion of territory was, contrary to conventional stereotype, important in South Asia and that sometimes boundaries were precisely demarcated. The editors concede, however, that "far from a lack of territory in pre-colonial India, it could be said that there was an excess of them. But these territories were multiple, sometimes discontinuous, and overlapping, as very different rights applied to the same tract of land" (28).

20. No doubt rice-growing peasants usually also, and where safe to do so, adopt the foot-dragging and dissimulation described in Scott's *Weapons of the Weak* (1985).

21. Van Beek (2001) describes how Ladakhis decided to claim Scheduled Tribe status in the 1980s, a self-ascription of backwardness that evidently would have been unthinkable in Ladakh twenty years earlier but had already begun in other parts of India. I have explored the tribe-caste contrast in the context of the Kathmandu Valley

in Gellner (1991). See Shneiderman and Turin (2006), Kapila (2008), and Shah (2010) on the politics of tribal status in India.

22. For more on the paradoxical ways in which Nepali ethnic activists' indigenist discourses invert traditional values, see Lecomte-Tilouine (2009).

23. See Shrestha (2011) for an overview of the border issues at stake between Nepal and India. The 'open' border is not guaranteed by any treaty; it was simply, until recently, taken for granted. The Nepal-India Peace and Friendship Treaty of 1950 guarantees the citizens of one country the same privileges as granted the citizens of the other, that is, reciprocal equal treatment of each other's citizens, without specifying that the border will be open.

24. An OBC (Other Backward Classes) movement has developed in these parts of the Nepalese Tarai, which is in effect a movement against Yadav dominance. This is doubly ironic because the language of 'OBC' has no official standing in Nepal at all, and because normally, in India, the Yadavs would themselves be considered paradigmatic OBCs.

25. On ethnic geography, see P. Sharma (2008); for caste and ethnic breakdowns by district according to the 2001 census, see CBS (2007).

26. The open border was blamed for the uprisings in Kathmandu, but, in view of the advantages (easy access to India and its employment opportunities), Jha (2007) concludes, "The border is the best thing to have happened for millions of Nepalis."

27. Although there is a long way to go before Madheshis are fully incorporated into Nepal's state structures, the fact that in the new republican setup following the abolition of the monarchy in 2006 both the president and the vice president are Madheshis is symbolic of a very real shift.

28. South and Southeast Asia do not seem to have developed the republican city states, rejecting monarchical rule, that emerged in Europe, though kings often had to contend with powerful aristocracies, as in Malla-period Lalitpur, Nepal.

29. See Mann (1993: ch. 3) for a theorization of the ever-increasing powers of the modern state.

30. As he has put it elsewhere, "The state's partially obscured view of borderland activities, the gap between people's understandings of what they are doing versus the state's, inconsistent notions of illegality, and the presence of other legalities across the border, all make, for the state, the borderland an area where by definition criminality is rife and sovereignty under constant threat" (Abraham and Van Schendel 2005: 25).

31. A cogent, book-length argument for the anthropological study of borderlands is made by Donnan and Wilson (1999).

ONE | ANASTASIA PILIAVSKY

Borders without Borderlands

On the Social Reproduction of
State Demarcation in Rajasthan

Attention
Before entering the lift, check whether lift is present or not
— Sign in a multistory building in New Delhi

The Idea of the Borderland

Since the latter half of the nineteenth century 'borderlands' have been a popular subject in writings ranging from geographical, ethnological, and travel to spiritualist, horror, and occult.[1] Adopted from its original geographical usage as a descriptor of frontiers of ecosystems or countries, the term has persisted across disciplines, genres, and time. Over the past century and a half no-man's-lands on moors and marshlands, frontiers of empires and civilizations, psychic realms between spirit and matter, and occult spheres dividing this world from the next have each been referred to as 'borderlands.' In all these genres they have been conceived as territorially and socially distinct regions surprisingly like the ecosystems, psychic states, or nation-states at the fringes of which they are found. Both Maud's (1904) Abyssinian borderlands and the ghostly borderlands of Hodgson's (1908) *The House on the Borderland* are spatially and socially separate lands, whether populated by barbarians or by ghouls. In the course of the twentieth century, the concept of the borderland obtained a new lease on life in the historiography of frontiers, particularly in the study of the American Anglo-Spanish, and more recently the

U.S.-Mexico, border regions.[2] Since the 1950s it gained currency in work on other parts of the world, passing over the course of the past decade into South Asian studies.[3] In this vast and rapidly proliferating literature the idea of the borderland has retained the shape it assumed in older genres of writing: the borderland of current historiography is a spatial unit, a sociospatially discrete zone.[4]

Baud and Van Schendel's (1997) account of borderland theory typifies this view.[5] The authors tell us that borderlands are *territorial units* "determined first and foremost by the spatial dimension. Borderlands are geographically defined areas that can be drawn on a map like any other region" (221–22). They further tell us that these areas are home to "borderland societies" with a distinctive sociocultural, linguistic, economic, and political character (227). In fact Baud and Van Schendel argue that the "borderland people" are so different from everyone else that they feel "ethnically and emotionally part of another, nonstate entity" (227, 233). More specifically they claim that these zones are home to a special "triangle of power relations between state, regional elite, and local people"; distinctive political alliances between local elites and the state; hubs of black economies; and "creole" or "synthetic" languages (219, 217, 234).[6] The idea of a distinct entity is further consolidated with the anthropomorphic image: the authors describe the borderland as a geopolitical organism with a distinctive character (that can be "quiet," "unruly," or "rebellious") and a life history that moves through "life-cycles" (from "embryonic" to "infant," "adolescent," "adult," and "declining"; 227–79, 223–24; see also Martínez 1994: 27–28). Though Baud and Van Schendel (1997: 225) themselves recognize this is "not completely satisfactory because of evolutionary and deterministic implications," the metaphor reflects their conception of borderlands as discrete entities with lives of their own.

On closer inspection, however, borderlands have proven resistant to being "drawn on a map like any other region" (Baud and Van Schendel 1997: 221), forcing Baud and Van Schendel to resort to subdividing them into the "border heartland," the "intermediate borderland," and the "outer borderland" on the basis of their spatial proximity to national borders and the extent to which these regions "feel the influence of the border" (222). The edges of these subzones and the relations between them have proven just as difficult to establish, prompting the authors to use a simile in place of a definition: "There is the *outer borderland*, which . . . is affected by the existence of the border in the same way that land protected by an embankment is affected by the sea.

In daily life the border hardly plays a role at all, but there is always a hint of suspense, a slight tinge of uncertainty. Just as a tidal wave may sweep far into the interior, so a political storm may suddenly engulf this zone and involve it directly in border dynamics" (222, italics in original).

In their description the parameters of borderlands blur even further with the admission that "borderlands may at times, though briefly, stretch to embrace entire countries" (222). Of course, when stretched to encompass an entire country, the category of borderland loses all of its heuristic force. And unless we assume linguistic and cultural homogeneity within states, the creole or synthetic language and culture (234) staked as a distinctive marker of "borderland societies" will appear no different from life most anywhere else. Neither are the "socio-political networks" characteristic of borderlands. Baud and Van Schendel's observation that historically in South Asia "borderland elites [such as *zamindars*] were well integrated into networks of state power" so as to "become important allies of the state in its efforts to control borderland society" (217) is equally true of contexts throughout the territories of South Asian states.[7] Collusion between state officials and local elites, flagged by Baud and Van Schendel as a special feature of borderlands, is another general quality of the political landscape in South Asia (e.g., Brass 1984, 1997). "Gangster rule" (Van Schendel 1993, 2002b) is likewise a trademark of politics *throughout* the territories of India, Pakistan, and Bangladesh, not just on their peripheries (e.g., Hansen 2001; Berenschot 2008; Michelutti 2008; Ruud and Price 2010). Policy and administrative differences within nation-states often affect economic processes no less than differences between them, so that an excise tax differential between two districts may generate "borderland economies" within nation-states as much as on their margins. Neither is smuggling, described as a quintessential borderland enterprise, confined to trade across national limits: smuggling hubs are often located in the heartlands of states rather than on their peripheries. While state rhetoric, as Baud and Van Schendel (1997: 231) themselves point out, "gives the entire border economy an air of stealth and subterfuge," smugglers know all too well that national border crossing is only one part of business whose impulse lies beyond border regions (de Wilde 2009).

The difficulties faced by borderland theorists in defining the object of their analysis are not merely a matter of empirical imprecision, but are an important clue to the nature of the problem at hand. In their preoccupation with defining the limits of borderlands as substantive entities—as territorially, socially, linguistically, and politically discrete zones—borderland theorists tend to forget about borders, which in their case really are the root analytical objects. Borders are meant to enclose and divide. And sometimes they do just that, producing a great variety of border scenarios, not all of which produce frontier-like situations or "borderlands." While some borders may function as frontiers populated by distinct communities of border-crossers (Hausner and Sharma, chapter 4, this volume), others are tightly sealed boundaries that create distinct populations on either side. (The Berlin Wall did not generate a borderland, however menacingly it may have affirmed its idea.) Borders are also conceptual objects that have different meanings in different circumstances; they can be perceived as fringes, frontiers, or national heartlands. While people on the U.S.-Mexico border may feel that they are on the outskirts of both states and part of a frontier, nonstate society, Kargilians living next to the symbolically significant India-Pakistan border think of themselves as residents of the Indian heartland (Gupta, chapter 2, this volume). The sense of border life may also permeate entire states; as Turner ([1893] 1920), the historian who gave us the concept of a frontier society, argued some time ago, life throughout the territory of the United States has been animated by the frontier spirit from the country's beginnings. The effect of national borders on local life often differs neither in kind nor necessarily in degree from the effect of other types of state demarcations on societies throughout the territories of modern states.

In this paper I argue against the claim that national borders everywhere are surrounded by borderlands imagined to be substantive, freestanding places. Borders are entities of a fundamentally different sort. They are not like the spaces they encircle and divide, and the moment they become spaces they cease to be borders. Borders enclose, separate, and bring spaces into relation. They are relational rather than substantive objects, which generate different sorts of relations within and between communities around them. To say that borders are relational rather than substantive entities is not to present them as any less 'real' or decisive. Indeed the border is the primary tool of the modern state and of modernity at large (Abrams 1988; Mitchell 1991; Scott 1998). And as we shall see in the ethnography that follows, the people in my study live and breathe borders. My ethnography further undermines the blanket application of the concept of borderland to regions around national borders by showing that various features posited by borderland theorists as distinctive markers of borderlands are just as present in the territorial heartland of the

Indian state. It shows that the effect of borders is not confined to the fringes of national states but that it spans their territories. In my case borders do not provoke their crossing but function as boundaries that in fact enclose and divide communities. They shape local lives no less thoroughly than borders between Mexico and the U.S.-Mexico or between Bangladesh and India, but they do so in quite different ways from those ascribed to many borderland scenarios.

The Setting

My ethnography focuses on an Indian community, the Kanjar, a caste that practices thieving (cattle rustling, household burglary, roadside burglary, opium theft) as a hereditary, caste-based occupation. The success of Kanjars' burgling business relies substantially on patronage by the police, with whom Kanjars have intimate and very regular dealings. Through this relationship, official demarcations—territorial and otherwise—have become not only a prominent feature of Kanjars' everyday lives but indeed a central structuring force within the community.[8] More specifically my study demonstrates how official policing parameters configure matters ranging from marriage alliances to professional relations, considerations of rank, and the nature of authority in the community.[9] Focusing on two key parameters of policing—the territorial layout of police jurisdictions and the divisions of rank among the staff of police stations—I show how the structural demarcation of the state, including but not confined to spatial boundaries, is projected onto and reproduced within the Kanjar community. With this order of administrative divisions at the heart of Kanjars' everyday lives and social organization, we can think of the community as a sort of "borderland society," but one that has little to do with the physical periphery of the Indian state: they live in rural Rajasthan, more than six hundred kilometers from the nearest national border. On a broader analytical level, my study suggests that the administrative structuring of the state and local social life occurs simultaneously, making the conceptual separation of "state" and "society" not only analytically problematic but also empirically inaccurate.

There are approximately 200,000 Kanjars living in South Asia today. Most of them can be found in the northern Indian State of Uttar Pradesh, and nearly forty thousand live in Rajasthan, where I conducted most of my field research (Census Commissioner of India 2011). Kanjars constitute one of several South Asian communities of professional thieves (Piliavsky 2011a). Professional raiding and thievery has long been and continues to be a standard political and governmental practice on the subcontinent, and communities of professional thieves continue to be employed as agents of protection, intimidation, resource extraction, intelligence provision, and dispute negotiation.[10] Under British colonial law such groups were persecuted, along with nomadic and otherwise "inconvenient" communities under the rubric of Criminal Tribe. Those who were designated as Criminal Tribesmen were subjected to a regime of special surveillance, "reclamation," and penal measures.[11] By 1952, when the Indian Criminal Tribes Act was repealed, ties between such communities and patrons among aristocrats and village communities were largely severed, and the former Criminal Tribesmen became increasingly dependent on patronage by police, with whom they had already become intimately acquainted in the days of the Raj. Today, while Kanjar thieves continue to find employment with local landholders, their most significant attachments are to the police, who offer them protection (or minimize predation) in exchange for intelligence, provision of muscle force, and a share of their spoils.

I conducted most of my field research in southeastern Rajasthan in a Kanjar settlement, which I will call Lakshmipura, in 2005 and again in 2007–8 (see map 1.1). For much of this time I lived in the home of a gang leader and a village chief on the rise. My discussion focuses on Lakshmipura and on the circle of its in-caste relations, which its residents refer to as their 'brotherhood' (*biradari*).[12] All settlements in the Lakshmipura brotherhood are located in Rajasthan, and most are in the southeastern district of Chittaurgarh. Their distribution, which is now all but confined to a section of a single administrative district, is a fraction of the former territorial span of the community, whose relations once stretched from Rajasthan to Punjab, Gujarat, and Pakistan. Reflecting on the recent history of Lakshmipura and its brotherhood, I describe the ways in which some basic features of the community—the extent of matrimonial and professional ties as well as the nature of communal authority—have been shaped along the lines that structure the work of the police in particular and the order of the state at large.

Loss of Guts

The Kanjars of Lakshmipura often lament the loss of *jigar* in their community. *Jigar* literally means "liver" but refers metonymically to "guts," a metaphor akin to our own. According to a local adage, "a man is only as big as his circle of relations,"[13] and a person who lacks bonds with brothers, patrons, and friends is not just isolated but effectively socially absent. The concept of jigar expresses this idea of a person who is not simply a part of but is essentially constituted by a circle of relations, the reduction of which amounts to a person's social hollowing or "gutting": the loss of jigar.[14] A man with no relations is no more than a dot on a social map.

Among Kanjars the lament of "lost guts" refers to some important recent changes in the structure of the community. Prior to independence the Kanjars in Lakshmipura (much as in other places) practiced a variety of itinerant trades, including genealogy, prostitution, and thieving. They often traveled across great distances and engaged a wide and varied circle of relations with patrons, relatives, colleagues, and friends. Although now most Kanjars in Rajasthan live sedentary lives, members of one community in the south of the province have remained itinerant genealogists and, as such, provide a present-day example of a former way of life among Kanjars. The extent of this community's travels and connections is comparable to that once engaged in by the Lakshmipura brotherhood, to whose currently narrow circle of relations it can be contrasted in its breadth. Every year these Kanjar bards travel as far as Ahmedabad, Delhi, and Bombay to record and perform genealogies for their patrons.[15] Each year they traverse the distance of more than two thousand kilometers and visit up to three hundred villages, settlements, and city neighborhoods on their way, usually staying in one place for no more than a night (see map 1.2).[16] En route they forge and maintain relations of patronage, friendship, and marriage, all of which are constitutive of their fraternity or "society" (samaj), as they call it. Although formally settled, Kanjar bards still exchange wives with communities in Bombay and Pune, retain patrons near Delhi, and visit cousins in Gujarat. They speak a number of languages and regional dialects and form marriage alliances with at least fifteen different Kanjar patriclans, whose members are involved in businesses ranging from alcohol distillation to the sale of watches and toys. The extent of their brotherhood is measured not simply in terms of the distance traveled but in the number and variety of persons to whom they relate. Patrons, acquaintances, and merchants with whom they trade on the way and families they marry along the route form a linguistically, economically, and occupationally heterogeneous—and socially rich—circle. As one Kanjar bard put it, the community's "wealth" (daulat), material as well as social, "is in [its] relations." "Our community travels far and has connections with all sorts of people and that is why it has respect (izzat)."

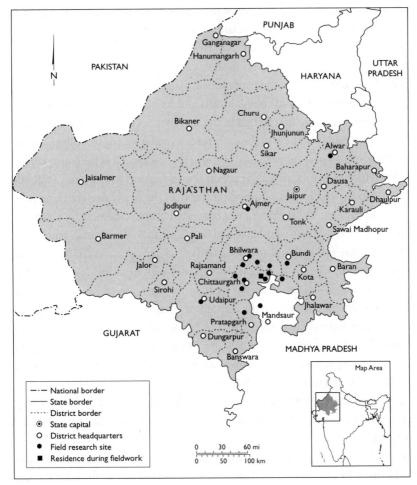

MAP 1.1. Location of field research sites in Rajasthan. (Lakshmipura is marked with a black square.) Drawn by the Cartographic Unit of the Dept of Geography, University of Cambridge. Reproduced with permission.

The reach of the Kanjar bard brotherhood stands in striking contrast to that of the Kanjars of Lakshmipura. Over the past four generations, the Lakshmipura biradari dwindled from a scale comparable to the Kanjar bards' to a community comprising a handful of neighboring villages within a forty-kilometer radius. The business of thieving and protection, in which most residents of Lakshmipura are nowadays engaged, has likewise become limited to a few neighboring villages and the jurisdictions of two police stations (*thanas*), on whose protection the success of the thieving business relies. In contrast to the Kanjar bards' biradari, relations within the sedentary Lakshmipura brotherhood are now restricted to a handful of villages and a few local patrons, most of whom are officers in the local police.

Such truncation of the fraternity is tied, via relations with the police, to the territorial demarcation of colonial India and its heir-republic.[17] The Kanjars of Lakshmipura were first settled in the area by the chief (rawat) of local nobility, who employed them in the early 1920s as a marauding force to aid in the suppression of a peasant uprising.[18] By 1930 the chief had lost the control of his fiefdom (thikana), and his Kanjar clients became subject to Criminal Tribe administration, which then assumed control over the newly declared Criminal Tribes in the area. Lakshmipura was converted into a settlement for Criminal Tribes and its residents were subjected to special surveillance and penal measures: regular roll call and irregular raids, a system of absentee passes, and preemptive or warrant-free incarceration. Between 1930 and 1956, when the Criminal Tribes legislation was at work in the area, the inspector in charge of the settlement left some of the community members alone in exchange for intelligence and a share of their spoils. A few Kanjar gangs were thus let loose onto the territory within the jurisdiction of the police station. After independence, police patronage carried on along similar lines, with thieves enjoying protection in the territories of their police stations.

Thus over time, the spatial limits of the biradari shrunk, eventually becoming effectively coextensive with the territorial limits of local police jurisdictions. Although the Lakshmipura Kanjars have occasional dealings with Kanjars in neighboring police jurisdictions, they now effectively imagine their community as territorially confined to the land under the jurisdiction of the local station. The continuous withering of ties with Kanjar communities elsewhere, which I discuss below, suggests that the identification of the spatial limits of the biradari with the police territory is not merely imagined. The official territorial markers now organize the Kanjar community no less than they organize the police.

Relations with the police have led not only to the establishment of a rigidly territorial system of thieving beats (with much hostility arising from the jealous guarding of their boundaries) but also to a significant reformatting of their network of marriage relations. The increasing concentration of the biradari within the jurisdiction of a single police station is reproduced in the decline of marriage ties with Kanjars in other police territories. More than half of the marriages that now take place in the biradari are confined to the

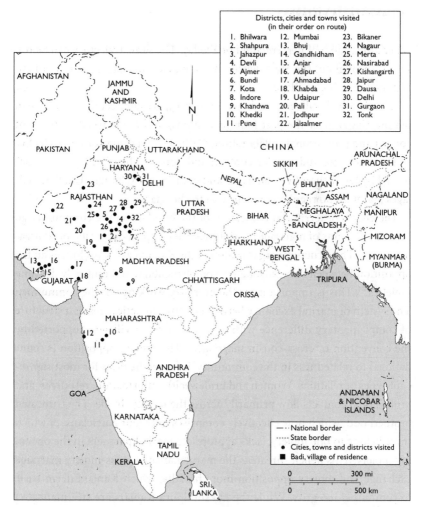

Districts, cities and towns visited (in their order on route)		
1. Bhilwara	12. Mumbai	23. Bikaner
2. Shahpura	13. Bhuj	24. Nagaur
3. Jahazpur	14. Gandhidham	25. Merta
4. Devli	15. Anjar	26. Nasirabad
5. Ajmer	16. Adipur	27. Kishangarth
6. Bundi	17. Ahmadabad	28. Jaipur
7. Kota	18. Khabda	29. Dausa
8. Indore	19. Udaipur	30. Delhi
9. Khandwa	20. Pali	31. Gurgaon
10. Khedki	21. Jodhpur	32. Tonk
11. Pune	22. Jaisalmer	

MAP 1.2. Locations visited annually by the Kanjar bards of Chittaurgarh district. Drawn by the Cartographic Unit of the Dept of Geography, University of Cambridge. Reproduced with permission.

jurisdiction of a single station (see map 1.3). The recent shriveling of the territorial stretch of marriage alliances follows a clear trajectory. Four generations ago Lakshmipura exchanged four women in marriage with villages in the nearby district of Bhilwara, four marriages were formed three generations ago (this time in a more populous village), one marriage alliance was forged two generations ago, and none was secured during the most recent nuptial round. Thus alliances with villages outside of the Lakshmipura police territory have dwindled from 24 percent and 17 percent of total marriage exchanges four generations ago to 4 percent and none today. The same trajectory can be observed throughout the State, where in some cases marriages are now all but confined to a single village.

'Closely allied' villages, as shown in map 1.3, are connected by more than ten marriages (over the past four generations) and are marked by frequent contact and professional collaboration;[19] 'allied' villages are connected by five to ten marriages and regular contact; and 'loosely allied' villages are connected by fewer than five marriages and occasional exchange. 'Unallied' villages maintain no regular contacts with the biradari.

The effects of territorial truncation of the biradari on the community go beyond the limits of marriage possibilities; they impact deeply its social organization.[20] The structural organization of the Kanjar caste (*jat*) hinges on the opposition between two exogamous, complementary, and mutually defining moieties.[21] This is important for the everyday workings of the community. The system of marital exchange between the two moieties creates a structure of complementary difference with alliances between villages, supported by the convention of cross-cousin marriage.[22] The moiety opposition is foundational to relatedness in the community: it forms the basis for most significant types of relations. Women and bridewealth, information, resources, and professional contacts flow primarily across the moiety divide. The truncated brotherhood, which now effectively comprises only four patriclans, of which three belong to one moiety, lacks appropriate marital partners in the opposing moiety. This deficit threatens the maintenance of cross-moiety marriage exchange and moiety opposition more broadly, which Kanjars deem basic to communal integrity. While the Lakshmipura Kanjars are still managing to find marriage partners in the opposing moiety, some of the neighboring biradaris, some of which are confined to a single village, started marrying within their own moieties and even within patriclans, committing incest, about which the Lakshmipura Kanjars whisper in tones of moral horror.

Policing and Raiding the Same Beats

The current shape of the biradari reflects the recent development of the 'special relationship' between the residents of Lakshmipura and the police.[23] In 1991 the Lakshmipura "Village Crime Note Book" on file in the thana reported an abrupt drop in property-related crime in the village, a change that

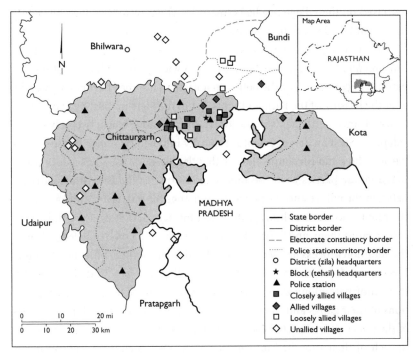

MAP 1.3. Villages of the Lakshmipura *biradari* and other neighboring Kanjar villages. Drawn by the Cartographic Unit of the Dept of Geography, University of Cambridge. Reproduced with permission.

coincided with a reported upsurge in thieving in a neighboring Kanjar village. One constable, who has been posted in the station for almost three decades, explained this reported shift. Rather than reflecting an actual decline in the thieving activities of the Lakshmipura Kanjars, the record indicates a transformation in the nature of the relationship between policemen and the Lakshmipura Kanjars from hostile to cooperative. This change was prompted by a large-scale pogrom that ravaged Lakshmipura in the summer of 1990 and the scale of which attracted much media attention, not only to the incident itself but also to the 'Kanjar problem'—including police predation—in the area. As a result of the 'incident' the police station staff, who stood by watching Kanjars get murdered and their houses blasted with dynamite, became subject to monitoring 'from above.' 'Coercive measures'—the filing of false cases, unwarranted arrests, beatings, and other forms of intimidation—previously exercised on the village residents (many of whom were therefore constantly on the run), had to be abandoned.[24]

These were replaced with milder measures, and Lakshmipura was 'adopted' (inf. *god lena*) by the police. 'Adoption' is a widespread Indian institution of patronizing criminals by the police; in Rajasthan it spread particularly rapidly after the passing of the Human Rights Act in the State in 1985. By 2008, of the sixteen Kanjar settlements in the local administrative block, twelve had been 'adopted.' Such an arrangement is typically initiated by senior house officers (SHOS), who establish connections with village leaders, usually heads of thieving gangs (or 'parties'), who become both informers (*mukhbar*) and mediators between the village and the police. In exchange for intelligence and a share of their loot, SHOS turn a blind eye to their informers' activities, avoid filing false cases against them, and 'write off' arrest warrants for a moderate fee.[25] By now the adoption process has been standardized to the point of bureaucratization. It is expected, for instance, that the SHOS will 'pass down' to their successors their informers, along with lists of reliable and unreliable informers, descriptions of their gangs and thieving beats, and other details noted in secret files of the police. It is expected that upon arrival in post the SHOS will pay a visit to each of their inherited informers and villages to confirm the continuity of the relationship. If faithfully nurtured, relationships between Kanjars and SHOS can outlast a given officer's tenure in post, with the result that the more sophisticated gang leaders can develop far-reaching and durable patronage bonds with officers beyond the limits of their block or even district.

As a result of police patronage, the more resourceful thieves become virtually immune to policing and prosecution in the *territory of a given station*, where their exploits are ignored, and indeed are often commissioned, by the police. The alignment of thieving beats with police jurisdictions spatially inverts the old convention of patronizing thieves, which assumed that the robbers employed by landlords and village communities would plunder *outside* of their employers' domains. Under police protection, robbers conversely run their business *within* the territory of their patrons' station. As a result, the neighbors of 'adopted' Kanjars are subjected to constant and frequent predation; after the adoption of Lakshmipura, for instance, attacks on the four immediately neighboring villages increased to a weekly average of four. The victims, naturally, retaliate by regularly beating, periodically murdering, and occasionally staging pogroms against their neighbors. Over the past twenty years twenty-four Kanjars were killed in the administrative block alone, and ten were murdered in the 1990 Lakshmipura pogrom.

Police patronage has further consequences for the structure of rank in the community. One of the results has been a growing class stratification among Kanjars. Adopted villages, families, gangs, and individual informers have come to form a wealthier and more educated class that increasingly refuses to mingle, marry, or even drink and eat with their lowlier caste-mates, whom they deride as 'orphans' (*anath*) or 'masterless men'.[26] This is not to say that the new conditions of police patronage have upset a prior state of harmony in the community, which has always been fractious (Piliavsky 2011b: ch. 2). Kanjar clans regularly bifurcate, villages split up, sons routinely leave their father's gangs, and brothers often quarrel.[27] The fragmentation prompted by current police patronage, however, is quite different. Whereas previously sections of the community would move away, today they remain in the same village, where they are separated only by mutual silence or violent and at times fatal conflict.

Such changes are inseparable from the territorial parameters of local policing practice. Today, as in the 1860s, when modern policing was being consolidated in colonial India, the distribution of police authority, the apprehension and prosecution of offenders, and the recovery of property are territorially structured (see figure 1.1). And the boundaries of police station jurisdictions are so jealously guarded as to be virtually impermeable to officers from other stations.[28] If an officer observes a crime just beyond the limit of his own jurisdiction, he is neither held responsible for nor indeed permitted to pursue it. This rigidly territorial system operates equally among Kanjars; their beats coincide with the territories of the stations, so that one can say that gangsters and the police operate within a shared territorial grid. Just like the officers, Kanjars avoid operations in unprotected territories, which are guarded as much by the police as by local Kanjars. Gangs do cross over into each other's territories, but they do so at the risk of being prosecuted and of initiating a gang war. The police hold local Kanjars accountable for thefts committed within their jurisdiction and lay claim to a share of the proceeds. When local gangs are thus forced to pay for the actions of others, they retaliate by raiding their neighbor's beat, which can in turn set off a cycle of cross-beat raiding, a chaotic and dangerous state of affairs that many would rather avoid.

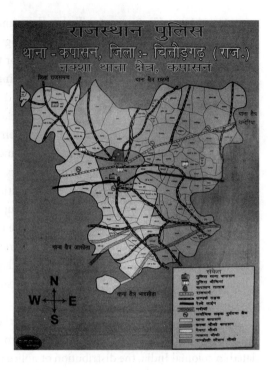

FIGURE 1.1. Police map in Rajasthan, 2008, showing the jurisdiction of a police station in southern Rajasthan and its territorial subdivisions (the boundary lines correspond to outpost jurisdictions and villages within them); such maps are usually displayed in police stations. Photo courtesy of A. Piliavsky.

Reproducing Divisions of Rank

Territorial divisions are not the only boundaries that shape the life of the community. The hierarchy of police ranks has likewise become a shaping force in Kanjar villages and gangs. Like the 'borderland peoples,' whose lives are inexorably linked to border administration, the Kanjar biradari has been deeply structured by the police ordering of rank.[29] The territorial arrangement of thieving beats in its own right reflects the hierarchical ordering of the staff of police stations. While the activities of Kanjar brotherhoods normally spread across the jurisdictions of one or two stations, the work of individual gangs relies on their patronage by individual officers. Just as the jurisdictions of police stations are subdivided into plots, each assigned to the care of one officer, the biradaris' territories are split up into beats belonging to individual gangs. The stability of police protection inside individual beats depends on the duration of officers' tenure in post. The lowest ranking officers—constables, head constables, and assistant subinspectors (collectively known as *sipahi*s [sepoys, foot soldiers] among Kanjars)—usually enjoy the longest tenure. While senior officers (inspectors and subinspectors) are frequently transferred, sipahis often remain in the same posting for many years, if not for the duration of their career.[30] This allows them to develop long-lasting relationships with local Kanjars. In fact because employment in particular positions (in the police as in other government services) is often inherited, the patronage of Kanjars by sipahi families can be maintained across several generations and even acquire the status of 'traditional' (*paramparik*) bonds.[31] Ties to individual officers further confine gangs to small patches of land allocated to those officers.[32] Kanjars protected by senior officers ('in-charge sahibs') have less stability, but their protection can be more effective and can extend to a wider territory.

Senior officers also patronize Kanjars, but the reasons for their patronage differ from those of their inferiors. While for subaltern policemen Kanjar exploits are primarily a source of immediate income, for senior officers Kanjars are most useful as agents of intelligence that boost their statistics, which aids their careers.[33] While junior officers encourage more thieving among Kanjars, senior officers promote informer activity. The roles of thief and approver are often at odds: informers for superior officers are often either kept uninformed or altogether excluded from gang activity by those allied with junior officers. Relationships between Kanjars and their sipahi patrons are often so intimate that the latter come to be thought of by Kanjars as members of their own gangs. Kanjars refer to their patron officers as gang 'chiefs' (*mukhya* or *sardar*) and call officers who betray them to rank seniors as 'informers' (*mukhbar*). For their part, constables refer to their Kanjar informers by first names and call them 'friends' (*dost*) or 'our men' (*apane admi*). The result is two classes: low-ranking officers and their Kanjar clients on the one hand and senior policemen and their informers on the other. The line of difference between the two is drawn both in the police stations and in the Kanjar settlements. It does not divide thieves from the police, but low-class of Kanjars and sipahis from the high-ranking officers and their Kanjar clients. This line is often marked by antagonisms that reverberate equally through Kanjar settlements and police stations. Senior officers protect their informers at the expense of junior colleagues' clients, and in turn junior officers compromise their superiors' informers. While constables bemoan the fact that their superiors 'spoil their work' (*kam bigarte*), SHOs complain that their cultivation of reliable sources of intelligence is constantly undermined by subordinates.

Police patronage also precipitates changes in the nature of communal authority among Kanjars. Although patronage by senior officers is commonly less stable than alliances with sipahis, it often entails more substantial privileges.

Kanjars under the tutelage of senior officers are much better positioned to have an arrest warrant written off, to settle a better deal when the need to pay off the police arises, or to have kith and kin released on bail. Resourceful Kanjars, who manage to maintain relationships with SHOs beyond the term of their local tenure can secure protection in other jurisdictions in the state and thus extend their beats and acquire greater political weight in the community. One of the outcomes is that the old system of elected community elders (*patels*) who acted as dispute arbiters is now being displaced by the new rule of *sardars* (bosses, gang leaders), who wield increasing weight in decision-making and resolution of disputes in the community. Successful clients of senior officers are not only immune to police harassment, they can also employ their connections to intimidate caste mates. While appeals by Kanjars (and other poor villagers) are typically ignored by the police, the sardars' complaints are taken seriously and occasionally even pursued. The growing presence of sardars in community councils (*jat panchayats*) also means that disputes are increasingly referred to the police, a change that signals not only a displacement of elders by gang leaders but a broader transfer of the community's legal apparatus to institutions of the state, on which the emergent class of sardars relies. Just as the Kanjars' thieving terrains replicate the territorial parameters of police jurisdictions, so does the rank order within the community replicate the hierarchies in police stations. Both police and Kanjar communities are now subject to a common order of rank, which equally operates in the populations of police stations and Kanjar settlements.

Borders without Borderlands

I share the borderland theorists' suspicion of 'state-centrism' in social science —the tendency to treat national states as undisputed entities and borders as their natural barriers (Baud and Van Schendel 1997: 235; Van Schendel and Abraham 2005). Yet it is precisely this suspicion that makes me uneasy with borderland theory, for I am not convinced that stretching borderlines into borderlands helps to dispel the delusions of state ideology. True, analyses of modern statehood cannot be conducted in the terms provided by the state itself, and we cannot treat national borders simply as given. Yet what borderland theory fails to recognize is the fact that the border is the key structuring mechanism of the state and, as such, should stand at the base of its analysis. This oversight leads to a paradox: instead of blurring borderlines, borderland theorists end up with their reification, drawing them on maps with thicker felt pens over and over again. As territorial entities with a distinctive political, economic, and sociocultural life, borderlands appear like replicas of the nation-states they circumscribe. Thus the implied proposition that everywhere national borders are flanked by distinct sociopolitical zones sharpens instead of blurring the official geopolitical picture. In this picture, where national borders have been extended into border zones, the global grid of national states retains its shape. While the statist narrative tells us that borders are substantive, freestanding things—on maps and on land—ethnography suggests that borders are a mechanism in the set of categorical distinctions we call the state. Borders are structural entities and as such can generate different effects in different circumstances. They can enclose as well as relate; they can form barriers as much as frontiers; they can facilitate their crossing as well as enclose and divide, functioning equally well both as limits and prompts for movement. On closer inspection it turns out that national borders generate different sets of circumstances, and some are not surrounded by socially, linguistically, or politically distinct zones that straddle them on both sides. Locally borders can be understood as limits, heartlands, or peripheries. Whether dotted with gunmen and lined with barbed wire or physically unmarked (as in the Kanjar case I have discussed), borders do not necessarily generate cross-border bonds but often produce differences, whether between Indian and Pakistani citizens or between gangs. As I hope to have shown, processes observed around national borders are also present deep inside the territories of states. In other words, there is no difference of kind (and often not even of degree) between national borders and the boundaries of provinces, administrative blocs, police jurisdictions, or other administrative divisions. Aspects of 'borderlands' are as vividly present deep within the territories of national states as on their peripheries. We may say that today we live in a world where the state is a borderland. In conclusion I would like to suggest that in our study of border situations we shift analytical weight from the imagined territorial entity of the borderland to the structural phenomenon of the border, lest we find ourselves—as the sign warns—in the wrong lift or, more disconcertingly, in thin air.

NOTES TO CHAPTER 1

Research for and the writing of this essay were made financially possible by the Rhodes Trust, the Wenner-Gren Foundation, the Ada Draper Fund, the RE Katz Fund, the Boston University Anthropology Department, the Oxford Institute of Social and Cultural Anthropology, Wolfson College (Oxford), and King's College (Cambridge). My attendance at the British Association of South Asian Studies Borderlands Workshop, for which this piece was originally written, was made possible by the British Academy. My field research relied on the generosity and patience of many, but I am especially indebted to the Karmawat, Chattrapal, Chundawat, and Nat families, as well as B. L. Sisodiya and Mahendra Singh Mewar. I thank David Gellner, Jonathan Norton, Alice Obrecht, Piers Vitebsky, John Dunn, the participants of the Research Associates' Seminar in Cambridge, and two anonymous reviewers for their comments. I have transliterated Indian terms phonetically and without diacritics.

1. In its earliest usage in the early nineteenth century, the term described moors and wastelands, particularly between England and Scotland (OED), later coming to be used interchangeably with 'frontiers' of the empire, such as the North-West Frontier (Holdich 1901; Maud 1904; Ethnographical Survey of India 1909). In fin de siècle literature across genres and subjects the 'borderland' was as widely invoked in descriptions of frontiers of the British Empire as in spiritualist periodicals (D. Jones 2009). Stead's *Borderland: A Quarterly Review and Index of Psychic Phenomena*, for instance, enjoyed very wide readership in the years of its existence between 1893 and 1897 (Baylen 1969). A wasteland populated by aliens, ghosts, and ghouls, the borderland became a prominent feature of fantasy literature, where it still retains currency: consider such diverse uses as Hodgson's (1908) horror novel *The House on the Borderland*, Boyd's (1922) *Borderland Experiences; Or, Do the Dead Return?*, Windling's (1986) urban fantasy novel series entitled *Borderland* (set in a dystopian metropolis Bordertown on the frontier between Elflands and the World), or a 2004 *Star Trek* episode by the same title.

2. This literature took its inspiration from the American historian Frederick Jackson Turner's essay "The Significance of the Frontier in American History," published in 1893, in which he advanced his famous thesis of the centrality of the frontier to American history.

3. See, for instance, Asiwaju and Adenyi 1989; Berdahl 1999; Donnan and Wilson 1999; Rösler and Wendl 1999; Van Schendel and Abraham 2005. On South Asia, see Samaddar 1999; Van Schendel 2002b, 2005a, 2005b.

4. This usage of 'borderland' draws on Bolton's ([1921] 1996) seminal *The Spanish Borderlands*, in which he defined the Spanish borderlands, the northern periphery of New Spain (stretching from modern-day Florida to California), as culturally and geographically distinct regions with a distinctive mixture of native and European population. The monograph set out an analytical paradigm for generations of historians to follow (Weber 1986; Sandos 1994), with 'borderland studies' developing into a field with its own professional associations, conferences and journals since then (e.g., Gutiérrez-Witt 1990: 123; *Frontera* 1976–84; *Journal of Borderlands Studies* 1986–present; *Borderlands* 2002–present). The sheer volume of such writing is reflected in the number of books written on the subject on the 500th anniversary of Columbus's discovery of America: the three-volume *Columbian Consequences* (Thomas 1989–91) and the twenty-seven-volume set of *Spanish Borderlands Source Books* (Thomas 1991). For overviews of this literature, see Stoddard et al. 1983; Valk and Cobos 1988;

Adelman and Aron 1999; Segura and Zavella 2007; Wood 2009. For some examples, see House 1982; Gibson and Renteria 1985; McKinsey and Konrad 1989; Martínez 1994.

5. Although varying in detail, Baud and Van Schendel's (1997) model does not substantially depart from the maxims of borderland scholarship. Thus my comments apply to the borderland theory at large, examples of which are too numerous to be discussed individually here.

6. The idea of a culturally and linguistically mixed society goes back to Bolton's ([1921] 1996) definition of Spanish borderlands and has remained a staple of borderland studies. Herzog (1990: 135), for instance, refers to such mixing as the "transboundary social formation." For further examples, see Nalven, ed., "Border Perspectives on the U.S./Mexico Relationship," special issue of New Scholar 9 (1–2), 1984.

7. Historians of colonial India have written extensively about the relationship between local landed elites and the colonial state. See, for instance, Stokes 1978; Singh 1988.

8. I describe the given Kanjar community as 'professional thieves' not simply because theft is the main source of their livelihood or because the planning and execution of raids, the negotiation of spoils, and dealings with law enforcement authorities are the main preoccupation of most men in the community. I do so no less because being a thief locates Kanjars within the larger society. They are thieves in popular and official rhetoric as much as in their own self-understanding. While being thieves makes for common assumptions of their guilt among neighboring farmers, court officials, and the police, the designation also gives Kanjars an important role within local society. It is precisely their reputation as thieves that gets them employed as watchmen (according to the local maxim of 'set a thief to catch a thief'), police informers, or 'raiders' by local communities (whether these be families, villages, or business partnerships).

9. The ethnography is based on eighteen months of fieldwork conducted in increments between January 2005 and January 2009.

10. For historical writing on the politics of raiding, see Wink 1986; Kolff 1990; Gordon 1994; Guha 1999; Skaria 1999; Mayaram 2003.

11. For more on the history of special surveillance and policing measures used under the auspices of Criminal Tribes legislature, see Nigam 1990; Radhakrishna 1992, 2001; Singha 1998.

12. The Kanjars of the brotherhood think of themselves as a distinct 'society' (samaj) and accordingly avoid marriage and even commensal relations with other Kanjars. On a daily basis, the conceptual integrity of this brotherhood is reified through the exchange of women, cattle, and information, through professional cooperation and its spoils, as well as by means of mutualities of lending, borrowing, and bail.

13. Jitna badha rista, itna badha admi. A common expression, ek-jan, ek-jigar (same birth, same guts), denotes "same caste, race, family, or sort; co-religionist; of the same parents" (Platts 1884).

14. Among Kanjars this metaphor carries quite literal significance as (goat or sheep)

entrails are basic to the structuring of Kanjar society. Each major rite, whether post-partum, marriage, or mortuary, is sealed with the exchange and sharing of sheep and goat meat, where entrails are given central attention. The consumption of different parts of the viscera expresses the binary division of the society into moieties. The moieties are distinguished on the basis of their customary consumption of gall bladder (*almoda*), and one of the moiety patron goddesses is actually called Almodi Mata, literally 'Gallbladder Mother.'

15. In Rajasthan only five Kanjar villages continue to make their living through bardic activities. However, at one time most Kanjars worked as genealogists. Some old men can still align Kanjar clans with erstwhile patron castes, and fewer have preserved 'copper letters' (*tamba pattars*) inscribed with genealogies of their patron communities, once used as proof of their relationship to their *jajmans*. The withering of bardic trade and its falling into disrepute is connected to the recent dwindling of patronage ties between genealogists and their patrons. The production of family histories, which once played a central role in the 'Rajputization' of hill communities such as the Minas, Kolis, Gujars, and Bhils in the nineteenth century (Sinha 1962; Parry 1979: 118–23; Kolff 1990: 110; Guha 1999: 114), has now lost much of its currency as a mechanism of social mobility.

16. The Kanjar community to which I refer here is one of three remaining Kanjar bard communities in southern Rajasthan and the only one practicing such trade in the Chittaurgarh district.

17. An entire generation of colonial historiography has dealt with the significance of territorial demarcation in the making of the colonial Indian state. Studies are too numerous to be listed or summarized in a footnote.

18. The use of such communities as thieving parties and 'intelligence agents' (as one Rajput patron put it) was (and to some extent still is) common practice among local Rajputs, so that most local Kanjars were originally settled by their Rajput patrons.

19. The nearby cluster of 'closely allied' villages is within the territory of an adjacent thana, which became a separate jurisdiction only in 1997.

20. One consequence of such shrinking is a narrowing of employment opportunities and hence the near-disappearance of the possibility of finding sources of livelihood other than theft. Young men with some schooling who are keen to abandon their fathers' thieving trade are hard-pressed to find a job, their reputation as thieves preventing their local employment as anything but watchmen or hired thieves; besides, the confinement of their spheres of acquaintance to a few nearby villages makes factory work in a town fifty kilometers away appear unthinkable.

21. Moieties are unified in their common relationship to the tutelary goddesses Almodi Mata and Ashapal Mata and the distinctive rites associated with these.

22. Such village alliances are virilocally arranged settlements often composed of members of a single clan or *got*. In marriage conventions, the structure of moiety opposition is expressed in the isogamous cross-cousin marriage arrangement. This does

not, however, mean that all spouses are actual first, or 'womb' (*saga*), or even traceable cross-cousins. In Lakshmipura marriages with womb cross-cousins (with mother's brother's daughters and father's sister's daughters) constitute 17 percent (11 of a total 65 marriages) and marriages with secondary cross-cousins constitute 32 percent (21 of a total 65 marriages) of existing alliances. Prescriptions of alliance with persons involved in such exchange (between maternal uncles, paternal aunts, and cross-cousins in other moieties) classify all persons of the other moiety, so that parents-in-law (*sasur* and *sas*), for instance, are commonly referred to as *mama* (mother's brother) and *dado* (father's sister), as are older men and women of the opposing moiety at large.

23. I have discussed elsewhere the intimate link between the establishment of the police and the criminalization of 'protection communities' in colonial India (Piliavsky 2013). Beginning in the early 1860s a number of policing measures (including the formation of penal colonies to systems of roll call and recruitment of informers) were applied to these communities, establishing connections of patronage between the Criminal Tribes and the police (Chatterji 1981; Freitag 1991; Singha 1993).

24. Between 1956 and 1991 the relations between the police and the Lakshmipura Kanjars were interrupted, the community no longer protected by the inspector of the Criminal Tribe colony and not yet taken under the wing of the new Indian police. 'Coercive measures' were halted after the Human Rights Act passed in Rajasthan in 1985.

25. Whereas unprotected thieves may get away after paying 100 to 200 percent of the value of stolen (or presumably stolen) goods in order to be cleared of the charge, protected thieves are normally expected to submit no more than 25 to 50 percent.

26. According to the Rajasthan Police Rules, a person can be listed as a 'history sheeter' when his or her criminal record reaches or exceeds thirty offenses. History sheeters are liable to random warrant-free searches and other otherwise illegitimate policing measures. Indian Penal Code Sections 109 and 110 are commonly applied, both prescribing preemptive penalties for supposed abetment of criminal activity. The process of forming a new class after adoption can be traced to the colonial period. In reformatory Criminal Tribes colonies headmen chosen from among inmates by overseers to help in the policing of the community received more land, were spared police predation, and often capitalized on the bureaucratic procedures with which they were entrusted (e.g., by selling absentee passes).

27. By established convention, boys between the ages of five and thirteen (before they begin married lives) 'abscond' (*bhag jate*) to their mother's natal villages, where they join a thieving party and learn the tricks of the trade. After returning to their home village, they maintain close professional ties to gangs in this village, whether they operate together with its gangs or establish their own.

28. According to the Rajasthan Police Rules, even if in hot pursuit, officers must obtain permission for the pursuit from the local police station, making tracking down offenders across the boundaries of police jurisdictions effectively impossible.

29. While such intimate involvement with the police is specific to the Kanjar

community, the lives of others in the area are no less (if less constantly) affected by differences in judicial, taxation, or other policy differences between states, districts, administrative blocks, police districts, or areas under judicial jurisdiction. For instance, because a trade tax does not apply in the neighboring State of Madhya Pradesh, the cash crops grown in the bordering districts in Rajasthan (making for the bulk of the local economy) are transported for sale to the Madhya Pradesh markets. Such transportation is often lengthy and costly. The goods may be sidetracked or fail to be sold, resulting in losses. The tax differential, however, has established a convention of sale, so that notwithstanding the risk (or even likelihood) of loss, farmers insist on selling their crops in Madhya Pradesh.

30. This system inverts official prescription. Although the Rajasthan Police Rules prescribe a maximum term of two years for these ranks, most commonly remain in their posting for many decades, if not for life. The stringently competitive system of promotions paired with virtually no financial incentives makes for virtually no movement between ranks on this level. Moreover while Police Rules prescribe posting outside one's native Judicial Circle, the vast majority of low-ranking officers are posted in their home villages. These days such administrative favors on the part of the posting authorities are considered simply part of the deal in the routine purchase of such positions.

31. In Rajasthan this trend of inheritance is particularly prominent in the Rajput and Mina communities. In 2008, out of the sixteen sipahi—the constables, head constables, and assistant subinspectors—in the local police station, twelve had been acquainted with the local Kanjars for more than ten years, and four had multigenerational relationships (two of these going back three generations) with them.

32. The strength of such alliances, however durable it may be at times, is rarely guaranteed; the protection of gangs and their beats can often be volatile. If expectations are not met, officers can betray their clients, and, as allegiances are not always seamlessly transferred, the transfer of shos often means a shift in the parameters of a beat, so that the layout of beats does alter periodically.

33. While locals often blame policemen for their greed (*bhuk*, literally 'hunger') and international observers are quick to describe such activity as 'corrupt,' the dire underpayment of such officers makes such collusion virtually inevitable. For the first five years in service, constables earn a monthly wage of 3,005 rupees. This is less than half of an average government schoolteacher's salary of 8,000 rupees. Senior officers do not work in 'the field' but are preoccupied with administrative work. Their promotion relies more heavily on their satisfaction of target quotas, or the percentage of reported cases investigated and resolved and offenders apprehended.

TWO | RADHIKA GUPTA

Allegiance and Alienation
Border Dynamics in Kargil

Kargil entered the imagination of the Indian nation in a significant way only after the 1999 war with Pakistan. It had been part of the much-contested line of control (LoC) between India and Pakistan ever since the ceasefire that drew up this de facto border in 1949. It was also a central battlefront in the two wars of 1965 and 1971. Yet it was only after the Kargil war of 1999 that it found a place on the mental map of the public in India. This is a map contoured by the mighty and forbidding peaks of the Indian Himalayas, which the Indian army recaptured from the 'intruders' across the LoC, colored by images of heroic men in battle fatigues, and held forth forever after as the country's victory symbol, be it in the media or other writing on the area. Kargil is the iconic border for those who believe the sovereignty of a nation-state is contained unequivocally by its territorial borders.

When I was embarking on my fieldwork, the reactions of family and friends amused me. Unfamiliar with the world of anthropology, some innocently remarked, "Could you not find any place to do your research in but a war zone?" My tailor in Delhi, when asked to stitch clothes suitable for the mountain climate, asked in puzzlement, "What will you do there? Are you going to do something in relation to the army?"[1] For all practical purposes, Kargil, even a decade after the Kargil war, continues for most Indians to be an out-of-the-way place inhabited only by sentinels. That there might be ordinary people leading ordinary lives in this area does not quite fit into the received images of the region. This chapter seeks to rectify this image and show that while the presence of the military has an important role to play in configuring the relationship of the people of Kargil both to the border and to the state, this is only one part of the story. It does not do full justice to the reality of the borderland in their lives. For that one must go beyond an understanding of the border as only a geographical and political boundary that divides one side from the other.

Unlike many other borderlands that are quite porous and thereby see both licit and illicit flows of people and goods across them,[2] heavy policing coupled with the natural barrier of the mountainous terrain permits few border crossings along the LoC in Kargil, especially after the 1999 war. The literature on borderlands has shown that border crossings are important to understanding the spatial and cultural organization of nation-states and the discourse through which legitimacy is sought (Horstmann 2004). Through her work in Northern Ireland Aretxaga (1998: 19) urges a reading of borders as spaces "where national imaginings are rendered unstable." In a similar vein, in her ethnography on Muslim pastoralist Jatts in Kachchh living along the border with Sindh, Ibrahim (2009) shows that their relationship to the border is dissonant with the official discourse of the the State of Gujarat in India. Contemporary Gujarat seeks to define its identity through a regional variant of Hindutva ideology, which ignores the historical sociocultural relationship between Kachchh and Sindh; however, the nomadic Jatts continue to embrace Sindh in Pakistan both symbolically and through migration (52). Thus whether through narratives of actual border crossings or symbolic attachments to spaces that cut across the official demarcation of culturally and ecologically homogeneous territories, work on borderlands has amply demonstrated that the border offers a different vantage point from which to view the nation-state (Wilson and Donnan 1998a). The analyses, however, tend to place borderlanders either in a position of encapsulation and accommodation within the bounded space of the nation-state or in a stance of resistance, often of a violent kind. It is difficult to apply this dichotomy to the relationship of people living in the Kargil borderland with the Indian nation-state. Kargilis relate to the nation-state in a multiplicity of ways, structured both by allegiance and by alienation, through the reality and the rhetoric of the border in their lives. This chapter attempts to convey the complexity of this relationship.

From 'Frontier' to Border: Historical Background

It is useful to remember that Kargil was historically a 'frontier,' a region not politically delimited by boundaries between states, nor was it a periphery or margin to the Indian nation-state as it is perceived today in the wider public imagination. Uberoi (1978: 74–75) writes, "A true frontier is an autonomous region which represents the conjunction, the unity and the opposition of two or more other regions, such that all of them together form a patterned whole in some one or other aspect of society and history." Said to be derived from *khar* (fort) and *rkil* (center), Kargil denotes a place between many forts, a central place where people could stay. Geographically Kargil is indeed located at a crossroads, equidistant from Srinagar, Leh, and Skardu (Baltistan) (see map 2.1). Culturally the ethnoracial mix of the inhabitants of Kargil represents the conjunction of all these regions. Sociopolitically, it represents the dividing line or "opposition" (74–75) between the Muslim and non-Muslim parts of Ladakh and Baltistan prior to the Partition of the subcontinent. Understanding Kargil as a frontier enables us to move away from viewing it merely as a political border between two nation-states and locate it within a longer historical span.

Prior to the Partition of India in 1947–48, Kargil, or Purig, together with Baltistan and Leh constituted the Ladakh *wazarat* (province), sometimes referred to today as Greater Ladakh. A key gateway between Central Asia and Tibet, it was a region with a long and rich history of cross-border ties forged by trade, religion, and political alliances extending as far as Yarkand and Kashgar toward the north, Tibet in the east, and the Kashmir Valley to the south (Rizvi 1996, 1999). This came to be reflected in the ethnic mix of people in the region. According to local historians such as Kacho Sikandar Khan, the Purigpa, the people of central Kargil, are the mixed descendants of two races, the Dards and the Mongols, who started intermarrying following the cessation of warfare between the two groups in the tenth century.

Kargil even today is a mosaic of several different cultures and languages. Three major ethnic categories make up its cultural fabric: the Balti and Purigpa (both a mix of Tibetan-Mongoloid and Aryan stock, speaking similar Tibetan dialects); Dards and Brogpa (both of Indo-Aryan stock and speaking an Indo-European language); and the Bhoto (Tibetan-Mongoloid, speaking Tibetan-derived dialects). Of these various groups, the Purigpa and the Bhoto are the largest. All these groups, along with other, smaller groups, some based

MAP 2.1. The position of Kargil in relation to neighboring regions.

on occupational status, were accorded Scheduled Tribe status by the central state in 1989.[3]

While much has been written about the cosmopolitan nature of Leh as an important entrepôt for trans-Himalayan trade (Rizvi 1999), Kargil is perhaps a frontier in the true sense of the term, for it represents the conjunction not only of different ethnoracial groups but also of religious regions.[4] While the majority of the people of Leh are Buddhists, with spiritual and religious links to Tibet, the people of Kargil and Baltistan are Muslims. Islam traveled to Kargil via Baltistan with preachers from Khorasan from the sixteenth century onward. Certain areas, such as Chigtan, remained Buddhist till as recently as a hundred years ago. Family genealogies in Chigtan often reveal Buddhist names just three or four generations back. Several villages in Kargil even today are a mix of Muslims and Buddhists. While the majority of Kargilis belong to the Twelver Shi'ite sect of Islam, a sizable population of Dard Sunni Muslims is found in the Drass area, whose genealogies can be traced to ancestors in Gilgit. Thus in the current geopolitical frame, Kargil marks the dividing line between the Muslim and non-Muslim worlds: Kashmir valley to the south over the Zoji-la Pass and Gilgit-Baltistan to the west are both Muslim, while Leh (Ladakh) to the east is predominantly Buddhist.

These religious differences were ignored in the creation of administrative units under the Raj. Ladakh and Gilgit came to be designated as wazarats, their fate conjoined with Jammu and the Kashmir Valley into a single administrative unit under the reign of the Hindu Dogra rulers of Jammu in 1901. Raja Gulab Singh, a feudatory of the Sikh Durbar in Lahore, had aligned himself with the British in the first Anglo-Sikh war of 1856. With the victory of the British, the treaty of Amritsar was signed and Gulab Singh was installed as the maharaja of the combined State of Jammu and Kashmir, including Ladakh (Bray 2005: 16). During the Dogra reign, Gilgit wazarat was leased to the British because of the strategic significance it held for them in the Great Game. The Dogra era is often recalled by Ladakhis as a time of great oppression. As an elder in Kargil put it, "The oppression was so great that when Zorawar Singh [a general in the Dogra army] attacked Skardu, it is said that women would jump off the fort into the Sindhu (Indus) River in order to escape being raped."

The Partition

As Sir Cyril Radcliffe was hurriedly dividing the pie between India and Pakistan, the question of the fate of the princely states came up. The majority acceded to India or Pakistan by the time of the 'transfer of power' in August 1947, with the exception of Hyderabad, Junagadh, and Jammu and Kashmir. Both Hyderabad and Junagadh had Muslim rulers over a largely Hindu population, while Jammu and Kashmir had Hindu rulers over a majority Muslim population. Unlike these other two 'problem' States, Jammu and Kashmir already possessed what Lamb (1997: 96) calls "an active and complex public political life of its own." After 1931 two major groupings in the Kashmir Valley, the National Conference and the Muslim Conference, came into existence. Both were opposed to the ruling Dogra dynasty, and their agitation produced a certain degree of constitutional development leading to the formation of a legislature, the Praja Sabha, in which franchise was organized on a communal basis. Lamb classifies public opinion in Jammu and Kashmir over the issue of accession into four broad categories:

1. Hindus in Jammu and Hindu Brahmin Pandits of the Kashmir valley supported the Dogras.
2. In Ladakh, a new Buddhist political consciousness had begun to crystallize, which tilted towards being with the Hindus.
3. The Muslim Conference, which represented the bulk of the Muslims in Jammu, and the more hard-line Muslims of the Valley opposed the idea of joining the Indian union.
4. The National Conference had a relatively secular outlook with a preference for an independent Kashmir. (my summary of Lamb 1997: 96–97)

Exceptions to this categorization were the Gilgit wazarat and the Baltistan portion of Ladakh, which generally subsumed the people of Kargil by virtue of religious affinity. Gilgit, which had been on lease to the British, reverted to the rule of the Hindu maharaja in 1947, without consultation with the people, the majority of whom were Muslim. There was latent resentment against this move, and thus, while the maharaja ruled, de facto it was the Gilgit Scouts (a paramilitary force originally raised by the British in the Gilgit Agency) who held real power in the region. The maharaja, in his prevarication over which dominion to join, signed stand-still agreements on 12 August 1947 with both India and Pakistan in a bid to maintain the status quo. In the meantime revolt had erupted in Poonch in the Kashmir Valley against Dogra rule. To contend with this, the maharaja, while packing his bags to retreat to the safe haven of Jammu, appealed to Indian political leaders for military assistance. The Gilgit rebellion finally broke out in early November 1947. A branch of the maharaja's army rebelled in Skardu, and groups of pro-Pakistani Gilgit Scouts entered and occupied Kargil, Nubra, Sham, and Zangskar. After several months of battle the Indian forces compelled them to retreat, and a cease-fire demarcating an arbitrary line of control was drawn up, fragmenting the Ladakh wazarat between the two nations of India and Pakistan. Leh and Kargil came under the administration of Jammu and Kashmir, while Baltistan and the Gilgit wazarat came to constitute the Northern Areas of Pakistan. Until 1979 Leh and Kargil together constituted the district of Ladakh, after which Kargil was designated as a separate district.

The LoC has been a flash point for the assertion of sovereignty by both India and Pakistan ever since, as evidenced in the ongoing dispute over

Kashmir, which has become central to the ideological opposition between the secular and the Islamic in South Asia. The people of Leh and Kargil had little say in their destiny being tied to the Kashmir Valley. The absence of the voices of the people of Kargil is particularly conspicuous in the history of the Partition in Kashmir. The sentiments of the Sunni Muslims of the Valley are well known, as are those of Buddhist leaders of Leh, who launched a struggle for autonomy from Jammu and Kashmir in 1989, alleging that the political conflict in the Valley had been eclipsing their developmental and political concerns (Behera 2000). While this feeling of neglect was shared by the Muslims of Kargil, they have never supported the demand in Leh for declaration of Ladakh as a Union Territory. The agitation for autonomy was framed in communal terms by Buddhist leaders, leading to a rigidification of religious boundaries and communalization of politics in Ladakh (Van Beek 1996; Aggarwal 2004). However, before discussing the impact of regional politics on the equation of Kargilis with the nation-state, I turn to a few Kargili voices on the Partition—an event not limited to 1947–48 for them, but extending to the subsequent wars between India and Pakistan in 1965 and 1971. The Kargil war shook most Indians, if only for a brief moment, out of their complacent assumption that the LoC was set in stone. For Kargilis, by contrast, the precariousness of this de facto border has always been a reality.

Partition Unfinished

People in Kargil were unaware of the first stirrings of Partition. In those days many men from Kargil migrated to Shimla in Himachal Pradesh and areas of Uttar Pradesh and Punjab in search of labor work. An elder in Kargil recalled that they first heard about figures like Nehru and Jinnah from these migrant laborers visiting home, while chatting at the *changra*, a place where the men of the neighborhood gathered socially. It was only with the rebellion of the Gilgit Scouts that the force of events struck Kargilis.

The Gilgit Scouts first captured Gilgit town and then, crossing Rong-yul, moved toward Skardu in January 1948. In the rendition of local historians in Kargil, the army of the maharaja of Skardu was besieged in Kharpo-Che, the fort at Skardu, and as the fighting continued there, a segment of the Gilgit Scouts moved toward Kargil.[5] At this time a thousand men of the Indian army came via Kashmir to Kargil. On 5 May 1948 Kargil was attacked. The Indian army was small, and the men fled to the Suru Valley, facilitating the movement of the Gilgit Scouts toward Leh. It is interesting to note the difference in the way the Gilgit Scouts are referred to. A Sunni intellectual whose ancestors settled in Kargil as *mulazims* (those in government service) of the Dogra regime referred to the Gilgit Scouts as the Pakistani army. A local Balti intellectual whose ancestors were traders settled in Kargil referred to them as those who freed them from the oppressive Dogra regime. According to him, many Kargilis from villages like Hardas, Tambis, and Poyen also joined the Gilgit Scouts. He added, "Up to then there was no Hindustan or Pakistan," suggesting that Kargilis were not participating in a coup against India. When the Gilgit Scouts captured the area near Basgo, forty kilometers downstream from Leh, detachments of the Indian army arrived. This, combined with the onset of the winter, forced the Scouts to retreat, fleeing to Skardu, thus freeing Kargil too. According to the historian Abdul Hamid Tanvir, "The Indian army attacked Kargil under the leadership of Brigadier Hiralal Atal via the Tik-Tik-Mo route and, finding Kargil empty, captured it." He added, "The people of Drass and Matayen [the last village before the Zoji-la, en route to the Valley] also helped the Indian army [see figure 2.1]. The people of Kargil also supported the Indian army and started helping it." The fighting continued until a cease-fire was declared in July 1949.

As elsewhere in India (Butalia 1998), silence enshrouds the Partition in Kargil. The subject seldom appeared naturally in the course of general conversations about the history of the region, as compared to the enthusiasm to talk about the history of *qadim* (ancient) Ladakh. The absence in Kargil of the violence and massive cross-border migration of populations that Punjab experienced at the Partition may in part account for this silence.[6] Another reason, however, which reflects the way the people of this region relate to the Indian nation-state, or 'Hindustan,' as they call it, may also offer an explanation for the scant mention of this critical event. When I asked them, perhaps unfairly, which side would the people of Kargil have chosen, had they been given a choice, I got two strikingly different responses. After some thought, the young Balti intellectual replied, "If the elders had been asked which side they would have chosen at that time, the response would have been Pakistan because of the *zulm* [oppression] of the Dogras." He added, "But people in Gilgit today are regretting that they went to Pakistan. At that time they were under emotional stress under Dogra oppression. There was no Pakistani in the Gilgit Scouts."[7] In contrast, the Sunni intellectual (of Kashmiri origin) immediately said, "Kargil always wanted to remain with Kashmir. There were

FIGURE 2.1. The Road to Drass, 2008. The mist-shrouded mountain in the background is under Pakistani control—hence the warning on the signboard. Photograph courtesy of R. Gupta.

trade relations, and most commodities came from Kashmir. The blockage of the road in 1948 led to a lot of difficulties in Kargil—a famine broke out . . . dead bodies were buried without a *kafan* [funeral shroud]. When the Indian army finally arrived people were very happy, as the road from Kashmir was reopened. Further, employment was provided to the local people as coolies, ponies [were] hired, and numerous appointments were made in the civilian administration."

It is clear that, despite the not so subtle difference in viewpoints, both historians ultimately converged on emphasizing the loyalty of Kargilis to Hindustan once the LoC had been drawn up. This loyalty to the Indian nation-state, however, is not a simple story of allegiance or submission to its dominant discourse. Different contexts and borders of a nonterritorial kind, such as those between different religious sects, enter the equation and complicate the relationship of Kargilis to the territorial border. Further, the story of the Partition of India in the Kargil sector continued to be scripted even after the drawing up of the LoC in 1949, as it shifted in two subsequent wars with Pakistan, in 1965 and 1971. Several villages experienced division and shuffling between India and Pakistan. The stakes of sovereignty vested in this region are reflected in the Kargil government website's proud proclamation in a random list of "highlights" or achievements of the district that villages like "Badgam, Lato and Hundoorman were annexed and added to Kargil in 1971."[8] Take, for example, the case of Badgam village.

The largely Shina-speaking village of Badgam, whose inhabitants claim descent from the Indo-Aryan people of Dardistan and are said to have settled there in *qadim zamana* (ancient times), lay within Pakistan until 1965. During the 1965 war, half of this village was annexed to Indian territory, while the other, marked off by a mere *nallah* (stream of water), continued to be under Pakistani control. Both parts of the village were united in 1971, when the second half was also brought under India. A much respected *shaykh* of this village related how he was separated from his younger brother in this shifting of territory between the two nation-states. His brother had been away for *ziyarat* (pilgrimage) to Iran and Iraq when the 1971 war between India and Pakistan broke out. Holding a Pakistani passport, he could never return to his village, as it was annexed by India during the war. Ever since, there has been a strong army presence. People say that sometimes their livestock stray over, but they are not allowed to go and fetch them. They complain about the meager compensation given for land lost to mining of patches by the Indian army and that mobile phones do not work in the village. On the whole, however, there is general acceptance of their fate. There is no mention of any sort of border crossing.

Living Close to the Line of Control

For villages like Badgam, Partition is not a 'critical event' that took place in 1947–48. Their recent inclusion in the Indian nation-state has left them in a liminal space: part of India, but not quite within the full vision of the Indian state. For the people of these villages, it is the army that is the predominant face of the Indian state. Unlike the civilian administration, governed by local politics, where the boundaries between state and society are blurred, there is a clear-cut distinction between people and state when it comes to the army. In the present day, for the most part, the army is seen as a benevolent force, ironically revealing the very liminality of such areas with respect to mainstream governance. The Kargil war of 1999 brought about a transformation in the relationship between the army and the people of Kargil.

As one crosses the Iqbal bridge over the Suru River while driving into Kargil town from the direction of Leh, a rock face proclaims, "Jawan aur awam, aman hai mukam" (Soldiers and people together and there is peace), signaling the nature of the relationship that the army claims to share with civilians in Kargil. This equation of brotherhood has been a recent development. Mistrust characterized the relationship between the army and local people before the Kargil war. Although the situation was markedly different from that in the Kashmir Valley, where much has been written about human rights atrocities committed by the armed forces, people in Kargil still feared the army.[9] Elders recall how, as children, they would run away and hide on seeing a soldier or vehicle approaching. It was only hesitantly (according to one of the many narratives surrounding the issue of local intelligence) that the people in the Drass and Batalik region reported to the army that they had seen Pakistani insurgents in the winter of 1998, fearing that suspicion might be cast upon them instead.[10] During the Kargil war itself, locals were indispensable to the army as guides and porters on the treacherous mountain terrain. Yet even then the army looked upon them with suspicion, alleging that they were in league with the insurgents. In a volume of recollections of reporting on the Kargil war, the journalist Sankarshan Thakur (1999: 12) recounts that one day, while driving back from Batalik to Kargil town, his driver, a local, was harassed and searched next to a Bofor's gun position near Apati, with the gunner saying, "This is no ordinary war. We are fighting a hostile enemy from hostile ground. There is little local support. You see this is not a war for Kargil; this is a war for Kashmir. We have had to fight Kashmiris to keep Kashmir. Trust is a tough thing." Another journalist describes local politicians telling him that they felt insulted when Kargilis were accused of being spies: "If we had not wanted the Indian army here the troops would never have been able to stay even a single day" (Jaleel 1999: 91).

This hurt runs deep, for even ten years later I was told the same thing time and again: that Kargil is the only Muslim-dominated area of Kashmir where militancy has not been able to strike root. When the Indian army realized that they could not have won the Kargil war without the support of the locals, the Sadbhavana (goodwill) program was established in 2001 under the leadership of Lt. Gen. Arjun Ray with the objective of building bridges between the army and civilians. Under this program, the army opened schools in remote villages, a disability center, skills-training workshops for women, and an apricot-processing center. Sadbhavana worked well as a confidence-building measure between the army and civilians. The extent of its success in terms of a sense of ownership by the locals is, however, questionable. While appreciated by Kargilis, there is still a pervasive perception that it is the army's program. Unlike local ownership of development schemes routed through the civilian administration, the sense of distance between Sadbhavana and civilians suggests a clear-cut boundary between the army, as one face of the state, and the people. In an analysis of the Sadbhavana program, Aggarwal and Bhan (2009) rightly argue that development interventions by the army, although not new as subsidiary to the role of the civilian administration in this domain, are becoming a means to legitimize increased militarization of democratic societies. However, when viewed from the perspective of the people, some have no choice but to rely on the military's development largesse. For this reason, despite the sense of distance from it, the army is an awkward but welcome presence in some villages closer to the LoC.

The increased presence of the army after the 1999 war spawned a parallel economy of goods sold on the black market to the benefit of locals and army alike. In villages close to the border, in the Batalik sector, for instance, locals found new avenues to earn income by driving taxis for the army, becoming porters, and renting out rooms to accommodate the influx of migrant Nepali workers. More important than this parallel economy, however, is the role that the army has been playing in sectors normally under the purview of the civilian administration, in this case, primarily the Ladakh Autonomous Hill Development Council. The case of Lato village demonstrates this.

The predominantly Balti village of Lato came into being after the 1965 war between India and Pakistan. Driving about fifteen kilometers out of Kargil town on the Srinagar Highway, the River Drass meets the Shingo. Near this junction, an old, nonmotorable wooden bridge connects the highway to the other side, leading to a rocky mule path that disappears into the mountainside. This is the road to Lato village, which lies four kilometers from the LoC. The inhabitants of Lato were brought down from their village of Drelung on the LoC as a temporary measure to protect them from Pakistani shells in 1965. Later, however, a full-fledged army picket was established in Drelung, and the people were permanently settled on an open plateau-like piece of land farther down the mountain, which is now the village of Lato. This land is uncultivable for lack of water. Even though the emerald-green waters of the Shingo swirl in the deep gorge below, the villagers lament that they are not able to use it for lack of appropriate technology and infrastructure. The main source of sustenance for the people of Lato is portering work for the army picket in Drelung. Water, a motorable bridge, and a road from the main highway constitute the long-standing demands of the people of Lato from the civilian administration. But their pleas have yielded only false promises. Inhabitants of Lato say, "Only the army has stood by our side. We don't exist on the map as far as the local administration goes." A young man commented rhetorically, "The authorities do not even know if we are a part of India or not."[11]

I visited the village of Lato on 16 August 2008, a day after witnessing the enthusiastic celebration of Independence Day in Kargil town. Lato had organized its own little celebration in the ground of the middle school, with the captain from the nearby army post acting as the chief guest to salute the parade of schoolchildren. Several people in the village gathered on my first night there to show me a video-recording of this function. Speeches and poetry by village intelligentsia reiterated the patriotism of the people of Lato to India.[12] The next day I was escorted with much enthusiasm farther up the gorge to get a view of the LoC, the pride evident among my companions at being the last sentinels of India. Yet for the people of Lato, the fervor of their patriotism is lost on the state. As long as they remain marginal to governance by the civilian administration, there is a perception of their being incomplete citizens of the nation. A military presence in the daily lives of people will always represent a 'state of exception,' even in the absence of violence.[13]

In his work on Siam, or modern-day Thailand, Winichakul (1994) has persuasively shown how the 'geo-body' of a nation is the effect of maps: the nation as a discursive construct comes into being through its territorial demarcation. He writes, "To a considerable extent, the knowledge about the Siamese nationhood has been created by our conception of Siam-on-the-map, emerging from maps and existing nowhere apart from the map" (17). It is not surprising that border villages like Lato and Badgam are invisible on maps of the region. But with their absence on the map, not only is the fragility of the boundary of the nation-state inadvertently acknowledged, but the inhabitants of these areas are also effectively excluded from the geo-body of the nation, as alluded to in the rhetorical statement from Lato about the civil administration not even knowing the village belongs to India. Zones of classification within border areas as being either 'inner-line' or 'accessible' thus allow certain regions to enter the geo-body of the nation more than others.

The question that needs to be raised is to what extent the neglect of the needs of Lato are entirely determined by their position as borderlanders. Is there a certain amount of rhetoric in their narrative of alienation? Or do they simply face a heightened version of the sociopolitical tensions experienced by other marginalized communities across the country? When does the border become a rhetorical, albeit legitimate, claim-making device? And how does the 'reality' of the border enter lives in other symbolic ways? I examine this question through the example of the Balti community in Kargil.

Symbolic Attachments across the Border: Kinship, Poetry, and Music

The people of Leh routinely refer to all Shi'a Muslims in Ladakh generically as Baltis (Grist 1998).[14] However, the Baltis are a distinct community whose ancestors migrated from Baltistan to Kargil and Leh before Partition. Most Baltis came to Kargil as traders, but some are also descendants of preachers who came from Baltistan. Three villages in Kargil district—Hardas, Lato, and Karkichu—situated on the left bank of the Drass, a couple of miles from the main Kargil town, are predominantly Balti. These villages came under the *jagir* (estate) of the raja of Kharmang, one of the valleys in the Skardu Tehsil. According to a Balti elder, the raja brought people from Hamzigund and Singkarmo and settled them in what is present-day Hardas. These villages provided a halting point for the raja during his travels. In Kargil town itself there are about five thousand Baltis, mostly living in a neighborhood called Balti Bazaar, one of the oldest bazaars of the area, where traders from Kharmang settled.[15] When the cease-fire was announced in 1948, the LoC cut through Balti-inhabited areas, separating people living in Balti Bazaar and villages like Hardas and Karkichu from their kin in Baltistan. The arbitrariness of this political boundary is perhaps most starkly experienced by the Baltis who continue to maintain strong symbolic attachments to their place of origin. The political stalemate between India and Pakistan made legal travel to their original homes impossible until the mid-1980s, and even today telephone lines to Pakistan remain cut off from the Indian side.[16] Despite these difficulties of travel and communication, Baltis on both sides have maintained strong affective and cultural links. This world of cross-border Balti relations brings forth the reality of the border in a way that is distinct from its political rhetoric.

As is characteristic of communities in exile, there is immense nostalgia for Baltistan among those few of the older generation of Baltis who remember a childhood unfettered by the border. Never able to return, they express a deep sense of loss for their homes, lands, relatives, and friends on the other side. Api Fatima,[17] a seventy-three-year-old from Balti Bazaar, one of the few of her generation still alive, came from Gandus village in the Kharmang Valley of Baltistan to Kargil on getting married at the age of twelve to her husband, who was a trader. She could never return to visit her natal family. A few years ago her elder sister in Pakistan sent Api a video cassette of her family. Api's daughter recalled that her mother started crying when she saw her family on the cassette, adding, "Now she keeps anything nice that she has for her sister in Baltistan." Meanwhile Api reminisced about her village in Baltistan, recalling the apples and apricots of her childhood. Another old gentleman in Balti Bazaar was more fortunate than Api Fatima. In October 2008 he had returned from visiting his brother in Pakistan for the second time. Trying to convey to me how "sweet" was the water of his village, Pari, in Baltistan, he remarked, "The water of Pari is the best in the whole *ilaqa* [region]. . . . Even black people become white after drinking it." As I was leaving, Apo dipped into his pockets and offered me a handful of dried apricots and small dried black currants called *basho,* saying, "These are special; they are from Baltistan." I bit into an apricot and told Apo how delicious it was. His lined face broke into a wide smile.

It is not only the older generation of Baltis who feel a strong attachment to Baltistan. A combination of needing to reinforce their identity as a minority and genuine curiosity have engaged the younger generation of Baltis in a vigorous cultural dialogue with their counterparts in Baltistan. This dialogue takes place in a variety of mediums. Most popular among these is the writing and recitation of *shairi* (poetry), a genre becoming increasingly popular in Kargil to express both personal and political sentiments. Poets like Sadiq Ali Sadiq, Bashir Wafa, and Septe Hassan Kaleem have been producing Balti verse that is much appreciated on both sides of the border. As people in Kargil began to obtain visas in the 1980s to visit Baltistan, some of these poets traveled there, returning with stories of the special *mushairas* (poetry sessions) organized in their honor and lamenting the 'shallowness' of Kargil's literary culture in comparison with Baltistan. Recordings of these mushairas are eagerly borrowed and circulated within the wider Balti community in Kargil, as are photograph albums of their visits. One day a young poet showed me a packet of souvenirs of his visit to Baltistan. Along with a CD of a mushaira in which he was honored and a photograph album, there was also a brochure of a shop in Skardu that makes furniture from local materials. The preservation of seemingly trivial material like this is an indication of how poignant the separation from Baltistan is for them.[18]

The Baltis in Kargil pride themselves on the preservation of their culture and language. Extolling the *adab* of Balti culture,[19] they would often joke that even their friends across the border have at times remarked that they speak a purer Balti, uncorrupted by the influence of Urdu, as has happened in Pakistan. Through vigorous cultural activism, the Baltis have been successful in having their language recognized in the Sixth Schedule of the Constitution of Jammu and Kashmir and have successfully lobbied for a weekly Balti program on Radio Kargil. Complaining about the insufficient appreciation of their language, a Balti activist lamented that this radio slot was given only on the ground that it would help to counter Pakistani propaganda on Radio Skardu. Such cultural activism is an example of how the Partition has shaped new, more conscious identities.[20]

In recent years traditional Balti has also been set to pop music to popularize and keep the language alive among the younger generation. Classical poems as well as modern-day lyrics penned by poets in Baltistan are set to music in Kargil, as religious disapproval of music is said to be less strictly enforced than in Baltistan. The cassettes and CDs produced in Kargil travel back to Baltistan with pilgrims from both sides meeting on the *hajj* or *ziyarat* in Iran, Iraq, and Saudi Arabia. A different genre of music travels from Baltistan to Kargil. *Qasidas* and *nauhas* from Baltistan are extremely popular in Kargil.[21] In fact the Baltis in Kargil take pride in having brought the 'culture of Islam' to Kargil. As the early preachers of Islam came to Kargil via Baltistan, the language of religious expression, especially hymns and elegies sung in Kargil even today, continues to be Balti. Radio Skardu has a wide audience in Kargil and is heard with particular enthusiasm in Balti settlements, especially by older uneducated women who do not understand Urdu. Another new medium of communication between people on both sides of the border that is becoming increasingly popular is the Internet. Some of the more savvy and educated young Baltis regularly visit Internet cafés in Kargil bazaar to chat in real time with friends and relatives in Baltistan, often even striking up cyber friendships with strangers through extended kinship and friendship networks. Thus territorial limitations are transcended through new trans-local sites, constituting new "pluri-local" spaces in the "transnationalization of social space" (Horstmann 2004: 7).

For all the nostalgia for Baltistan, the vibrant cultural conversation between the two sides, and a shared realization of the need to keep their culture alive, there is no desire among the Baltis of Kargil to return to their original home-land in any sort of permanent way. They consider themselves fortunate to be Indian citizens. It is not just a comparison of the cultural and religious ambi-ence between Kargil and Baltistan as related by those who made the journey to Skardu and beyond that is voiced. Nostalgia for the past and longing for people, places, and things from Baltistan and Gilgit are tempered by knowledge of the pragmatic conditions of daily life, witnessed firsthand. Those who have been to Baltistan come back shocked at the price of basic commodities like cooking gas, for instance, in comparison to the prices in India. Further, there is an acute awareness of political alienation among the people of Gilgit-Baltistan and sectarian violence against the Shi'a in Pakistan. Political marginaliza-tion in Gilgit-Baltistan has given rise to nationalist movements demanding autonomy from Pakistan, sometimes expressed through calls for the revival of Greater Ladakh. A Balti writer in exile in the United States writes, "We started a weekly magazine called *Phayuli Spera*, or Talk of the Fatherland. We exposed the fact that Islamabad imprisoned and tortured Gilgiti freedom fighters who had protested the 1948 annexation. We also informed our readers that UN resolutions actually demand that the Pakistan Army withdraw from Gilgit and Baltistan" (Hussanan 2008).[22]

Responses to political alienation have also been manifest in less overtly political forms, such as through cultural activism that seeks to distinguish the identity of this region from that of Pakistan. MacDonald's (2006) work describes how tropes of Tibetan authenticity and 'culture' are being appropri-ated from a transnational discursive realm to foreground Baltistan's 'Tibetan' past in order to extricate the region from the dominant negative represen-tations of Pakistan in the Western world. Efforts are being made in Skardu to revive the Bodik (Tibetan) script and folk music and preserve remnants of Buddhist monuments.[23] While this cultural activism is echoed by Kargili activists, their goals are entirely different from those in Baltistan. Activists in Kargil are seeking to reclaim the region's more 'composite' heritage from the threat posed by purveyors of a more puritan reformist Islam, while cultural activism in Gilgit-Baltistan is an expression of political alienation from the Pakistani state.[24] The cultural exchange between the two sides of the border, or what MacDonald terms "trans-border incipient identity formation," is often expressed as a call for the revival of Greater Ladakh. From the perspective of the Kargilis, this in no way poses a challenge to the sovereignty of the Indian nation-state. In their perception, the revival of Greater Ladakh will enhance trade across the border and ease overland travel to Baltistan and Gilgit. There is little discussion of any dissolution of political boundaries in their imagination of Greater Ladakh.

The Border in Regional Context

The desire continually to reassure the state of their allegiance is not limited to those who live close to the LoC and are often portrayed as 'outsiders' within intraregional ethnic politics, such as the people of Badgam and Lato or the Baltis. More than any other factor, it is perhaps this sentiment of straining to belong and be accepted as loyal citizens of the Indian state that unites all Kargilis. This is manifest not only in heightened displays of patriotism at official state functions or in more quotidian forms of expression such as poetry, but also in explicit endorsement of nationalist ideologies. The way Kargilis constantly extol the doctrine of secularism, despite being aware of its contradictions in practice, is particularly striking. This can only be understood by seeing how the border dynamic in their lives is shaped by their relationship of allegiance and alienation to the Kashmir Valley.

Kargil's relationship with Kashmir has always been somewhat ambivalent, colored by the sectarian difference with the predominantly Sunni Valley. Besides the discrimination that Kargilis experience in their dealings with the State administration or the generally negative attitude toward the Shi'a, the sectarian difference becomes paramount in their unequivocal condemnation of separatist movements in the Kashmir Valley. Kargilis have sought at every opportunity to distance themselves from the politics of the Valley in this respect, of which their heightened displays of patriotism are a symbolic expression. Yet at the same time Kargil sees its destiny as being entwined with that of the Valley. This is evident in the fact that Kargil has never supported Leh's demand for Union Territory status, despite sharing with it the sentiment that Ladakh's development suffered needlessly from the political conflict in the Valley. However, the relatively rapid pace of development in Leh, coupled with the communalization of politics in the region, has led to Kargilis feeling underconfident, vulnerable, and insecure vis-à-vis the Buddhists of Leh. As a result they derive a sense of security in the shelter of their religious affinity with Kashmir, overriding the sectarian issue. They fear even greater perceived marginalization by being clubbed together with the Buddhists of Leh in an administrative entity independent of Kashmir. This sheltering aspect of Kashmir has, however, been a double-edged sword for Kargilis, as it has also been responsible in large part for their invisibility to the Indian public. Until the 1999 war, when the people of Kargil were able to convince the state of their patriotism to India, they were simply assumed to be Kashmiris, subsumed under a pan-Muslim label and subject to the same sorts of discrimination, prejudices, and suspicion that Kashmiri Muslims face beyond the confines of Jammu and Kashmir.

Kargil's double bind in relation to Kashmir became evident in the summer of 2008, when the ruling Congress–PDP (People's Democratic Party) coalition allocated about forty hectares of forest land in the Valley to the Amarnath Shrine Board to build shelters for Hindu pilgrims. This created a furor in the State, and allegedly separatist parties in the Valley united to launch a protest against what they deemed a communal act. This in turn instigated counter-protests by Hindus in Jammu. Public support for demonstrations both in the Valley and in Jammu was reported by the national press as being second in scale only to the outpouring of people's sentiments when the insurgency was at its peak in the early 1990s. In August 2008, as thousands of Kashmiris marched to the LoC, toward the Pakistani town of Muzaffarabad,[25] people in Kargil were much more preoccupied with the upcoming elections to the local hill council. The Amarnath land transfer issue was a topic of discussion but subsidiary to the council elections. While Kargilis remarked upon the disproportionate killing of Muslims who violated curfews as compared to the Hindu protestors in Jammu, clearly conscious of the breakdown of the secular discourse of the nation-state, they generally adopted a quiet stance toward the whole controversy, dismissing it as yet another instance of the political manipulation of religious sentiments. One day in August, however, all the shops in the bazaar suddenly closed their shutters in the middle of the afternoon as Kargilis staged a march to express solidarity with the Kashmiris. However, rumors had it that this march took place under pressure from the PDP in Srinagar and not at the behest of the villagers. A few young men at the head of the procession in the bazaar shouted condemnatory slogans against India. Not only were these universally condemned by Kargilis across local political factions and dismissed as being the work of youth who did not belong to Kargil, but the protest was also quickly truncated for fear that it might go astray. A rhetorical call to march toward Skardu was also made, but nothing came of it. This instance clearly shows that Kargilis, despite their close relation to Kashmir, do not want to be associated with separatist sentiments. Even though there is an implicit acknowledgment that ultimately Kargil will always want to be with Kashmir, regardless of the nation-state in which it is located, by virtue of basic religious affinity, the preferred choice of Kargilis is to be with India. And as long as Kashmir is with India, all the energies of Kargilis are consumed by aspirations and plans to develop their own region. Thus, despite the token protest march in solidarity with Kashmir over the Amarnath Shrine Board issue, the attention of the people of Kargil was really focused on the imminent hill council elections.

The Border Fades Away?

All major decisions and funding on regional development in Ladakh are taken by the Ladakh Autonomous Hill Development Council (LAHDC), with separate branches in Leh and Kargil. Of the civilian developmental apparatus, the LAHDC is perhaps the most powerful state institution in the region. When the provision for setting up the LAHDC was first granted in 1996 in response to the struggle for autonomy and Union Territory status by the Buddhists of Leh, it was rejected by Kargil, fearing that it would threaten their ties with Kashmir. Over the next few years, however, Kargilis saw the immense power and funds vested in the council in Leh and decided to set up the Kargil Council in 2003. At its inception, the majority of the people in Kargil did not really understand the full import of the LAHDC. By the time the second elections came around in 2008, an acute political consciousness had developed within Kargili society.

Kargilis have been able to assert their voice with much more confidence after the Kargil war, which established their loyalty to the nation-state. This has manifested itself in a search for the region's own, unique identity, or what might be termed a "creative project of self-definition" (Tsing 1993: 18).[26] Continually underpinned by the desire to 'catch up' with Leh and the Kashmir Valley, the quest for modernity has been central to this project of self-definition. However, given the ethnic and cultural diversity in the region, the only common feature that offers coherence to the region is religious identity. Thus any embrace of modernity must also be reconciled with notions of religiosity. For if development as it is widely understood entails Western-style modernization, how could Kargili society achieve this without losing their religious identity and mooring? These questions instigated religious factional politics in Kargil, wherein two factions, the Islamia School and the Imam Khomeini Memorial Trust, appropriated different ideological strands from the wider Shi'a universe as they grappled with this issue. While the former initially subscribed to a more quietist and traditionalist stance, advocating the separation of religion from politics, the latter was more influenced by Khomeini's ideology, that religion and politics are inextricable. This factional struggle came to play itself out within the arena of local democratic politics in the 2008 elections to the hill council. Every individual in Kargil was aligned with one or other of these two factions. As a result, politics seeped into very basic social units, whether at the level of the family, wider kin network, neighborhood, or village. However, despite being enmeshed in factional politics, people in Kargil were fully aware of the detrimental impact of religious politics on society. They challenged political leaders to remain focused on issues of development and governance. Religious discourse came to be expressed in the language of politics and vice versa. It was rare to find mention of the border as a significant factor influencing people's everyday lives, except as a claims-making strategy.[27]

Although both Kargil and Leh receive equal central government funding through its various schemes, such as the Border Area Development Program, Kargilis point to various issues of neglect. These include civilian flights being allowed to operate from the Leh airport but not from Kargil, recruitment into Ladakh Scouts (a division of the army which, before the Kargil war, allegedly recruited mainly Buddhists), and the difficulty in getting the FCRA permit that allows local organizations to receive foreign funds, making it difficult for already reluctant external NGOs to work in Kargil, while Leh is overrun by them. These issues dominated the promises that politicians made to people while campaigning for the council elections. Increasingly Kargilis have been attributing their perceived neglect by the central government to discrimination against Muslims. Although none of these allegations made by Kargilis is false, they are imbued with rhetoric. Kargilis are well aware that their own socioreligious compulsions have historically in part been responsible for their 'late development'—which they admit to candidly in private conversations.

They also berate Kargili politicians for not being able to mobilize additional central government attention using the sympathy that the Kargil war garnered for the region. Although Kargilis lament that they have not been given enough due recognition of their patriotism, the war nonetheless enhanced the symbolic significance of their strategic border position. It is in such complaints about politicians' failures to mobilize resources that the border acquires great rhetorical value.

EVEN THOUGH the history of Kargil as a frontier region, its symbolic attachments and conversations across the LoC, and the presence of the army all present a picture of it as the quintessential borderland, the concerns that shape everyday life present quite another image, one in which the border is no longer a 'state of exception' but a space where people face a heightened version of the same socioeconomic and political tensions confronting citizens in other parts of the country.

The factors at play in the hill council election of 2008 brought into the open the latent tensions in Kargili society, many of which are a reflection of issues visible in other parts of the country and the nation-state at large. Thus the border for the most part fades into the background of the surrounding mountains.

Elections to the hill council reflected how a certain democratic space had been seized by the people of Kargil to effectively blur the boundaries between the people and the state (Gupta 1995). Unlike the relationship with the army, the state in this guise does not remain a distant monolithic entity. Kargilis, I suggest, have come to see in the hill council a possibility of 'owning' democracy and thereby becoming 'full citizens.' To that extent the borderland no longer remains a margin to any 'center.' Instead it lies at the heart of the sociological project of the nation-state. From this perspective, often the invocation of the border is rhetorical. But this rhetoric is as important as the reality of the border, for it reveals the contradictions inherent in the discourse of the nation-state through which it seeks to legitimate itself. Yet, as I have sought to show, allegiance to the nation-state and its discourse is not simple and unqualified. The contradictions inherent in the discourse of the nation-state emerge particularly at the level of regional politics with Kashmir and Leh.

We have been urged to go beyond the concept of the margin in spatial terms and to use it instead as a "device for critical thought" (Dube 2004: 23; compare Das and Poole 2004). The reality and rhetoric of the borderland in Kargil make it a double signifier: it is a territorial margin that takes us to the center of the state, revealing the contradictions that underlie its discourse. This revelation, however, is not made through a simple narrative of alienation from the nation-state. The relationship of borderlanders to the state in Kargil is more nuanced. It defies any easy categorization of Kargilis either as manipulated subjects of the state or as those offering a radical stance of resistance. The stance offered is context-dependent as well as different in relation to the various guises of the state.

NOTES TO CHAPTER 2

1. The bulk of the fieldwork for this research was undertaken between 2007 and 2009 for my DPhil thesis (Gupta 2011). Data were collected through participant observation and semistructured interviews. In some cases the names of my interlocutors have been changed for the sake of privacy.

2. For examples, see chapters 3 and 4, this volume.

3. As Van Beek (1996: 122) has argued, this classification reproduced the census categories developed by the colonial administration. However, the classification is not faithful to self-ascriptions of ethnic identity among some groups of Ladakhis. Yet even though the cataloguing of these identities had "little or no grounding in social practice" (Van Beek 2001: 375), they have become an important means of accessing state concessions and benefits. This has also led to an increasing consciousness of ethnic identity in the region.

4. Aggarwal's (2004: 14) general reminder that "Ladakh [should] be viewed, not merely as a frontier of either peace or hostility, but also as a cultural crossroad; not an isolated periphery, but a place located in an orbit of national and transnational networks of travel, trade, migration, knowledge exchanges, political alliances, and conflicts," is particularly applicable to Kargil, given its predominant association with the Kargil war in the national imagination.

5. The remarks here and in the rest of the paragraph have been culled from extensive conversations in 2007 and 2008 with Abdul Hamid Tanvir and Sadiq Ali Sadiq, well-known poets and historians in Kargil.

6. Van Schendel (2005a: 28) rightly points out that studies of the Partition have taken Punjab as a model. He has argued for further research on this event as it was experienced in other parts of the subcontinent.

7. Political alienation from the Pakistani state in Gilgit-Baltistan has led to the rise of 'nationalist' movements that have reversed the meaning attached to the victory of the Gilgit Scouts. Since 1992, the Jang-i azadi of 1947–49, celebrated as Independence Day on 2 November every year, marking freedom from Dogra rule, has been redesignated Yaum-i Shuhāda (Day of Martyrs) as a symbol of protest against the Pakistani state (Sökefeld 1997: 77).

8. See "Main High Lights of District Kargil," accessed 5 September 2010, kargil.gov .in/others/highlights.htm.

9. Basharat Peer (2008) provides an account of his childhood in Kashmir when the insurgency was at its peak, describing numerous incidents of harassment and violence by the army.

10. One version of the story on local intelligence is that people did not report it for fear that the army would suspect them, while another story reported that some local shepherds had pointed this out to the army, but the information was ignored.

11. Van Schendel (2005a: 59) describes a similar narrative of alienation in the village of Malopara near the border crossing of Bongaon-Benapol in West Bengal, which is completely at the mercy of the Bangladesh border guards for all their needs, as it has been neglected by the Indian developmental apparatus since Partition.

12. The enthusiasm of the people of Lato for showing me the recording of the Independence Day celebration in their village can be seen, in Aggarwal's (2004: 17) terms, as the "performance of border subjectivity." She argues that celebrations of events like Independence Day constitute the "performance of official nationalism," which is, however, "riddled with internal ambiguities" (31).

13. 'State of exception' is a phrase coined by Agamben (2005) to describe the suspension of a regular juridical order, characteristic of militarized zones.

14. The 1909 "Settlement Report of Ladakh and Baltistan" too refers to all Shi'a 'Mohamedans' as Balti or Brogpa. This classification stands at odds today with the rise of a relatively new Purigi identity, a contentious issue culturally and politically.

15. A rough estimate provided by Balti Bazaar inhabitants in 2008.

16. When it became easier to obtain visas to travel for the purpose of meeting relatives, Kargilis lamented that they had to take a circuitous route from Kargil to Skardu via Leh or Srinagar to Delhi, from Delhi to Islamabad, and from there to Skardu on the Karakoram Highway, even though Skardu is a mere eight hours by road directly from Kargil.

17. *Api* in Balti means grandmother and is used generically for old women out of respect and affection. Similarly, *Apo* (grandfather) is used for old men.

18. While these objects attain significance through the meaning that 'human actors' give them, one could also consider them in their own right to view them as "things-in-motion that illuminate their human and social context" (Appadurai 1986: 5).

19. *Adab* denotes an inherent sense of sophistication, courtesy, and depth of a culture.

20. Compare Van Schendel (2005a: 33). The inclusion of Balti and not Purigi in the Sixth Schedule of the Jammu and Kashmir Constitution is becoming an increasingly contentious issue in Kargil, in the context of the recent rise of a Purigi identity. Interestingly Balti was included in the Sixth Schedule on the basis of the pre-Partition census of 1941, which included Baltistan, and thereby showed a numerically larger number of people who considered Balti to be their language.

21. *Qasidas* are religious songs sung on joyous occasions, while *nauhas* are rhythmic dirges that accompany mourning and flagellation during Muharram.

22. Note that the Gilgit Scouts are referred to here as 'freedom fighters,' reflecting how meanings attached to the struggle for freedom against Dogra rule—*Jang-i-azadi*—by the Gilgit Scouts are being radically reversed.

23. The Tibetan script is referred to as Bodik in Ladakh and probably derives from *Bod-yig* in Lhasa dialect, literally meaning 'Tibet-writing/letter.'

24. Borneman (1997: 96) describes the relationship between East and West Germany during the cold war as "asymmetrical mirror images of each other." He argues that "these states were involved in what Hegel . . . called a 'struggle to death': seeking recognition of self without having to recognize the other in turn." The relationship between Kargil and Baltistan is the reverse. A large part of Kargili self-recognition takes place through comparisons of differences and similarities that have emerged in the lives of people from these two regions in the postcolonial state. In other words, Kargil and Baltistan seek recognition of the self *through* recognition of the other over the border.

25. Marching toward Muzaffarabad was symbolically significant, for it is the capital of Pakistan-administered Kashmir just across the LoC.

26. In her ethnography of the Meratus Dayaks of South Kalimantan (Indonesia), Tsing (1993) shows how the asymmetries created by administrative practices and regional economic differences, which marginalize the Meratus, became the starting point for the negotiation of their cultural identity.

27. I have dealt in detail with factional politics along religious lines in Kargil in my DPhil thesis (Gupta 2011). Aggarwal (2004: 76–77, 78, 201–3, 210) also touches on the subject.

Naturalizing the Himalaya-as-Border in Uttarakhand

The Himalayas, running for 1,500 miles across the north of the Indian sub-continent, are widely considered to form the 'natural' northern frontier of the nation-state of India. The 'abode of snow,' the translation of the Sanskrit word *himalaya*, encircles India, separating her from Central Asia. Textual references to the delimiting of Hindustan by the mountain chain can be found as early as the *Vishnu Purana* (ca. first century BCE), which calls them the "shield of India" (Woodman 1969). The *Mahabharata* and the *Ramayana*, two key Hindu mythological texts, constantly refer to the holy Himalayas at the periphery. Kautilya's political treatise, the *Arthashastra* (ca. fourth century BCE), defined the natural boundaries of the dominion of a Chakravartin raja (supreme wielder of the wheel of law or paramount lord) as "extending north to south from the Himalayas to the sea and measuring [a] thousand *yojanas* across" (quoted in Chakravarti 1971: 2).

The natural demarcation of India by the Himalayas is a trope that resur-faces constantly in British colonial-era accounts as well. Thomas Holdich (1901: 280), for instance, described them as "the finest natural combination of beauty and barrier that exists in the world. . . . Never was there such a God-given boundary set to such a vast, impressive and stupendous frontier." Lord Curzon (1907: 24), who had served as viceroy of India (1899–1905), in his 1907 Romanes lecture entitled "Frontiers" said, "Backed as they are by the huge and lofty plateau of Tibet, the Himalayas are beyond doubt the most formidable natural Frontier in the World." The postcolonial Indian state's self-representation of the 'Motherland' constantly refers to the naturalness of her 'god-given' boundaries. For instance, the enormously popular Incredible India campaign,[1] launched by the government of India in 2002 to promote tourism, begins its introductory description of India thus: "India is set apart from the rest of Asia by the Himalayas, the highest, youngest and still evolving mountain chain on the planet."

In fact the Himalayan ranges do not constitute an unbroken wall but possess a number of traversable passes that have always facilitated contact in the form of travel, migration, and trade beyond the Indian subcontinent. Donald Moore (2005: 7) directs our attention to "political technologies" that "produce territory including its presumed 'natural frontiers.'" Following Moore's injunction to analyze the production of territory, I suggest that the demarcating effect of the Himalayas is the product of certain historical conjunctures and of particular state policies. I locate my effort in studying the creation and maintenance of a border within a small portion of the long Tibeto-Indian interface: the district of Chamoli in the Garhwal Himalaya in the north Indian State of Uttarakhand. Over the ten months that I spent in Chamoli conducting doctoral fieldwork, the 'naturalness' of the border with Tibet/China was impressed upon me by state and nonstate agents alike. The current lack of friction with China on the Chamoli border was considered a derivative of precisely this aspect of 'naturalness.' The slightest historical research into the formation of the borders of present-day Chamoli district, however, brings to the fore what Moore describes as "the production of territory." In this paper I begin with a brief recounting of the history of present-day Chamoli to describe the colonial policies of conquest and mapping and the postcolonial efforts to impose these very maps and boundaries. The border, it appears, is not only not 'natural' but also remains a bone of contention between India and China. Moving on from a brief historical exegesis, I ask how, on an everyday basis, the imaginary of the 'natural' Himalayan border maintains itself in the district by, once again, focusing on certain technologies, "technologies of the imagination" (Sneath et al. 2009).

Historicizing Uttarakhand

Uttarakhand is a small Himalayan State in northern India bordering China (Tibet) and Nepal (map 3.1).[2] Present-day Uttarakhand comprises thirteen districts divided into two administrative divisions, Garhwal and Kumaon.[3] The boundaries of Garhwal and Kumaon have been modified with surprising frequency over time. The ninth century saw the emergence of a large kingdom spanning both Garhwal and Kumaon as well as western Nepal; it was headed by the Katyuris, who ruled from Katyur-Baijnath. In the twelfth century there was an invasion into this area by the Mallas, hailing from western Nepal. This marked the liquidation of the centralized Katyuri kingdom and paved the way for the rise of several smaller independent principalities in this region, each of which was confined to a few valleys. The exact number of principalities is disputed. Some say there were fifty-two in Garhwal, while others believe that the principalities, which were known as *gadha*, exceeded sixty-four. In contrast, in Kumaon there were only six principalities.[4] These principalities existed, it seems, in a state of constant struggle with one another until they were undone by two large north Indian dynasties in the middle of the sixteenth century (Joshi 1990). King Rudra Chandra (ca. 1565–97 CE) brought all of present-day Kumaon under the sway of the Chandras (Atkinson 1881: 542–44), and in Garhwal it was Ajaypala (ca. 1500–1547 CE) who subjugated the rest of the principalities (Joshi 1990). This marks an important period in the history of Uttarakhand as we know it now, for this is arguably the first time that the regions of Garhwal and Kumaon surface as two distinct political entities. Henceforth the boundaries of what constitutes Garhwal and Kumaon might change, but they are recognized as two distinct sections of this central portion of the Indian Himalayas.

Conventional histories of Uttarakhand regard it as being subjected to two different colonial regimes, first that of the Gorkhas, then that of the British. Beginning at the end of the nineteenth century, Gorkha rule in Kumaon (1790–1815) and Garhwal (1803–15) is widely considered to be an oppressive period of the region's history.[5] The British claimed to have "rescued the inhabitants of Kumaon and Garhwal from the yoke of their oppressors" when they defeated the Gorkhas in 1816 (letter from Adam, secretary to the government, quoted in Joshi 1990: 103), culminating in the Treaty of Sagauli. The defeat of the Gorkhas brought all of Kumaon directly under the British East India Company. A portion of Garhwal, the present-day districts of Tehri and Uttarkashi, were 'returned' to Sudarshan Shah, the son of the former ruler of Garhwal. The British entered into an agreement with him whereby Shah was installed as king of a truncated Garhwal, west of the Alaknanda and Mandakini rivers. Srinagar, the capital of undivided Garhwal, was also given to what was now called British Garhwal, forcing Sudarshan Shah to construct a new capital at the confluence of the rivers Bhagirathi and Bhilangana at Tehri.[6] Hence

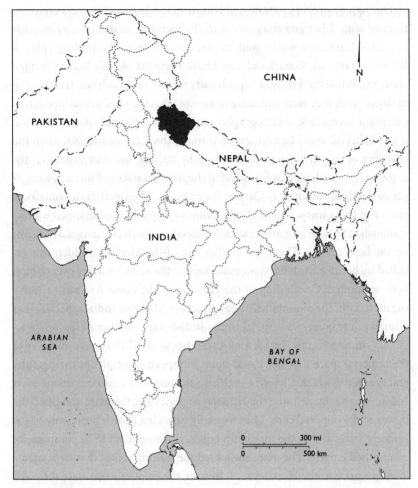

MAP 3.1. Uttarakhand in India.

three new political entities came into existence in 1816: the princely state of Tehri-Garhwal, British Garhwal, and Kumaon. Further, under the Treaty of Sagauli of 1816, the eastern section of the Gorkha Empire was restored to Sikkim, and the Gorkhas were left with the territory that roughly corresponds to present-day Nepal. The outcome of the Treaty of Sagauli of 1816 can be seen as the carving out of a border between British India and the Gorkha Empire, or what are now the states of India and Nepal. All of present-day Uttarakhand was included in what was then called the United Provinces.

Through control of Garhwal and Kumaon, the British acquired a common frontier with Tibet and thus access to the lucrative trans-Himalayan trade in *pashm* (cashmere wool), gold, borax, and salt from the trading cities of Bokhara, Yarkand, Samarkand, and Lhasa along the old Silk Route (Rangan 2000: 73). While the Treaty of Sagauli had granted the British vast tracts of Himalayan land, they were still quite unsure of what they had actually acquired due to the severe lack of cartographic accuracy of the area. Britain's interests, it was believed, could be best served through the accurate measurement and mapping of the territory under control, by etching out neat frontiers, "the razor's edge on which hang suspended the modern issues of war or peace, of life or death to nations," as Curzon (1907) put it. The Great Trigonometrical Survey of India was set up in 1802 in order to map all of India, which was accomplished by 1870 by mathematically extending a web of triangulated forms on the land surface. The Great Indian Arc of the Meridian, which this resulted in, became the longest measurement of the earth's surface ever to have been attempted. Concluding in the Himalayas, the Great Arc was to "solve the mystery of the mountains" (Keay 2000: 15). Mapping India, especially her Himalayan frontier, was crucial to the British for a number of reasons, succinctly summed up by Zurick and Karan (1999: 103): "They gave an order to the imperial space that was based upon European principles of cartography and geometry, which allowed the British to construct a rational image of its Indian empire. By defining the Himalayan periphery, the maps solidified the power of the imperial core. They formally extended British hegemony to the princely states and to the mountain tribes, showing them to be components of a unified empire. The maps measured the trading routes that were such a lucrative prize in the Himalaya. . . . In sum, the frontier maps were the colonial keys to subjugating both the lands and the peoples of the mountains."

Inheriting the Frontier

The maps that these politicohistorical processes produced were indeed considered by colonial administrators as "keys to subjugating" the lands and peoples they governed. Maps are what James Scott (1998) has aptly termed "state simplifications" or techniques that allow officials to grasp what are otherwise complex realities through their reduction to schematic categories. State simplifications such as maps do not depict 'reality out there'—if such a task was even possible. Yet such depictions of what is officially designated as being reality have powerful effects (Scott 1998; Van Schendel and Abraham 2005). The numerous maps drawn up during the colonial era created two realities: the official establishment of the demarcation of British India and the distinction between India and Tibet, at least from India's perspective. As we shall see, China had quite a different understanding of the mapping of Tibet and India.

I have offered a somewhat superficial history of the production of a very specific portion of the border of a region that is aptly described as Northern South Asia.[7] This border was inherited by the postcolonial state, with the Indian Independence Act of 1947 defining the territories of India as those "under the sovereignty of His Majesty, which immediately before the appointed day (15th August 1947) were included in British India, except the territories which, under subsection (2) of this section, are to be the territories of Pakistan." At this period Tibet served as a buffer between India and China. The Chinese invasion and conquest of Tibet in 1950–51 was to erode this protective cushioning between India and China, particularly as one of the avowed objectives of the Chinese move into Tibet in 1950 was "to stand guard on the frontiers of China" (Chakravarti 1971: 10).

In pursuance of a neighborly relationship China and India signed a treaty in 1954, the Agreement on Trade and Intercourse between the Tibet Region of China and India, which proclaimed eternal friendship between the two on the basis of *Panch Shila*, or the five principles of peaceful coexistence, including mutual respect for each other's territorial integrity. Despite the Panch Shila agreement, very soon afterward a series of border disputes took place between the two states over the question of what constitutes the boundary of Tibet. The first of many disputes took place in Chamoli's adjoining district of Pithoragarh at a place that India calls Bara Hoti and the Chinese call Wu-Je. This is a grazing ground about sixteen thousand feet above sea level, close to the Tun Jun La Pass between present-day Uttarakhand and Tibet. To date there is no agreement on the geographical location of Bara Hoti/Wu-Je. India claims it lies two miles south of Tun Jun La; China says it is twelve kilometers to the north of the pass. In the summer of 1954 the Chinese complained that over thirty Indian troops armed with rifles had crossed over the Niti Pass; India denied this claim. In 1956 both sides decided not to exercise jurisdiction over this area until the dispute over it was settled (Woodman 1969: 229–32).

From 1959 onward there was a series of transgressions along what was

understood by the Indian government to constitute the Indian border, ranging from Ladakh to Assam, with the most significant transgressions at Longju
to the south of the McMahon line. In response to the notes of complaint written by the Indian side to China on 8 September 1959, Chou En-lai wrote a
letter to Nehru to say that the boundary between India and China had *never
been delimited*. The response to this statement by the government of India is
worth quoting in detail: "The Sino-Indian boundary, based on custom and
tradition, follows natural features, and for the major part this customary and
traditional boundary is also confirmed by treaty and agreement. This boundary throughout has been fixed and well-known for centuries. According to
international usage and practice, a customary boundary which follows well-
known and unchanging natural features like main watersheds stands defined
and does not require further and formal definition" (White Paper No. iii, p.
85, quoted in Chakravarti 1971: 15).

Evidently China did not agree with what India understood to be the customary boundary following 'natural' features, for in 1960 Bara-Hoti and other
neighboring Indian posts of Lapthal and Sangchamalla near Niti Pass in present-
day Chamoli district were claimed by China as forming one composite area of
two hundred square miles of Tibet without any intervening wedges of Indian
territory (Woodman 1969: 270–72). The growing rift in diplomatic relations
and the need to police what had until now been presumed to be an undisputed
customary border led to the creation of a series of smaller districts alongside
the Tibetan border in present-day Uttarakhand. On 24 February 1960 an area
of 9,125 kilometers on India's frontier with Tibet was converted into a district:
Chamoli (Pahari 2005: 19). Present-day Chamoli includes the critical passes
of Niti and Mana. The creation of a smaller unit of governance on the border
with a hostile and powerful neighbor was done, according to those I interviewed in situ, for greater ease of administration with an eye to increasing
surveillance, expanding state power, and quelling and controlling local dis-
satisfaction with the nation-state. The creation of Chamoli and other, smaller
districts right along the Indo-Tibetan border can be read as a mechanism to
relieve the anxiety of the policing of borderlands that the modern state has
to contend with. Two years later the Sino-Indian border war broke out. Even
though the war did not take place directly in Chamoli, it did have the effect of
sealing off the all-important passes of Niti and Mana from all forms of trade
or travel between India and Tibet. In one fell swoop the 1962 war converted
an ancient trading route into what Ispahani (1989: 3) terms an "anti route,"

FIGURE 3.1. Uninhabited Bhotiya summer village, near the border in Chamoli, Uttarakhand, 2007. Photograph courtesy of N. Mathur.

or what "creates pressure against movement—it limits, restrains, or 'channels' it—where routes facilitate broader movement."

The Mana and Niti passes (map 3.2) are considered two of the most navigable routes into Tibet, as is evident from the large number of travelers who wrote of passing through them, as well as the large volume of trade that was conducted via them. In recognition of this, both Mana and Niti were on the list of the six mountain passes that the Sino-Indian agreement of April 1954, the now infamous Panch Shila, had opened up for travel by pilgrims and traders. The Bhotiyas of Kumaon and Garhwal traditionally conducted commercial interactions with the Hunias of western Tibet (see figure 3.1).[8] Local accounts made it clear that trading relations continued between the Bhotiyas of Chamoli district and Tibet through Mana and Niti right up until the Sino-Indian border war of 1962. From being habitations on prominent border passes, Mana and Niti have been converted, after 1962, into border villages. They have become the Himalayan borderland not just politically and in the concomitant representations on maps and other official documents but, perhaps more importantly, in the narratives and imaginaries of the space of the Indian state itself. It is to this imagination of the Himalayan borderland that I turn now.

The Imaginary of the Himalayan Borderland

Over 2006–8 I conducted sixteen months of doctoral research in Uttarakhand, of which ten months were spent living in Chamoli district (see map 3.2). I resided in the district's administrative headquarters town of Gopeshwar, where I was following through on the implementation of antipoverty legislation by the local state. I spent vast amounts of time in government development offices in Gopeshwar and in other scattered locations around the district, accompanied officials to villages for events such as monitoring and evaluations, and independently visited various villages in order to gauge the operations of the development scheme I was interested in. My original research focus, then, was not on imaginaries of space, nor had I chosen my field site due to its location on the borderland. Over time, however, I grew increasingly interested in how residents of Chamoli, officials and nonofficials, described what it felt like to live in a 'remote' Himalayan borderland (see Mathur 2010). In this section I dwell on the complete lack of ambiguity with which they considered the border between India and Tibet/China that coincides with the northern edge of the district to be a 'natural' one. This frontier was, I was repeatedly told during my time in Chamoli, entirely peaceful, as it has been since time immemorial.[9] Because it was a 'natural border' it was not considered a "sensitive border" (Van Schendel, this volume). This recurrent discourse of naturalness gives rise to an ethnographic question: What allows for such an imaginary of the Himalayan border to be constructed and maintained?

Prima facie, the answer would seem to lie in the scores of maps, some of which I reproduce here, that produce powerful visual depictions. Scott (1998), Van Schendel and Abraham (2005), and Keay (1983), as mentioned earlier, refer to maps as tools that might not represent reality but do aid in the work of statecraft through the clearing up of geography and the establishment of neat schemas. Benedict Anderson (1991: 164) has studied maps as an "institution of power" that, along with the census and the museum, "profoundly shaped the way in which the colonial state imagined its dominion." Rather than merely focusing on their utility, that is, the work that maps do in the governance of states, Anderson focuses on how maps, disseminated in print form, aid the very imagination of a national community. A recent work on the anthropology of the imagination urges ethnographers to "explore the heterogeneous processes through which concrete imaginings come about" (Sneath et al. 2009: 9). In order to do so, the authors advocate a "focus on the

MAP 3.2. Chamoli district, Uttarakhand.

concrete processes by which imaginative effects are engendered, or, what we call 'technologies of the imagination'" (11). The term 'technology' is utilized in a dual sense: colloquially, in order to refer to material artifacts, but also more indeterminately, as a "particular kind of theoretical object" (18), as a "wider repertoire of objects and practices that bring about imaginative effects" (20). I have been arguing that the Himalayas are imagined in Chamoli as constituting the 'natural' frontier of the nation-state of India. What technologies empirically allow for such an "imaginative effect" of naturalness to be created and maintained?

The Sensorial Border

The first and most fundamental of such 'technologies,' if it is not sacrilegious to term them thus, are the mountains themselves. The Himalayas are, as is well known, the highest mountains in the world. As one travels north in Chamoli, they exponentially grow in height, imbuing one with the sense of a solid wall-like formation. As one nears the Nanda Devi (7,817 meters), the second highest mountain in India and the patron goddess of Uttarakhand, for instance, one is struck by a ring of mountains that stretch on as far as the eye can see, with twelve of the surrounding mountains exceeding 6,400 meters. When positioned within the northern edges of the district, one can clearly understand what made Curzon (1907: 7) describe mountains as a "natural frontier," as "the earliest of all barriers," "the most durable and the most imposing." The sheer gargantuan physicality of the seemingly insurmountable mountains of the upper Himalayas is in itself enough to convince one—resident and visitor alike—that there really is nothing that lies beyond these towering snow-clad peaks. The narrative of the 'naturalness' of the Himalayas as a border, then, is propped up by the affective experience of space.

The Mapped Border

Sensory experience finds affirmation in textual materials issued by the Indian state such as maps and school books. Bénéi (2000), following Anderson, has studied the banal modes in which nationalist ideas are taught in Indian schools with a focus on language deployed, the quotidian ritualization of the worship of the nation, and the utilization of the student's body itself as a pedagogical tool. Similar processes were evidently at play in schools in Chamoli, and though I did not study them in detail, I was constantly struck by the image of the map of India or Uttarakhand that was to be found everywhere in the district: in the offices of senior officials; on wall paintings in government buildings; on large billboards proclaiming the achievements of the state, with a photo of the chief minister beaming down upon the viewer; in children's textbooks and storybooks; in newspapers and magazines; in pamphlets and brochures issued by the state; on calendars that hung in shops. Many of these maps were what Anderson (1991: 175) describes as "logo-maps," a "pure sign, no longer compass to the world," with all political and physical features removed from it. The shapes of India and Uttarakhand as pure symbols are widely available all over Chamoli district. Just as popular as the logo-maps are idealized maps depicting temples and other religious sites, tourist maps showing areas of interest, and artistic maps beautifully portraying the state and pointing out important places (see map 3.3). Interestingly most of these maps depict nothing to the north other than a vast empty space called China and/or Tibet. For Anderson, such logo-maps "unconsciously reinforce the developing imagined ties" (176); I would argue they also create the effect of the end of India. In the two border villages of Mana and Niti, named after their location in the vicinity of the passes into Tibet, villagers proudly told me that they stand on the nation's frontier: they inhabit a space where Hindustan abruptly terminates to give way to some distant and unknown world called China. They substantiated their assertion by gesticulating to the towering mountains that dwarfed us, by references to 'any map' (one young educated man told me to look up Google maps), and, most critically, by invoking their centuries-long role as forming the boundary of Hindustan.

The Traditionally Sacred Border

Maps, school curricula, and other such materials that emanate from state sources can be seen as a technology contributing to the imagination of the Himalayas as a natural frontier. I would argue, however, that of even greater import was the diffuse ensemble of narratives and processes that impinged upon everyday life in various oblique ways, thus creating and heightening a sense of living on the borderland. Primary among these was what the Indian state took recourse to in its fraught dealing with China and what the local residents take great pride in: 'custom and tradition.' 'Natural' geography combines with tradition and custom to make the Himalayas function as the northern protector of India. This is most clearly evident, residents of Chamoli would argue, in the abundance of Hindu myths and legends about the Himalayas. The district possesses one of India's most ancient and vital Hindu shrines, the Badrinath temple.[10] Badrinath serves as a central identifier for residents of the district, and they frequently refer to it as their place of origin rather than saying they come from Chamoli district. The centrality of the

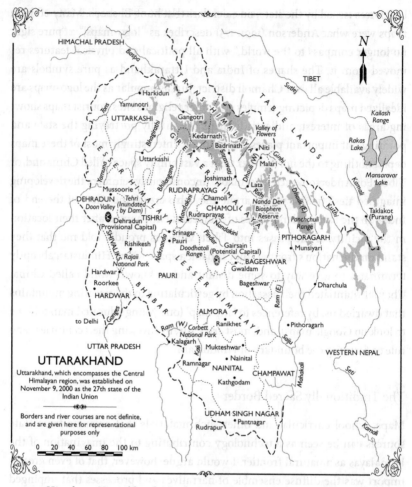

MAP 3.3. Himalayan Uttarakhand. Map by Rajiv Rawat. Reproduced with permission.

Badrinath temple within the district and its importance as an imagined tip of India cannot be overstated when seen from the perspective of Hindu cosmology. Diana Eck (1998) points out that in the eyes of the Hindu pilgrim the entire land of India constitutes a sacred geography. The circumambulation of the sacred land comprises the four *dhams* or "abodes" of the divine at the four compass points: "Badrinath in the north, Puri in the east, Ramesvaram in the south, and Dvaraka in the west . . . they are part of a very important symbolic geography which constitutes what Hindus mean by 'India'" (65).[11]

Prominent religious sites aside, every single bit of Chamoli is littered with references to Hindu mythological tales. Sacredness is etched into the very landscape, which has historically served to attract a variety of mythological heroes. A prominent local tale, for instance, tells of the unhappiness the Hindu god Shiva felt on living across the border in Tibet on Mount Kailash, which is believed to be his original abode. Unhappiness with Tibet, the tale goes, made Shiva cross over the border into India to set up a home near Badrinath. At Badrinath his wife, Parvati, was outwitted by the naughty god Vishnu, and they had to move house to a place near Kedarnath. At one place in Chamoli there seems to exist an unnatural gap between two huge mountains near the village of Malari. Legend has it that the gap arose due to the thievery of the monkey-god Hanuman, who features prominently in the Hindu epic the *Ramayana*. The local story describes Hanuman flying over to Chamoli to look for a precious herb that can be found only here. Unable to distinguish the many herbs that grow in this region, Hanuman actually picked up an entire mountain and flew across to Lanka (present-day Sri Lanka), carrying the mountain with him to deliver it to Lord Rama. So popular is this story that an official sign recounting it has been set at a point from where one can view the protruding space between two mountains. It is for this reason that all references to Hanuman have been deleted in local Garhwali performances of the *Ramayana* that take place annually during the festival of Dussherra, which marks the return of Rama from exile. Valmiki himself, the author of the *Ramayana*, is said to have written the epic while meditating in a cave near the Badrinath temple. The heroes of the other major Hindu epic, the *Mahabharata*, are also believed to have visited Chamoli in their quest for nirvana at the very end of their lives.

The number of local tales is endless, and I provide but a sample of them here to point out how Chamoli is imagined simultaneously as central and eternal to the Hindu nation even while it is positioned at its very edge. According to local accounts, Hindu gods either lived here or came seeking something, be it a precious herb or salvation or the solitude to meditate and pen the greatest of all Sanskrit epics. The sacred geography of the region does not remain the mere stuff of legend but often slips into other avenues. The very name of the State itself is an obvious instance. Uttarakhand, the name with which this region was referred to in Vedic scriptures, means quite literally 'a piece of the north,' a signifier of the fact that since the Vedic period this region has been recognized as a critical northern component of Hindustan. In Hindu scriptures the

Himalayas are called Devalaya or 'the abode of the gods.' Uttarakhand has chosen the very same phrase as a sobriquet for itself, prominently on display throughout the State on billboards and posters and in paintings, magazines, newspapers, and the speeches of politicians and bureaucrats.

The Criminal Border

Sacred as the outer periphery of the Indian nation-state might be, it still possesses its criminal side. Criminality too in Chamoli was spoken of as a 'natural' feature of life on the (natural) border. The notion of "the borderland as an area where by definition criminality is rife and sovereignty under constant threat" (Abraham and Van Schendel 2005: 25) was accepted especially by state officials. During my period of residence in Chamoli, the police and the forest department of the district struggled to prevent the smuggling of Yarchagumba *(cordyceps sinensis)*, or what is referred to in Hindi as *keedajadi*, a unique herb-cum-fungus believed to be an alternative to Viagra. Keedajadi is to be found only in the upper reaches of the Himalayas, in the districts of Chamoli and Pithoragarh in Uttarakhand. At the end of winter, with the melting of the snow, it is to be found in abundance. 'Smugglers' organize villagers to pick this precious and rare herb, pay them some nominal amount, and then take it across the border for sale at 100,000 rupees for one kilogram in Nepal and China. Interestingly it is believed that this smuggling is organized by Nepalis, who find it easy to cross the Indo-Nepal border in Uttarakhand as well as to sell the smuggled goods in markets in Nepal or China. During my stay in Chamoli such 'Nepali smugglers' were arrested on several occasions. For example, on 14 June 2007 the Garhwal edition of the Hindi language newspaper *Amar Ujala* carried a long story on the arrest of three people for smuggling keedajadi. It included a color picture of three chastened-looking men seated on the floor, the legs of their apprehenders visible directly behind them. The story identified them as "three Nepali people" who were nabbed red-handed by the police, who had been tipped off on their illegal possession of vast quantities of keedajadi on the Chopta-Gopeshwar road. The police caught the three Nepalis with 330 pieces of keedajadi, which would have sold for approximately 200,000 rupees in the international market. On cross-examination it was found that the three were planning to smuggle them to Nepal. The story ends by explaining that smuggling is a common activity in Uttarakhand, even though the forest department and the police are on full alert to stem the problem.

In my interviews with officials of the forest department in Chamoli as well as in the reportage in the local media, it was clear that smuggling of medicinal plants and herbs is a regular feature of life in Chamoli. It was difficult to control, claimed local agents of the state, due to the perennial problem of 'understaffing,' which leaves them without enough manpower to function as a gatekeeper state that is capable of enforcing complete closure of its edges. Further, the police and forest guards are often complicit in this illegal flow of keedajadi, if not directly responsible for this lucrative trade, which exhibits the incoherence of the state as a unified machine working, on the face of it, on similar principles of legality and illegality. Veena Das (2004) has poignantly described such blurrings as the "illegibility" of the Indian state, namely, moments when the zones between legality and illegality, state and nonstate melt away. Officials in Chamoli located the problem of cross-border smuggling of precious herbs squarely within what can be termed a 'problem of place,' with the character of the borderland constituting a problem in and of itself. Smuggling, officials explained to me, is a problem that is endemic to life in a borderland.

The borderland that local state officials were referring to was not merely Chamoli, the land on the border between India and Tibet/China, but, more expansively, a space that falls between the wider contours of India, Tibet, and Nepal. As I mentioned previously, Uttarakhand shares an eastern border with Nepal. It was evident from the multiple stories emerging around the sale of keedajadi that the goods were crossing over to Nepal in the hands of Nepali 'smugglers,' not to the closer border of Tibet, before they made their way into China via Nepal. The Nepal border is not that far away, and it is easy for Nepalis to travel around Uttarakhand unnoticed. Unlike the seemingly impermeable Sino-Indian border in Chamoli, the Indo-Nepal border is considered 'open' (see Hausner and Sharma, this volume). The local state officials had a broader notion of what constitutes a borderland than what one would get from merely looking at maps in relation to a point or by thinking of the international border as the one to be found in closest proximity.

The issue of the illegal smuggling of medicinal plants and herbs from Uttarakhand remains a key problem for the state, so much so that in April 2008 the minister of environment and forests in the lower house (Lok Sabha) of the

Indian Parliament in New Delhi was asked what measures had been taken to prevent this 'illegal exploitation and smuggling' out of Uttarakhand.[12] In May 2008 the Uttarakhand government decided that the one way to stem smuggling was by legalizing the extraction and sale of keedajadi and empowering the *van panchayats* (forest councils) to control it. In other words, the manner in which the state countered an illegal flow was by partially legalizing the very same process that had until recently been totally banned. While the vexed issue of illicit flows of keedajadi was handled by bringing the flow into a state-recognized, legalized domain, no such action can be taken for the sale of tiger and leopard skin and body parts. Poaching of big cats is an even more pressing issue than the smuggling of medicinal herbs given the national and international attention paid to these highly endangered animals. Further, poaching of animals and birds is believed to be undertaken by 'nationals,' whereas the Nepali population is widely believed to trade in the sale of keedajadi specifically. Also the impermeability of the Sino-Indian border comes up for question on this front as it is widely believed that the flow of animals and birds occurs across this border just as much as the Indo-Nepal border.

I merely flag the flow of poached animals here in relation to the flow of keedajadi to show that the idea of 'the border' is complex and sometimes contradictory. On the one hand, it is an extremely broad concept moving beyond literal, proximate borders to encompass a wider imaginary of a region suspended on the nation's edges. Simultaneously each border is differentiated and contextualized on the basis of parameters such as the sort of objects and people that cross through them, on the degree of their 'naturalness' or constructedness, by the level of surveillance they require to be upheld, by their permeability, their physical distance from one another, their historic roles in shaping the lives of the region, and so on. Focusing on illegal flows of goods shows the inherently destabilizing effects of the seemingly rationalized practices of state demarcation through official boundary making via simplifications such as maps, as well as the limits of state power to impose its official writ. Simultaneously the everyday talk of criminality, its frequent reporting in the local media, its discussion in the Indian Parliament, the changing of laws, and cries for stricter regulation and policing of the borderland were all processes that contributed to keeping alive and indeed enhancing local people's sense that they existed at the nation's frontier.

The Empty, Remote Border

In conclusion, I posit narratives of place as a key technology that aids the imagination of the Himalayan borderland.[13] Daphne Berdahl (1999: 8), in her ethnography of a village on the border between East and West Germany, moves from analyses of the literal border to the figurative border, from an analysis of the concrete wall to the "wall in our heads," to demonstrate that borderlands should be seen as "places of intense and inflexible lucidity." The border in Chamoli symbolized by the wall of the Himalayas was also a symbol of the location of Chamoli as occupying the literal and metaphorical edge of the Indian nation-state. The metaphorical understanding of the border as signifying distance, to the point of exclusion from the Indian state, which is seen to be residing in capital cities such as Dehradun (capital of Uttarakhand) and New Delhi (the national capital), comes across clearly in the narratives of state agents posted to Chamoli who lived and worked out of the district headquarters of Gopeshwar.

'A remote town on India's border with Tibet/China high up in the Indian Himalayas'—this is how Gopeshwar is almost universally defined. Substitute 'town' with 'district' and you get the regular definition of Chamoli.[14] Given the distance from large urban centers such as Dehradun and Rishikesh, the difficult terrain, and the poor transportation infrastructure, it is not surprising that the adjective 'remote' was used most often to describe this town and district. Initially I took it to be a description of a 'fact,' yet gradually I realized that the utilization of such signifiers had multiple implications for the manner in which this space is lived. Remoteness that arises from being placed on the border leads to neglect, to an emptying out of the space, to being ignored, to being forgotten from the national consciousness, and to a lack of 'development' (*vikas*). In my very first conversation with the incredulous district magistrate of Chamoli, he warned me off living in Gopeshwar as it is so 'remote.' "Why would you, or anyone else for that matter, want to ever live in this border district?" he asked me in shock. In official circles there is a well-known 'fast fact' about Chamoli, which is that only one of 'the three Ps' can bring you here: promotion, probation, or punishment. Most commonly Chamoli was a punishment posting, sometimes a promotion (as was the case with the district magistrate, who was posted to Chamoli just before I left but who told me that he wished he had not been promoted if living in Gopeshwar is what it entails!), and often a probation to measure your guts and your willingness to work. In other words, a posting to Chamoli was held in very low esteem by the upper echelons of the bureaucracy. Senior officials carefully informed me of how postings in the state are decided for civil servants. The most junior or the ones in "need of being fixed or punished" were posted to the border districts as far as possible from the action in Dehradun. The ones next on the seniority or punishment scale would be posted in the belt adjoining the outlying district, and so on in an increasing order of seniority and decreasing level of punishment, as one came closer to the capital. Only the chosen few—the most senior, the most deserving, and the ones with the best connections to their political masters—get to remain in Dehradun. The hegemonic representation of the mountains emanated from the large, powerful, heavily populated towns in the plains that believe the mountains, especially the farther they are from the centers, are 'remote' and 'backward.'

In her analysis on the production of difference in Indonesia's upland Sulawesi frontier, Li (2001) notes that hill people also judge each other by a set of standards derived from and centered on the coast. Much like the mountains of Uttarakhand, in Sulawesi too the farther away in the mountains people live, the more backward they are considered to be. Li interprets such representations as "indicators of the hegemony of cultural standards defined on the coast in hill people's assessment of social worth" (58). Naturally such a representation of the 'backwardness' of the more 'remote' mountainous region, particularly the borderlands, was not swallowed by all the *paharis* (mountain people) in Uttarakhand, especially those who proudly identify themselves with the *pahar* (mountains) and Chamoli. The more senior bureaucrats, however, function within a world that is structured by and operates on the dictates of Dehradun and Delhi. For them, even if they hail originally from the mountains, it is these worlds that constitute the center. They themselves took their borderland outposts as constituting a slight upon their professional capacities. For them a posting to the frontier was akin to being sentenced to a metaphorical prison. A posting to Gopeshwar was often described as being sent to *kala paani*, another name for the notorious Cellular Jail, set up on the Andaman islands in the Indian Ocean by the colonial British administration after the Indian rebellion of 1857. Literally it means 'black water' and refers to exile. A posting away from Gopeshwar was described metaphorically by officials as a release from prison (*jail se rihan hona*). When I went around the various offices in the town to make my farewells at the time of my own departure, nearly all the officials congratulated me on having served my time in jail. At farewell parties for officials, the speeches were always loudly congratulatory on the richly deserved release from time out on the frontier, the escape from the constraints of this remote, underdeveloped place. The relief was palpable on the faces of those who were 'escaping,' the verb most often deployed to refer to leaving this distant borderland. Descriptors such as 'remote' and 'under-developed,' metaphorical comparisons of the district with grim prisons, and long-winded narratives spun around the emptiness of this space by a particular class of the district residents contributed greatly to the imaginary of a distant space on the very tip of the nation-state, an empty periphery from which one must seek release at the earliest opportunity.

Through the course of this chapter I have elaborated on the manner in which a border comes to be carved out as a product of historical and state-led processes and how it continues to be maintained in the popular imagination of local residents as a 'natural' border through the operation of an assortment of material artifacts, narratives, and everyday processes. An eclectic assortment of technologies—maps, pamphlets, the mountains themselves, local myths and tales, prominent Hindu temples, illegal flows, and narratives of emptiness emanating from local elites—do the work of maintaining the imaginary of an Asian borderland constituted by the highest mountains in the world.

NOTES TO CHAPTER 3

Thanks are due to all participants of the Borderlands workshop. I am especially grateful to David Gellner and David Sneath for their careful readings of drafts of this essay. I hope the residents of Chamoli will find something of interest in my take on their naturally exquisite borderland habitation.

1. See "Geography," Incredible India, accessed 17 March 2009, www.incredibleindia .org/newsite/cms_page.asp?pageid=391.

2. Uttarakhand became the twenty-seventh State of the Republic of India when it was carved out of its 'parent-State' of Uttar Pradesh in November 2000. Containing a population of 8.48 million, it is considered a Himalayan state, as 90 percent of its landmass is officially classified as 'hills' (47,325 sq. km. is mountainous, with 3,800 sq. km. falling in the Tarai plains). A sharp increase in out-migration from the hills to big cities in the plains since the creation of the new State has been commented upon but not yet substantiated with empirical studies. The census data, though not up to date with trends since the creation of the State, give us some hints as to this pattern: taking the case of Chamoli district, its population as per the 2001 census is 369,198. There has been a substantial decline in the decadal growth rate, from 21.97 over 1981–91 to 13.51

over 1991–2001. My own research in the region clearly brought home the aching desire among most of the inhabitants of the district to escape to urban centers in the plains to seek out education, employment, and a better standard of living.

3. In addition, the large plains district of Hardwar is not inserted into either of these divisions but stands apart as a division-less district.

4. Interestingly local accounts as well as administrative records on Uttarakhand all point to the comparative ease in governing Kumaon due to its large valleys, unlike the more rugged, mountainous terrain of Garhwal.

5. The Gorkhas introduced a new land and revenue management system in the occupied territories, which included ten kinds of taxes (Atkinson 1881: 462). Inability to pay the dues led to a form of slavery in which the defaulters were forced to sell themselves or their relatives to the Gorkhas. The *Gazetteer* of the Garhwal Himalaya quotes a figure of twenty thousand people sold during the Gorkha occupation (Walton 1989: 126).

6. After 190 years the town of Tehri was entirely submerged by Asia's highest rock-fill dam, named, with no awareness of tragic irony, after the very town it was drowning out of existence. The 2400 MW hydro-power project, which officially started functioning in July 2006, is spread across forty-five kilometers of mountainous terrain and is believed to have led to the eviction of at least 100,000 people resident in and around what used to be the town of Tehri.

7. For a more detailed analysis of the production of the 'colonial state space' for all of India, see Manu Goswami's (2004) *Producing India*. Goswami builds on Lefebvre's conception of the state as a spatial framework of power to highlight the processes whereby "the conception of India as a bounded national space and economy was brought into being historically" (5).

8. Ramble (1997: 391) has written in the context of Nepal, "Literally, a Bhotiya ('Bhote') is someone from Bhot. 'Bhot' in turn derives from the Tibetan word 'Bod' meaning Tibet, via the late Sanskrit 'Bhotah.'" Ramble's analysis of the designator 'Bhotiya' in Nepal holds true for the scenario in Chamoli as well: "As an ethnic term, Bhotiya has traditionally included various 'Tibetanoid' populations, and it has also been used as a non-ethnic legal designation" (409). In India Bhotiyas are currently listed by the Indian constitution as a Scheduled Tribe, which allows them access to certain positive discrimination policies.

9. The skirmishes at nearby Bara Hoti and the still unresolved status of the two hundred square miles of disputed Himalayan tracts were never mentioned during my stay in Chamoli. In the everyday functioning of the local state's outpost in Chamoli, located at the district headquarters of Gopeshwar, this zone is a forgotten space where herdsmen, primarily Bhotiyas, from the Indian side of the border still take their goats for grazing as the seasons change. Despite their Scheduled Tribe classification, which serves as a recognition of their legal status as bona fide citizens of India, the Bhotiyas

remain stigmatized by the majority non-Bhotiya population in Chamoli as faintly foreign, which allows them to move in and out of nonstate spaces such as Bara Hoti.

10. Badrinath, along with Kedarnath, Gangotri (the source of the Ganges), and Yamunotri (source of the Yamuna River), is part of the Hindu *char dham yatra* (four abodes pilgrimage) in the Himalayas. Of the four *dhams*, Badrinath (in which Vishnu sits in a meditative pose) is widely considered the holiest, with Kedarnath (a Shiva temple) just behind it in terms of the local evaluation of holy Hindu sites.

11. In 1997 the district of Chamoli was broken down to form the new district of Rudraprayag. The division of Chamoli transferred the temple of Kedarnath from the bounds of the district to Rudraprayag, which is still lamented as a singular loss by local residents. Chamoli also possesses Hemkund Sahib, an important Sikh *Gurudwara* (temple) located en route to Badrinath temple.

12. "Lok Sabha Questions," April 2008, accessed on 30 April 2009, http://164.100.47.132 /LssNew/Questions/questionlist.aspx.

13. See Cons (this volume) for a comparable emphasis on narrations and what they might tell us about the sense of belonging to a space.

14. Situated at a height of 1,308 meters above sea level, with a population of 19,775 according to the 2001 census of India, Gopeshwar is to be found at a distance of 280 kilometers from Dehradun and 235 kilometers from Rishikesh (the nearest railhead). The patchy roads on which one has to navigate eight to ten hours of a rough car or bus ride, zigzagging up and down mountains and valleys to reach the town, makes Gopeshwar the quintessential "out-of-the-way place" so favored by anthropologists in the past for their seeming pristineness (Tsing 1994: 280).

FOUR | SONDRA L. HAUSNER | JEEVAN R. SHARMA

On the Way to India

Nepali Rituals of Border Crossing

National boundaries may appear clearly in the maps and documents of state and other international agencies, but from the perspective of a migrant, a border looks different. Not only do borders mark the periphery of a state, but they are an essential feature of national identity. As such, they become the locations of state mechanisms that serve primarily to regulate population movements and where, as every chapter in this volume shows, states can maintain and put on display structures of difference. In this chapter, we attempt to understand the state boundary between Nepal and India from the vantage point of those actors whose movement transcends it and who thereby directly experience and confront its authority. We could think of large flows of unskilled labor migrants—often the poorest populations, and so the most dispensable but also the least desirable—as a kind of tacit agreement between states about where workers most benefit the market (Portes 2008). But that analysis would not adequately consider the perspective of those who are doing the crossing, namely those who by leaving are made to feel just how deeply they undermine or betray the state's raison d'être. From the perspective of the migrant, border crossing should instead be seen as a ritual of mobility enacted against the ideological authority of the state.

A national boundary is a necessary precondition for the integrity of state coherence. Kearney (2004: 133) suggests that borders accomplish this in two principal ways: first, they support the 'classificatory' mission that categorizes the identities of persons on either side of the border (as well as those who cross it); second, they filter forms of economic 'value' that flow across them, such that borders usually serve to uphold class structures. In short, borders make sure that the right people stay in and the wrong people stay out. But by crossing borders emigrants diminish the salience of national boundaries and present a challenge precisely to republican ideology. Migrant mobility testifies to the failure of the power that has let them down. To put it more strongly, whether as victims or agents of the global market for labor, land migrants who cross a national border effectively undermine the whole idea of statehood and national boundaries; cross-border migration acts against the very defining power of the state. Piliavsky (this volume) warns us not to consider international borderlands as so very different from interiors, but here we suggest that it is at international border crossings where the dynamics between a state and its nationals (never mind its markets or its foreigners) are most apparent.

Most of the Nepali migrants we spoke with (between 2004 and 2007, at five places along the Nepal-India border) would rather not have migrated to India.[1] With insufficient food, land, work, or cash income in their villages, our informants sustained long-held patterns of cross-border labor migration from Nepal to India. The decisions made by able-bodied men, women, and families to leave their homes in search of work opportunities in Indian cities show in no uncertain terms that Nepal is unable to give its people work or sustain them. If people vote with their feet, labor migration demonstrates that the capacity of the Nepali state is diminished. Since Nepal is unable to provide sustenance or support, migration to India becomes a self-preserving move toward independence—a coming-of-age ritual—for the young unmarried men who initiate their generation's flow across the border. Later they may marry (usually in Nepal), and if in due course they settle in India for extended periods of time, they may ask family or village members to accompany their wives to India to join them and mostly end up retiring back in their villages in Nepal (J. R. Sharma 2008).

As far as women's migration was concerned, public campaigns against trafficking were so closely linked to mobility that for a woman to cross the border was automatically to place her in a marked category of risk, which seemed to justify the state's taking control for her protection (and through the implicit trope of purity). Trafficking was twinned with migration when it came to women's movement in both local and global discourse (and at every level in between) in the perception of female migrants' willingness—or unwillingness—to traverse or transgress borders or boundaries. If it was feared that migrating women were victims of trafficking, it was because the transnational governance agenda has prioritized the market as in some sense the only viable challenge to the state. And if the labor market is the lens through which the state may legitimately (in the transnational or globalized world) filter its citizens at its border, women's migration will similarly be regulated through the discourse of labor or, as in this case, gendered or sexed work. Had the transnational development industry recalled the equally pressing imperatives of kin relations at the level of people's lived experiences (alongside the aspirations for class mobility and the capacity to participate in a cash economy), it might have anticipated just how many women crossing the Nepal-India border were going to India to meet fathers, husbands, and kinsmen.

For the purpose of our chapter, the border should be understood not just as the boundary line demarcating two states—in this case, Nepal and India—but also as the range of technologies, sociocultural instruments, and personnel that define and patrol it. As Kearney (1995, 2004) has demonstrated, the border is a place where states may assert their independence from each other as well as wield power over that which they still contain. Borders are not in fact geographical lines in the sand, but rather emerging locations in the relations between states and their peoples. Kearney differentiates between a border and a boundary, but from the perspective of a land migrant, they are one and the same, insofar as getting across them presents an enormous ordeal. Farrelly (chapter 8, this volume) suggests that even in a borderless region "there is a process of hardening the state in places that matter"; it is thus that the border, a place that matters a great deal to the state (and indeed might be said quite literally to define it), poses a journey with much at stake. For an overland labor migrant, borders are where the state makes itself felt and must therefore be approached with the right attitude: crossing might best be understood as a ritual that involves delicate negotiation with an authority at the height of its power. But once you make it to the other side, the state no longer has a claim over you and stands to lose its veneer of transcendence, as when the curtain is pulled aside to reveal the Wizard of Oz as a cowering figure standing behind a velvet drape.

In the context of Nepal, and from the perspective of Nepali migrants, we take three sets of state or state-sanctioned actors at the national border with India—state police and customs officials, the NGO Maiti Nepal, and private transporters and agents—to see how border crossing is negotiated, what dangers are posed, and who might occupy the role of transcendent authority. If, as we are suggesting, the ritual of border crossing subverts the dominance of the nation-state, we are interested in the interactions between migrants on the one hand and the state and its representatives on the other. We ask whether these interactions—taking place as they do at a heightened moment of spatial and experiential liminality—might be usefully understood not only as rituals of departure but also as rituals of transgression. If borders are places of significance for both states and land migrants, it is because they are the last place the former can claim any territorial sovereignty over the latter and the first place a national can shake free of the state's dominion.

A History of Border Crossing from Nepal to India

The unique arrangement of an open border between Nepal and India has facilitated population movement across the state boundary for centuries; people living on either side of the boundary have always maintained economic, cultural, and familial links. Following the typology constructed by Oscar Martínez (1994), the Nepal-India border can be interpreted as 'interdependent borderlands' "in which the societies on both sides of the border are linked symbolically, leading to a considerable flow of economic and human resources across the border" (Baud and Van Schendel 1997: 220). Significant numbers of people cross the border into both countries from both directions; we focus on Nepali migrants traveling from Nepal into India (see figure 4.1).[2]

Starting with recruitment into the army of the Sikh ruler Ranjit Singh and then systematically into the British army in India in the nineteenth century, migration from Nepal to India has been an immensely popular practice among a very large number of men from rural Nepal. There is historical evidence that state policies and agrarian relations during the eighteenth and nineteenth centuries forced peasants in the hills to move off their land and seek their livelihoods elsewhere, including and most notably multiple Indian cities (Regmi 1978). In contemporary times there are probably more than two million Nepali migrant workers in India (compare Seddon et al. 2002, who estimated one million a decade ago). About 90 percent of these migrants are believed to be male (J. R. Sharma 2008). Remittances sent from India that are largely outside the official banking system continue to contribute to the economy and livelihoods in Nepal at very high levels.[3]

Migration and mobility in search of work is not a new phenomenon in Nepal; there is historical and ethnographic evidence that Nepalis have long been a mobile population (Hitchcock 1961; Hutt 1989; Pfaff-Czarnecka 1995).

FIGURE 4.1. Indian gate marking the border at Biratnagar, viewed from Nepal, 2009. The inscription on the gate, dedicated to the memory of Jayaprakash Narayan, records that it was built by the MP Sukhdev Paswan. Photograph courtesy of D. N. Gellner.

We might think of the eighteenth and nineteenth centuries when the state redistributed agricultural lands, thereby forcing peasants from the hills to move off their land and either into the Nepali Tarai or across the border to India as the *first wave* of migration. The *second wave* of migration, in the mid-twentieth century, marks an even more dramatic rise in rural-to-urban migration both within and outside of the country (Gellner 2013).

The *third wave* of migration started in the mid-1980s, accelerated in the 1990s, and dramatically increased in the twenty-first century, when the Maoist insurgency spread throughout Nepal. Hill men continued to migrate to India and began to migrate to the Gulf and Malaysia, not only as a way to keep money flowing to rural families but also as a strategy to protect young men who might be vulnerable to forced recruitment by the Maoists (Bruslé 2010). This period marks the age of rising expectations among young Nepalis, when the aspiration to migrate and participate in the world of modernity and in the consumption of commodities and global places was universalized (Liechty 2003). This is also the period when increasing numbers of Nepalis began to use labor recruitment agencies and agents to facilitate their migration out of Nepal, especially when going beyond the traditional destinations in India.

Of course, neither historical nor contemporary Nepali migration to India is exclusively about labor; a large number of Nepalis cross the border for other purposes, including medical, educational, pilgrimage, and familial purposes and for employment in multiple sectors. We have come across ascetics who travel around the Indian subcontinent in search of excitement and fun (Hausner 2007b) and many young men who migrate to Indian cities in search of movies and other consumption opportunities in an environment of urban bustle (J. R. Sharma 2008). But most male land migrants are intending to find work. From the perspective of Nepali migrant laborers, travel to Indian cities forms an important part of their life and livelihoods; migration provides household income, to be sure, but also an opportunity to participate in the consumption of regional and global markets, goods, and experiences (J. R. Sharma 2008). We document our fieldwork with Nepali migrants crossing the Nepal-India border to elucidate some of the ways the Nepali state enforces its boundary. Interestingly, unlike the situation at many state boundaries or immigration checkpoints in the world—consider the war-zone frontier that Gupta describes in this volume—the Nepali state appeared to us less concerned with monitoring the incoming flow of migrants from India than with interrogating the steady outgoing flow of labor migrants from Nepal.

The Nepal-India Border

Such a history of migration shows in no uncertain terms that a border is more than a physical demarcation between states; it is instead produced by a set of dynamics that arise in response to regional and international labor relations. Nevertheless the geography of Nepal as a state has contributed to the historical production of this particular land border—a place where, ironically, it is very apparent that there is no natural justification for a division between states: the south of Nepal runs imperceptibly into the Indian Gangetic plain. As is well known, Nepal is a landlocked country surrounded to the east and west by the mountains of India and to the north by the formidable natural border of the Himalayas. That Nepal's only access to seaports is through India and that Nepalis have depended on Indian labor markets for centuries has made Nepal highly dependent on India. In contrast to the almost insurmountable border with its northern neighbor, China, Nepal shares an open 1,751-kilometer

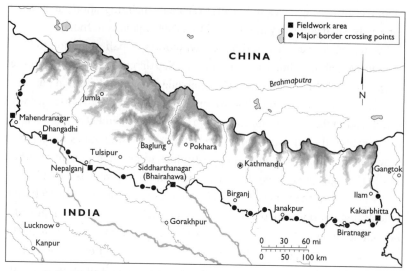

MAP 4.1. India-Nepal border crossing points.

border with India, which people of both countries may readily cross at any point and at any time, ostensibly without producing an identity document. The border between Nepal and India is marked by twenty-two official crossing points that are patrolled and manned by Nepali and Indian security personnel; unlike the mountainous borders that Mathur describes on the northern rim of Uttarakhand (chapter 3, this volume) or that Mishra describes in Arunachal Pradesh (chapter 6, this volume), the balance of the border in the Nepali Tarai is open, dry land, unfenced and unmonitored, through which any Nepali or Indian citizen may pass without hindrance (see map 4.1).[4]

Historically speaking, the open border between the two states is as old as the demarcation itself. The Nepal-India Peace and Friendship Treaty of 1950 formally gave citizens of both countries equal employment rights in the other country and the right to unhindered passage across the border. The 1950 treaty and the letters of exchange that followed state that neither country may unilaterally introduce travel provisions that might restrict free movement of people across the border. Article 7 states, "The governments of India and Nepal agree to grant, on a reciprocal basis, to the nationals of one country in the territories of the other the same privileges in the matter of residence, ownership of property, participation in trade and commerce, movement and other privileges of a similar nature."[5] However, it should be noted that in practice

Indians are not allowed to own property in Nepal and can set up a business only with a Nepali partner. India has not formally protested this practice as a violation of the 1950 treaty because similar stipulations operate in its own border regions, such as Kashmir and Arunachal. The treaty of 1950 does not explicitly discuss any issues relating to migrant workers and their rights; these discourses emerged later, mainly in the 1990s, after the first wave of democracy and decentralization.[6]

Neither the colonial regime in India nor Nepali rulers showed much interest in controlling the border, thus giving rise to the waves of migration described earlier, for at least two reasons. First, an open border facilitated the flow of cheap labor from Nepal into India, especially the recruitment of hill men from Nepal into the British Army (commonly known as Gurkhas; Des Chene 1991). Second, it facilitated the flow of raw materials from Nepal into India and, in reverse, the flow of commodities and goods manufactured in India into the Nepali market (Blaikie et al. 1980). As a result, no official system of formal record keeping was ever established, especially because people crossing the border were not required to carry identity documents.

The contemporary monitoring of the border is much different. An increasingly vocal national debate on ethnic politics and citizenship (in tandem with a widely held public view in Nepal that personhood requires such paperwork) has meant that most migrants feel obliged—and go to considerable effort and expense—to procure identity cards. Issues surrounding the regulation and flow of people across the border have become areas of public debate in Nepal with the growth of civil society and NGOs since the 1990s: discussions on the economic consequences of migrants on either side of the border; the harassment of Nepali migrants into India (or Indian migrants into Nepal); the trafficking of Nepali women into Indian cities; the smuggling and illicit trade across the border; crime and terrorism; the border encroachment by India, among others, all point to the critical role the Nepal-India border plays in conceptions of Nepali statehood.[7]

Similarly the Nepali media frequently reports on issues of Indian dominance in Nepal—whether it be regime change, political processes, unequal bilateral trade, unequal treaties, or violence and armed conflict in Tarai.[8] The first nine of the Nepali Maoists' forty demands, with which they launched the People's War in 1996, were designated "concerning nationalism"; seven of the nine points directly related to the border or to India or Indian domination of the Nepali culture and economy (Thapa 2003; Sharma 2010).[9] Although it might be seen as granting access to India, many Nepalis consider the treaty to have served India's interests exclusively, and it has generated heated debate (Hoftun et al. 1999: 261). We might argue that Nepal benefits from the ability of Nepali migrant workers to move to India for employment and other opportunities, but the dominant perception within Nepal is that the treaty has facilitated large-scale immigration of Indians into Nepal and domination of the Nepalese market by Indian goods and businesses and boosted the Indian economy through a flow of cheap labor from Nepal. The conclusion among the Nepali Maoists at least was that the treaty has been detrimental to Nepal's development and sovereignty; they have consistently demanded that it be revised.

With the spread of the Maoist insurgency in Nepal after 1996, and in view of their links to Naxalite movements in India, the Indo-Nepal border came under intense bilateral scrutiny, with increased surveillance on both sides. Indian security personnel at the border began to ask for 'citizenship cards' from Nepalis traveling to India after the 2001 State of Emergency in Nepal. In November 2001 the Indian government designated the Nepali Maoists a security threat to India, labeling them a terrorist organization. On 11 September 2004 the *Kantipur* daily newspaper reported that both the Indian ambassador to Nepal and the foreign secretary of India repeated that the Maoist insurgency in Nepal was a threat to India as well as Nepal, after which the Indian state established a further presence at the border by deploying more security forces. Certain critical events like elections in either state or increased violence in a border area results in the tightening and sealing of the border for a period of time. Even without a legal requirement to do so, scrutiny at the border has intensified.

Migration as a Ritual between States

For some, the crossing of the border is an option, while for others it is an existential issue. It is often the latter, those that must find a way across the border if they are to survive, who find it the hardest to cross, if only because they are deemed undesirable by the border gatekeepers who maintain control over entry and exit.— Newman 2006a: 178

Jeevan: It was about eleven in the morning, in mid-October, and a Bahun man of thirty-four with two of his nephews (about eighteen and twenty years old) were about to leave for Delhi, India. He was returning to work in Delhi after the Dasain holidays.[10] At this time he was taking two of his nephews for the first time to Delhi, with the aim of finding them employment. He had already found a job for one as a domestic worker; given the demand for domestic workers in Delhi, he was hopeful that he would be able to find work for the other one soon.

The departure was an emotional scene lasting about twenty minutes. Around a dozen family members and neighbors gathered in front of the house. The two boys in their new clothes were staring at their family members and seemed both nervous and shy. At the same time, some members of the family, neighbors, and friends were teasing the two boys for going to be *lahures*, the term for those who sell their labor in a foreign country.[11] Signifying good luck for the journey, those who were leaving had red *tika* on their forehead and carried fruit (guava).[12] They were carrying only two small bags with a change of clothes. The boys were asked to take care of themselves and not to become involved in immoral work or behavior, to "do well" and send news regularly. The uncle assured his brothers and sisters-in-law that he would take care of their boys and that they need not worry about them. As they left, all the family members and neighbors gathered and watched them walking away until they disappeared along the trail that led to the main road. In response, the three men turned back frequently and waved. One of the mothers had tears in her eyes, but the grandmother said in an authoritative voice that she should stop crying at the *sait* of travel.[13] As soon as the three men had disappeared from view, those left behind returned to their usual routines.

Whether or not accompanied by elders, the departure of young village men is a common scene in the hill villages of western central Nepal. Playing loud Bollywood music, the buses to Butwal in the plains depart every twenty or thirty minutes from the noisy bus park, each carrying between twenty and forty passengers. From Butwal their journeys continue to the Indian border at Sunauli, where they separate, traveling to different destinations either by train or by bus.

Let me turn now to my experience of border crossing with a group of Nepali migrants traveling to the Indian city of Mumbai. During my doctoral fieldwork in 2005 I accompanied a group of three Nepali migrants (one of them was returning to work in India, while the other two were going to India for the first time) who were excited to be going to India. As we prepared to travel to the border town of Sunauli, the returnee migrant told us that it was important to look confident at the border crossing, otherwise they might be harassed by police or other officials, including "strange-looking people" who would try to cheat us. We were going to be confronted by the state or state-sanctioned authorities. He told us that we needed to be extremely cautious while traveling, as people could not be trusted at this juncture of the journey. We were told not to panic and to avoid showing any signs of nervousness. With the mounting pressure from the heat and the fear, there was an uncomfortable anxiety in the group when we left Bhairahawa. My fellow travelers avoided eye contact with border officials, including the police and customs officers. As we were crossing the border, we were extremely conscious of how we held our bodies and how we were being perceived by others.

Sondra: The vast majority of Nepali migrants are men,[14] but women do cross the border. In 2005 most women we met were traveling to join husbands already working in India.[15] They were excited about the prospect of new locations and family reunions, but tremendously nervous—and usually quite ignorant—about the mechanics of travel. It was unbecoming for a woman to travel alone, and most women migrants were accompanied by male family members, who were charged with knowing the routes, destination addresses, and modes of travel and who were also in charge of the money for the journey. Almost all women migrants we spoke with were entirely inexperienced in the ways of journeying; if for some reason a woman was separated from her male kin, she would have no information or means to continue the journey, nor, in some cases, would she know how to return home. Buying bus tickets, using telephones, and articulating destinations fell entirely outside the purview of women.

More surprising were the straightforward interrogations that would take place at the border. If a group of two included a young woman (seemingly either a brother and sister or a young couple), each person would be taken aside and interviewed separately. If the stories did not match, it was assumed that the young man must intend to traffic the young woman, and they would be summarily turned around. (This policy may sound sensible, but it is misplaced; if a young man *did* have plans to traffic his attractive young companion, he would likely just walk her through an open field and rejoin the main transportation routes once they were safely in India, or wait until the border guards were engrossed in interrogating someone else.) I saw one couple turned around after their respective interviews—they were not permitted by the NGO staff member to pass through the Bhairahawa border to Sunauli—because their stated intentions were dubious. To me, it looked like they were trying to elope (they came from the same village, and they were young and holding hands), but the NGO official decided that it was too risky. On another occasion, in Kakarbhitta, an NGO staff member appealed to a border policeman to stop a migrant couple who tried to dodge the booth.

Sometimes a large group of villagers would travel together through a border post; if women were included in their number, they would be allowed free passage only after marriage certificates were produced. With a widespread cultural ethos that questions women's movement (Bennett 2006), it was not hard to get swept up in questioning female—especially girls'—mobility. On one occasion I met a young girl of thirteen eating her rice alone. When asked whom she was traveling with, she indicated a group of rowdy men drinking whisky at another table in the border *dhaba* (roadside restaurant), and I found myself raising the alarm bell. The girl was detained in the NGO transit home at the border for four days while her father took time off from his job at a restaurant in Delhi to come and retrieve her. Drunk as they may have been, the rowdy men who were his village kin were doing him a favor. He had asked them to accompany his daughter to Delhi—they were traveling from the village to India in any event—and they were doing his bidding.

What emerges from our field experiences is that border areas are designed to monitor and demarcate those people and goods traveling through them; they are not just boundaries separating two nations. Nervousness about interrogation or security procedures at checkpoints—clearly a constructed domain of authority—was widespread, and both men and women who were crossing the border experienced a combination of fear, pressure, and powerlessness. On the other hand, excited anticipation about what lay ahead—India, a reunited family, new work opportunities, and the possibility of wider life experiences in new locations—made the tension and uncertainty worthwhile. Widely publicized narratives of 'girl trafficking' made migration through the border a particularly gendered experience; having a woman—especially a girl—in the traveling party brought about heightened scrutiny, extensive interrogation, and sometimes extended periods of detention.

Maintaining the border involves a range of bureaucratic, legal, and other personnel to regulate citizen mobility and exercise (or at least perform) authority over people who travel across or transcend the border. Such an apparatus of state and nonstate actors sometimes engages with migrants in the name of protection but sometimes poses a set of prohibitive or abusive dangers themselves. Thus the border is a site where the state is made visible as an unquestioned or transcendent authority—and in anticipation of which young travelers engage in ritual preparation—only to be revealed as a power that cannot be sustained.

The State of the Border at the Border of the State

The three sets of actors that we identify and discuss next occupy different positions in their relation to statehood: the state itself, an NGO (which is state-sanctioned, especially in this case), and private agents and transporters, who have to receive state permission to function. We dub all three sets of actors arms of the state (although they are so to varying degrees), in that they both enable and are (therefore) enabled by the state. At the broadest level, we can understand them as gatekeepers—quite literally—who serve to maintain the coherence or integrity of the state (in the case of police, army, or customs officials, who stand to gain as much as anyone by its strengthening) or the explicit values or priorities endorsed by the state (in the case of the NGO that acts with local, state, and multilateral support of antitrafficking campaigns). Private agents could be seen as more of a direct challenge to the state but could at the same time be seen as expressions of the endorsement of market structures (labor and otherwise) that the state now holds out to both the transnational rule of global elites and to its citizens as its main legitimating promise.[16]

STATE POLICE AND CUSTOM OFFICIALS

Police and customs officials, particularly the Armed Police Force on the Nepal side and the Indian paramilitary Sashastra Seema Bal, are clearly visible at the border, possibly as the most prominent demographic and certainly as the most apparent representatives and even icons of the state. Police and custom officials from both India and Nepal occupy the no-man's-land on the road that crosses the border. They keep a constant eye on people and goods moving across the border. Migrants are stopped and their bags are searched. These uniformed officials speak to migrant travelers in a commanding voice, and it is rare that someone migrating through the border will not face these officials in transit. Such encounters mean that migrants are made to feel extremely conscious of their vulnerable position.

Jeevan: After getting off the bus on the Nepal side of Sunauli border, we took two rickshaws at the border to reach the bus station on the Indian side, where we could get a bus to the train station in Gorakhpur. The combination of pressure to be seen as confident on one hand and fear on the other was palpable as we approached. As our rickshaws headed toward the border crossing, two Nepali policemen standing at the side of the road beckoned to us. They stopped our rickshaw, looked through our bags suspiciously, and began to ask questions. Where had we come from? Where did we want to go, and why? Questioning by authoritative policemen was a regular feature at the border, and yet it was nonetheless frightening and humiliating.

As we moved forward on the Indian side of the border, our rickshaw was stopped initially by Indian police and then by Indian immigration officials. Two policemen sitting on chairs on the left side of the road called us to them, using their long stick. We went to them and stood obediently. Commandingly they asked us in Hindi, "Where have you come from? Where are you going? What are you carrying?" Without waiting for our answers, they searched our bags. In an attempt to defuse the tension, one of them jokingly asked if we were Maoists or had any links with the Maoists.

More recently, in 2010, I crossed the border in Mahendranagar by *tanga* (a horse-drawn carriage) with three young men who were leaving for Delhi. The tanga took an hour and a half to cross a twelve-kilometer border zone from Mahendranagar, on the Nepal side, to Banbasa, an Indian market town where we could get buses for our onward journey. Our tanga crossed the Nepali checkpoint just before no-man's-land. It was guarded by Nepali armed police force, who did not stop us for checking. After the checkpoint on the Nepal side, we continued on a dirt road. After about five minutes, the tanga helper asked us to get off, and we had to stand in a queue to be questioned and inspected by a member of the Sashastra Seema Bal. He looked inside my bag and asked if I was a student. I told him that I was going to Naini Tal for my holidays, and he let me go without further questions. Each and every traveler was questioned and their bags inspected. As we remounted the tanga and continued, we found that the border gate was closed. It was 6:15 P.M., and we were told that the border gate closes at 6.00 P.M. We were told that this was a regular occurrence and the gate would open after paying a bribe to the official who controlled the gate. The helper of our tanga collected five Indian rupees from each passenger and passed the money to the official, and the gate opened after about twenty minutes.

On the same trip, as I was crossing the border to return to Nepal, my rickshaw was stopped by customs officials on the Indian side. They asked me to get out of the rickshaw and enter the small hut where two customs officials had their office. After asking a couple of questions regarding where I had come from and where I was going, one of them directed me to look at a cloth banner which read both in Hindi and English that travelers into Nepal are not allowed to carry Indian currency notes worth 500 rupees. Then he asked me if I had read and understood the notice, and also whether I was carrying such paper notes. As soon as I replied that I had understood the notice and did not have any 500-rupee notes, he asked me to empty my pockets and started to frisk me. He searched all of my pockets and asked me to remove my shoes. The other official simultaneously opened my bag, emptied the contents on the table, and looked inside all the clothes I had packed. I kept repeating that I did not have any 500-rupee notes. They agreed to release me from their 'inspection' once I told them that I work for a university and had previously studied in India. After inspecting my ID card, they finally let me go. I was quite relieved, as I had heard rumors of customs officials 'threatening' and 'looting' money from Nepali migrants. Once I reached the Nepal side, I met a middle-aged man who had had 3,000 Indian rupees taken by the same customs officials, all in units of 100 rupees. Border crossing involved encounters with various authorities who made the travelers feel very vulnerable and powerless.

MAITI NEPAL

Maiti Nepal is an NGO that has been running antitrafficking programs in Nepal since 1993. Following the public proclamation that Nepali girl trafficking to India was rampant (the oft-used figure was eight thousand Nepali girls annually), Maiti Nepal (and a number of NGOs following its lead) established checkpoints in eight border areas, alongside police posts, to monitor any migration that might be a foil for smuggling a girl into India for illicit sex work. There are at least two or three Maiti Nepal staff who carry out surveillance at each of the eight border crossings; many of the staff are returned 'rescuees,' that is, girls or women who have worked in brothels in India and who have either been unable or opted not to return to their home villages.

Supported by the police, Maiti Nepal staff question migrants and verify their documents in order to gather information that will help them ascertain whether a girl or woman is migrating under acceptable circumstances. None of these procedures is a mechanism of state law; they are instead a testament to the state's commitment to combat trafficking. However, in practice, Maiti border checkpoints require people who cross the border to prove their identity (although, again, there is no legal requirement to carry documentation at a formally open border), and the people are often interrogated. From the perspective of migrants we spoke to, Maiti Nepal staff are "just like police," although the stated intention of these border agents is to protect women.

Sondra: For the women migrants with whom I spoke, and the male kin who accompanied them, the greatest source of tension (and the most detailed preparations for) crossing the border centered on what was viewed as an inevitable encounter with the Maiti Nepal girl-trafficking prevention checkpoint. I was shown photographs and identity cards that were procured in district headquarters, proving marriage, sisterhood, or daughterhood. The more evidence that could be proffered to prove the legitimate status and relations of a woman migrant and her companion, the higher the chances, it was felt, that crossing the border would be permitted: the more formality the arrangement appeared to have, the less Maiti Nepal would question the relationships or motives for the migration.

Although there is no legal provision for the state, let alone a nongovernmental organization, to stop migrants, Maiti Nepal appeared to have an unwritten authority to which even state police would defer. I saw couples turned around, disallowed from crossing a border that is legally open to everyone; girls separated from village members for interrogation and eventual sequestering; and women who appeared to be practicing sex workers hotly pursued by Maiti Nepal staff trying to prevent their crossing. The sheer potential of the border as a checkpoint location is one reason Maiti Nepal antitrafficking policies have centered there, but unquestioned assumptions about the safety of the home state, the parallel dangers of the foreign state, and the inherent transgression of cross-border travel are also at work. The border is a site of passage, and so the obvious place, ostensibly, to divert the threat of the Other.

Jeevan: Maiti Nepal had a small office at the Sunauli border with two members of staff constantly checking the movement of women and children over the border. At the time of crossing the border, I saw a Nepali family (a man, a woman, one son, and one daughter about sixteen to eighteen years old) questioned by a couple of Maiti Nepal's staff, dressed in their uniform of a light pink *kurta surwal* with a brown *dupatta*. There was also a couple crossing the border who were stopped and questioned again. The frustrated husband was trying to convince the staff that his wife was accompanying him to Mumbai, where he worked, but he was not believed. He had never had to prove to anyone in the village that they were husband and wife. Initially the wife kept quiet but later spoke in anger to the staff, saying that they were creating a problem unnecessarily. The couple did not have a recommendation letter from the VDC (the office of the village administration), which the Maiti Nepal staff requested. It was eventually the argument of the wife that allowed them to move on. Other people crossing the border made remarks that this was a typical scene. Later I met the couple in the railway station in Gorakhpur; they told me that they were unnecessarily given trouble by "those people," as the wife referred to the Maiti Nepal staff. During our conversation, the wife asked me, "Now you tell me, now we need documents to prove that we are husband and wife. Why don't they go to our village and ask for it?" The helpless husband stood beside his wife and smiled at me as his wife continued to complain.

PRIVATE TRANSPORTERS

As discussed earlier, transportation plays a key role in border crossing; migrants have to take one vehicle to cross the border, followed by a separate vehicle to continue to their destination. Border crossing is not served by a single and straightforward transport system. Often migrants and other travelers have to take at least three or four different modes of transport to cross the border: a typical sequence involves (1) a bus to the nearest town or city bus stop; (2) a small jeep that carries the travelers from the city bus stop to the border town; (3) a rickshaw that carries the traveler from the border town to the other side of the border; and (4) some mode of transport from the other side of the border to the destination.

With this elaborate system in place, migrants must depend upon the networks of private transporters who in turn exercise authority—and sometimes abuse them—as they cross the border; private transporters often cheat migrants and use force. Migrants are often asked to pay the same fare more than once and are frequently robbed; travelers take precautions by traveling in groups and keep money hidden in inside pockets, by avoiding anything to eat given by strangers, and by avoiding overnight stays in hotels. Migrants spoke about being looted in the border areas when they were returning home with savings. Places like Gorakhpur and Sunauli were considered to be the worst places for being cheated and threatened.

Jeevan: Before we reached the bus stop on the Indian side of the border in Sunauli our rickshaw was stopped by two threatening men who wanted us to buy bus tickets from them to travel on their bus. Scared as we were, we said that we would like to go by jeep (which is much faster and more comfortable for the same price), but they forced us to buy tickets and travel on their bus.

When I objected, they physically forced us to take the tickets and travel on the crowded bus, standing for about three hours to Gorakhpur. While I had traveled to India by road before as a student, I had never previously had such an experience (probably because I always traveled with my middle-class friends in good clothes and we spoke English to officials). When I resisted (in Hindi), we were told, "Go, go, go back to Nepal. . . . There's nothing to eat [in Nepal], so you come here [to India]. . . . Go, go, get out of here." ("Chalo. . . . Chalo bhago Nepal jao. . . . Kuch khaneko nahi milta, phir chale aate ho. . . . Chalo . . . chalo . . . bhago.") I was pulled aside by a fellow traveler who asked me not to argue. He told me that this was a very common experience at the border and advised me to keep quiet. The experience was frightening; we felt helpless and forced to obey. The feeling of insecurity was deep.

On the bus there were many Nepalis (most of them were men, but a few women accompanied their husbands) watching each other, which made me feel more relieved. A loud Bollywood film song was playing in the background. A man working in the Indian army (*lahure*) was standing in the bus next to me. Referring to the earlier use of force, he told the conductor that he should have let the passengers choose which bus to travel on and so have the chance of obtaining a seat. In reply, the conductor simply used abusive words to insult him. It was a very tense and frightening moment as the conductor with his associate tried to drag the lahure out of the bus. Realizing the difficult situation, the humiliated lahure and the rest of the people kept quiet. Despite the village meaning of *lahure* as a brave man, this lahure was in a vulnerable position and he had no other choice but to keep quiet. In stark contrast to his respectable position in his home village, he was humiliated here in front of his fellow countrymen.

The Liminality of Borders

From the moment of departure, elements of ritual mark Nepali migration. If we recall that rites of passage mark a transformation in status or lifestyle, then clearly migration across the Nepal-India border, most commonly to alter one's economic status and gender identity, qualifies as a rites of passage. In referring to the 'sait of travel,' a village member wishes to mark the transitional quality of the journey. In adorning young men with tika powder and marigold garlands, families acknowledge an upcoming migration as a ritually powerful time. In the first stage, the migrant prepares for the change that will occur as a result of the departure, a process that involves bidding farewell to the old life in the village. It involves carrying money, wearing new clothes, and being accompanied by a known guide. The departure encompasses manifold goodbyes and displays of love, tears, nervousness, shyness, and excitement.

Such a ritual to precede departure may be enacted in anticipation of the dangers of encountering the state (as one of multiple transcendent forces that may stand in the way of successful passage). Or the trials of border crossing may conceptually map onto the already heightened transition of travel, regardless of whether a particular journey is designated as a migration or a pilgrimage. Either way, crossing the border marks the passage into a new nation-state and a new status-state as well, such that an unemployed village youth becomes a Nepali migrant worker in India and in turn has the opportunity to become a lahure or a *jagire* (a successful man) rather than stay a *phaltu* (a useless man) back in his village (J. R. Sharma 2008).

If travel is generally considered an experience of transition and therefore a potential danger, crossing the state border may be seen as the literal manifestation of liminality. Migration through the India-Nepal border means departure from a known home place and the performance of going through a specific zone of checks, controls, and customs. That the border represents a liminal passage—complete with somewhat altered experiences and fears of the unknown—so that a new phase of life can begin seems clear. To return to classic studies of ritual, migrants crossing the border can be said to be "betwixt and between the positions assigned arrayed by law, custom, convention and ceremonial" (Turner 1995: 95). Seen from the perspective of migrants, borders may be interpreted as a site of deference to or defiance against the state: passing through it may be or feel like a pilgrimage to transnational opportunity.

In the internationally designated no-man's-land between Nepal and India, we see how the spatial dimension of liminality between nation-states is reflected in migrant experiences: by moving toward and passing into a liminal zone, the migrant is marked as the ambiguous and vulnerable person that he is. Consider how we were instructed to hold our bodies in a particular way, to look confident and not panicky; we were asked not only to perform our resistance to marginality but also to experience it. Humiliation was a punishment for crossing the border, a way of disciplining migrants as they were about to became (low) wage earners in India. While it is 'legal' to cross the border, the police, NGOs, and private transporters dealt with migrants as if they were 'illegal migrants' or 'criminals'—people who, by migrating, exposed the ideological integrity of the nation as false.[17] The state is shown to be unable to adequately sustain its people and to be complicit with global labor flows whereby the most marginal are the most expendable.

Nepal-to-India labor migration (and the marriage migration that follows from it) is thus cast as legal but illicit (in Abraham and Van Schendel's [2005] terms) from the perspective of the state, even though it benefits all parties. In order to obfuscate the weakness of the state as well as the complex market and transnational dynamics that effectively undermine it further, the border becomes a zone of transgression and danger. The state and its operatives may not prohibit crossing, but they may make it as difficult, frightening, and foreboding as possible; if you want to engage in the illicit activities of departure or moving between states, you will need to pay the price. Simply leaving Nepal is considered a dubious act—a kind of treason—and it thereby becomes a treacherous affair in the lore that surrounds travelers (especially women) who travel alone, the way migrants are roughed up at the border, and the kinds of unchecked abuse agents and transporters may enact against those who are seen as marginal not only in their socioeconomic status but in their traveling state.

Borders pose a hypothetical contour to the definition of the state, and those who wish to contain the nation will try to ensure that boundaries are monitored, overseen, and maintained. Recall that there is no legal provision to prevent crossing the Nepal-India border; all the charades of confidence, trust in the returnee migrants, reliance on male gatekeepers for women migrants, and elaborate preparations for the inevitable demands for identity documents are constructions of the state that are in no way required or supported by law. Control over migrants where there is no rule of law might therefore be seen as the attempt to assert state integrity, such that the rituals of migrant departure and transition are acted out against the ostensible but ultimately ineffective power of the nation.

States make boundaries literal: a migrant who passes through a border to the other side reminds the authorities of the state that it too may be transcended. Migration challenges the underlying principle of the state, namely, that people stay where they belong. Structures of authority are thereby questioned in the act of transgressing an international border; quite apart from the material incentives to harass and humiliate migrant travelers, the operatives of these structures will be invested in making the journey difficult. From the perspective of the migrant laborer or his family, however, even as they may be humiliated, the latent power of freedom from the state's inadequacies—and the accordant danger of liminal passage and all that lies ahead—is directly experienced by Nepalis on their way to India. Borders make liminality (and the powers and dangers that attend it) real to migrants, just as cartographers make borders real to politicians.

In the designation of no-man's-land, in the experience of vulnerability, and in the clear tussle of power between migrant and official (the migrant may have to pay a bribe to a customs official or Maiti Nepal may prohibit a woman from crossing), we see an actively re-created tension between the citizen and the state. Will the traveler cross? At what cost to him—and at what cost to the state, now shown up not only as too weak to provide sustenance but also as corrupt, irrational, and prohibitive in the face of its failure? Are customs officials who have to be bribed any different from the voracious demons that have to be pacified in other South Asian rituals, or indeed from any upwardly mobile civil servant? That Nepali laborers engage in a ritual of migration between states seems true both geopolitically and phenomenologically: the political and the personal are here again shown to be equivalent.

NOTES TO CHAPTER 4

1. Fieldwork was done by each of us in a series of border points, in somewhat differing contexts: Hausner (2005, 2007a) led a team for Save the Children's Himalayan Field Office that conducted research in Kakarbhitta, Bhairahawa, and Nepalganj at the end of 2004; Sharma (2007) conducted extensive fieldwork in Bhairahawa-Sunauli in 2005 as doctoral research and in Dhangadhi-Gauriphanta and Gaddi Chauki-Banbasa in February–March 2010. Sharma's fieldwork focused on the lived experiences of male migrants traveling to Indian cities and towns; Hausner led fieldwork focused on migration and trafficking as linked discursive fields that moved between the border town and the international development organization.

2. It is important to note that crossing the border in one direction is not the same as crossing it in the other, since the border depends on two different regimes of state power, which shape the experience of departure from and entry into their respective national spaces. During our fieldwork we did not focus on Indian travelers crossing the border to Nepal, and therefore we are unable to make any statement about their experiences.

3. Close to US$1 billion in total remittances to Nepal were reported through the formal banking system in 2004–5, although this amount was not all from India (Singh 2006). An estimate in the mid-1990s suggested that the annual aggregate value of

money sent (or brought) back to Nepal from India has been substantial, probably between 25 and 30 billion Nepalese rupees, or about US$450 million to US$500 million (Seddon 2005).

4. These twenty-two are formal transit points where customs and security are present, but people living close to the border cross it via many other small roads and paths along the Nepal-India frontier. There are six formal immigration points along the Nepal-India border: Banbasa/Gaddi Chauki, Dhangadhi, Nepalganj, Bhairahawa (Siddharthanagar), Birganj, Kakarbhitta. The geography may in parts be similar to the Bangladesh-India border, where the border is closed and has by contrast been heavily monitored for close to forty years (see, for example, chapters 9 and 10, on the Bengal borderlands, in this volume).

5. See www.nepaldemocracy.org/documents, accessed 30 May 2013.

6. The document from the International Organization for Migration that finally ensured the rights of migrant workers and their families (according to the sending countries, at any rate) was ratified by the UN in 2003 (IOM 2003; see also UN RES/57/201).

7. Mathur (chapter 3, this volume) discusses how the issue of illegal smuggling of medicinal plants and herbs from Uttarakhand remains a key problem for the Indian state.

8. In his book *Regionalism and National Unity in Nepal*, Frederick Gaige ([1975] 2009; see also Friedman 2005) writes that the issue of national integration in Nepal is directly related to India-Nepal border problems. In the context of national integration and Nepal Tarai, he identifies four types of border-related problems: border demarcation, outlaws and political terrorists operating on both sides of the border, smuggling, and migration of settlers from one country to another. (Whether all—or which—of these are perceived as problems by the state depends upon its political relationships with its neighbor at a given moment in history, of course.)

9. See also "40 Point Demand," accessed 20 May 2013. www.satp.org/satporgtp/countries /nepal/document/papers/40points.htm.

10. Dasain is the biggest festival among Hindus in Nepal. The festival is held on the tenth day of the light fortnight of the month Asvin (September/October) in honor of the goddess Durga.

11. This term is associated more specifically with Nepali men's recruitment into foreign armies or, derivatively, police forces (British, Indian, Brunei, etc.). The word *lahure* comes from the name of the city of Lahore in Pakistan. It was originally used to refer to the hill men who went to Lahore to enlist in the army of Sikh leader Ranjit Singh in the early nineteenth century.

12. A *tika* is a small mark placed on the forehead as part of religious worship or ritual.

13. *Sait* means the ritually favorable time for a specific action. Her point was presumably that tears should be reserved for inauspicious occasions, such as mourning a death.

14. Indeed state and NGO concerns about the potential dangers of conflict-induced migration were likely misdirected when they focused on the travels of women: they should have been equally or more focused on the dangers faced by young men (Hausner 2005).

15. I refer to members of my 2004–5 Save the Children-U.S. research team: Rita Dhungel, Ganesh GC, Prerna Rai, Archana Thapa, and Luna Thakur.

16. Given that the entire stretch of the border was like a busy market—with stalls, eateries, hotels, restaurants, telecommunication shops, and travel agents—it would seem that consumer consumption is at the very least tolerated if not actively encouraged by the state. It is perhaps not too farfetched to see a parallel between the state's transcendent authority and that of the transnational marketplace.

17. We might view border-crossing Nepali migrants as *homo sacer*, in the language of Agamben (1998).

The Perils of Being a Borderland People

On the Lhotshampas of Bhutan

This chapter responds to Baud and Van Schendel's (1997) call for bottom-up perspectives on borderlands, using oral history, by considering the experiences of the Lhotshampas of Bhutan. Baud and Van Schendel compare borderlands to "an accordion that contracts and expands to the pressures of social, economic and political developments on both sides of the border" (225). While an extensive literature addresses "how states have dealt with their borderlands," historians have "paid much less attention to how borderlands have dealt with their states," which results in the presentation of borderland people as "passive and reactive" (234). By contrast, the study of borderlands "assigns an active historical role to borderlands and their population" and redresses "the imbalance of 'state-centred' studies" (234). Such research requires the use of oral history to reconstruct borderland people's self-images and perceptions and to explore how these influenced their political, social, and economic behavior (242).

The Lhotshampas are an ethnic Nepali people who migrated from Nepal and India to Bhutan, where they settled along the Bhutan-India border between 1865 and 1930 (Hutt 2003: 24). They are a typical 'transborder people' since they share cultural values and the Nepali language with ethnic Nepali groups both India and in Nepal. As a transborder people the Lhotshampas' national loyalties are questioned by dominant ethnic groups in Bhutan. Such experiences are similar to the Madheshi people of Indian origin living in the Nepalese Tarai, who are considered 'foreigners' and often face social discrimination and difficulties accessing citizenship papers (Pradhan 2002: 17). Both the Nepalese and the Bhutanese state have pursued nationalist policies designed to homogenize the population through the imposition of the prevailing group's culture, language, dress, and religion. The dominant narrative told in the refugee camps and by human rights groups presents the Lhotshampas as victims of a cruel regime, which tried to 'Bhutanize' their ethnic Nepali citizens. According to such accounts, the Lhotshampas responded to a new 'one nation, one people' policy by protesting against the government and defending their right to maintain their distinct cultural and linguistic identity. The Bhutanese government suppressed this dissent, precipitating the flight of over eighty thousand Lhotshampas, who became refugees in Nepal in the early 1990s. However, the oral histories, collected from refugee adults in Nepal and presented here,[1] demonstrate that this history becomes significantly more complicated if the perspectives of southern Bhutanese villagers are considered alongside those of the Bhutanese state and the elite and well-educated refugee leadership.

This ethnographic research was conducted among Bhutanese refugees in Kathmandu and in camps in eastern Nepal for eleven months over two fieldwork trips, from September 2006 to March 2007, and from August 2007 to January 2008.[2] During this period the refugee community was politically divided over long-term solutions to their situation. This was precipitated by a burgeoning Maoist movement in the camps and the U.S. government's offer of resettlement places for over fifty thousand refugees. However, by the time I returned to Nepal and visited the camps and Kathmandu for two weeks in January 2009, resettlement had begun and most refugees had applied for this process. By mid-2011 over fifty thousand Bhutanese refugees had departed Nepal for third countries.

My research participants included refugees of all ages living in the camps, in addition to families and individual refugees living illegally in Kathmandu and Damak. I moved regularly between these three field sites and lived with a Bhutanese refugee family in Damak between September 2007 and January 2008. My research activities were conducted in both English and Nepali. I used a number of different research methods to allow for the collection of varied data and to enable cross-checking and triangulation of findings. These included traditional ethnographic research methods, such as participant observation, genealogies, oral histories, and semistructured interviews, as well as participatory research methods, which engaged young refugees in the research process.

The Creation of a Borderland People

Although monastic Buddhism was introduced to Bhutan from Tibet as early as the seventh century (Schicklgruber 1997; Pommaret 1997a), the country was not unified until the arrival of the first shabdrung or dharma raja (religious king), Ngawang Namgyal, in the seventeenth century (Rose 1977: 24). The shabdrung, who was the first theocratic ruler, "created something akin to a 'Bhutanese culture' in the 17th Century," and since this period "successive rulers have made attempts to induce the many different groups of Bhutanese to accede to a common cultural legacy and tradition" (Schicklgruber 1997: 16). Following the first shabdrung's death, the various leaders who occupied the throne "were more inclined towards religious than political activities," resulting in a period of internal instability and political turmoil (Pommaret 1997a: 206). In 1907, recognizing that the dual system of religious and secular rule no longer worked effectively, the religious and secular leaders offered the throne to the most powerful among them, Gongsar Ogyen Wangchuck. This initiated a system of hereditary monarchical rule.

Borders and their control have long been sensitive issues in Bhutan, and the northern border with the Tibet Autonomous Region continues to be undefined in spite of ongoing negotiations with the Chinese authorities concerning its demarcation (Whitecross 2009). The country's current southern borders were formed in the late nineteenth and early twentieth century partly as a result of disputes with the British government in India. Conflict over access to the Bengal Duars region resulted in the Anglo-Bhutanese war of 1864–65, which was concluded in the 1865 Treaty of Sinchula. This treaty gave the Duars to the British, in return for an annual cash subsidy paid to the Bhutanese. A further consequence of the Sinchula Treaty was British encouragement of large numbers of Nepali immigrants arriving in Darjeeling and Sikkim, some of whom eventually settled in Bhutan (Sinha 2001: 27).

Bhutan's people are collectively known as Drukpas, "a term which derives from Druk Yul, the name of the country in Dzongkha" (Pommaret 1997b: 43). The majority of Bhutan's people "are of Mongoloid stock" and speak languages belonging to the Tibeto-Burman family (43). The Ngalong in the west originated from Tibet, and their language, Dzongkha, was decreed by the king to be the national language in 1961 (van Driem 1994). The Sharchops in eastern Bhutan speak another distinct language. Both the Sharchops and the Ngalongs follow a Tibetan form of Mahayana Buddhism, although the

Drukpa Kagyü tradition is commonly practiced by Ngalongs in western Bhutan, and the Nyingma is predominant in the east (Hutt 2003: 5). Many Nepali and other non-Bhutanese authors assume that Bhutan's royal family "belongs to the 'ruling' Ngalong group that is counterposed to the Sharchopa" of eastern Bhutan. However, "the Wangchuck dynasty is mainly of a stock from the central districts of Kurtoe and Bumthang" (Phuntsho 2006).

Since the early twentieth century "the ethnic and linguistic character of the narrow southern belt has changed considerably due to the progressive arrival in this region of people of Nepali descent" (Pommaret 1997b: 58). The southern-dwelling Lhotshampas,[3] sometimes referred to as Nepali Bhutanese, include "peoples from a range of different ethnic and linguistic backgrounds" whose ancestors migrated from Nepal itself or from the Nepali-speaking part of Darjeeling in West Bengal a few generations ago. The Lhotshampas are predominantly Hindu, and some belong to caste groups, such as Brahmins, Chhetris, and Dalits. Additionally, and as in the Nepali society from which they originate, there are other ethnic groups represented among the southern peoples, such as Rais, Limbus, Gurungs, and Tamangs, some of whom practice Buddhism. Despite these differences, Santosh (a Gurung) told me, "In Bhutan we were all stuck together and we called ourselves Nepali-speaking Bhutanese people. Sometimes we called ourselves Gorkhas." Although Richard White-cross reports that some southern Bhutanese self-identify as Drukpas (personal communication, September 2009), my refugee informants always used the term to refer to the northern, Buddhist peoples of Bhutan.

The initial policy toward the south was isolation, enacted by restricting the Nepali Bhutanese to this region (Rose 1977: 47). Lhotshampas were not allowed to own land in the north, and many did not learn to speak the Dzonghka language. The king's first official royal tour to the region occurred as late as 1957 (Dhakal and Strawn 1994: 146–47). By the time the Bhutanese authorities became involved in the government of the south, "the Nepali Hindu south had run its own affairs for more than half a century with minimal contact with the Drukpa Buddhist north" (Hutt 2003: 145). This allowed the "area of Bhutan most susceptible to rapid economic development and ideological penetration from India" to be populated "with a community that had not been integrated either socially or politically into the broader Bhutanese society" (Rose 1977: 47). The Lhotshampas experienced further differential treatment from other ethnic groups. From the late nineteenth century onward, the Nepali population was required to pay taxes in cash and labor, whereas the Drukpas in the north provided their taxes in kind and labor until 1960 (Hutt 2003: 74). The Nepali settlers were taxed more heavily (76) and, prior to the 1950s, were not admitted to the police force and army on the same terms as other ethnic groups (Rose 1977: 113). Their residence in the country was perceived by some to be tenuous until official citizenship was granted to all Bhutanese (including the Lhotshampas) in 1958 with the promulgation of the Nationality Law of Bhutan (Rose 1977: 111; Hutt 2003: 134–37).

Regional political changes, including the British departure from India in 1947, inspired early political activism in southern Bhutan in the 1940s and 1950s (Hutt 2003: 113–16). Although accounts are contradictory, refugees informed Hutt that agitation began because "at that time equal opportunities were not given" (115) to the southern Bhutanese. In the late 1940s a movement known as Jai Gorkha sought support for "an agenda of social reform and development" in southern Bhutan (116). In 1952 the Bhutan State Congress (BSC) was formed across the border in the Indian State of Assam by a group of Nepali Bhutanese, who demanded a democratic system of government and equal rights for Nepali Bhutanese with regard to taxes and recruitment to government administration and military forces (122–23). The BSC organized public demonstrations in Bhutan that failed to attract popular support among the Nepali Bhutanese population (Rose 1977; Hutt 2003) but nevertheless were repressed by the Bhutanese authorities (Joseph C 1999: 65).

The third king, Jigme Dorji Wangchuck, acceded to the throne in 1952 and introduced many reforms during his twenty-year reign, which transformed Bhutan's political and administrative structures (Rose 1977: 38). He established the Tshogdu (a body of people's representatives) in 1953 and initiated the first five-year development plan in 1961, which put Bhutan on the road to modernization. In 1965 he created the Royal Advisory Council, which enabled members to "draw the king's attention to matters of national importance" (Hutt 2003: 133). It is likely that the BSC's activities were "taken as a warning" since the government's attitude toward the borderland in the south notably changed and "efforts were made to encourage the Nepali-speaking southerners to identify with the nation" (Hutt 1993: 11), including the 1958 nationality legislation, which Whitecross (2009: 13) argues was a direct response to the BSC's demands. Financial incentives were introduced to encourage marriage between northerners and southerners. Southern Bhutanese were politically represented and occupied many senior government posts, as well as being recruited into the army and the police force (Hinton 1996: 26). In addition to the government's strategy of advancing the Dzongkha language, southern schools continued to teach Nepali and Sanskrit (Hutt 1993).

The government's attitude toward the southern Bhutanese changed under the fourth king, Singye Dorji Wangchuck, who came to the throne in 1972. During the 1980s the government began to push for a national identity that promoted the idea of "a united and homogeneous Bhutanese populace" (Whitecross 2009: 15) and which was felt by the southern Bhutanese to reflect Drukpa culture (Strawn 1994). This resulted in new government policies, including a stricter citizenship law passed in 1985, which required people to be able to speak the Dzonghka language and to prove their residence in Bhutan before 1958 to qualify for automatic citizenship. The 1985 Act made it more difficult for non-Bhutanese women who married Bhutanese men to gain citizenship, while their children were no longer entitled to citizenship by birth since they only had one Bhutanese parent (Hutt 2003: 148–49). In 1988 a census in the south reclassified many Lhotshampas who had previously been granted citizenship cards as nonnationals. Lhotshampas brought their grievances about the census process to Tek Nath Rizal, a southern Bhutanese member of the Royal Advisory Council. After Rizal raised the matter with the king he was expelled from the Royal Council and imprisoned for three days. He left for Nepal shortly afterward (Hutt 2003: 197–200). Rizal was later extradited from Nepal and imprisoned and allegedly tortured in Bhutan.

One Nation, One People:
Imposing Bhutanese National Identity

The Lhotshampas may be considered a "transborder people" (Baud and Van Schendel 1997: 233, citing Weiner 1985), since they share the Nepali language and cultural practices with Nepali-speaking people both in India and Nepal. In such situations, where citizens of a nation-state share an ethnic identity with those across the border, their political loyalty is very commonly called into question. Of central importance in borderlands is the division between citizens invested with rights and duties, and aliens, who are excluded from being members of nation-states (Baud and Van Schendel 1997: 214–15). In southern Bhutan (and in many other places) the border does not coincide with cultural or linguistic divides but cuts across them (see map 5.1). In these contexts, Baud and Van Schendel assert, state policies "often evince a preoccupation with establishing new cultural divides that coincide with the border,"

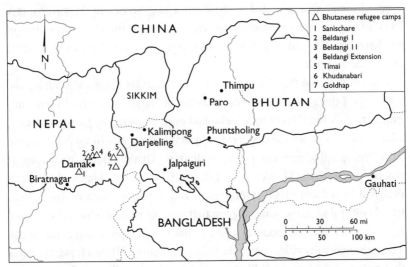

MAP 5.1. Bhutan and neighboring areas. In December 2011 it was decided to move all remaining refugees to Beldangi, as over half had left for third countries.

meaning that "symbols of national unity" (e.g., national language or dress) "take on a special, more emphatic meaning in borderlands" (233). In keeping with these trends, the southern Bhutanese experienced the state's efforts to promote a homogeneous national identity as an attempt to achieve the "Bhutanization" (Dhakal and Strawn 1994: 201) of the Lhotshampa borderland population. This involved the introduction of policies that not only sought to give "the Nepali Bhutanese a separate identity—a feeling of being Bhutanese— from their neighbours across the border" but also aimed to produce differences in "the outward appearance and everyday activities between those across the border and the citizens of southern Bhutan" (201).

In 1989 the government adopted a 'one nation, one people' policy, which aimed to preserve a distinct Bhutanese national culture through the enforcement of Driglam Namzha, a traditional Buddhist code of dress and etiquette. The dress law was strongly imposed by local officials, with fines for those who refused to conform, and was resented by many southern Bhutanese. Bidwan recalled, "This was a new way of dressing. People had to buy new clothes, which were expensive." Nikhil told me that "some Lhotshampa people who went to hospital without wearing national dress were not treated." Apparently others were prevented from getting married wearing traditional Hindu clothing. Some refugees assert that girls and women were required to cut their hair short, although this is denied by the Bhutanese government (Hutt 2003: 175). In 1989 the government removed the Nepali language from the curriculum of southern schools, and Nepali textbooks were reportedly burned by government officials (185).

According to the Royal Government of Bhutan (RGB 1992: 32), during the 1988 census the government became aware of "large numbers of illegal immigrants flooding the country," who had been attracted by free health care, education, and other development projects in southern Bhutan since 1961. This demographic pressure rendered Bhutan's Drukpa Buddhist culture at risk of "extinction" (Thinley 1994: 72), which necessitated laws and policies designed to address illegal immigration and to retain Bhutan's distinct national cultural identity. Some suggest that the government's fears also related to the impact of rapid modernization in Bhutan (Joseph C 1999; Hutt 2003). These changes are evidenced by the following figures. Hinton (1996: 18) notes that in 1987 the economy of Bhutan was "based primarily on subsistence agriculture, which provided a livelihood for about 90% of the population." The Bhutan government recently reported that "the share of agriculture in GDP has dropped from the over 50% levels in 1986 (and before that) to 22% in 2006" (RGB 2007: 3). The economic importance of the south, where many industries (e.g., cash crops and hydroelectric power) are located (Hutt 1997: 139), suggests that "politico-economic control of southern Bhutan became unavoidable to help maintain the Ngalong dominance of the state establishment" (Joseph C 1999: 182). These issues highlight the necessity of attending to the relationship between the political, economic, and cultural effects of borders. In this case, the political and economic value of the southern borderland contributed to clashes over what constituted 'Bhutanese' cultural identity and the nature of citizenship rights and duties.

Since the Lhotshampas are part of a 'transborder' group of Nepali-speaking people, regional political developments involving members of this ethnic group in Sikkim, India, and Nepal intensified the perception of the southern Bhutanese as a threat. In 1975 political unrest involving ethnic Nepalese in Sikkim caused the former state, where Buddhist monarchs had also ruled, to lose autonomy and be subsumed by India. In Sikkim the demographic changes caused by large-scale immigration of ethnic Nepalese were perceived to have resulted in the monarch's loss of power, which fueled fears in Bhutan. However, despite these similarities, there were also many differences in the political and demographic situations in Bhutan and Sikkim (Rose 1977; Hutt 2003). Yet the

Bhutanese government feared that if their new citizenship laws were "circumvented," the "indigenous" Bhutanese would be "reduced to a minority in their own country, as has happened to the indigenous people of Sikkim and the neighbouring hills of Darjeeling and Kalimpong" (RGB 1993: 40). These concerns were exacerbated by a violent Gorkhaland movement in Darjeeling (for a separate State within India, no longer part of West Bengal) between 1986 and 1988. This was led by ethnic Nepalis and "must have played a major part in convincing the Bhutanese government that political activity among the Lhotshampas should be prevented at any cost" (Hutt 2003: 195–96). The Gorkhaland movement revived the fear in South Asia of a plot to create a 'Greater Nepal,' since its leader, Subhas Ghising, "used the idea of Greater Nepal in the late 1980s to extract political concessions from New Delhi" (Dixit 2003: 323). The Bhutanese government justified their new citizenship policies on the basis of the Greater Nepal conspiracy, arguing that members of the "minority ethnic community" were attempting "to turn themselves into a majority through illegal immigration in order to take over political power" (RGB 1993: 34).

Conflict in Southern Bhutan: "Two Sides to the River"

Following the introduction of new government policies in the late 1980s, political tensions mounted in southern Bhutan. By 1992 over eighty thousand Lhotshampas had departed for refugee camps in eastern Nepal (AI 1992). There are two opposing interpretations of the events that preceded their departure. The RGB and its supporters allege that southern Bhutanese dissidents engaged in violent and subversive activities against the state, which posed "a threat to Bhutan's survival as a distinct political and cultural entity" (RGB 1993: 1). Therefore the RGB arrested a small number of criminals and 'terrorists.' When large numbers of southern Bhutanese began leaving, the RGB expressed surprise at this "disturbing trend," claiming that "no force whatsoever has been used against them" and that the king had made "appeals to the Lhotshampas not to leave the country" (16).

In contrast, according to the refugees and their supporters, the southern Bhutanese peacefully objected to the government policies, which they felt directly attacked their distinct culture and language, and requested political reforms. In response, the government branded "all the activists and the supporters of the movement as anti-nationals" and "sent the Royal Bhutan Army to crush the movement" (AHURA 2000: 9). This resulted in "mass arrests, flogging, torture, rape, arson, looting and plunder" (HUROB 1992), which "compelled the innocent Lhotshampa villagers to flee Bhutan" (Rizal and Yokota 2006: 124).

Drawing on the existing literature and refugees' oral history, the following account of "the southern Bhutan problem" (RGB 1993) attempts to make sense of such contrasting interpretations by acknowledging that, in the words of one southern Bhutanese man, "there are two sides to the river." In response to the government's new policies, some southern Bhutanese established organizations to demand respect for their cultural rights. The Students' Union of Bhutan was formed in 1988 in Sherubtse College in eastern Bhutan. Between 150 and 200 southern Bhutanese members organized peaceful demonstrations within the college and circulated pamphlets on human rights and democracy. Students and lecturers at the National Institute of Education were involved in the People's Forum for Human Rights (PFHR). This organization was established in June 1989 and headed by Tek Nath Rizal, who had already fled to Nepal. The PFHR produced pamphlets encouraging southern Bhutanese to unite to protect their culture, such as the following: "It is time for us to shout to the power in Thimphu 'Liberty, Equality and Fraternity' and bring down the 'Bastille.' It is time to say ourselves, Bhutanese Nepalese, unite, we have nothing to lose but gain. The hour has struck for the historic conflict. We the Bhutanese Nepalese have a culture we cherish, a language we speak, a dress we wear, a religion we follow. They are all ours. They are part of our identity. We shall not allow any power to take them away from us. We shall resist, we shall fight to the last man of our race all repressive laws intended to wipe out our identity. THIS DOCUMENT IS A PROTEST AND A PROPHECY" (from PFHR pamphlet written in English and quoted in Hutt 2003: 200, original emphasis). In addition to student-based organizations, one author records the reemergence of the BSC (Parmanand 1998: 134), and at the village level, Bidwan told me, "political leaders who were active in the 1950s gave out pamphlets on human rights and democracy."

Although Amnesty International (AI) did not consider the PFHR pamphlet to be advocating aggression against the state of Bhutan, it has often been quoted as evidence that the dissidents planned to overthrow the Bhutanese government (Hutt 2003: 200), which referred to the PFHR's literature as "seditious" (RGB 1993: 7). Whatever the early dissidents' intentions, the Bhutanese government acted swiftly to quell their resistance. Between October and December 1989, forty-five people active in organizations protesting against the government policies were arrested, including Tek Nath Rizal, who was extradited from Nepal with the assistance of the collapsing Panchayat regime (Hutt 2003: 201–2). Following these arrests, by late autumn 1989 several hundred mostly male activists had fled Bhutan and "taken refuge in a tea plantation in Garganda, West Bengal, whose manager, an Indian Nepali, was sympathetic to their political cause" (202). It was here that the Bhutan People's Party (BPP) was formed in June 1990 and "plans were made for a programme of political action across southern Bhutan" (203) to demand civil rights and democratic reforms. Contact was reported between the Bhutanese activists and the Gorkhaland movement in India, and "during the early stages of the 'movement,' some Lhotshampa activists adopted violent tactics similar to those adopted by Gorkha National Liberation Front (GNLF) extremists in India." Such tactics included pressuring ethnic Nepalis to support the movement financially and threatening them with violence if they did not attend protests.[4]

Allegations of "violent activities by government opponents, whom the government termed *ngolops* or 'anti-nationals,'" were first reported in February 1990 (AI 1992). On 2 June 1990 the severed heads of two men, both southern Bhutanese government officials, were found in a bag by the Gomtu River in Samchi district (AI 1992; Zeppa 1999; Hutt 2003: 203). The RGB associates these murders with the BPP's inception and reports that an attached letter warned that "all those who supported the Royal Government would meet the same fate" (Hutt 2003: 203). According to refugees, this incident gave credence to the BPP's threats that nonsupporters would "lose six inches" (i.e., their head: *chha inchī ghatāune*) or that they would find their "head in a bag, body in the river" (*tāuko jholāmā jīu kholāmā*). From mid-1990 onward the government claimed that the 'antinationals' (including members of the BPP) increased their violent activities, including kidnapping and murdering civilians (AI 1992). While AI "is not in a position to confirm" government figures on such incidents,[5] the delegates were able to interview victims and their relatives, "who reported incidents of kidnapping, beheading, extortion, torture, and other abuses by opposition groups, which had occurred in the south mainly during 1990" (AI 1992). Some refugees described a campaign of violence conducted by the BPP to ensure support for their movement among the southern Bhutanese population. Their methods included forced 'donations' in cash and kind, the demand that at least one member of every household join the party, kidnaps of and attacks on those perceived to be nonsupporters, and theft of animals. They also engaged in military activities, such as bombing government buildings. The AI report is consistent with these memories. It states that villagers told delegates they were pressured into selling their crops to pay 'donations,' were threatened if they refused to comply, and that threats were sometimes carried out.

Refugees described a situation wherein they were caught between the government and the BPP: "If people did not give donations or take part in the movement, the BPP said that they would shoot them with a gun. But if people did give donations or took part in the movement, then they were targeted by the government" (Manisha). These difficulties caused some southern Bhutanese to leave Bhutan. Suraj recalled, "In the area where we lived, the villagers were stuck between the antinationals and the Bhutanese government. My father said we could not continue to live like this, so we left." While Hutt (2003: 203) concludes that it is impossible to assess the scale of "the violent aspect of the Lhotshampas' resistance," he correctly asserts that "the assassinations that did take place can only have strengthened the position of hardliners in the Bhutanese government." Arguably the BPP violence played a significant role in hardening the government's attitude toward all southern Bhutanese. Ranju certainly saw it in these terms: "If people had not done criminal activities like this, then the government would not have chased us out." She also explained that the Bhutanese government had been more sensitive to the needs of ethnic Nepalese than is often reported: "They made us wear *gho* and *kira* to school, but the thick cloth was too hot for the climate in the south, so they changed it to a cotton version, which was more comfortable." She concluded, "If people had slowly tried to ask the government to change the policies, instead of using violence and trying to make huge changes all at once, then I think the government would have listened and we might still be living in Bhutan."

The government's approach toward the 'southern problem' was further influenced by mass demonstrations in September 1990. These demonstrations were called by the BPP and other organizations in all southern Bhutanese districts and were attended by a large number of people, including children (Hutt 2003: 207). According to Hutt, the dissidents maintained that the "marchers' purpose was to submit the BPP's demands to district offices," while government sources alleged that national dress items were burned and census records were removed from offices (208). The government further claimed that "all the male demonstrators, and even some of the women, came armed" with *khukuri* knives and that "there were militants dressed in camouflage uniforms and armed with guns and bombs amongst all the mobs" (Department of Information, quoted in Joseph C 1999: 145). The political activists, however, maintained that the protests were peaceful, yet "suddenly the RBA [Royal Bhutan Army] opened fire upon the crowd and charged them with bayonets resulting in the deaths of several people and injuring scores of them" (INHURED quoted in Joseph C 1999: 146). Despite reports in the Nepali press that the Bhutanese government killed over three hundred demonstrators in Samchi district (Hutt 2003: 209), the AI (1992) delegation "found no evidence to support these reports."

There are further questions concerning the motivation of the demonstrators. Hutt (2003: 207) acknowledges that "a measure of coercion" was imposed on participants by the political parties yet judges that "it is unlikely that the small number of activists ... could have exerted this measure of control over what was still largely a conservative agrarian population." While it is true that some people "willingly decided to come forward to take part in the procession" (Santosh), other refugee informants, such as Siddharth, insisted they were compelled to attend due to threats of violence: "I was forced to take part in the demonstration because the BPP made threats that if people did not support them they would lose six inches." Schoolchildren too were also pressured to go: "A group of Nepali people came to the school shouting slogans. The teachers hid inside the toilets because they were scared. The teachers closed the school and ran away. The protestors took students above Class 4 to the demonstrations. They burned the students' national dress in the market" (Bina).

Other refugees confirmed that BPP members forced southern Bhutanese to burn their national dress: "We hid our gho and kiras, but the BPP party members came to search our house and they found our national dress and burned it" (Amita). Although informants described the demonstrations in some districts as peaceful, in others refugees recalled that "all the boys were walking at the front carrying weapons" (Sabita). These memories suggest that many accounts of the 'peaceful' protests and indeed the wider political tensions in southern Bhutan underestimate the level of coercion exercised by members of the BPP over the Lhotshampa population.

After the 1990 demonstrations the Bhutanese government began identifying and subsequently arresting participants and supporters, most of whom left Bhutan following their release from detention (Hutt 2003: 214). Those arrested reported torture and ill treatment in jail, including being forced to perform incongruent acts that violated their cultural or religious beliefs (Hutt 2003: 215). Bina explained, "The army took one of our relatives to jail. He was vegetarian but they made him carry meat outside in the sun every day."

Many "human rights and political activists and influential people in the villages who were alleged by the government authorities of being involved in the movement" began leaving the country in 1990, "fearing persecution or because of continuous harassment" (AHURA 2000: 77). Schools and health facilities in southern Bhutan were closed; this was interpreted by Lhotshampas as a collective punishment (Hutt 2003: 220). Development projects in the south were halted; the government attributed this to the disruption caused by "large-scale acts of terrorism unleashed by the anti-national elements" (RGB 1992: 48). New rules were introduced requiring people to produce a No Objection Certificate (NOC) to access government employment and educational institutions (Hutt 2003: 217). These certificates were acquired from the Bhutanese police force and provided proof that the holders "had not taken part in oppositional activity, and were not related to anyone who had" (217). Children whose parents had participated in demonstrations or were suspected of supporting the democracy movement had problems enrolling in school. Rumors circulated that members of the Bhutanese army were raping girls and women in the south, which contributed to the sense of insecurity among the Lhotshampas and was a factor in their decision to leave the country. In addition to violence perpetrated by the BPP, there were also village militias formed by northern Bhutanese, which were established to defend the country against 'anti-nationals' (219).

Beginning in 1991 it appears that "a systematic eviction of southern Bhutanese" began through the government's use of 'voluntary migration forms' (VMFs), which many southern Bhutanese were pressured to sign, sometimes following physical violence and coercion (AHURA 2000). Southern Bhutanese report being advised by village leaders or ordered by government officials to leave the country. Bina's account of how her family came to leave Bhutan is typical: "The Mandal [local headman] told my father that he had to fill in a form to leave the country or he would be arrested. Many people were leaving the country, and it was risky for my older sisters because of the army's activities. After my father filled in the form in Dzongkha, we were taken for photos. They told us to stand in a line and show our teeth [smile]. Later we realized the statement said he was happy to leave the country and was going willingly."

The Association of Human Rights Activists, Bhutan undertook a survey of

4,553 households (49,909 refugees) in the camps. The organization collected information on reasons for leaving the country and time of departure and digitized the nationality documents of the refugees. Their report stated that 99.82 percent of those surveyed possess "incontrovertible evidences of Bhutanese origin and nationality" (AHURA 2000: 76–78). The main reasons recorded for leaving include harassment by security forces of those people who had paid donations to the movement or taken part in demonstrations; family members of those arrested were told to sign VMFs to secure the release of their relatives; family members of those who had already fled the country were told to leave; detainees were threatened with rearrest if they did not leave the country after being released; village heads ordered certain families to leave on the instruction of the government authorities; and those deemed nonnationals in the census or 'antinational' following agitation were evicted (82–83). Most refugees left Bhutan in 1991 or 1992 (77).

Oral History:
Experiencing the 'Southern Problem' in Kharpani Village

Kharpani village is situated in southern Bhutan close to the Indian border.[6] Villagers recall that problems started when the Bhutanese government introduced new policies "almost overnight" (Bidwan). Beginning in 1989 people in the south "suddenly had to wear national dress even if they were only going to the market" (Bidwan). In school too the government changed the rules. "Before," Ranju recalled, "we wore skirts and shirts to school. But then we had to wear gho and kira, and Nepali language was removed." Students were also intimidated by government officials. Ranju, who was a teenager at the time, was taken to the police station since she was playing outside the school but not wearing national dress. She and the other girls in her class were "given a warning that if we hadn't cut our hair by a certain date, the school would cut it for us." Long hair for women is valued in Nepali culture, while northern Bhutanese women wear their hair short. Many southern Bhutanese began to feel "frustrated with the way we were being treated by the government" (Bidwan). Some Kharpani villagers became involved in underground human rights groups.

Shortly after the BPP formed in June 1990, Ranju heard in school that the heads of two southern Bhutanese government officials had been found by the river: "It was clear that if people did not support the BPP, they would face the same consequences." The BPP were active in the area and built a training camp just over the border from Kharpani in India. One Kharpani villager, Ganaraj, became a local BPP leader. He started collecting 'donations' from other villagers and recruiting new members. The BPP members also stole people's cows, hens, and other animals. Tarak was pressured to join the BPP as "it was compulsory that from every household, at least one person had to join the party. From my house I was the person who had to go. We knew that if we refused to go, there would be serious consequences." The BPP members said that if people didn't support them, "it would be like 2 June [1990] and people would lose six inches." Ranju's younger brother, Umesh, who was fourteen when he was forced to join the BPP, estimated that there were between eighty and ninety people from Kharpani village living in the camp.

During the day the BPP recruits did military training. Every few days Tarak engaged in "action and counteraction against the army." He detonated bombs that had been built with electric poles stolen by BPP members. At night the recruits kidnapped southern Bhutanese who had not paid their 'donations' or who were accused of spying for the government. Umesh remembered, "During the kidnaps there were thirty people surrounding the house. One person would go to the door of the house and pretend to be a relative and call the person to the door. Someone would grab the man and others would threaten to kill anyone else who came out of the house." The victims were taken over the border to the training camp, where BPP members "asked them questions and hit them and shouted allegations at them" (Tarak). The BPP members "used to beat people mercilessly" (Umesh), breaking bones and knocking out teeth. Some BPP recruits were forced to participate in kidnapping their relatives and neighbors. Umesh was present when his great-uncle was kidnapped because he could not afford to pay his donation. Another villager, Parul, had to show the attackers the way to his father's house. On one occasion Ganaraj had a disagreement with the Drukpa husband of a southern Bhutanese woman from Kharpani. That evening, with the help of ethnic Nepalese Indians from across the border, Ganaraj came to his home, knocked him unconscious, and brought him to the training camp, where he was murdered.

In 1990 the BPP organized demonstrations against the Bhutanese government's policies. Due to fear of repercussions, most Kharpani villagers felt compelled to attend. Ranju's father, Hari, a well-respected community leader and religious man, was asked by the BPP to lead the demonstration in this area. Ranju recalled, "That day we were told we shouldn't go to school or we would lose six inches. We marched across the bridge and shouted slogans." Shortly after the demonstration, Hari left the village to visit a temple in India. Ranju felt scared when the army came to the village: "As I had taken part in the protest, my mum sent me to hide in the bush when the army came to the village because we heard they had taken photographs of the people in the demonstrations."

The army started arresting people who were involved in the demonstration and told others to leave Bhutan. When the first family left the village, "the army came and used *roti* flour and banged gongs to force the family out. The Drukpas use the same method to chase away evil spirits" (Ranju). Government officials began searching for Hari. Ranju's brother Padam recalled, "The government said my father was from the BPP. Our block head came in the evening and informed my mother that our father should not come back to Bhutan from India, as he would be arrested. The next morning Ranju and I left for India to find my father. We met him and told him not to come to Bhutan." Ranju and Padam's mother crossed the border later that day. After spending some months in India, the family went to the refugee camp in Nepal.

While Hari's family left before he could be arrested, others were not so lucky. Parul was identified as a BPP member and was jailed for one year, during which time he was tortured. Intimidation and extortion by the BPP continued. Ranju's grandfather regularly had to give donations to Ganaraj, who came from the refugee camps. In return he ensured that Ranju's grandfather's house was not raided by BPP members. Ganaraj was arrested by the Bhutanese government in 2000 and remains in jail. After individuals left for the refugee camps, their remaining family members experienced harassment or arrest and were not entitled to the NOCs, which continue to determine access to jobs, travel documents, and educational opportunities. Some family members lost their government jobs due to having relatives in the camps. Of the fifty-five households in the village prior to 1990, thirty-five became refugees in Nepal. Their land was redistributed to eastern and northern Bhutanese people who now reside alongside the remaining Lhotshampas.

A Borderland People in Exile: Bhutanese Refugees in Nepal

The Lhotshampas first crossed the border from southern Bhutan into India. However, the Indian government was unwilling to grant asylum to the refugees: "We asked the Indian government for shelter in camps. We went to the district officer to ask for permission, but then the police came and dismantled our camp. The Central Reserve Police loaded the refugees into vehicles and sent us to Nepal" (Krishna). The first refugees from southern Bhutan arrived in late 1990 in eastern Nepal, where they settled by the Mai River in Jhapa district (Hutt 2003: 251). The number of refugees steadily increased throughout 1991, reaching a peak in mid-1992 of up to six hundred people arriving each day (257). By mid-1994 over eighty-six thousand Lhotshampa refugees were registered in Nepal (HRW 2003). A 2007 census determined that the number of refugees had grown to 107,923 (WFP and UNHCR 2008: 5), with the increase in population due primarily to the refugee children born in the camps. Like many other refugees around the world, the Bhutanese "are not legally permitted to work, own land, leave the camps or engage in political activities" (Muggah 2005: 157), enforcing their dependency on international aid.

Despite being extolled by the international aid community as model camps (Muggah 2005), the Bhutanese refugees faced the social and economic problems common to protracted camp situations: "Now people are frustrated and blame each other for mistakes. We live in *jupāpātī* [slumlike bamboo huts] in a small area very close to each other. It is like keeping rice in a pot—it naturally gives a bad result. Or if you keep bamboo shoots in a bottle the taste turns sour. This is the same as living in the camps for seventeen years with no hope—nothing is there" (Santosh) (see figure 5.1).

While the refugees demonstrated high levels of social (physical and educational) well-being, they also experienced "unusually high levels of mental illness" (Muggah 2005: 159). Many were separated from parents, siblings, and other relatives, heightening the emotional impact of living in exile: "I worry about my mother because she feels alone, but living away from her I cannot give her all my support" (Bidwan). The refugees were sometimes able to meet relatives still residing in Bhutan at the India-Bhutan border, and some occasionally crossed the border in secret to visit their former homes. However, these encounters were fraught with tension, due to fears that the Bhutanese authorities might find out and arrest those still living in Bhutan. Such meetings were necessarily infrequent and in many ways intensified the emotional distress at being unable to maintain close relations with their families. The incidence of suicide among refugees was approximately four times higher than in the local Nepalese population (HRW 2003). Refugees also frequently reported other social problems, including alcoholism and domestic violence, which were perceived to have increased with the length of their stay in the

FIGURE 5.1. Empty plot in Beldangi 2 refugee camp, now used to grow vegetables, January 2009. Once refugees have departed for a third country, it is compulsory to deconstruct their dwelling. Behind the plot stands a standard toilet outhouse. Photograph courtesy of D. N. Gellner.

camps (HRW 2003, 2007; Muggah 2005). The frustration and social decay caused by the protracted situation made finding a solution a priority for many refugees, some of whom took political action to achieve this.

After the Lhotshampas fled to Nepal, numerous human rights committees and political parties were formed, and these operated alongside the already existing groups established in southern Bhutan. However, there were concerns among some refugees about close associations between human rights groups and political parties. A member of AHURA said, "We felt that a human rights organization should be independent and should not be a fundraising organization for political parties." All the groups advocated repatriation and human rights protection, while the political parties also campaigned for multiparty democracy in Bhutan (Hutt 2003: 260). It should be noted that calling themselves human rights groups and distancing themselves from political parties lent legitimacy to the activists who did so and served to draw international attention away from the BPP's acts of violence and intimidation in southern Bhutan.

FIGURE 5.2. Two young girls in Sanischare refugee camp, Nepal, standing next to a solar oven provided by the Vajra Foundation as an alternative to coal or wood for cooking, January 2009. Photograph courtesy of D. N. Gellner.

Despite these differences over political strategy, attempts at cooperation have been made under umbrella groups. In 1995 and 1996 camp-based refugees initiated the Appeal Movement Coordinating Committee to hasten repatriation, which included a 'peace march' from the camps to Bhutan (Hutt 2003: 261). According to a founding member of AHURA, the march was intended "to bring the refugee issue back into the radar as it had faded from international attention." Participants walked from the camps toward Bhutan, but most were arrested after crossing the Indian border and sent back to Nepal. Those who reached Bhutan were arrested or immediately ejected. The idea of the peace march has endured, however, and similar attempts to return peacefully on foot have been repeated by various refugee organizations.

For many years most refugees expressed a wish to repatriate to Bhutan, and the United Nations High Commissioner for Refugees emphasized return as the most desirable solution. The government of Nepal has "always advocated for an honorable and respectful repatriation of the refugees," I was told in 2007 by an official working in the refugee section of the Home Ministry. It held a total of fifteen bilateral meetings with Bhutanese government representatives to this end between 1993 and 2003. The Bhutanese government claimed most of the 'refugees' were "people of Nepali origin from the north-eastern states of India and other areas," invited by the 'anti-nationals' to "inflate" their numbers (RGB 1992). In 1993 the Bhutanese and Nepali governments established a Ministerial Joint Committee to seek a solution (Hutt 2005: 48). In 2001 these negotiations culminated in a process of joint verification (JV) to determine the national identity of the camp residents. When the results of the JV process in Khudanabari camp were finally announced in 2003, only 293 individuals (2.4 percent of the camp population) had been identified as genuine Bhutanese with the right to return to their country (Hutt 2005: 49). Frustrated by this outcome, some refugees attacked the Bhutanese members of the JV team. This halted the process, which was never completed in the other six camps.

The failure of the JV process caused many refugees and international actors to conclude that a negotiated repatriation to Bhutan was currently impossible and inspired new activities aimed to reacquire citizenship for the refugees. In October 2006 the U.S. government offered resettlement places for sixty thousand Bhutanese refugees, and other countries committed to resettle smaller numbers. Many refugees welcomed the chance to move to countries where they would eventually be eligible for citizenship. However, others opposed the proposal of any durable solution except repatriation. Motivated by the political impact of the Maoists in Nepal, a Bhutanese revolutionary movement was launched by camp-based refugees in 2003 and also operates in southern Bhutan (Adhikari 2007). The Communist Party of Bhutan (CPB) asserts that the monarchy must be overthrown by force in order to achieve civil rights in Bhutan and opposes the resettlement process, which it terms a U.S.-Bhutanese conspiracy "to stop the people's war in Bhutan and protect the Wangchuk regime" (as reported to me by a refugee who attended a CPB meeting in the camps in February 2007). While some refugees chose to support the CPB, the party capitalized on the example set by the Nepali Maoists, whose brutal treatment of individual nonsupporters was effective in achieving compliance. One refugee man remarked to me, "Because the Nepali Maoists set a precedent with people who did not cooperate with them, it is not necessary for the Bhutanese Maoists to have to do the same."

These contrasting perspectives on the refugees' future produced severe political tensions in the camps, resulting in collective violence against pro-resettlement refugees in May and August 2007. Despite these hostilities, the resettlement process quickly accelerated. The CPB continued to demand that the Nepal government stop the resettlement process and threatened to launch attacks if these demands were not met.[7] However, by February 2009, over ten thousand Bhutanese refugees had been resettled in third countries, including the United States, Australia, and New Zealand.[8] Meanwhile a Bhutanese communist leader told me in January 2009 that 160 refugees had crossed back over two international borders (Nepal-India and India-Bhutan) to begin their revolutionary struggle in Bhutan: "We have five teams of guerrillas inside Bhutan, working in the west, central and eastern side." He confirmed that these guerrillas receive support and arms from other communist groups operating in India and depend on southern Bhutanese villagers for "rice, shelter, shoes, and sleeping bags." Based on the activities of the CPB in the refugee camps and the methods employed by the Nepali Maoists, it is likely that some southern Bhutanese villagers feel compelled to assist the cadres due to fear of violent repercussions. These activities are likely to impact negatively on those Lhotshampas remaining in Bhutan; indeed, by January 2009, according to this same CPB leader, fifty Bhutanese citizens had been arrested for being members of the party.[9]

THIS CHAPTER has explored the experiences of the Lhotshampas of Bhutan, offering an analysis of how the state's presence is felt in borderland areas and how borderland people interact with the state. The Lhotshampas are a borderland people whose arrival in southern Bhutan coincided with the beginning of a process of state building. When the Bhutanese government tried to introduce a homogeneous national identity to match the country's political borders, some Lhotshampas protested against these policies, which they felt attacked their ethnic and cultural identity. Lhotshampa political leaders, such as Tek Nath Rizal, attempted to defend the southern Bhutanese people's cultural and citizenship rights to the government. After these negotiations failed to achieve the desired result, some Lhotshampas engaged in peaceful and/or violent protests against the 'one nation, one people' policy. When the government crushed this dissent, the Lhotshampas crossed an international border to escape political repression and eventually found international protection as refugees in Nepal.

This conflict precipitated the flight of tens of thousands of Lhotshampas. While refugee and Bhutanese government interpretations appear to be contradictory, they are both partial versions, each containing and excluding important elements. As my informant suggested, there are indeed "two sides to the river," and "two things cannot be denied: the government discrimination and the BPP pressure" (Bidwan). Yet in Bhutan only one side of this story is told and accepted: the violence on the part of 'antinationals' and BPP members. While in the camps across the Indian and Nepal borders it is the other side of the story—the government oppression—that is the dominant narrative of the past.

However, although the Bhutanese government's and refugee political activists' accounts of the conflict are diametrically opposed, the oral histories collected from refugee adults allow an alternative story to be told. As Baud and Van Schendel (1997: 212) assert, "Rather than focusing on the rhetoric and intentions of central governments, we look at the social realities provoked by them." The voices of refugee adults describe the experiences of a small number of people from a borderland village where political activists were able regularly to traverse an 'invisible' national boundary to promote political awareness and the rights of Lhotshampa communities. Their memories emphasize the perspectives of ordinary villagers caught between the Bhutanese state and local political activists, demonstrating that, as Baud and Van Schendel argue, it is necessary to consider "the triangular set up within border regions," where the state, the borderland elite, and local inhabitants engage in social and political struggle (241–42). These triangular interactions are missing from most accounts of the Lhotshampas' exodus, which usually favor either the government or the refugee leaders' version of events. This results in a lack of attention to the experiences of ordinary citizens, many of whom have been residing in long-term camps since the early 1990s and whose lives have been affected by the political rhetoric and actions of the government and regional elite.

Finally, the Lhotshampas' transborder identity, as members of a group of Nepali-speaking people in this region of South Asia, highlights the importance of considering borderlands on both sides of an international border. Regional developments such as demographic and political transformations in Sikkim and the violent Gorkhaland movement in West Bengal contributed to the Bhutanese government's fears over the national loyalty of their Nepali-speaking borderland population. These concerns were exacerbated by the Lhotshampas' cross-border connections, which allowed activists to establish oppositional political parties (e.g., the BSC and the BPP) and receive support from Nepali-speaking people on the Indian side of the border. Such cross-border affiliations continue to influence social and political realities today, as the CPB receives training and arms from revolutionary groups in India and from the Maoists in Nepal to further its goal of revolution in Bhutan. In this case, the political, economic, and cultural impact of borders encompasses borderlands in three states: India, Bhutan, and Nepal. These nations are all implicated in the conflict and its aftermath, which has resulted in the existence of long-term camps in eastern Nepal and the refugees' ongoing attempts to return to their homeland and to instigate political change there.

NOTES TO CHAPTER 5

1. All names have been changed to protect the identities of informants.

2. The research was part of my DPhil in international development studies at the University of Oxford. I am grateful to the Economic and Social Research Council U.K. for funding this research.

3. Lhotshampa is the Dzongkha name for ethnic Nepali Bhutanese, meaning 'southern border dweller' (*lho*—south, *tsham*—border, *pa*—suffix meaning people).

4. Desai's (2006) award-winning novel includes an account of GNLF violence.

5. "An article in Kuensel on 7 March 1992 quoted the Home Minister as saying that current figures for murder and kidnapping by 'anti-nationals' stood at 39 and 180 respectively" (AI 1992).

6. 'Kharpani' is a pseudonym to protect the identities of informants, whose names have also been changed. I have chosen not to name the district in which this village is situated. All these histories were collected in the Bhutanese refugee camps from people I consider to be reliable informants, in Ranju's case in November 2006, for most of the others in November 2007.

7. See November 2008 CPB Press Release, in possession of the author.

8. See International Organization of Migration report, accessed 20 May 2009, www .iom.int/jahia.

9. The CPB is believed to have divided into two factions in 2008, led by Commander Birat and Commander Vikalpa, respectively. While their anti-resettlement activities in the camps have dwindled, the Bhutan News Services report that one branch has since employed explosives in Bhutan (Mishra 2010).

SIX | DEEPAK K. MISHRA

Developing the Border
The State and the Political Economy of Development in Arunachal Pradesh

Arunachal Pradesh, situated in the extreme northeast corner of India, is characterized by an extraordinary degree of ecological, institutional, and cultural diversity. The State has undergone remarkable economic changes within a comparatively short period of time. The relatively isolated economies of the tribal communities of the area, which were later reorganized as Arunachal Pradesh, were gradually integrated into the larger economy only after independence, and more particularly after the Indo-China War of 1962. The State's economy has not only experienced a remarkable growth over the past decades; it has diversified from a localized, nature-based subsistence economy into a thoroughly integrated market economy, notwithstanding the continuing significance of some of the traditional economic institutions. The predominantly barter economy has been almost completely transformed into a monetized economy within a relatively short time. Market institutions are still underdeveloped in many respects, and there are many regional variations in the degree of integration with the market economy, but a remarkable feature of the transformation process is the way the ecological, historical, and policy-induced specificities of the State have shaped the trajectories of economic change.

Arunachal Pradesh shares 1,746 kilometers of boundaries with the neighboring countries: 160 kilometers on its western frontier with Bhutan, 1,146 kilometers to the north with Tibet (China), and 440 kilometers to the east with

Myanmar. In the south Arunachal Pradesh has a State boundary mainly with Assam and Nagaland (see maps 6.1 and 8.1). The overwhelming significance of Arunachal Pradesh as a 'border state' has not only shaped the politics of governance of the region; it has had significant implications for the development process as well. Understanding the interactions and interdependencies among the local state, the market, and the 'community' in the region provides fresh insights into the diverse ways in which the 'identity' of the agents remains crucial to the nature and outcomes of transactions, both economic and political.

In this chapter I focus on the interactions between the state, market forces, and the communities of Arunachal Pradesh. Among the many specificities that have shaped the transformation of Arunachal's economy, three significant dimensions deserve special mention: the ecological specificities of a hill economy;[1] the institutional complexity underlying the use of and access to the various forces of production such as land, forests, and labor; and the historical role of the state as the prime mover of economic transformation. I argue that the nature of state intervention in Arunachal's economy as well as the character of local governance have also been influenced to a considerable extent by the perceived significance of Arunachal Pradesh as a sensitive border State. Institutional diversity, which itself is an outcome of the specific ways the state, market, and community institutions have interacted with each other, remains a key feature of the economy in contemporary Arunachal Pradesh, and it plays a central role in determining the nature of economic transformation in rural Arunachal Pradesh.[2] In the complex interplay of state power, market forces, and the community, the strategies adopted by various agencies and actors cannot be explained without reference to the proximity of borders.

I present a historical perspective on the borders with particular reference to the recorded history of trade across the Himalayas. Contrary to the post-independence perception of Arunachal as 'isolated,' historical evidence suggests that trade between the Assam plains and Tibet flourished throughout the region that is known today as Arunachal Pradesh. I briefly outline administrative and political developments in Arunachal to bring out some important implications for the process of economic development. Subsequently I discuss the nature of government intervention, its role in the creation of a market economy, and the various ways community institutions have been transformed as a result of these changes.

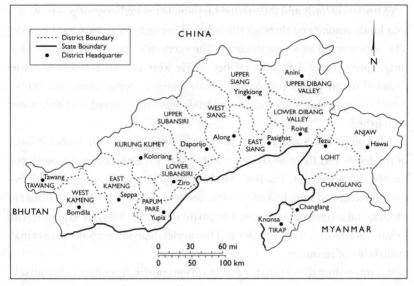

MAP 6.1. Arunachal Pradesh and its districts.

Borders in Historical Perspective

The tribal communities of Arunachal Pradesh are generally described as iso-lated from the mainstream, but long before the present day there were signif-icant exchanges and contacts both among these communities and with the Tibet in the north and Assam in the south (Ray 2005). As the region wit-nessed continuous migration flows from both Tibet and Myanmar, many of the ethnic groups had strong kinship ties with their relatives living beyond the borders. The borders, for them, were artificial constructs imposed by distant powers.[3] Moreover, as chronicled by anthropologists, the borders that mat-tered most for indigenous communities were village boundaries or the moral and social boundaries of the community.[4] Physical boundaries between states were, by all accounts, fluid. With colonization came the need and justification for clearly demarcated, cartographically supported borders. In this part of India at least, the borders did not exist on the ground for those living near them, even after lines were drawn and defended by the 'modern' nation-states. People living near the borders maintained their ties with their neighbors, un-less physically prevented from doing so (see map 6.1).

Historical records and folk narratives point to the exchange of goods of various kinds among and through the tribes of present-day Arunachal Pradesh. The region acted as a continuum in the economic and cultural space that linked present-day Assam and Tibet. There were various established trade routes through which people and goods traveled, negotiations and transactions were carried out, conflicts and feuds were encountered, and links were established.

The composition and volume of trade depended upon the resource base of the tribes and their needs and surpluses. But the economic ties were not limited to trade alone. The livelihoods in this mountainous region were interdependent and were linked to resources available at different locations, altitudes, and geographical spaces. The pastoral communities, for example, had to move across different altitudes and territories depending upon the seasonal availability of resources.

It is interesting to note that, while in various postindependence discourses, the Northeast region in general, and Arunachal Pradesh in particular, is routinely described as a remote, exotic, and distant frontier and the history of the region 'since time immemorial' is described in narratives of isolation and stagnation, the economic, social, and cultural disruption that has been engineered by the creation of borders, has hardly been discussed. India's independence and the partition of the country dislocated and created hardships for peoples living across the borders. While the violent and forced eviction of people across the western border has remained a constant reminder of the pains of nation making, the Partition in the northeastern frontier has remained obscured for a long time, at least in official narratives.

The significance of borders for present-day Arunachal Pradesh is obvious. But it is important to note that the severity with which borders restricted the movement of people and commodities was not the same everywhere. Depending on the nature of relations between India and its eastern neighbors, which has not remained constant over the past six decades or so, and the degree of strategic significance of the borders, some of them were relatively strictly monitored and others were allowed to remain porous. This continues to be so even today.

In order to make sense of how the indigenous populations living along the borders perceive these borders, it is important to take note of the history of migration and trade in the region. Historical evidence shows that the tribal communities of Arunachal Pradesh have had a long tradition of trade relations with the neighboring populations of Tibet, China, Myanmar, Naga Hills, and Assam.[5] While Assam is called the Eastern Gateway for the passage of people, commodities, and ideas between India and China (Chatterji 1955), before the British period through which all the border countries were connected Arunachal Pradesh was a commercial and military route.[6] During the precolonial period the hill tribes carried on barter trade with Tibet, China, Bhutan, Myanmar, and Assam due to ethnic ties, *Nyetsang* (family friends and trading partners), and geographical proximity (Bhattacharjee 1997, 2002; Mibang 2002; Salam 2008). Trade through hill passes, or *duars*, contributed to the affluence of the chiefs who controlled them.[7]

There were two trade routes from Tawang to Tsona in Tibet: the Bumla route and the Zemithang route. A market was appended to each duar through which trade was carried on. Besides the periodic markets, annual fairs were held in some of the duars, like Udalguri and Daimara. There were also two other principal trade routes in the Siang district that passed through Bori and Bokar countries to the Tibetan plateau (Kumar 2002). Pangsu Pass in Pakai Hills was one of the trade routes to India from the upper part of Myanmar. Although the extent of early border trade across the Pangsu Pass was not as voluminous as trade with Tibet, the trade route connecting Sadiya, Hookong Valley, Mougong, and Bhamo went up to Ava and onward to southwest China (Sebastian 2002). The tribes of Arunachal Pradesh not only bartered their own products to Tibetans and others across the borders and in the marts; they also acted as intermediaries between different trading communities of Assam, Tibet, and Burma. Thus trade relations along both the eastern (Myanmar) and western (Tibet) borders were an important aspect of the tribal economy in this region even before the colonial period (Government of Arunachal Pradesh 2009: 45–48).

Silk, tussa, rice, iron, lac, skin, buffalo horn, pearl, and more were brought from Assam to Tibet, while Arunachalis bartered pepper, ginger, wax, ivory, cotton, wool, gold, yak tails, rubber, elephants' tusks with Assam for salt, cloth, glass beads, utensils, and agricultural implements. In a traditional cross-country trading system, traded items also varied from tribe to tribe. Bhuyan (1974, quoted in Bhattacharjee 2002: 35) writes that "the Mishimis living in the hills to the north of Sadiya brought with them Lama swords and spears and the vegetable poison known as Mishimi tita, and these they exchanged for glass beads, clothes, salt, and honey. The Abors and Miris brought pepper, ginger, munjit, and wax. The Singphos used to bring ivory in considerable quantities."

In the Tawang belt of the Mon region, where maize, millet, and barley were the staples, rice was procured from Udalguri and other places and was bartered with rock salt from Tibet (Dutta and Jha 2002). The periodic bazaar of Tsona was usually held on the fifth, seventh, and eleventh months of the Tibetan calendar. Apart from the rice and rock salt trade, the items traded at Tsona Bazaar included chili, millet, *chhurpee* (dried smoked cheese), dry meat, animal fats, dye, local paper, incense sticks, vegetables, fruits, wool and woolen garments, blankets, and other traditional local garments. Thus the traded items included not only immediate necessities but also culturally significant items used in religious rituals. Within the tribal communities of Arunachal Pradesh, these items were often markers of social prestige and status.

However, these exchanges and the social interactions underlying them were not entirely smooth. For example, Mibang (2002) points out that, although the Adis, particularly Boris and Bokars, had a traditional barter system with Tibet for articles like raw hides and chilies in exchange for rock salt, woolen clothes, swords, vessels, and ornaments, the Minyong group among the Adis were very suspicious of contact with others, presumably due to the absence of related ethnic groups across the border. There is little evidence about how, if at all, trade was regulated; perhaps the market was controlled by the local administration. In the Mon region in western Arunachal Pradesh, trade was supervised by Dzongs (the local administration), and the Tawang monastery regulated the rock-salt trade (Salam 2008). The expansion and consolidation of colonial rule to these frontier areas altered the context of trade across the Himalayas. Annual trade fairs were organized by colonial authorities as part of the strategy of maintaining cordial relations with tribal chiefs and also to expand trade to Tibet through the region (Sikdar 1997). Gradually the traditional payment of *posa* to tribal chiefs was monetized and they were encouraged to buy different commodities from the fairs.[8] During the colonial period, trade with Tibet declined significantly due to the supply of salt by the British, which was the most important item of Tibetan export. The opening up of regular permanent markets and shops as well as domestic trade hastened the decline of this trade.[9] Although the British initially wanted to open up the trade routes and rail link from Sadiya to western China via the Mishimi Hills, the idea had been abandoned due to strained Sino-British relations in the early years of the twentieth century.

Trade was only one of the means of interaction among the people across the present-day borders. Pilgrimage, inter- and intraclan social interactions, movement of people in search of better livelihood options, and the seasonal migration of pastoralists constituted other dimensions of cross-border linkages. In relatively isolated habitations across the Bhutan and Myanmar borders such interactions continue to be a significant aspect of people's survival. So far as the Indo-China border is concerned, the 1962 Indo-China War was definitely a watershed. Movements across the borders were severely restricted, and it was the pastoral people who were most severely affected by this development. In Tawang district in western Arunachal Pradesh, for example, many of the tribal people depending upon livestock lost their grazing grounds as the border management was tightened. On the other hand, in many places trade in livestock and movements of herders across the border continue, although to a lesser extent than before. Notwithstanding the posturing of the respective states, on the ground borders remain porous and negotiable in many contexts. The consolidation of security and military establishments has meant a disruption of these flows, but sporadic and clandestine contacts continue among the people living on either side. The nature of these contacts varies from the trade in legal and illegal goods to social visits. Some of these transactions are regulated and monitored through border posts, but many are informal and illegal. Occasionally such transborder contacts have led to conflicts as well.[10]

To sum up, contrary to the assumptions of isolation, fixity, and remoteness, many of the tribal communities of Arunachal Pradesh have long been interacting with each other as well as with the people living in the Assam plains and Tibet. Permanent and semipermanent migration of populations has always been and remains an important aspect of the economic and social landscape of the region.

Consolidation of Administration

During the colonial period the area was largely unadministered. Hence the governance structure of the tribes, which itself was very diverse, remained significant for a longer period in these areas than in other parts of India. Though the colonial encounter had a profound and long-term impact on the local economy and society (Sikdar 1982), village councils and chieftainships continued to be important.[11]

The Inner Line Regulation, enacted by the British Indian government in 1873, restricted the entry of outsiders to the area. As per the provisions of this Act, people from other parts of the country cannot enter the State without the permission of the government. They also cannot own any fixed assets in the State. Colonial interests and perceptions dictated this restriction, which was aimed at keeping the tribal populations free from unwanted migration from other parts of India.[12] In the context of the Chittagong Hill tracts, where a similar policy was followed, Van Schendel (1992: 111) writes, "Far from being a charter for regional autonomy or a protection of 'tribal' rights (as some would have it) it marked the onset of a process of 'enclavement' in which the hill people were denied access to power and were subordinated and exploited directly by their British overlords." Arunachal Pradesh remained less closely integrated into the empire than the Chittagong Hill tracts, but the implications of the policy of exclusion have remained significant, even during the postindependence period.

Thus modernization is, for the most part, a postindependence phenomenon in Arunachal Pradesh, beginning gradually with the establishment of a direct administrative structure in the State (Luthra 1993). For many years after independence, the area earlier known as North Eastern Frontier Tracts and renamed North Eastern Frontier Agency (NEFA) in 1954, was under the Ministry of External Affairs of the government of India. Although constitutionally NEFA was a part of Assam, the NEFA administration was not fully integrated with that of Assam. It was administered directly by the governor of Assam, who acted as the representative of the president of India. The Legislative Assembly of Assam did not have the authority to enact laws for NEFA. Although the first general election in India was held in 1952, the adult franchise was not extended to Arunachal Pradesh for a long time because of a special provision of the Representation of People Act of 1951.[13] The Bordoloi Subcommittee, which was appointed in 1950 to recommend an administrative framework for tribals of Assam and other unrepresented people, was also not in favor of extending the franchise to the people of NEFA on the grounds that the level of consciousness among the tribals was very low (Chaube 1999: 193). The Panchayati Raj institutions of local democratic governance introduced modern participatory political processes to the State only in 1969.

The 1962 war with China exposed the vulnerability of the Indian state in the region (Maxwell 1970). The Indian leadership made concerted efforts to address the weak administrative integration of the area in its policies for the region in subsequent periods. In 1972 NEFA was made a Union Territory and was named Arunachal Pradesh under the North Eastern Reorganisation Act of 1971. This Act provided Arunachal Pradesh with one seat in the Rajya Sabha (upper house) and another in the Lok Sabha (lower house), to be filled by presidential nomination. It was only in 1977 that the first general elections on the basis of universal adult franchise took place.

In 1987 the Union Territory became the twenty-fourth State of India. With the granting of the statehood, the establishment of institutional infrastructure in this hilly and sparsely populated land was further consolidated (Government of Arunachal Pradesh 2006: 3–9). The State was granted special status in the constitution, which entitles it to receive liberal financial assistance from the center. The special powers enjoyed by the governor of Arunachal Pradesh have continued to be a bone of contention between the center and State leadership.

The Political Economy of State-Induced Transformation

For a number of historical, political, and strategic reasons, the state has played a central role in modernizing and thereby increasing the productive capacity of the economy. There are basically three sources of the liberal grants that Arunachal receives from the center. The first is the statutory transfers made on the recommendation of the Finance Commission. The second is the plan assistance by the Planning Commission. Third are different centrally sponsored schemes by different ministries of the central government.

As an example of Arunachal's economic dependence on central government, in 2008–9 the percentage share of own tax revenue to gross state domestic product (GSDP) was only 3 percent.[14] During the seventeen years from 1986–87 to 2002–3 the real inflow to the State increased at a constant annual growth rate of 2.55 percent. The inflow of funds from the center constituted about 80 percent of the total revenue of the State (Government of Arunachal Pradesh 2006). So far as the composition of the central inflow is concerned, the share of grants in total inflow has increased in recent years, from 68 percent in 1997–98 to 82 percent during 2002–3.

Jairam Ramesh (2005), a politician from the Congress Party and a minister in the central government, argues that the central policies toward the Northeast have passed through four different phases: the Culture Paradigm, influential in the 1950s and the 1960s, viewed the Northeast as a "phenomenally diverse mosaic of cultures which have to be preserved and enriched"; the Security Paradigm, which came into greater prominence in the wake of the Chinese invasion of 1962, saw the Northeast as a "strategically significant region not only in a geographical sense but in a larger geopolitical sense of

India's role in East Asia and Southeast Asia"; the Politics Paradigm, which acquired relevance in the 1970s, was based on the presumption that lack of political representation in 'mainstream' democratic processes has led to the alienation of people of the region. Thus the creation of new States was part of a policy to accommodate subnationalist and ethnic aspirations within the broad framework of parliamentary democracy; the Development Paradigm of the 1980s is an economic response premised on the belief that "if we build schools, bridges, internet centers, IITs [branches of the Indian Institute of Technology] and refineries, the people will be happy. Give them development and they will forget about problems of identity, problems of assertion, problems associated with creating a nation out of essentially tribal communities. Thus the 1980s was the period marked by a substantial increase in public expenditure in this region." Since the 1990s, one may add, another phase in the dominant thinking about the Northeast has been added: the neoliberal paradigm, linked with the much-hyped transnational dimension through India's Look East Policy (compare Farrelly, in chapter 8, this volume). For entirely different reasons, both critics and policymakers for the region seem to agree that once international trade and markets take over, the highways linking the booming economies of Southeast Asia and China with that of India through the Northeast will also bring peace and prosperity to the region.[15] Ramesh (2005) himself argues that "the future of the Northeast lies in political integration with India and economic integration with Southeast Asia."

Many analysts believe that the political decision to create a number of small States in the region did not pay adequate attention to the question of their economic and fiscal viability (Sachdeva 2000; Rao and Singh 2004). The States of Northeast India, including Arunachal Pradesh, have been heavily dependent upon central government assistance and are routinely described as States facing a severe "fiscal crisis" (Sarma 2005), mainly because of their low internal revenue-generation capacities. While this 'asymmetric federalism' has acted as a means of preserving the unity of India in the face of secessionist movements (Rao and Singh 2004), the center's policy has also been blamed for the crisis of state finances in India, particularly in the case of the special category States.[16] Political commentators like Sanjib Baruah (2003a), however, argue that this policy of creation of unviable States, which are perpetually dependent on the center for their day-to-day survival, has given rise to a 'cosmetic' regional federal order, in which the center retains sufficient control to achieve its strategic and developmentalist objectives. The heavy dependence on central assistance has also meant that there is little local control over development schemes. The centrality of the government sector in general and public administration has shaped the growth trajectory of the State to a great extent.

The other significant aspect of the 'developmentalist' vision in this border state is the interrelationship between the security and developmental aspects of government spending in general, and in infrastructure in particular. As noted by Baruah (2004a), the state has always placed heavy emphasis on building roads. Poor connectivity to the plains was a major reason for the military debacle in the 1962 war with China. In subsequent decades considerable effort was made to develop road connectivity in this difficult terrain, a process that has been termed 'nationalizing space' (Baruah 2003a, 2004a). The construction of roads, mostly by the Border Roads Organisation, has had many significant consequences for the State's economy, both intended and unintended. First, most of the roads were developed in a north-south direction, connecting the borders with China to the plains of Assam, which probably makes sense from the security point of view, but it also means that to visit one district headquarters from another, the people of Arunachal have to travel a long distance through Assam.[17] Second, these roads have become so significant for the people that the settlement patterns in the uplands have undergone significant changes. Many villages have shifted from old sites to newer sites nearer the roads. This has led to the creation of multiclan, multitribe villages with several implications for control and management of community resources, including land and forests. Third, in the construction of roads local people were employed as contractors, which not only cemented the relationship between the locals and the administration but also played a catalytic role in creating a local contractor class.

State, Market, and Community

These specific characteristics of Arunachal Pradesh play an important role in creating the overall context in which the political economy of development is shaped by the actions and inactions of various forces—local, national, and international. In this analysis, I attempt to understand these processes by looking at the ways the local State, market forces, and 'community' interact with and influence each other.

As discussed earlier, in Arunachal Pradesh most villages had some institutional mechanism such as a village council to manage and safeguard property rights in land and forests. While in some areas the institution of chieftainship was well developed and individuals derived their rights of ownership from the village chief, in many areas the village council, consisting exclusively of adult males, was the basic institution of decision making, conflict resolution, and collective action (Misra 1979; Das 1995; Dutta 2003; Pandey et al. 1999). The traditional shifting cultivation system was based upon elaborate networks of informal contracts and on cooperation, as well as on resource pooling, risk sharing, and mutual insurance mechanisms. Verrier Elwin, an anthropologist and advisor to Prime Minister Nehru on tribal affairs, firmly believed in the democratic ethos of these institutions. He advocated that state policy should encourage these micro-institutions as the building blocks of democratic governance of this region (Elwin [1957] 1999). The Nehru-Elwin policy was unequivocal in its belief that tribals should not be overwhelmed with change.[18]

The anxieties and the utopian vision of the Indian administration in these border regions are best captured by Elwin ([1957] 1999: 146, emphasis added) in A Philosophy for NEFA: "Every official is an ambassador and the frontier people's idea of India will largely depend on his behaviour. They will judge not by what they are told, but by what they see. India is becoming real to them, and if they can blend a pride in their own culture with a pride in the greater Indian culture of which it forms a part, they will be not only politically but psychologically integrated with the rest of the country. *This task of emotional integration is of special importance in the remote areas along the international boundary.*"[19] Although this policy was advanced primarily at the level of rhetoric, particularly after the 1962 war,[20] the anxieties of managing and controlling a border region remained at the core of the administrative practices on the ground. A significant outcome of this process was that involving the locals, however superficially, became one of the conscious strategies of the State administration.[21] In the absence of a representative governance structure at the beginning, this involved inviting the local chiefs and influential persons to be part of the governance structure 'informally,' a policy that had its origin during the colonial administration. As the institutions of democratic governance started taking root in the State, the older generations of leaders were gradually replaced by the 'new elites.' However, the elites, both old and new, derived their legitimacy as representatives of their respective communities. To a great extent, contemporary politics in Arunachal Pradesh continues to operate in this broad framework of communal representation (Ghosh et al.

2005). Hence the politics of identity and difference plays a long-enduring and important role in such a framework of governance.

To put this argument in context one needs to understand the historical trajectories of the politics of identity and difference in Northeast India, which, as elsewhere, has a long and complex history. The colonial project of building the empire and the postcolonial politics of nation building are the broader processes in which the ethnic landscape of Northeast India has taken shape. The extraordinary ethnic diversity in the region makes its politics complex and fragmented, but the roots of the fragmented nature of the polity do not emanate from the coexistence of diverse ethnic groups alone. It also has resulted from the multiple ways external forces such as the state and capital have interacted with this diversity. One of the ways state and markets have interacted with and changed the ethnic landscape of the region, at least since the encounters with colonialism, is the way property rights over crucial livelihood resources have been altered or created. The micro-ethnic communities had their respective institutions of governance at the community level, and these institutional arrangements not only regulated the religious and social life of the members but also governed access to a range of tangible and nontangible resources that were crucial for the survival of the people. Depending upon the resource endowment position and the particular history of the community, its rules might be well defined or ambiguous, strictly or loosely applied. But the state-induced move toward modernization and integration of the local economies with the broader regional and national economies led to significant alterations in the way property rights were created, destroyed, or rearranged to suit the demands of the changing economic and political contexts. These ethnically inflected property rights were protected by various policies, including restrictions on land transfer and mobility of labor and reservations in jobs, government contracts, and business licenses, all of which give people a strong vested interest in communal identities (Harriss-White et al. 2010). There is a common tendency to view these changes through the binary prisms of 'destruction of the old and creation of new' institutional forms. A detailed study of the changes in various dimensions of property rights and institutional mechanisms, however, shows that the transition has been complex (Harriss-White et al. 2009). It involved destruction, survival, adaptation, and modifications of the precapitalist institutional structures, along with the creation of newer institutional forms. The institutional diversity and complexity that underlie such transitions are to be seen not simply as leftovers of the past but as the defining characteristics of the nature of capitalist transition in the region. Adding to the specificities of the situation is, of course, the continuing significance of the traditional institutions governing access to natural resources. The state and market forces are constantly interacting with and, by implication, changing various dimensions of the resource-management practices in Arunachal, but, as of now, the institutional milieu is defined more by heterogeneity and hybridity than by institutional convergence. In a recent field survey in eleven villages in five districts of Arunachal Pradesh, Harriss-White et al. (2009: 512) found that "institutional adaptation, continuity and hybridity are as integral to the emergence of the market economy as are the processes of creation of new institutions and demise of others. There is no necessary correspondence between the emerging commercialization of the different productive dimensions of the agrarian economy. These uneven processes are deeply influenced by existing and emerging power relations and by the state."

As noted, in Arunachal Pradesh nearly 63 percent of forests categorized as 'unclassified state forest' are in fact in the hands of village communities and clans. However, the effective control of these forests varies considerably among different communities. Individual property rights over land in practice coexist with de jure collective rights in forests. Irrespective of the precise nature of property rights regimes operating at the ground level, there is an unmistakable tendency toward de facto privatization of the ownership or at least use rights over forests. The individual ownership rights, particularly in regard to alienation rights, are necessarily subject to community control in many areas (D'Souza 2001: 46; Mishra 2006; Harriss-White et al. 2009), but the exploitation of forest resources, particularly timber, before the imposition of restrictions by the Supreme Court of India has certainly weakened the ethos of collective management. Apart from the environmental impact of deforestation, induced by the wanton exploitation of the 'common' forest for private gain, the institutional impact was that the traditional rules of resource use, which had been designed in a resource-abundant context and hence involved almost no cost for monitoring, became redundant so rapidly that communities did not have the social capital to address the problem. The emergence of a labor market itself transformed the labor-sharing practices, and since most of the traditional institutional mechanisms were based upon the implicit assumption of labor shortage, their distributive egalitarianism lost the capacity for conflict-minimization (Mishra 2002, 2004).

The transformation of property relations has hastened the processes of peasant differentiation. Landlessness has increased, although there is a great degree of unevenness in the process.[22] It is important to note that this shift from a communal economy to increasing economic and gender differentiation did not occur primarily because of factors like internal population growth (although migration from outside has played a significant catalytic role) but because of state interventions in terms of discouraging shifting cultivation and the provision of incentives to 'progressive' farmers to grow commercial crops. In such contexts the state, on the one hand, has facilitated the emergence of private property rights through a series of direct and indirect measures, while on the other hand, by not taking cognizance of the move toward privatization, by remaining at best a passive observer of it, the state has virtually left the process in the hands of 'traditional' community institutions. These institutions, notwithstanding their other strengths as institutions of decentralized, local-level governance, are hardly 'participatory' when it comes to women and other socially marginalized groups (Krishna 2004; Goswami 2002; Mishra and Upadhyay 2007).

An important dimension of the development process in Arunachal Pradesh is the reworking of the 'traditional' community identities under the influence of the state-led modernization drive. It is widely recognized that "ethnicity is not a primordially given essence, but the outcome of complex socio-cultural and political processes of labelling and identifying people" (Peters 1998: 400; see also Collier 1998). The politics of identity and difference in Arunachal Pradesh, as elsewhere, involves considerable rediscovery and invention of the past in the light of the present. It has been influenced not only by the introduction of electoral democracy but also by the unequal distribution of the fruits and burdens of economic prosperity. Ethnic politics in Northeast India have been an important aspect of the transition in the region, particularly in the context of the heavy military presence of the state and its relative inability to protect the life, livelihoods, and dignity of its citizens (Baruah 2003b, 2004b). The relative weakness of the state in safeguarding property rights and enforcing contracts typically creates the space for the emergence of ethnic groups to provide private means of securing property rights (Bates 1998).

Unlike in many of the northeastern States, where this has resulted in the proliferation of numerous insurgent groups defending the interest of specific ethnic communities, in the case of Arunachal Pradesh it has led to competition and bargaining among different tribal groups to acquire a larger share of government resources—a form of 'quiet pressure' exercised from within the system (Mishra and Upadhyay 2007). In contrast to the Naga movement for secession and autonomy, and many similar movements across the northeastern region (see Joshi, this volume), Arunachal Pradesh has witnessed ethnic tensions operating within the framework of popular democracy. Not that there has never been any attempt to create pan-Arunachal military groups. Several little-known groups, such as the Arunachal Dragon force, have been formed in the past, but none of them has been successful in creating durable, violent, secessionist or ethnic movements in the State. Ethnic tensions between numerically dominant ethnic groups such as the Nyshi and the Adi have emerged as a distinctive feature of local politics. The demand for separate autonomous area councils for the Buddhist communities in western Arunachal Pradesh (Tawang and West Kameng), the eastern 'Naga' tribal areas bordering Nagaland, and also for the tribal groups in central Arunachal Pradesh symbolizes the struggle for better resource allocation in the framework of ethnic competition. Although so far these tensions have been relatively free from the extreme forms of violence witnessed in other parts of the region, there have been reports of coercion and violent attacks against individuals belonging to particular groups during periods of ethnic tensions in the State. Such incidents, with the sole exception of the actions of Naga militant groups in eastern Arunachal Pradesh, have not been able to or even attempted to seriously challenge the legitimacy of the Indian state.[23] Nevertheless the overall framework of ethnic politics has weakened the 'universal' principles of civic rule to a considerable extent and has provided substantial scope for community leaders and elites to exercise control over the everyday politics of survival and accumulation.

As elsewhere, the benefits of the identity-based mobilization of public opinion have not necessarily been shared equitably within the groups in whose name the demands for more resources from the governments have been placed. Ethnic claims and ethnic action, although purporting to be designed to serve the ethnic collectivity, may in practice serve the mobilizers more than the collectivity they claim to represent (Das Gupta 1988: 145–46). It is generally the traders, politicians, and bureaucrats who corner a substantial proportion of the gains of such collective articulation of demands. It often happens that the principles of democratic rights, equality, and justice, which are invoked when claiming benefits for ethnic or identity-based groups, are not necessarily considered legitimate when the rights of underprivileged groups of individuals within the ethnic group itself are at issue (Mishra and Upadhyay 2007).

The other significant dimension of this transition, noted in Harriss-White et al. (2009), is that it is basically the nonagricultural surplus that has been the moving force behind this transition. Access to political power and resources of the state acted as key factors in the creation and sustenance of this surplus flow. Another source of surplus for the local elites, until recently, was the huge profits from the timber trade. Although timber was by and large controlled by large-scale business from outside the State, the local business class, as junior partners and facilitators, managed to corner a substantial share for themselves. Some of them invested the surplus in establishing sawmills, plywood factories, and transportation businesses. "Although in the first instance the timber trade appears to be independent of the state, the manner in which the state allowed the plundering of the commonly owned forests for private profit makes it clear that state support and protection was essential for the timber trade. While the forest department of the State government retained control over the supply of permits to cut trees, these permits were issued with such frequency and under such a framework of political patronage that community control over forests remained at best a minor irritant ... for the traders," whether from indigenous tribal groups or from outside the State (Harriss-White et al. 2009: 537).

Since state support was crucial for the surplus extraction activities of the elites and access to the resources of the State was being governed within the framework ethnic politics, it was quite natural for the elites to protect the institutional diversities that provided scope for them to exercise control and power at the local level. To put it rather crudely, the ability of the local elites to draw a share from the State's resources or to extract a rent from the State or from outsiders, depended upon their ability to perpetuate the politics of ethnicity and difference and also on their capacity to represent their 'community' in the competition over tangible and nontangible resources. Thus while the State has been influential in initiating the capitalist transition and also in changing community institutions in diverse ways, the overall framework of ethnic politics has created the context in which the politics of democracy and state intervention is being played out today.

THE STATUS OF Arunachal Pradesh as a 'frontier' and a 'border State' had a profound impact on its political economy of development. From the early years of the postindependence period the Indian state has taken a cautious and special approach to this mountain State. This paper has focused on some important aspects of this process by looking at the interactions among the local state and market forces and the community at the grassroots level. I have argued that historically this region was part of a trade route through which there was a continuous flow of people, goods, and ideas, but the consolidation of administrative and security structures reduced such flows. Although, in practice, people living in relatively isolated pockets have contacts with those living outside the borders, the frequency of such contact varies from locality to locality. The state has tried to consolidate its position not only by strengthening its military presence along the borders but also by making special efforts to bring the tribal communities and their organizational structures within the fold of the civil administration. In its anxiety to gain legitimacy and acceptability among the people in the border areas, it has made many special provisions that have resulted in a situation wherein the politics of identity and difference have come to play a very significant role. The state has not only modernized the administration; it has also acted as the prime mover of economic transformation. This has altered the very foundations of the local economy and has resulted in the creation of new types of property rights over resources that are crucial for the survival and accumulation strategies of individuals and households. Institutional diversity and complexity has helped the small tribal elite to take advantage of the situation. This elite has managed to acquire resources both from the state and from the community through negotiations at various levels. Being a 'border' region has, in many significant ways, shaped the political economy of development in Arunachal Pradesh.

NOTES TO CHAPTER 6

This paper draws upon the ongoing collaborative research undertaken by the author with Barbara Harriss-White, Department of International Development, University of Oxford, and Vandana Upadhyay, Department of Economics, Rajiv Gandhi University, Itanagar, Arunachal Pradesh. Some of the arguments presented here have been discussed at greater length in Harriss-White et al. (2009). This paper was written when the author was a Commonwealth Visiting Fellow at the Oxford Department of International Development, Queen Elizabeth House, Oxford University. It has benefited from the comments from participants at the BASAS annual conference at Edinburgh University. Special thanks are due to David Gellner and Barbara Harriss-White for their insightful comments and support. Thanks to Dr. Padmini Pani of CRSD, JUN, for help with drawing the original map for Map 6.1.

1. The total geographical area of Arunachal Pradesh is 8,374 hectares. Of the total reported area under land utilization about 94 percent is covered by forest. Mountain specificities, such as inaccessibility, fragility, marginality, and diversity, have significant implications for the local economies (Jodha 2001).

2. Against the claim that rapid economic changes and capitalist transformation of the economy result in increasingly anonymous, depersonalized, and voluntary economic exchanges among agents, Harriss-White et al. (2009) argue that the 'identity' of the individual remains key to the economic transactions that take place.

3. This assertion is based on interviews with village heads and elders in West Kameng and Tawang districts in western Arunachal Pradesh carried out in 2002 and 2007. Several scholars, however, point to the frequent 'boundary disputes' among tribal chiefs and the Ahom rulers, hinting at the possibility of emergence of nascent states even during the precolonial period (Jha 1997). Mishra and Thakur (2004), while discussing the conflicts between the Ahom kings and the Noctes over salt wells in the latter's region, argue that even during the thirteenth century there was already a crystallization of the territorial state of the Noctes.

4. Intervillage, interclan, and intertribal warfare, feuds, raids, and kidnappings were the rule rather than the exception in those days.

5. Salam (2008) provides a detailed account of the traditional trade routes through Arunachal Pradesh. On the international boundary line, Arunachal Pradesh has as many as thirty-five natural passes, but the main trade routes passed through just eight of them: the Beelting/Namstring Pass near Lumla with Bhutan, the Kenzamanee near Zimithang with Tibet, the Bumla Pass near Tawang with Tibet, the Lola Pass near Mechuka with Tibet, the Domla Pass near Monigong with Tibet, the Landupgo, Simula, and Lusala passes near Gelling with Tibet, the Thochu Pass near Kibithow with China, and the Pangsu Pass near Nampong with Myanmar.

6. See Pemberton 1835; Gait (1905) 1926. On the basis of Pemberton's report, Hamilton described the trade relations between Assam and Tibet: "Tibetan caravans conducted by 20 persons used to come down annually to a mart of Chouna to the Assam border after two months' journey from Lhasa and conveyed silver bullion to the amount of about one lac [100,000] of rupees, and a considerable quantity of rock-salt for sale to the Assam merchants at Geegunshur, four miles away. The large quantities of rice brought by the merchants at the latter place were purchased and imported into Tibet from Assam by the merchants. Tussa silk cloth, iron and lac found in Assam, skins, buffalo horns, pearls and corals, first imported from Bengal, were traded by the Assamese merchants. The Tibetan merchants brought woollens, gold-dust, salt, musk, horses, Chinese silk, etc. The annual fair was temporarily stopped due to Burmese occupation. Attempt was made to revive it in 1833. The fair was started at Udalgiri later on" (Mackenzie 1884 quoted in Kumar 2002: 52).

7. The most important of the duars were Kariapara, Charduar, Naoduar, Chaiduar, and Sadiya (Bhattacharjee 2002).

8. During the reign of the Ahom ruler Pratap Singh (1603–41), "the Akas, the Dufflas, the Miris, and the Abors" were granted the right of levying posa, which, apart from the annual collection of goods in specified areas, included labor service of the Assamese peasants for which they were given corresponding remission from the state's revenue demand (Mackenzie 1884: 27 cited in Mishra 1983). With the advent of British rule attempts were made to fix the amount of commodities to be paid to each of the tribes (Bose 1979: 136–46; for a discussion of posa, see Jha 1997). The British, who referred to posa as "blackmail, blackmail levy or compensation levy for blackmail . . . within a short period of 25 years of their rule, commuted it into money terms and made the tribal chief and leaders agree to receive the amount each year directly from the Deputy Commissioner's office" (Mishra 1983: 1838). Other scholars have viewed posa differently, regarding it as a 'rent' for using the plains that belonged to the tribal people. Fürer-Haimendorf (1982: 27), for example, writes, "The officers of government had generally considered *posa* as a form of tribute with which in the early days of British rule the hillmen had been bought off from raiding the plains, but I am convinced that in this they were mistaken and *posa* was really a kind of rent for land belonging to the Miris and other hillmen by right."

9. Later the Indo-China border conflict put a complete halt to the already low-scale border trade.

10. An officer in charge of a subdivision on the India-Bhutan border disclosed that he was in regular touch with his counterparts across the border. They try to solve minor disputes among the people, mainly through informal negotiations. The conflicts generally relate to disputes over grazing rights, transborder land rights, and trade in livestock.

11. Outlining the transformation of Kebangs, the traditional institution of Adis, during the British period, Elwin ([1957] 1999: 158–59) wrote: "Official Gams, as the Headman are called in Siang, were appointed, one for every clan in the village. . . . Their appointment changed the *Kebang* to some extent, for they naturally became members and caused the authority of the priests to decline. They introduced the official element that had previously been absent. . . . [A] more elaborate institution known as the *Bango* was introduced under official inspiration. The *Bango* represents a number of villages and . . . is mainly concerned in settling inter-village disputes."

12. In the words of Elwin ([1957] 1999: 66), "The Inner Line Regulation was enacted in 1873, not with the aim (as is so often thought) of isolating the hill people from the plains, but to bring 'under more stringent control the commercial relations of British subjects with the frontier tribes.'"

13. Constitutional orders VII and VIII withheld from NEFA the right of representation to Assam and central legislatures.

14. "Own Tax Revenue as % of GSDP from 1997–98 to 2008–09," Databook for DCH,

28 March 2011, accessed 22 April 2011, planningcommission.nic.in/data/datatable /2803/tab_98.pdf.

15. The Vision 2020 document that has attempted to provide a road map of development in the region also emphasizes the scope for making the northeastern region the eastern gateway of India (Ministry of Development of North Eastern Region and North Eastern Council 2008). Situating the Look East policy in the context of development policy in the Northeast, Baruah (2004a: 22) writes, "If the Look East policy is to live up to its potential of becoming Northeast India's road to peace and prosperity we will have to face up to the risks that exist and actively assess and manage them. That would mean taking a long-term view and synchronising our foreign policies towards China, Myanmar, ASEAN—as well as towards Bangladesh and Bhutan—and our domestic policies vis-à-vis Northeast India. Building roads can deliver results only if they are part of a comprehensive transnational region-building project informed by a long-term strategic vision." It is important to note that even authors like Baruah, who have criticized the 'developmentalist' vision that characterizes state intervention in the region, tend to believe that market-led integration of the Northeast with neighboring economies will, in the final analysis, be good for the people of the region.

16. In 2001–2, Rao and Singh (2004: 15) pointed out, "non-special category states on average raised revenues to finance over 50 per cent of their current expenditure whereas in special category states it was just about 20 per cent. Thus, central transfers financed more than 80 per cent of the expenditures of special category states. In per capita terms, transfer to special category states is more than four times that of the average transfer received by general category states." Rao (n.d.: 11) has noted that although the per capita GSDP of the special category states is higher, the tax/GSDP ratios in the special category States are lower than in the general category States. "This is partly because, in these States there is not much production activity and the government administration is the major determinant of the GSDP. Further, size of their tax base is smaller than what is indicated by the GSDP, because a significant proportion of government spending spills over the jurisdictions." Although "the revenue bases in the special category States are low, their average per capita current expenditure are higher than not only the all-State average but also the average of high income States. . . . Of course, the higher than average per capita expenditures in special category States cannot be entirely attributed to their inherent cost disability. This may also be due to bad fiscal management."

17. Geogang Apang, one of the key politicians of the State and a long-serving chief minister, often complained about the rule that he has to get permission from the army authorities to construct roads in the border areas.

18. The Nehru-Elwin policy specified five fundamental principles of development: "1) People should develop along the lines of their own genius and we should avoid imposing anything on them. We should try to encourage in every way their own

traditional arts and culture. 2) Tribal rights in lands and forests should be respected. 3) We should try to train and build up a team of their own people to do the work of administration and development. Some technical persons from outside will no doubt be needed especially in the beginning. But we should avoid introducing too many outsiders into tribal territory. 4) We should not over administer these areas or overwhelm them with a multiplicity of schemes. We should rather work through and not in rivalry to their own social and cultural institutions. 5) We should judge results not by statistics or by the amount of money spent but by the quality of human character that is evolved" (Jawaharlal Nehru, foreword to Elwin [1957] 1999: xiii).

19. Nehru, Elwin claimed, was in complete agreement with him on this. He quotes Nehru: "An officer in the tribal areas . . . must be prepared to enter [local people's] huts, talk to them, eat and smoke with them, live their lives and not consider himself superior or apart. Then only can he gain their confidence and respect, and thus be in a position to advise them" (Elwin [1957] 1999: 147).

20. After India's defeat in the Indo-China War of 1962, the Nehru-Elwin policy of gradual integration of the NEFA, often called 'isolationist' and 'a legacy of the colonial policy' toward the region, came under severe criticism (Baruah 2003a: 919). The post-1962 period witnessed a rapid expansion and consolidation of administration in the region (Government of Arunachal Pradesh 2006).

21. The need for such a policy arose from the fact that the subjects, at least in the beginning, did not necessarily identify with the Indian administration. Asan Riddi (2004: 54), an indigenous scholar from Arunachal, reflects upon the attitude of the older generations of elders from his Tagin community toward education: "Their belief was that if their children get education, they would become *Nyeme-Nipak-Ni* (Tibetan and Indian government people); in that case, (they) would not be able to own the *Geda-Eshi* (land and water) of their parents." I too noticed this ambivalent attitude toward both Indian and Tibetan authorities while interviewing older village chiefs in the villages of Tawang and West Kameng districts.

22. See Fernandes and Pereira 2005; Salam 2007; Harriss-White et al. 2009; Mishra 2002.

23. The emergence of an 'Arunachalee' identity has been a complex process intertwined with the political economy of development through state intervention. Numerous tribal groups residing in then North Eastern Frontier Agency were brought under the State of Arunachal Pradesh by state intervention from above. During the movement against the Chakma refugees in the late 1980s and early 1990s, student groups such as All Arunachal Pradesh Students' Union tried to forge unity among all tribal groups of the State against the 'outsiders.'

The Micropolitics of Borders
The Issue of Greater Nagaland (or Nagalim)

As an Indian national, every time I go to Nagaland I have to make a mandatory visit to Nagaland House in Aurangzeb Road, situated at the heart of Lutyens' New Delhi to obtain an Inner Line Permit, known in common parlance as an ILP, to enter the State.[1] Once inside Nagaland State, I am also required to go to the district commissioner's office within a seven-day period to get the permit extended for a period of three months. Each time I have to supply my photograph and the name of my local guarantor and host. The very fact that as an Indian citizen I need an ILP to enter a border area in my own country speaks volumes about the nature of the northeastern border and how the colonial legacy has continued to keep the area inaccessible and under state control.

This chapter delineates how the situation of Nagaland on the borders of Indian territory has had a determining influence on its people, its politics, and the development of ethnicity, which at its extreme is expressed in the desire for sovereignty. The development of such political sentiment can be traced throughout the postcolonial history of the past seventy years. The internal competitiveness for hegemony along 'tribal' lines within the Naga nationalist movement in conjunction with the obsession of the different sides—the government of India; the Indian Federal States of Assam, Manipur, and Arunachal Pradesh; and the Naga nationalist groups—with where the borders of Nagaland/Nagalim should be, and the modern demand and assumption that there should be clearly marked and unambiguous borders, are what keeps the conflict so intractable.

The Inner Line

The Inner Line and excluded territories were administrative measures deployed by the British to keep a check on the usurpation of land by entrepreneurs during the nineteenth-century 'tea rush' in Assam in the area bordering a loosely demarcated territory known as the Naga Hills district (Baruah 2005: 92–93). The Inner Line regulation also distinguished the administered territory from the fuzzily defined unadministered area which lay beyond British control (Yonuo 1974: 94). The Inner Line was a constantly shifting 'boundary'; as the 'frontier' moved, so did the Inner Line.

In the 1830s the British East India Company began to explore the eastern borders of Assam for possible tea plantation.[2] They secured the region by restricting entry to what was declared in official terms 'wasteland' (Baruah 2005: 91–95; Guha 1991; Gangopadhyay 1990). The communities living in the 'wasteland' beyond the 'frontier,' including the ancestors of the present-day Naga, did not have any say in this expansion. After the 1850s the presumed 'empty tracts' were also used for settling migrants from other parts of India who worked as seasonal labor in the tea plantations as well as to settle migratory groups such as the Kuki people from the neighboring Manipur Kingdom.[3]

The administered part, known as the Naga Hills district in the colonial period, along with the unadministered territory, is mountainous and covered with thick tropical forest and lies between the plains of the Brahmaputra River in Assam and the Chindwin River in Myanmar (Burma).[4] This region has been home to many different communities, which formed a buffer between Burmese, Assamese, and Manipuri kingdoms (Roy Burman 1968). James Scott (2008; see also Scott 2009) describes the upland northeastern region of India as part of a nonstate space, which is one way of contrasting village republics with larger kingdoms. Based on the historical literature and colonial archives it would seem that this buffer zone was not specifically under any one kingdom's control; rather it was at the margins, with some villages having reciprocal relationships with the kingdoms (Barpujari 1992).

The historical records, or Buranji, of the twelfth-century Ahom rulers, a Tai people who had conquered parts of Assam, mention land deals with the neighboring hill communities identified by the name of their villages (Barpujari 1992; Baruah 1999). In the eighteenth century the Burmese defeated the Ahom kingdom and then were themselves defeated by the British in the first quarter of the nineteenth century. The Anglo-Burmese Treaty of Yandabo in 1826 also included transfer of the hill region between Assam and Burma to British India. With a view to finding a direct land route to Burma from Assam, British exploratory expeditions were sent into what later came to be known as the Naga Hills. When British interests conflicted with the villages, several punitive expeditions were sent into the hills to coerce the communities to enter into a settlement with the British.

Franke (2009) reiterates the point that annexation of the northeastern region by the British was not a reluctant act but was part of the imperialist strategy of expansion and search for new resources to increase revenue (see also Baruah 2005; Yonuo 1974: 95; Hilaly 2007). The nineteenth century was the time of exploration and survey. The discovery of oil reserves in 1889 at Digboy in Assam and coal in the surrounding region resulted in the building of the railways in the northeast (Hilaly 2007).

That the railway network in this part of India, Northeast Railways, was renamed Northeast Frontier Railways in 1958 raises the question of whether the northeast is a frontier only for the railway network or remains a frontier region, preserving the old sense of a moving border between a known territory beyond which lies as yet unknown land. Certainly since precolonial times this geographical area has been a 'frontier' region in sharing borders, but also cross-cutting trading networks, with what we now know as China, Myanmar, and Bangladesh (see Baruah 2005, 2009; Van Schendel 2005a; Robb 1997; Mishra, this volume). In other words, when and how do such regions become regarded as borders at one time and as part of a nation-state at another?

Nagaland, one of the seven northeastern States of India, shares its border with Myanmar and, for the government of India, is strategically located as part of a buffer against neighboring China and Myanmar. Since the Sino-Indian War of 1962, China has laid claim to the Indian State of Arunachal Pradesh, which lies to the north of Nagaland and borders Tibet, China, and Myanmar. It ignores the McMahon line, about 885 kilometers long, drawn in 1914 during the British colonial period as an outer line and international border along the northeastern Himalayan crest, which brought the trade center of Tawang (now in Arunachal Pradesh) into British Indian territory. The various 'frontier tracts,' identified as Balipara, Sadiya, Mishmi, and Tirap by the British colonial administrators, were renamed North East Frontier Agency by independent India in 1954 and now form the State of Arunachal Pradesh.

Unlike the formation of West Pakistan and East Pakistan (Bangladesh since 1971), where the 'known' land was divided between two countries, causing tremendous upheaval, leading to mass movement as well as large-scale massacres of people, the formation of India's northeastern border is said to have been more speculative. In the popular imagination an arbitrary line was drawn over the Patkai ranges when Jawaharlal Nehru, prime minister of India, and U Nu, the prime minister of Burma, flew over the area to determine the international boundary, thus unwittingly dividing villages perched on the mountaintops between the two nations. On both sides the area is envisaged as remote, with freedom of movement by local communities for sixteen kilometers on either side of the border. In recent years the Myanmar junta has helped the government of India by destroying the camps of two Naga nationalist groups on their side of the border. This tacit understanding between India and Myanmar is perhaps the basis for the government of India's diplomatic silence on issues of democracy in Myanmar.

Compared to India's northwestern border with Pakistan, which has been in national and international focus since 1947, the northeastern border with Myanmar has received only intermittent attention. The formation of East Pakistan (now Bangladesh) took away a large tract, leaving only a thin corridor strip about twenty kilometers in breadth that connects the rest of India to the seven northeastern States. At a conference on Asian borderlands held in Guwahati in 2008 an Assam government minister claimed that the northeast is equidistant to Hong Kong and Delhi and questioned the very term 'northeast,' asking, "'Northeast' of what?"[5] Of course, in nationalist narratives distance is measured from the capital city of the country. But 'the northeast' has always evoked the idea of a very distant place. As Baruah (2005) rightly points out, a posting to the northeast still carries a stigma of 'punishment' imposed on central government employees, despite the fact that they enjoy a hardship allowance and an income tax break.[6]

The seven northeastern States (earlier constituting most of undivided Assam) now have an equal status with other States in India. On the one hand, some of these northeastern States (e.g., Nagaland, Mizoram, Arunachal Pradesh) can be regarded as nonstate spaces according to Scott's (2008, 2009) argument in that they were not previously part of any kingdom. On the other hand, the large number of rebel movements in the northeast seeking autonomy or sovereignty demonstrates that they no longer wish to remain nonstate systems and that the days of viable nonstate space are gone. The demand for a 'greater' Nagaland (or Nagalim) is intended as a move toward formation of a nation-state of their own.

FIGURE 7.1. On 18 November 2006 a special reconciliation ceremony was held in Naga-land between the clans of A. Z. Phizo and T. Sakhrie. T. Sakhrie, the first general secretary of the Naga National Council and Phizo's trusted lieutenant, was murdered in 1956 after he rejected violent rebellion (see chapter 7, note 7). Photograph courtesy of V. Joshi.

Riots and Reconciliation

On 22 February 2009 a mass convention for reconciliation was held in Kohima, the capital of Nagaland.[7] This was a part of the ongoing attempt by Naga civil society organizations, comprising the Naga Baptist Church Council, Naga Mothers' Association, Naga Students' Federation, Naga Ho Ho, and Naga People's Movement for Human Rights (NPMHR), to bring together the different rival factions of the National Socialist Council of Nagaland/Nagalim—NSCN(IM), NSCN(K), NSCN(Unification)—and Naga National Council (NNC-Accordist and NNC-Non-Accordist).[8] As one unit they would then be able to negotiate with the Indian government. Among those present were also international representatives of the Quaker group and Baptist World Alliance. However, factional killings and attacks have continued between NSCN(IM) and NSCN(K), indicating the arduous process of reconciliation and the difficulties that the sharing of power poses for nationalist groups, especially the two main NSCN factions (see figure 7.1).

In 2010 the Indian government was engaged in negotiations with only one group, the NSCN(IM), concerning sovereignty and the unification of the Naga area, although it had cease-fire agreements with both NSCN groups. In 1997 a cease-fire was announced with NSCN(IM) and ground rules were laid. In 2001 a cease-fire was also agreed between the Indian government and the NSCN(K) group. There is a Ceasefire Supervisory Group, led by a chairman (the first chairman until 2008 was Lt. Gen. [Ret.] R. V. Kulkarni) from the government of India, personnel from the Assam Rifles and Indian Army that are stationed in Nagaland, Nagaland State home commissioner, Nagaland State police chief, and the representatives of the two NSCN factions. Cease-fire talks are also held separately with each faction.[9]

These were followed in the same year, 2001, by revised ground rules for the cease-fire agreed with both NSCN factions:

- NSCN will notify list of all its camps to the [Cease Fire Monitoring Committee] who after due consultation would declare them as the designated camps. In the interest of promoting peace process, there would be no parading (either in groups or individually) of NSCN cadres in uniform and/or with arms. For the present, this would cover all populated areas, public transport and Highways.
- The concern that forcible collection of money on essential supplies and intimidation of individuals including Government officials were taking place was denied by the NSCN. However, in the interest of promoting the peace process, the NSCN representatives agreed that the above activities would be prevented.[10]

The cease-fire with both factions was limited to the territorial boundaries of the present State of Nagaland. The attempt by the NSCN(IM) group to extend it to "all the Naga inhabited area" was rejected by the government of India on the following grounds:

In a federal structure, the Union Government is required to consult the State Governments, and at the time of the first agreement with the NSCN(I/M), such consultation has taken place only with the Government of Nagaland. . . . The term 'Naga areas' is vague and has not even been defined. NSCN's repeated references to the Naga areas have given a feeling of unrest and apprehension in the minds of the other State Governments, as indicative of your claim for Greater Nagaland directly or indirectly. While agreeing with the cease-fire between the Govt. of India and the NSCN as two entities, it has never been the intention of the Govt. of India that it should be interpreted by NSCN(I/M) as a step directly or indirectly towards recognition of any claim to Greater Nagaland. The intention was only to maintain peace with the NSCN as an Organisation, and to extend the area of peace in the North East.

Yet, the Govt. of India stands by its commitment to the cease-fire agreement with the NSCN(I/M) as an entity with a view to furthering the cause of peace. The Govt. of India would consider extension of cease-fire with the NSCN(I/M) to other areas in the North East subject to the condition that NSCN(I/M) accepts and agrees to issue a statement that extension of cease-fire to other areas will not be interpreted by them as a step towards recognition of their claim to Greater Nagaland.

As mentioned above, extension of cease-fire to other areas would require consultation with the concerned State Governments. The Govt. of India agrees to hold this consultation process in an agreed time-frame.[11]

Then, also in 2001, the government of India issued a statement to the effect that the cease-fire would be extended to all Naga-inhabited areas in the northeast. This was received with trepidation by the Manipur State government and was interpreted as the central Indian government's agreeing to the NSCN demands for a 'Greater Nagaland.' A series of violent riots in Manipur resulted in the hasty removal of the offending phrase.[12] The Cease Fire Monitoring Committee's jurisdiction is limited only to Nagaland State. There are designated camps for the NSCN(IM) and NSCN(K), but the factions have nevertheless allegedly extended their camps in Naga areas in Manipur,[13] Arunachal Pradesh, and North Cachar Hills district of Assam. Extortion, violent clashes between the two NSCN factions, and the killing of civilians have continued in these areas as well as within Nagaland.[14]

By 2010 Nagaland had a putatively democratically elected State government, which was a coalition between regional and national parties and separate parallel governments that are run by three Naga factions. Both the NSCN factions call their parallel governments the People's Republic of Nagalim, while the NNC's body calls itself the Federal Government of Nagaland, or FGN. English-language newspapers in Nagaland provide daily reports on the intra-factional fighting, as well as publishing rejoinders issued by factions and appeals by civilians to stop the extortion and killings.

The power structures of the elected government have been weak from the very inception of the State of Nagaland. As Baud and Van Schendel (1997: 228) note, "The position of the regional elite weakens because it is exposed as an agent of the state rather than a protector of local rights and concerns." Nagaland State before its inauguration was governed by an interim body of 'tribal representatives' comprising councilors from the dominant Ao, Angami, and Sema (now Sumi) communities who were members of the Naga People's Convention and were not supportive of sovereignty. The first government was formed by these representatives. The first Legislative Assembly elections in 1964 were contested by two parties but won by the party considered closer to the central government of India. However, internal divisions among the Naga, that is, between the nationalists (who were known as the 'undergrounds'), and those who were 'overground' and trying to run the Nagaland State, over the issue of sovereignty were also augmented by suspicion that the former had been 'bought' by the government of India. The increase in armed 'insurgency' during the mid-1960s to the late 1970s resulted in the imposition of President's Rule in Nagaland, that is, the suspension of the State Legislative Assembly. In the past thirty years the national political parties, such as the Indian Congress, have found a foothold in the State. Most Naga politicians (including the chief minister of the State in 2011) have at one point or another been members of the Nagaland Congress Party. The State politicians have made alliances even with the so-called Hindu national parties, such as the Bharatiya Janata Party, when it was the ruling party in India.

The Quest for Sovereignty

How the Naga national movement has reached this juncture has been a long, winding process. Sifting through the literature on Naga politics written by both Naga and non-Naga writers is like opening a Pandora's box—or perhaps a can of worms. The literature is full of details of various rounds of negotiations, the signing of accords, and programs.[15] Most such accords have succeeded only in dividing the Naga, creating suspicion, and causing the assassination of moderate Naga by their radical comrades. Since the early years of Indian Independence in 1947, alleged Indian high-handedness in political negotiations and the forceful suppression of the Naga movement have simply fueled Naga demands for sovereignty. There is some truth in the claim that the alienation of the Naga peoples is directly related to blunders committed first by the India Committee and then by brutal army action by the Indian government to quell the Naga armed uprising.[16]

At present, and despite some autonomy secured in 1963 through the creation of the State of Nagaland within India, many Naga are divided over the issue of full independence and sovereignty. My impression is that most Naga believe that full sovereignty (i.e., independence) is ultimately the only answer. But for many also the long decades of factional strife, intimidation, and extortion by the Naga 'nationalists,' all of which have continued despite the cease-fire agreement, does not portend a bright future for an independent Nagaland. The present atmosphere is such that very few are able to express critical opinions openly. Those who do are immediately threatened for having put themselves before the greater Naga cause.

As an indication of this, the NNC/FGN's Yehzabo (constitution) declares that "a Naga who undertook oath of allegiance to the Indian Constitution clearly betray[s] Naga nation" and "cannot serve the interest of Nagaland." It asserts that it is the Naga people who occupy Nagaland and that India cannot resolve the conflict through the creation of an administrative entity with no basis in history. It further cautions that whoever attempts "to subvert the authority of the FGN and NNC shall be judged according to the National Resolution passed on 27 April, 1955 at Lakhuti."[17]

By contrast, in 2000 a pamphlet appeared entitled "Bedrock of Naga Society," produced by the Nagaland Pradesh Congress Committee and written by S. C. Jamir (2000), a former chief minister of Nagaland. The pamphlet criticized the demand for Naga sovereignty and challenged the assumption that Naga existed as an independent nation before the British annexed parts of their territory. It began with the following statement: "The 16-Point Agreement of 1960 came about when the Naga were going through the worst of times. But it was also one of the best things to have happened to the Naga people because it led to the birth of Statehood—on whose firm foundation our society is built. In a larger form of things, due to the Agreement, for the first time, the world recognised the territory of the Naga as Nagaland." The pamphlet was vehemently denounced in Nagaland by the political parties and the nationalist factions for distorting historical facts and as an attempt to divide the Naga (Baruah 2005: 111–12). The protestors staged public burnings of the pamphlet. The Naga Students Federation office in Kohima displays a framed burned copy of the pamphlet to denounce the "divisive politics" of Jamir (Lotha 2008: 55). One of the bureaucrats who allegedly coauthored the document has been threatened by the NSCN(IM) group. The publication came at a time when peace negotiations between NSCN(IM) and the Indian government were taking place. It is alleged that, in 2004, Jamir was sent out of the State to become governor of Goa in order to allow for smoother peace talks.

Such was the controversy that by the time of the 2008 general elections in Nagaland the pamphlet had been withdrawn by the Congress Committee. However, the pamphlet touched on two sensitive issues at the heart of the present Naga movement: sovereignty and the unification of all Naga-inhabited areas—that is to say, an independent Greater Nagaland. The precise area covered by greater Nagaland, or Nagalim, as it is now called by NSCN(IM), is quite vague. Contradicting their earlier position in the pamphlet, the Nagaland Congress Party included the demand for Greater Nagaland in its 2008 election manifesto. The present coalition government of the State of Nagaland, known as the Democratic Alliance of Nagaland, has also taken on the agenda of Greater Nagaland.[18]

The present quest in the Naga movement for sovereignty and the formation of Nagalim or Greater Nagaland clearly invokes a narrative not only of an imagined community but one based on continual reconstructions of history. Van Schendel (2005a: 4) notes that "dominant historical narratives may sacralize borderlands and make them pawns in the 'performance' of sovereignty. Borderlanders may develop counter-narratives (e.g. irredentist ones) in which the historical significance of the border that separates them is minimized. In other words, borderlands are often battlefields of historiography, of the politics of selective remembering and forgetting." Despite the many internal differences, there is broad agreement among the various strands of Naga nationalism that Naga sovereignty and unification should be based on the following points:

1. The Naga were always independent and were a nation before the British annexed part of their territory.
2. The Naga are one people but divided into many groups that have similar cultural traits. Naga have common ancestors and arrived at their present habitat after migrating from the north and/or from the east (Burma). Ptolemy is quoted as the oldest source mentioning hill tribes living on the northeastern fringes of Assam.
3. The Naga are Christian and speakers of Tibeto-Burman languages.

4. As far back as 1929 Naga had submitted a memorandum to the Simon Commission declaring their intention to be independent. This was signed by educated Christian Naga, mostly from the Angami community, who worked for the British administration as clerks and interpreters.

Invoking an 'Ethnie'

These claims are far from uncontroversial. The argument that Naga are one people, a nation, and were always independent before the British annexed part of their territory may be regarded as part of the process of constructing an 'ethnie' (Smith 1984, [1994] 1998: 709). As is often the case in such situations, the term 'Naga' has no known or agreed origin.[19] Conjectural suggestions abound: that the name was derived from the Sanskrit *nāg* meaning 'mountain,' or *nangā*, the Hindi/Sanskrit for 'naked,' or from the Kachari *nok*, meaning 'a warrior,' or from Burmese *nā kā* meaning 'those with pierced ears.'[20] The Naga themselves never had a common term for the different communities that occupied the hilly tracts. Some of these communities had different terms for themselves from those used by their neighbors. The term 'Naga' itself was used by outsiders, especially the British, when they came in contact with hill communities during the surveys for tea plantations in Assam from the 1830s onward. The Naga were divided into *pakka* (real) and *kachcha* (raw, half-baked) by the British during their first contact with the hill communities. The pakka Naga resided in the northern areas and "went naked," whereas the kachcha lived in the southern areas and wore a "short black hobbled kilt" (Hutton 1965: 16). The oldest documents that mention contact with the hill communities living on the east of Assam are the twelfth-century chronicles, or Burunjia, of the Ahom rulers (Barpujari 1992). The hill communities were named after their villages or the dominant village in the cluster and further divided into Bori (tame) and Abori (untamed), depending on the distance from the Assam plains and their relationship with the Assamese.[21] The Ahoms were Tai people who moved westward, passing areas inhabited by the hill communities now known as Konyak, Tangsa, and Nocte. The legends and folklore of these hill communities also provide an oral account of such contact. Ptolemy's mention of hill tribes in the area (150 CE) is taken as further confirmation of early Naga presence (Shimray 2005; Sanyü 1996; Iralu 2000).

Currently the name Naga is used as a suffix after the individual name of the group, for example, Ao Naga, Phom Naga, Konyak Naga, which asserts both the individual identity of the group and their collective ethnic identity. What constitutes the collective identity of the entity Naga is based on certain institutional similarities and on material culture (Lotha 2008). But some groups sharing similar cultural traits do not identify with the Naga nationalist movement. Depending on the benefits of exclusion and inclusion and the coercive tactics used by the Naga nationalist groups, some groups identify themselves as Naga and others do not (see also Longkumer 2010).

The legends reinforce this sense of diversity counterbalanced by common identity. Some of the central and southern Naga, for example, the Angami, Lotha, Sema, Chakesang, and Rengma, share a common legend of origin; their ancestor, Koza, is said to have come from the south, settling at Kezakenoma, with the community then dispersing in various directions from Chiteba, where an old pear tree is said to mark the site of dispersal (Joshi 2012; Lotha 2008). On the other hand, the Ao, Sangtam, Yimchungrü, Phom, Chang, and Khiamniungan of north and northwest Nagaland believe that they migrated from the east. The Ao and Sangtam, in addition, also have the same myth of origin, which claims that their ancestors emerged from the six sacred stones at Longtrok. Recent excavations at the place have indeed revealed ancient settlement patterns and artifacts belonging probably to the Neolithic period.[22] A common theme in the various tales of migration is of emergence from the mouth of a cave or an opening in the earth. Here it is interesting to note that we have oral genealogical evidence from the recent past of people having a common origin but within a few generations developing some linguistic, ritual, and material cultural diversity. If such diversity could arise from a common origin so swiftly within living memory, it certainly could have happened less recently, as indicated in the older legends of origin of certain Naga groups.

A common feature in some legends is that ancestors of Naga peoples as well as those of the plains people were brothers. A number of folktales illustrate the cunning of the plains people. The Tangkhul of Manipur trace the origins of the Meitei and Tangkhul as well as other Naga groups (in Nagaland) to a pair of brothers who migrated from the east (Myanmar). The younger brother settled on the fertile plains, while the elder brother went to the hills to avoid heat and mosquitoes. The descendants of the elder brother thus spread northward, becoming the ancestors of all the Naga communities, and those of the younger brother became ancestors of the plains-dwelling Meitei people (Horam 1975: 25–26). This view of all the varied Naga communities coming from a single direction suits the nation-building aspirations of the NSCN(IM) group and is quoted frequently in the writings on Naga nationalism by Tangkhul scholars (see Horam 1975, 1988; Vashum 2000; Shimray 2005). This is in contrast to the early colonial writings. Hodson (1911: 8–9) mentions that there are three different legends of migration among the Tangkhul, and one of them points to Naga, Kuki, and Meitei having a common ancestor who had three sons. Other myths of origin and migration that have become popular in recent Naga writings point toward a possible migration of some groups from the north (i.e., from China). Thus the website of the Unrepresented Nations and Peoples Organisation (UNPO) claims that "the Naga are [a] racially and ethnically distinct people. Today there are 16 major and 20 minor tribes with a total population of a little over 3 million. About 95% of the Naga are Christian. The Naga people originally came from Mongolia, migrating to Nagalim in the 10th century B.C."[23]

Any scholarly writing that is seen as a challenge to the rhetoric of unity based on an oral history of migration is rejected by most Naga decision makers. For example, a book by Purtongzuk Longchar (2002), an Ao historian, which deviated from the Ao Naga myth of origin and dispersal from the Longtrok site near Chungliyimti village, was not accepted by the Ao council even though the writer had based his conclusions on oral narratives collected from different Ao villages. Longchar was eventually forced by the Ao Council to apologize publicly and withdraw his book.

Diversity is further evident in the plethora of languages and dialects in use among Naga. The official language of the proposed Nagalim is English, as is already the case in the present Nagaland State, in recognition of the many Tibeto-Burman languages and dialects spoken by Naga. The other, more extensive lingua franca spoken by Naga in Nagaland is Nagamese, derived from Assamese, an Indo-Aryan rather than Tibeto-Burman language, whereas in Manipur the Naga lingua franca is Meitei or Meiteilon, the Tibeto-Burman language of the Vaishnav Manipuri/Meitei population. In the past few years concerns have been voiced by public intellectuals regarding the preference for Nagamese over English as the language of conversation among people belonging to different tribes, and of Nagamese over Naga languages in urban families. The objection is essentially political because Nagamese is seen as an extension of Indian hegemony by virtue of its basis in Assamese and Hindi. On the other hand, T. Muivah of NSCN(IM), recognizing the popularity of Nagamese in Nagaland, has begun to address his meetings in Nagaland in both English and Nagamese.

Naga see themselves as distinct from the rest of India, while recognizing the internal complexity of their identity as a people. Some Naga scholars (Sanyü 1996; Lotha 2008) identify unifying traits, such as the erstwhile practice of cloistering or *genna*,[24] status-gaining 'feasts of merit,' an egalitarian social system based on age sets, clans, and the past tradition of headhunting. Some of these features are in fact common not only to Naga groups but also to a number of neighboring communities within northeast India as well as those farther afield in Southeast Asia (Kirsch 1973; Woodward 1989; Lehman 1989; Blackburn 2007). At a micro level some Naga communities have dissociated themselves from their earlier colonial classification, in some instances coalescing different groups into one unit. The group classified by the colonialists as Eastern Angami thus declared themselves a separate tribe from other Angami in the 1960s. They took on the name Chakesang, comprising Chakro, Kheza, and Sangtam. (Sangtams have since left the union, but the group name of Chakesang continues to be used by the other two.) Three groups, Zeme, Liangmei, and Rongmei, came together in the 1970s to form the Zeliangrong 'tribe' under the influence of Gaidinliu, the charismatic Heraka leader. The group labeled as the 'naked' Rengma in colonial writings are now a separate group called Pochuri, distinct from the rest of the Rengma grouping. The Tikhirs, who are claimed as one of their clans by the Yimchungrü, have been striving for separate group status since the 1990s.[25]

The difficulty in discerning the boundaries of Naga groups extends to overlaps in material culture and language. Moreover it is difficult to demarcate physically Naga territory from that of the neighboring groups who live in mixed villages at the boundaries of the Naga nation or Nagalim as proposed by the NSCN(IM). The situation regarding the proposed Assam-Nagalim borderlands is no different from that of the Indo-Myanmar border (Goswami 2007, 2008). Where the Naga area ends and non-Naga area begins is a question that cannot be easily answered. There are overlaps between neighboring communities. We can agree with Van Schendel (2005a: 9) that "borders not only join what is different but also divide what is similar." Naga nationalists claim that Naga communities are spread over an area of 120,000 square kilometers (map 7.1). The UNPO website describes Nagalim as

> situated between China, India and Burma. Nagalim occupies a compact area of 120,000 km² of the Patakai range between the longitude 93° east and 97° east, and in between the latitude 22.5° north and 28° north which lies at the trijunction of China, India and Burma. The part of Nagaland ruled by India consists of territory which today is administered by four different administrative units, the states of Assam, Arunachal Pradesh, Manipur and Nagalim.
>
> The eastern part of Nagalim, ruled by Myanmar (roughly 100,000 km²) has been placed under two administrative units, those of the Kachin state and of Saganing [Sagaing] division.[26]

Religious Reinforcement

A key part of the rhetoric of contemporary pan-Naga identity focuses on the dominant religion of (mainly Baptist) Christianity.[27] Christianity is seen as the unifying force that has brought together Naga from different groups in an evangelistic mission. The Christian character of independent Nagaland was first put forward by the NNC, although the Constitution of the Naga Federal Government gave equal rights to the animist Naga. The present NSCN(IM) leadership emphasizes Christianity in their motto "Nagaland for Christ." When Nagalim was inducted as a member of UNPO, the leaders presented the president of the organization with a cloth inscribed with this motto. Thuingaleng Muivah, the leader of NSCN(IM), has been quoted as saying that his is an evangelistic mission,[28] a statement that has been criticized by some church leaders as having a 'jihadi' connotation. Though almost 90 percent of Naga are Christian, not all of them follow Baptist Christianity. Since the 1950s other denominations have made their way into Nagaland; Catholics and various Revival churches, such as Pentecostals, Seventh Day Adventists, and Jehovah's Witnesses, have churches in several towns and villages, especially in the southern Naga area.[29] The 10 percent of the non-Christian Naga follow animism. A large percentage of Zeme Naga who live in Peren district of Nagaland and the North Cachar Hills district of Assam are followers of Heraka, a charismatic cult begun by Gaidinliu in the 1930s.[30] This has brought the Zeme into confrontation with the NSCN(IM), who are keen for them to convert to Baptist

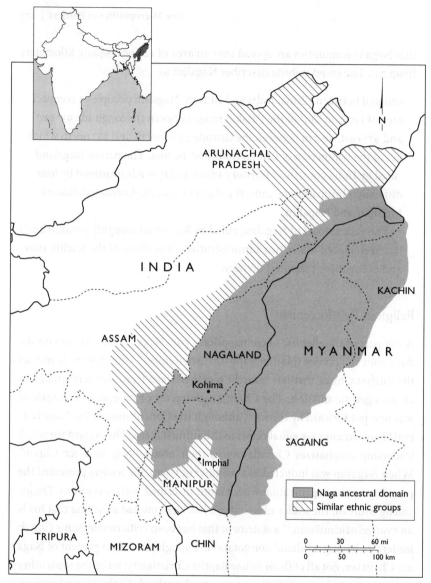

MAP 7.1. Nagaland and area claimed by Naga nationalists as part of Nagalim or Greater Nagaland and based on a map available at www.nagalim.nl (accessed 12 September 2012).

Christianity.[31] Across the border in Myanmar, NSCN has been instrumental in the Christian conversions among Myanmarese Naga (Jacobs et al. 1990). The Christian discourse is such that Vashum (2000: 99–100), writing on the Naga national movement, states that NSCN's split into two factions in 1993 was linked to the inability of the then vice chairman of NSCN, Sagwan Sankai Khaplang, to follow the strict discipline of the Christian life and give up the use of alcohol and narcotics.

Much earlier the issue of religious differences became a feature, though not the only one, in Naga attempts to gain recognition and of colonial responses to such claims. In 1927 the Conservative government in Britain appointed an Indian Statutory Commission, popularly known as the Simon Commission after its chairman, to decide the political future of India. The Simon Commission was boycotted by the Indian National Congress, the Muslim League, and other organizations as no Indians were included. However, the Naga, who were not a part of the mainland Indian freedom movement, sent a letter to the Simon Commission in 1929 expressing their wish to be recognized as separate from the rest of India and sought an independent status at the end of the British rule. The argument they put forward was similar to that expressed separately by Robert Reid, who was the governor of Assam, and also by J. H. Hutton, an anthropologist and former district commissioner of the Naga Hills, that the Naga peoples were different in their customs, religion, and governance from the mainland and plains Indians (see Elwin 1961).

The 1929 memorandum by the Naga to the Simon Commission declaring their intention to be independent is put forward as an argument in support of the claim that the decision to be independent had been made by Naga even before India itself became independent in 1947. The memorandum cited fear of Hindu hegemony and 'forcible' conversion, singling out their concern that they would be discriminated against both by Hindus and by Muslims over their diet of pork and beef. The memorandum was signed by a group of educated Christian Naga, mostly from the Angami community, who worked for the British administration as clerks and interpreters. Among them were two pastors. At that point in Naga history only some 13 percent of Naga were Christian (Baptist).[32] About two thousand Naga men had already experienced World War I when they were sent as part of the French Labor Corps in 1917 (see Balfour in Hutton 1921: xvi–vii). A group of Naga who returned from France, together with those who were employed as government officers and interpreters (Dobashi), formed a society called the Naga Club in 1919. Major conversions to Christianity took place after the 1944 Battle of Kohima in which Allied forces, with the help of the Naga, halted the Japanese incursion. Many Naga also converted to Christianity in the mid-1970s, when a massive Christian revival wave swept through Nagaland coinciding with brutal Indian army action against Naga nationalists and civilians (Luen 2009).

The Origins of the Nationalist Movement

After the battle of Kohima in 1945, Charles Pawsey, then deputy commissioner for the Naga Hills, formed the Naga Hills District Tribal Council to bring the Naga together for the postwar reconstruction program (Ghosh 1982; Singh [1972] 1995; Hutton 1945). Within a year it acquired political overtones and in January 1946 changed its name to the Naga National Council (NNC; Singh [1972] 1995: 89). Allegations and counterallegations have been made against each other by the Naga since the inception of the NNC. The diaries of Mildred Archer, who accompanied her husband, W. G. Archer (posted as additional deputy commissioner), for six months to the Naga Hills in 1947, reveal the developments that led to the demands for independence by the Naga National Club.[33] The Ao and Lotha members of the NNC were initially not in favor of independence as proposed by the Angami, fearing Angami hegemony in an independent nation. In 1947 the NNC members agreed to autonomous status within Assam with a ten-year interim government at the behest of the Ao members, who stated their apprehension regarding the viability of an independent Naga nation with no source of revenue and no armed forces to control the unadministered territories, where 'headhunting' raids were the norm.[34] Finally, in this stalemate, and at the suggestion of the deputy commissioner for Naga Hills that the Naga should present a united front to the All India Constituent Assembly, the NNC then turned in support of the Angami demand for independence to take effect after ten years of being an interim part of Assam. "This interim government was to have full powers in respect of taxation, legislation, the executive and the judiciary, while a guardian power was to give it a financial subvention, and to place some armed force at the Nagas' disposal."[35] However, the subcommittee on the constitution of Naga Hills of the All India Constituent Assembly (which included only one Naga among its seven members), rejected this proposal of a Naga interim government.

After much deliberation between the NNC leadership and the last British-appointed governor of Assam, Sir Akbar Hydari, a nine-point accord for an interim government for ten years was signed in June 1947. The Naga communities represented by the signatories were the Western Angami, Eastern Angami, Kuki, Kacha Naga (Zeme), Rengma, Sema, Lotha, Ao, Sangtam, and Chang. These communities were within the British administrative boundaries. The sixth point of the accord on boundaries stated, "Boundaries—That present administrative divisions should be modified so as (1) to bring back into the Naga Hills District all the forests transferred to the Sibsagar and Nowgong Districts in the past, and (2) to bring under one unified administrative unit as far as possible all Naga. All the areas so included would be within the scope of the present proposed agreement. No areas should be transferred out of the Naga Hills without the consent of the Naga Council" (Yonuo 1974: 174). The ninth point of the accord regarding the future of Naga at the end of the ten-year period was, however, disputed by the members of the Naga Council. It was seen as ambiguous and was interpreted by some members as equal to their gaining independence from India at the end of the ten-year arrangement. The ninth point stated, "Period of Agreement—The Governor of Assam as the Agent of the Government of the Indian Union will have a special responsibility for a period of 10 years to ensure the observance of the agreement, at the end of this period the Naga Council will be asked whether they require the above agreement to be extended for a further period or a new agreement regarding the future of Naga people arrived at" (174–75).

Angami opinion was divided on this. The Kohima group of Angami agreed to go with the accord, whereas the Khonoma group demanded full independence at the end of ten years and rejected it. A delegation led by Zapu Phizo, an Angami from Khonoma village, went to Delhi to put forward their case to Gandhi as well as talk to Jinnah. However, within a few days of signing the accord the Delhi Committee visiting Assam allegedly brushed aside the agreement, suggesting that Naga should send a delegation to Delhi. The Naga were then left with no clear idea as to the future of Naga Hills. In the meeting of the NNC that followed just before Indian Independence, the Naga once again disagreed over the issue of their own independence. On 14 August 1947 Zapu Phizo, leading the breakaway section, declared Naga independence. However, the telegrams he sent to the newspapers, the United Nations, and the Indian government were intercepted at the Kohima post office, and thus never reached their destination.[36] The Naga declaration of independence therefore went unnoticed by the press. Meanwhile in Kohima, the non-Naga (Mizo) wife of the British government employee Kevichusa (who was then assistant to the deputy commissioner as well as a leading Angami from Khonoma village) hoisted a black Angami Lohe cloth as the independent Naga national flag in the compound of their house, situated below Kohima village, near Mission Compound. This angered the Kohima Angami, who did not support independence and who also interpreted the hoisting of a Khonoma cloth as an extension of Khonoma village's hegemony over Kohima territory. Charles Pawsey, then district commissioner for Naga Hills, had the cloth taken down to disperse the angry mob.[37]

In 1950 Zapu Phizo was made the leader of the NNC. In 1951 the NNC conducted a plebiscite on the issue of Naga independence. It is alleged that 99 percent of Naga supported the ballot with their thumbprint. However, the plebiscite did not include eastern Naga (currently Tuensang, Longleng, and Mon districts). The issue of the colonial division of Naga into administered and unadministered has continued to be relevant to the present political divisions. The Eastern Naga Peoples Organization and Eastern Naga Students Organization strive to gain an equal footing in decisions regarding the political future of Naga by emphasizing that they have always been independent, even of British colonial rule. During the army action by the Indian government in the 1950s, the eastern groups of Naga along the Indo-Burma border had also joined the fight against the Indian army, and this is put forward as a counterargument to those who question the inclusion of all Naga in the plebiscite by NNC (Iralu 2000: 78). Naga training camps were also established among the eastern Naga villages.[38]

By the mid-1950s there was once again a division between moderates and radicals among the NNC, which eventually resulted in the resignation of high-profile members such as T. Sakhrie and Dr. Imkongliba, who were against the use of violence for gaining independence. Both were assassinated by Phizo loyalists for their moderate views in support of autonomy within the Indian Union. In 1960, after protracted army action,[39] a peace accord was signed between the Naga People's Council and the Indian government which became the basis for the formation of Nagaland State in 1963. The State comprises the erstwhile Naga Hills and Tuensang Area, which includes parts of unadministered territory that lay between the Naga Hills district and Burma during British rule.

The Thirteenth Amendment Act of the Constitution of India (1962) gives more autonomy to the Naga through special safeguards, which cannot be withdrawn unless the Legislative Assembly of Nagaland decides to pass a resolution against them. Thus the Nagaland State Assembly retains authority over (1) religious and social practices of the Naga; (2) Naga customary law and procedure; (3) the administration of civil and criminal justice involving decisions according to Naga customary law; and (4) the ownership and transfer of land and its natural resources (Singh [1972] 1995: 101). With these constitutional safeguards, the Naga are in a privileged position, as they have private ownership of the land, forest, and water resources, unlike in the rest of India, where water and forest resources are owned by the government.

However, the formation of the State yet again divided the Naga into those who supported the State and those who wanted independence and unification of all Naga areas.[40] By then the Tangkhul, Mao, and the non-Naga Kuki of Manipur had joined the Naga national movement.[41] The Nagaland State boundaries did not include these areas. The new State also did not get the land that had been transferred to Assam during colonial rule. Thus two kinds of government came into existence in Nagaland: the elected State government and the parallel 'underground' government, called the Federal Government of Nagaland, with their leader, Phizo, living in exile in London. The protracted conflict continued. Two more accords were signed: first, the Peace Accord in 1964, and then the Shillong Accord in 1975, which was formulated during the Emergency Rule in India. Both these accords created further divisions. Phizo's silence on the Shillong Accord, in which Naga signatories had agreed to abide by the Indian Constitution, resulted in the formation of a breakaway group in 1980 called the National Socialist Council of Nagaland, which was led by Thuingaleng Muivah, Isak Chishi Swu, and Sagwan Sangkai Khaplang. In 1993 NSCN itself split into two groups following an allegation by Khaplang that Thuingaleng Muivah and Isak Chishi Swu were making a deal with the Indian government. (As noted earlier, Khaplang's personal commitment, or lack of it, to Christian standards of behavior was also said to be an issue.)

Differences in ideology as well as 'tribal' group identities have played a part in these fissiparous nationalist politics. The NNC at its inception was dominated by the Angami and Ao members. The first split in Zapu Phizo's NNC saw the separation of the Sema group, which eventually surrendered in the 1964 Peace Accord. In the 1980s the formation of NSCN passed on the leadership of the nationalist movement to Naga who mainly hailed from communities that live outside the boundaries of the present State of Nagaland.

At present Naga are divided along party lines, with each party adhering to different aims with regard to the political status of Nagaland. The moderates believe in more autonomy within the Union of India, which the present State of Nagaland currently enjoys, while the extremists favor secession and

FIGURE 7.2. Memorial to A. Z. (Zapu) Phizo (1904–90), Kohima, Nagaland, 2011. It reads, "Father of the Nation, here rests the man who gave his all for the nation." On the plinth is a quotation in Tenyidie and English: "Our land is our heritage, to none shall it be surrendered: as whetstone our opponents sharpen us." Photograph courtesy of V. Joshi.

independence. At present there are at least five different State-level political parties (some of which are linked to the national parties of India, such as the Indian National Congress, Bharatiya Janata Party, and Rashtriya Janata Dal) and three main underground organizations. It is common local knowledge that during State elections the NSCN factions back candidates from rival groups. NSCN(K) is said to side with the Congress Party, whereas NSCN(IM) has its sympathy with the present State government of Nagaland formed by the coalition Democratic Alliance of Nagaland.

The Demand for Redrawing Borders

In recent years the demand for redrawing the borders of Nagaland has become a key issue for Naga nationalists with differing views on where the borders should be. As mentioned earlier, at the inception of the Naga movement in the 1940s the demand for the unification of Naga areas did not specifically include the hill districts of Manipur and the villages across the border in Burma (Myanmar). However, over the past two decades the inclusion of these areas has become central to the demands for an independent Greater

Nagaland or Nagalim. In the internal politics of the nationalist movement this demand for a Greater Nagaland has further consequences that go beyond independence claims and fuel the regional politics of leadership, 'tribal' hegemony, and the continued political stalemate with the government of India. Paradoxically this nonresolution of the conflict prolongs and so benefits the fundraising efforts of insurgent groups and delays the intractable problem of which of the rival groups would assume power in an independent Nagaland.

The divisions are evident in the visualization of Nagalim or Greater Nagaland by each of these groups. The NSCN(IM) in its negotiations with the Indian government is demanding the consolidation and unification of all Naga areas within the Indian union. These comprise two districts of Arunachal Pradesh (Tirap and Changlang), three districts of Assam (North Cachar Hills, Karbi Anglong, and parts of Sibsagar, Jorhat, Tinsukhia, and Dibrugarh, including the oil fields), and four districts of Manipur (Ukhrul, Senapati, Chandel, Tamenlong—almost two-thirds of the present State). The northern Naga areas in Myanmar are not part of the demand made to the Indian government but are shown on the Nagalim map of NSCN(IM). The Naga villages in the northern Myanmar portion are controlled by the NSCN(K) faction, but the southern Naga regions in Myanmar include some Tangkhul villages. The inclusion of the Assam oil fields, especially the region explored by the Indian Oil and Natural Gas Commission (ONGC) and found to have substantial reserves, is aimed at capturing the revenues from their exploitation. In the popular imagination in Nagaland it is claimed that Nagalim has immense natural resources of crude oil, natural gas, coal, and semiprecious stones. No evidence has yet been offered to support these claims. However, crude oil exploration by ONGC in the Champang region of the Lotha Naga-dominated district of Wokha was stalled after NSCN(IM) cadres threatened ONGC employees in 1994.

The Khaplang-led NSCN, on the other hand, demands a Greater Nagaland that does not include Manipur, especially the Tangkhul-dominated Ukhrul district, Tangkhul being rejected for fear that they might take control of an independent Nagaland. Naga within the State of Nagaland support integration with the areas in Assam, but in what can only be called 'kitchen talk' or private views, they are not in favor of integration with other Naga areas, especially Tangkhul. Most are now weary of the constant demands made by the two NSCN groups. They complain that the leaders are both from outside Nagaland State: Muivah is a Tangkhul, and Khaplang is a Heimi from Myanmar.[42] Since Zapu Phizo's death in 1990, the NNC has dwindled in scope, overshadowed by the larger and better organized NSCN groups. As mentioned earlier, in Nagaland State–level politics the demand for Greater Nagaland has been included in the manifesto of both the Nagaland Congress Party and the present coalition government, the Democratic Alliance of Nagaland.

The three major factions have parallel governments, each with its own constitution and departments of finance, publicity and information, foreign affairs, and defense. So far negotiations have taken place only between the Indian government and the NSCN(IM) group. The latter wants all negotiations to be unconditional and outside the scope of the Indian Constitution. To this effect it has proposed a 'federal' system in which Nagalim will have its own way of governance (apparently not based on democratically elected government), with a separate flag, its own army to maintain law and order, but using the Indian currency and allowing the Indian government to be responsible for foreign affairs and defense.[43] However, the Indian government insists on reaching a solution within the framework of the Indian national constitution. The result is a persisting stalemate. The Indian Constitution has provisions for changing the boundaries of constituent States of the federation, allowing decrease or increase of a State's area as long as both houses of Parliament agree on the issue and India's overall territorial integrity is maintained, as stated in the Preamble to the Indian Constitution.

The NSCN(IM) maintains that it is the sole representative of the Naga peoples. On this basis it had previously rejected any demands for reconciliation with other factions. It has publicly denounced the Khaplang-led group as being antistate and accepting funds from the Indian Intelligence Agency. Similar allegations have been made against the NSCN(IM) leadership by the Khaplang group.

In 1992 NSCN expelled the Kuki of Manipur from the Naga nationalist movement, simultaneously issuing a notice to all Kuki residing in southern Nagaland to leave. Prominent Kuki civilians were killed. In 2006 the NSCN(K) group issued a quit notice to the Tangkhul Naga living in Nagaland. Such quit notices inadvertently ignore the social realities of the present State of Nagaland. For while there are divisions along tribal lines, in urban centers there are intertribal marriages between Kuki and Naga and between Naga of Nagaland and Manipur. Some Nagaland State bureaucrats hail from other northeastern States as well from 'mainland' India.

Since the cease-fire agreement of 1997 the NSCN(IM) has increased its support base in Nagaland and, against the cease-fire rules, has continued to recruit cadres and collect taxes from all households, businesses, and government departments. About 25 percent of the salary of a government employee is claimed in taxes by the factions. Taxes are also collected from people living in the areas claimed as part of Nagalim. Ransom demands from both Naga and non-Naga (in common parlance, 'nonlocals') have continued. There have been claims that countries sympathetic to the Naga nationalists have supplied them with funds as well as arms, even from across the Indian Ocean (Shimray 2005). The flow of money from the center to the northeastern States provides a constant supply and inadvertently finances the insurgency (Nag 2008). Ramesh (2005) illustrates the total dependence of the northeastern state economy on the central funds (see also Mishra, this volume). Eighty percent of the Nagaland State budget is financed by the central government. On top of that, funds for development are constantly given to the States. If not claimed, these funds do not lapse but go back to the corpus, unlike the yearly funds available to other Indian States. The present 'Look East' policy of the Indian government has meant that northeastern States are now in an even better position to demand funds for infrastructural development, which may indirectly go into funding the insurgency (compare Farrelly, chapter 8, this volume). This is in contrast to the beginnings of the nationalist movement, which was based on what Elwin (1961: 75) saw as the "simplistic" claim by Naga that they could sustain themselves through hard work by tilling their land, depending on a subsistence economy.

WHAT SUSTAINS the Naga nationalist movement is the colonial experience, conversion to Christianity, and education of a people projected as a Christian population distinct from their Hindu, Muslim, and Buddhist neighbors. This is combined with the living memory and memorialization of sustained brutal army action by India during the 1950s and 1970s and the deployment of the controversial Armed Forces Special Powers Act since the 1960s, which has not been repealed.[44] In addition the geographical advantage of the mountainous landscape, forest cover, proximity to the international border, and guerrilla war tactics have helped the nationalist movement in the past to evade the Indian armed forces after the ambushing of army convoys and during the army's 'combing' operations against the insurgents.

The Naga secessionist movement has continually raised issues of ethnicity and identity. Paradoxically, while seeking overall Naga autonomy, the movement has experienced rivalry and competition among its members, which have been expressed through, and so have reinforced, internal boundaries and distinctions of 'tribe.'

Underlying the fragmented quest for sovereignty is the relationship between the plains and valley dwellers and the hill dwellers. The legends relate the separation of brothers and the cunning of the plains people, which is reflected in the demand for independence by a section of Naga. Coexisting with this is what Van Schendel calls selective remembering and forgetting, a distortion of history into modern time. As Van Schendel (2002a) has emphasized, the northeastern borderlands of India sit at the confluence of three world areas: South Asia, Central Asia, and Southeast Asia. The communities that live in this 'Zomia' region all fall in the margins of their main area.

On the one hand, as Van Schendel (2005a: 12) points out, states presume that "the borderland is considered to be 'known.'" At the same time, "state elites of the region have displayed a pervasive concern with sovereignty, security and territorial control. They have kept the borderland fairly inaccessible and this also has dissuaded academics from studying it" (12), thus creating "geographies of ignorance" (Van Schendel 2002a). This view is clearly applicable to the Naga area. The Inner Line Permit that was introduced in 1853 by the British colonial administration was retained, initially, at the behest of the Naga leaders (Yonuo 1974: 174). Its continued use in the northeastern States, especially Nagaland, is a direct consequence of the political situation. It dissuades Indian academics from entering an area out of fear for their security. It creates suspicion of 'Indian' researchers as being covertly engaged in intelligence gathering.[45] Any research on the politics of the Naga movement that is not explicitly in favor of nationalist demands may also be viewed with suspicion by the vigilantes of the movement (such as the Naga Students Federation).

Thus alongside the paradox that borders are at the center of state definition and reality, there is a second paradox that applies to situations such as that of Nagaland. In the struggle over borders between competing secessionists on one hand and the federal state on the other, prolonged nonresolution of the conflict may benefit both sets of combatants. Thus the regional factions can defer the seemingly impossible task of converting severe political division into a unity government, and the Nagaland State government can continue to reap economic benefits in the form of subsidies from the central government (a considerable percentage of which is siphoned off to the rebel movements as a 'tax'). At the same time the federal state of India exploits this political uncertainty by continuing to deploy armed forces along its national borders, and so preserves a buffer zone between itself and other nation-states.

NOTES TO CHAPTER 7

1. An Inner Line Permit is needed by Indians to enter some of the northeast Indian States. Foreigners require a Restricted Area Permit (RAP), which is obtained through the Indian Consulates. Beginning in January 2011 the RAP requirement for foreigners (except from Afghanistan, China, Bangladesh, and Pakistan) for Nagaland was lifted provisionally for one year to improve tourism in the State. However, ILP regulations for Indian citizens continued. Ministry of Home Affairs, Government of India, FAQs on Protected Area Permit and RAP, accessed 19 October 2011, mha.nic.in.

2. After the Indian Sepoy Mutiny of 1857–58, the East India Company was dissolved and the administration of India passed to the British government. The capital of British India was moved from Calcutta to Delhi.

3. Land was given to tea plantations under the Waste Land Grant Rule of 1838. The conditions were liberal, and revenue rates were very low (Gangopadhyay 1990: 134; compare Baruah 2005: 92). Guha writes that by 1901 tea gardens occupied nearly one fourth of the total settled area in Assam (Guha 1991: 191; cf. Baruah 2005: 93). Carving out tea plantations restricted the movement of the local population to forest paths. See also Joshi (Patel) (1994).

4. In 1989 Burma was renamed Myanmar by the new military regime.

5. "Northeast India and Its Transnational Neighbourhood," Asian Borderlands Research Networks Conference, Indian Institute of Technology, Guwahati, January 2008.

6. It has to be remarked that even today non-Naga do genuinely find conditions difficult in Nagaland.

7. Reconciliation among warring factions and between the families of victims of underground violence and the underground is now seen as essential for any meaningful unity among the Naga. In October 2008 a football match was organized by the Naga Baptist Church Council between a united team of Naga nationalists and Naga civil society members. In November 2006 a large gathering of all the clans from Merhema ward (*khel*) of Khonoma village and the representatives of civil society organizations was held to commemorate the fiftieth anniversary of T. Sakhrie's death. The occasion also highlighted the reconciliation between the clans of Sakhrie and Phizo (Dolie). An elder of Dolie clan apologized to the Sakhrie clan for the assassination. Sakhrie was the right-hand man of Phizo until his fallout and was brutally tortured and killed (Nibedon [1978] 1983: 70–72). He was labeled a traitor on account of his moderate views supporting autonomy within the Indian Union. See also the website of Unrepresented

Nations and Peoples Organization, www.unpo.org; Sanjoy Hazarika, "Let the Bloodshed End," www.hardnewsmedia.com, accessed 10 November 2008.

8. NSCN(IM) is the National Socialist Council of Nagaland/Nagalim—Isak Chishi Swu and Thuingaleng Muiwah (at Camp Hebron, Diphupar, Dimapur); NSCN(K) is National Socialist Council of Nagaland–Sagwan Sankai Khaplang; NSCN(Unification) comprises members of the IM and K factions who came together to form a united National Socialist Council of Nagaland (at Camp Khehoi, Dimapur).

9. I happened to be at the venue of two such meetings in January 2008, a government guesthouse in Kohima, where I stayed with a colleague. On our arrival we were stopped by the armed guards outside the gates of the guesthouse to allow the "important meeting" to finish and to wait until after the "parties" had left. Later we were told in hushed tones that the meeting was between the representative of the NSCN(K) group and the Ceasefire Monitoring Committee's chairperson. A couple of days later we chanced upon a large gathering for another "important" meeting. On this occasion the semicircular space in front of the guesthouse building was surrounded by vehicles with red lights on top, pilot jeeps, and several men sporting AK-47 assault rifles. It turned out to be the Ceasefire Monitoring Committee's High Command meeting with the NSCN(IM) group representative, 'Brigadier' Phunthing, and some of his comrades. The High Command comprised the army chief of staff, the director general of Nagaland Police, the Nagaland home commissioner, the Assam Rifles chief, and the chairperson of Ceasefire Monitoring Committee. These meetings had urgency as President's Rule (the suspension of the State Legislative Assembly) had been declared in Nagaland on 4 January 2008, after a no-confidence motion was passed in the Nagaland Legislative Assembly against the ruling coalition just months before the Assembly elections were due to be held. Meetings were to assure that no untoward activity should take place in the run-up to the elections. The Nagaland public was visibly relieved at the imposition of President's Rule as there had been rampant extortion of money in the preceding months by the 'national workers' (as the insurgent outfits call themselves).

10. From *Fault Lines: Writings on Conflict and Resolution*, South Asia Intelligence Review, South Asia Terrorism Portal, retrieved 20 January 2009, www.satp.org.

11. *Fault Lines*, South Asia Intelligence Review. See K. Padmabhaiah, "Territorial Cease Fire with NSCN IM," South Asia Terrorism Portal, accessed 19 January 2009, www.satp.org.

12. R. Koijam, "Naga Ceasefire and Manipur," The Hindu, 13 July 2001, accessed 19 January 2009, www.hinduonnet.com.

13. See news report on NSCN(IM) camp in Shirui, Ukhrul district, Manipur and the clash in January 2009 with Assam Rifles: "AR-/NSCN-IM Gun Battle in Ukhrul," *Morung Express News*, 12.08.2009, accessed 23 May 2013, www.tangkhul.tangkhul.com.

14. In February 2009 the subdivisional officer and his two staff members from Kasom Khullum in Ukhrul district were abducted and then killed by the NSCN(IM)

cadres. After public protest at these "senseless brutal" killings, the NSCN(IM) from Camp Hebron in Nagaland issued a statement that they had set up a "fact-finding committee and exemplary punishment will be meted out to the cadres who have committed the crime." See "A New Definition of Barbaric Killing Invites 48 hrs Gen Strike" and "NSCN(IM), Naga Organisations, Others Decry Slaying of SDO and Two Employees," *The Sangai Express*, 17.02.2009, e-pao.net/GP.asp?src=1. .180209.feb09; 'Finally, IM Hands over Hopeson Ningshen to CBI, Remanded to 15 days," *The Sangai Express*, 29.05.2009, e-pao.net; "Naga Army not to Spare any Cadre Involved in SDO Killing," *Hueiyen News Service*, 21.02.2009, e-pao.net/GP.asp?src=20.220209.feb09; "Manipur Protests Continue," *Assam Tribune*, 26.02.2006, www.assamtribune.com; 'SDO Murder: People Want NSCN (I-M) Cadres to be Taken to Task," *Times of India News*, articles.timesofindia.timesofindia.com; all accessed 23 May 2013.

15. For examples, see Nuh and Lasuh 2002; Vashum 2000; Horam 1975, 1988; Shimray 2005; Iralu 2000; Rammuny 1988; Nibedon (1978) 1983, 1981; Luithui and Haskar 1984; Rustomji 1983; Sema 1986; Singh (1972) 1995; Maxwell 1979; IWGIA 1986; Yonuo 1974; West 1999.

16. See Luithui and Haksar 1984; Iralu 2000; Chasie 1999. The brutality of the Indian army is also the subject of Naga literature, for example, *These Hills Called Home: Stories from a War Zone* by Temsula Ao (2000). She was awarded the Padam Shri, a civilian honor, in 2007 by the government of India.

17. Shevohü Keyho, "Let Our People be Aware," *Morungexpres*, accessed 23 May 2013, www.nagalim.nl/news/00001139.htm. See also Nuh and Lasuh 2002.

18. In early 2010 the Democratic Alliance of Nagaland government again addressed the demand for a return to Nagaland of the areas in Assam that had been transferred during the colonial period. However, when the central government asked for submission of the original maps, these could not be found, so the issue remains unresolved.

19. I have sometimes been asked in Nagaland whether I knew the first usage and origin of the term 'Naga' as I am a researcher. Such queries are not unusual: Burling (2007) writes that he was often asked about the origin of the Garo by the Garo themselves.

20. See Hutton 1921; Elwin 1961; Ao 1970.

21. See also Hutton 1965: 16. The labels for objects collected for European museums from these hill communities in the nineteenth century show a similar trend. While some objects are identified as Ao, Angami, or Rengma, others bear Assamese village names for hill communities such as Bordoria or Namsangia. See Joshi 2008a.

22. Excavations were carried out around Longtrok in 2006–8 by a team of Naga archaeologists led by Tiatoshi Jamir (Jamir and Vasa 2008).

23. See 'Nagalim' www.unpo.org (retrieved 10 December 2008). See also Burling (2007) for similar views on the migration of the Garo peoples of Meghalaya.

24. The term *genna* derives from the Angami word *kenyü*, denoting prohibition on movement and cloistering. It has now become part of the Naga lingua franca.

25. This insistence on a separate identity is also related to positive discrimination in

terms of reservation in government jobs for backward tribes that Nagaland State follows as part of national policy in India for the integration of the 'backward' communities into the mainstream. The Naga themselves are part of the Scheduled Tribe classification and benefit from reservations in government jobs and educational institutions.

26. See "Nagalim," accessed 10 November 2008, www.unpo.org. Nagalim became a member of UNPO in 1993 after concerted efforts by NSCN(IM).

27. For a comparable case from Myanmar, see Gravers 2007; Sakhong 2007.

28. See also Shimray 2005: 158–60.

29. See Joshi (2007, 2008b, 2012) on Christianity among the Angami Naga.

30. See Kabui 2004; Yonuo 1974; Longkumer 2007.

31. A similar line of argument is dominant among the Mizo, who have marginalized the non-Christian communities in Mizoram since the signing of the Mizo Accord with the Indian government and the subsequent formation of Mizoram state in 1987 (Das 2007: 40–42).

32. Eaton (1997: 246) provides comparative statistics from the census of India for the percentage of Naga that were Christian in 1881–1990.

33. See Mildred Archer, "Journey to Nagaland, An account of six months spent in the Naga Hills in 1947," typescript, Pitt Rivers Museum Archives, University of Oxford. They are also available online in the Naga database at www.alanmacfarlane.com. Of course, such writings are selective, subjective, and open to debate for the accuracy of their historical content.

34. See M. Archer diaries, 1947, and W. G. Archer papers and tour diaries, 1946–48, Naga database, www.alanmacfarlane.com.

35. Mildred Archer, "Journey to Nagaland."

36. The postmaster passed the telegrams to Charles Pawsey, the last British district commissioner of Naga Hills, who in turn decided not to send them. W. G. Archer diaries 1946–48, Naga database, www.alanmacfarlane.com.

37. W. G. Archer manuscript notes and diaries 1946–48, Naga database; Sentsi 2004. Anungla Aier and Easterine Iralu helped me confirm that the Angami cloth that was hoisted was in fact black-colored *Lohe*, which is common to both Kohima and Khonoma Angami villages.

38. See Lintner (1990) for his account of travel through these camps to reach the Kachin Independence Army in Burma.

39. According to reports by human rights groups (IWGIA and NPMHR), in the 1950s and 1960s ruthless actions, including the burning of villages, were undertaken by the Indian army. Monuments to those who died fighting the army are prominent among the Angami. In Jotsoma village the martyrs' graveyard overlooks the village. In the same village, in a *thehuba* (public meeting place), is a lasting inscription on a flat rock that informs readers that Jotsoma village was burned by the Indian army in 1956. Such monuments are a constant reminder to the younger generation of the ongoing war

for Naga freedom. The brutality of the Indian army is also the subject of recent Naga literature (see Ao 2000).

40. Sema 1986: 59–72; Singh (1972) 1995: 98; Rustomji 1983: 69; West 1999: 38–39; Gundevia 1975; Horam 1975, 1988. Elwin (1961: 670) writes that when demand for Nagaland State was accepted by the Indian government, the pastors in the radical NNC group used the biblical text of Exodus 32 to denounce the move and draw parallels between those who accepted the creation of Nagaland State and the worshiping of the Golden Calf by the Israelites while Moses was away in the mountains.

41. The Tangkhul considered themselves exploited and marginalized by the Meitei of Manipur. However, Baruah (2005: 115), writes that this claim is contentious, as Manipuri kings have had Tangkhul generals and since the formation of Manipur State there have been two Tangkhul chief ministers.

42. Khaplang has sometimes been erroneously identified as a Konyak, a group that is similar to the Heimi.

43. See "India's Hidden Wars in the North East Nagas Float Federal Model," UNPO, 06.10.2006, accessed 2 February 2009, www.unpo.org.

44. See Figures 7.1 and 7.2. Names of nationalist martyrs on public memorial stones and epitaphs are a constant reminder of the nationalist movement.

45. A Naga researcher working in the Northeast in a community different from his own was under suspicion by both the Indian army and the Naga nationalists (Longkumer 2009).

Nodes of Control in a South(east) Asian Borderland

Asia: South by Southeast

It is a peculiar feature of contemporary scholarship on the regions that we habitually know as 'South Asia' and 'Southeast Asia' that there is little traffic between their respective epistemic cohorts. In the past, scholarship that vaulted across the imaginary dividing lines between the Indian subcontinent and the countries of mainland Southeast Asia was relatively common. As recently as Hall (1955), Coedès (1968), and Mabbett (1977), scholars developed a deep understanding of the connections between the two regions. Knowledge about South Asia, particularly with respect to the texts and languages of ancient civilizations, was once considered almost essential for scholars of Southeast Asia. Moreover writing on India, both during and after the British colonial period, naturally carried much scholarly interest to Burma and beyond.[1] Anglophone scholars in particular were engrossed by the ongoing histories of contact and conflict that distinguished so much of the common experience in those parts of Asia subject to British colonial ambitions. Shared linguistic, historical, cultural, and religious experiences once guaranteed that from Colombo to Kengtung and from Pegu to Bodhgaya there was strong appreciation of shared inheritances. Such appreciation has not dissolved entirely, but in an era when contemporary geostrategic and political concerns generally take precedence, the cross-fertilization of scholarship between South Asia and Southeast Asia has been on the wane. There is instead a persistent tendency to focus on contemporary cohesions and divisions without sufficient attention to historical connections and fault lines.

This tendency challenges today's scholars who hope to find new ways of exploring the borderlands of South Asia and adjacent regions. For instance, among many scholars it is commonly taken for granted that the Association of Southeast Asian Nations (ASEAN) and the South Asian Association for Regional Cooperation (SAARC) delineate distinctive regional, indeed *associational* territories that are mutually exclusive and coherent to the extent that they *should be* relevant to current political, economic, and cultural concerns. But are such accidents of history and strategy really the best we can do? We could, with good reason, start by asking what such regions look like when seen from their respective borderlands. What is the difference between SAARC and ASEAN, or between India and Burma, when we try to straddle their shared frontier? Simply taking aim at the arbitrariness of these modern groupings— and their curious logics of geostrategic togetherness—is not the point. Attacking the construction, cohesion, and consistency of these groupings is a largely fruitless exercise.

Rather scholars should analyze what the presuppositions and implications of particular geopolitical groupings are, and why they become accepted.[2] What is most striking about such regional groupings is precisely that the arbitrariness of dominant international relations logics is often uncritically replicated in academic discussions and structures. Conversations, for instance, between scholars focused on Bangladesh and Thailand are far less common than the relative global positions of those two countries would suggest. South Asia and Southeast Asia can appear to be very far apart. So can we imagine studies of the South(east) Asian borderlands that bring knowledge about both South Asia and Southeast Asia into a full and useful conversation?

These are not entirely original questions; they draw their inspiration from the contrarian framework introduced by the Dutch social scientist Willem van Schendel's (2002a) article on regional knowledge in Asia. That article is now famous for its provocative effort to challenge area studies knowledge by suggesting that between South and Southeast Asia, and East and Central Asia, there may be an alternative region: the area Van Schendel dubs 'Zomia.' For Van Schendel, Zomia seemed to have "missed out" when the scramble for scholarly prestige occurred during the nineteenth and twentieth centuries. Few if any academic programs were built on explicitly 'Zomian' foundations, and, as a result, the highland 'peripheral' areas that fall within Zomia failed to garner significant attention. An anthropologist of highland Southeast Asia, Jean Michaud (2010: 199), insists that "what is commendable about Willem van Schendel's idea is his call to academics to pay more attention to areas and societies dwelling on the periphery of bona fide states and civilizations, which are otherwise neglected as merely peripheral, exotic, or backward."

What Van Schendel could not have foreseen is that within a decade of publishing his contrarian, even heretical ideas about area studies in Asia, Zomia has gone on to generate a new subgenre of debate about spatial control, cultural politics, and social change in the areas that fall *between* the standard blocks of area studies. The resulting debate has seriously stretched the original terms of his Zomia argument. And the apotheosis of Zomia came with the publication in 2009 of James C. Scott's award-winning *The Art of Not Being Governed: An Anarchist History of Upland Southeast Asia*.[3] This chapter is not the appropriate place to review Scott's evidence and argument in full, but needless to say he has produced a book of such scope and ambition that it is difficult to imagine the argument that I make here without some reference to his intervention and its aftermath.[4] In one of the most impressive surveys of the Zomia topic, the anthropologist Hjorleifur Jonsson (2010: 196) suggests, with a cadence that is very relevant to my argument here, that "to [a] considerable extent, area scholars are confined to one side of the border(s) and not interested in hinterland regions."

Why are scholarly specialists of South Asia or Southeast Asia so apparently disinclined to take on the challenge of studying borderland and interstitial areas or to cross regional borders completely? There are some obvious explanations that are a consequence of the ways junior scholars are funded and supported, which are then reinforced by the difficulty of learning new languages and the reluctance of senior scholars, conscious of rising standards of cultural competence and faced with numerous administrative burdens and little time for scholarship, to carve out new areas of research. Shifting a research focus from, say, Bangkok or Kolkata to an adjacent borderland area happens often enough, but it is far rarer for scholars to leap entirely away from their existing comfort zones. Justifying such flagrant border hopping can prove difficult, especially when crossing the prevailing regional boundaries of scholarship almost always opens up new vulnerabilities for those who come to a field with fresh ideas but perhaps without the requisite area studies training.

Why does this matter? Zomia is central to the interstitial zone where China and India rub together. Anyone intrigued by the future of *any* Asian region must be interested by this geographic reality. Moreover anyone intrigued about the future of war, counterinsurgency, postconflict development, narcotics production, people trafficking, migration, disease, or capitalism will also want to understand Zomia. It sits at a strategic crossroads of what we currently understand, and yet the way the world is carved up hides it from view. That is the original, polemical point Van Schendel wanted to make about the area studies knowledge we take for granted.

An Argument about Nodes of Control

My justification for introducing this chapter in terms of the politics of area studies knowledge is that the rest of my argument, drawing on Van Schendel's and Scott's contributions about Zomia, is really part of a conversation about borders—in our minds and on our maps. Is it acceptable for a self-styled Southeast Asianist (trained in the languages, politics, and histories of that region) to write with any authority on South Asian topics? I sometimes wonder whether the very foundations of what we think we know in the social sciences is so heavily conditioned by an inheritance of concepts and language and politics that it remains difficult to realistically stretch the boundaries of the existing regions. In response, this chapter is an attempt to explore places that fall, somewhat inconveniently, between dominant areas of study—in this case the borderlands between South Asia and Southeast Asia.

The focus in this chapter is two such places: Myitkyina, in northern Burma, and Miao, in northeast India. The local lingua franca of both towns is a Tibeto-Burman language incomprehensible to Burmese speakers or to speakers of Assamese. These are also places heavily connected to government projects and to the nation-state-making endeavors of postcolonial Asia. Both towns have experienced the arrival of outsiders from other parts of Burma and India, respectively, and the cultural influences that new settlers, media, and education have dispersed. These two towns are also tied up with a number of local antigovernment movements, some of which still maintain insurgent (or potentially insurgent) militias. The paradox of control and conflict defines government efforts to manage potentially rebellious parts of Zomia.

My argument is that in the borderlands where South and Southeast Asia meet, governments have sought to impose what I call 'nodes of control' to manage the potential challenges to their rule in these somewhat unruly areas.

One of the key points made by both Van Schendel and Scott is that in Zomia's interstitial borderlands it is the governments from lowland centers that have often struggled to exert full control. For hundreds of years there have been regular rebellions and revolts that have challenged such rulers. Scott goes so far as to assert that "state-repelling" cultures have evolved to make the peoples of Zomia less "legible" to the governments that hope to govern them. It is such ambitions of government—in conceptual, historical, and contemporary terms—that are the focus of this chapter.

In considering these arguments we should begin in Southeast Asia 'proper' with Thongchai Winichakul's influential discussion of Thailand during the colonial period. He introduced the memorable and widely cited point that a regime of mapping shaped the "geo-body" of Thailand. According to Winichakul (1994: 129), in the triumph of this new logic the "ultimate loser was the indigenous knowledge of political space. Modern geography displaced it, and the regime of mapping became hegemonic." In the Thai case, the new logic of modern geography brought a number of disparate political realms into a single national embrace called *chaat thai*, the Thai nation.[5] For Winichakul it served to make heterogeneous peoples 'Thai' and allocate them a supposedly cohesive, even uniform national identity. Even more significantly for Winichakul's argument, this historical process gave the Thais a map. The distinctive shape of Thailand was made possible only when technologies of mapping helped to define rigid national borders. And as other technologies of government in the region improved, the obvious ambition of central authorities (and not just the Thais) was to consolidate and demarcate their spatial control (as described also by Sturgeon 1997). This spatial control legitimized and maximized other opportunities for remaining in authority.

This 'geo-body' (of Thailand or of other states) displaced a system of spatial organization that predated these colonial impositions in the region. Indeed one of the points that Scott reinforces in *The Art of Not Being Governed* is that before the imposition of fixed borders many peoples of the region were free to wander, anarchically if you will, in ways that defy today's firm classifications. This idealized, borderless, transnational realm of interchange and conversation can be positioned as the antithesis of the border-mapping, fence-building world that Winichakul described so well. Sturgeon (2004, 2005) shows how the Akha traverse the borderlands between Thailand and China; she presents them as effective and flexible negotiators of border arrangements, undermining the supposed rigidity of some national frontiers. Van Schendel (2002a), as noted earlier, made a key intervention in this discussion when he pointed out that South, Central, East, and Southeast Asia, as imagined by scholars, are historical and geopolitical accidents. He then outlined a huge area between the 'areas' of scholarly attention and, more important, in between the various nation-state political systems: this area he named Zomia.

In Van Schendel's argument, it is countries like India, Bangladesh, Burma, Thailand, and China that have historically struggled, and struggle even today, to rule the parts of their territory that fall inside Zomia. He posits that people in Zomia, whether they live in Thailand, India, or Bangladesh, perhaps have (or had) more in common *with each other* than with their lowland neighbors. Thus the Lahu (in southern China) and the Naga (in northeast India) share commonalities that they may not share with their immediate lowland (i.e., Han Chinese and Assamese) neighbors. Such matters have now been explored by Scott (2007, 2009), who, for the better part of the past decade, has devoted his attention to explaining the historical details of Zomia. He actually focuses on something more specific: a region he calls "eastern Zomia." The two towns, Myitkyina and Miao, that I discuss in later portions of this chapter are right at the heart of this region.

The eastern Zomia region, for Scott, is a "state-repelling" space where the locals went to great lengths to minimize their legibility by government. He calls the locals—the Jinghpaw, Lisu, and others—"barbarians by choice." With titles like "Why Civilizations Don't Climb Hills" and "Zomia: The Last Great Enclosure Movement and Stateless Peoples in Southeast Asia" Scott toured the world lecturing on his conceptualization of this region and its history. Scott's (2009) monograph makes it clear that for him, at an uncertain moment, perhaps sixty years ago, the dynamics of Zomia were fundamentally changed by the implementation of new systems of government, with new technologies of control, mobility, and power projection.

Until that moment Scott is relatively comfortable with an exposition that prioritizes the state-evading practices and the state-repelling spaces of a Zomia that are beyond the easy control of governments. His anarchist resistance paradigm may warm the hearts of those who assume that a pattern of resistance to the nation-state is at the heart of local lifestyles and cultures. His enunciation of state-resisting forms in eastern Zomia is clarified by what he describes as the "last great enclosure" (Scott 2009: 11). In his neat explanation this enclosure, mimicking what happened in Europe in centuries past, was a "truly imperial project, made possible only by distance-demolishing technologies (all-weather roads, bridges, railroads, airplanes, modern weapons, telegraph, telephone, and now modern information technologies including global positioning systems)." Scott goes on to argue that this project "is so novel and its dynamics so different that my analysis here makes no further sense in Southeast Asia for the period after, say, 1950" (11). He emphasizes that the history of state evasion he describes appears to end in almost all areas with "modern conceptions of national sovereignty and the resource needs of mature capitalism" (11).

What has happened to Zomia—the land in between South, East, Southeast, and Central Asia—over the past sixty years? I suggest that it has been slowly and quite surely displaced: in all the places that matter to them, the governments are in charge. Zomia has been pushed out by what I prefer to describe as relatively muscular nodes of government authority. These sites of control, centered on towns like Myitkyina and Miao, have made for a stark change of circumstances in areas where a long-standing (i.e., Zomian) political and cultural orientation has been rapidly changed by the needs of governments that feel compelled to implement, and then maintain, new forms of spatial governance. Zomia may, as such, remain in isolated places far from sites of economic, strategic, and other significance. Wherever the government decides it does not need a presence—in unimportant hamlets, by the sides of little creeks, on lonely mountain passes—it can afford to withdraw. In the political systems of contemporary Zomia there is a process of hardening the state in places that matter and withdrawing from places that do not.

It follows that nodes of control have been established in the parts of the South(east) Asian borderlands that are most important for the survival of the central government systems. This is not a unique situation, but in the context of both the Zomia model and our understanding of area studies knowledge it is significant. A borderless realm that serves to disrupt nation-state frontiers and goes beyond area studies boundary-making projects is an intuitively attractive idea. What I hope to show, however, is that Zomia's borderless ideal has now been managed by nodes of control and that area studies in Asia must reconcile the difference in knowledge that follows scholarly inquiry in different but adjacent parts of the world. The idea of nodes of control helps to describe power projection and maintenance in the 'geo-body' in a way not captured by Winichakul's analysis. These nodes of control are the middle ground (as hinted at in works on borderlands like Jonsson 2006 and Giersch 2006). And as strategic nodes—along the various borders, the major transport and commercial routes, and the main population centers—they serve as sites where the governments have firmly fortified themselves. Thus Scott was right that something changed with the arrival of modern state-making technologies; the area he calls eastern Zomia is no longer what it was. But he misjudges contemporary Zomia if he imagines that Zomian forms of action and thinking are no longer found and no longer relevant today. State control is still incomplete and fragile in some border areas, even while it is relatively secure at the nodes.

Nodes of Contest and Control

Myitkyina and Miao sit on opposite sides of a national border close to the edge of what is usually considered South Asia, where the mountains and forests blur into Southeast Asia and into the southernmost areas of Tibetan settlement. At this far frontier, in areas where South Asia knowledge starts to fray, there is a long border between India and Burma. That border—which snakes 1,463 kilometers from Arunachal Pradesh in the north down past Nagaland, Manipur, and Mizoram—not only separates the Republic of India and the Union of Myanmar but serves to delineate two regions of area studies concern. One side of the border, on Indian soil, has tended to be the preserve of South Asia expertise, while the other side is supposedly captured by Southeast Asian studies.

MYITKYINA

Happily, from the Myanmar government's point of view, Myitkyina is one place where Zomia (and all it arguably represented) has been thoroughly displaced. With a name that means 'near the big river' (on the eastern flank of the town the Ayeyarwady River is almost one kilometer wide), Myitkyina is a bustling entrepôt of approximately 150,000 people and the capital of the Kachin State. It is also the heart of the Myanmar government campaign to control northern Burma in a context where decades-old cease-fire agreements are being tested by robust government efforts to finally remove potential armed opposition from Burma's soil.[6] Those efforts led, on 9 June 2011, to the breakdown of the seventeen-year cease-fire between the Kachin Independence Army and the Myanmar government. Once fighting recommenced, Myitkyina became ever more important as a node of control. It is ringed by large Myanmar military bases, with the headquarters of light infantry battalions, regional air force units, and special operations elements all nested in the immediate vicinity. Myitkyina is, in that sense, a garrison town. However, one quarter, Shatapru, was dominated under the cease-fire by the local Jinghpaw elite,[7] including many Kachin Independence Army commanders and their families. Elsewhere in Myitkyina the population is more or less evenly split between Jinghpaw and ethnic Burmese, with smaller numbers of residents hailing originally from China and India. Because it is a node of control, government efforts to entice ethnic Burmese migrants continue, and in many parts of Myitkyina the Burmese are now in the majority; they continue to arrive in greater numbers than any other group (see map 8.1).

A series of northern commanders of the Myanmar Defense Force (*tatmadaw*) have increasingly controlled all of the important aspects of the town on behalf of the Myanmar state. Zomia, that historical region of rebellious sentiments, requires vigilance on the part of a Myanmar government that has sought to neutralize its most ferocious opponents, including some of the locals in the Myitkyina area. Throughout the period of cease-fire negotiations, which began in 1989, Myitkyina was a key site for making truces and agreeing to terms. In these dealings, the overarching authority of the northern commander stands in stark contrast to the lack of political power allowed any ethnic minority group, especially the populous and militarily competent Jinghpaw. In most cases, the Myanmar government succeeded in its efforts to discourage the resumption of armed conflict, but in 2011 the government provoked a confrontation, whether or not they intended to. The northern commander may have initially anticipated the Kachin would comprehensively avoid a new conflict. Instead they defended their territories against government incursions, precipitating ferocious offensives and counterattacks. Kachin Independence Army guerrilla units were dispatched to target strategic sites, including in Myitkyina.

During the years of cease-fire the Jinghpaw leadership and their Myanmar government counterparts could meet and do deals in Myitkyina. In Myitkyina the local ethnic armies (the Kachin Independence Army, the New Democratic Army–Kachin, and the Lasang Awng Wa Peace Group), their commercial partners, and intelligence networks all had a substantial presence, as did some companies from elsewhere in Burma closely associated with the Myanmar government. During those years business in northern Burma was explicitly bilateral, and everyone, no matter how much they disliked the government,

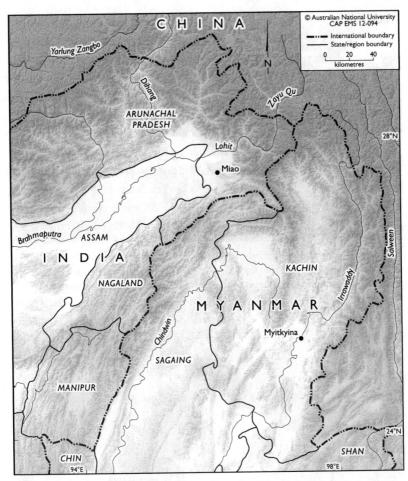

MAP 8.1. Kachin State within Burma. Original map by Australian National University, College of Asia and the Pacific, Education and Multimedia Services. Reproduced with permission.

was forced into a pattern of government-centric collaboration. This is one factor that continued to reinforce the negotiated nodular control that the Myanmar government claimed. The resumption of hostilities has reemphasized the need of the Myanmar authorities for the control of this node. Even, or especially, under conditions of civil war they do not claim authority to the same extent on every inch of their territory but have instead chosen to concentrate their interests and defenses. Based on my discussions with individuals who

FIGURE 8.1. Kachin Chinese tourists, who have come over the border into Burma to celebrate the pan-Kachin Manau festival in Myitkyina and are dressed in Kachin costume, pose with Myanmar Army soldiers, January 2011. Photograph courtesy of N. Farrelly.

FIGURE 8.2. Soldiers of the Myanmar Army's Northern Command guard the entrance to the Manau festival grounds in Myitkyina, January 2011. The banner reads (in both Jinghpaw and Burmese), "Kachin cultural Manau festival." Photograph courtesy of N. Farrelly.

are key players in this system, such collaboration ultimately requires that the government never takes too much. During the cease-fire, compromises flowed in both directions; those arrangements ended with the new civil war.

One of the explanations for such substantial compromise was that lucrative commercial interactions were premised on a degree of cooperation. The major jade mines at Hpakant, in the western part of the Kachin State not far from the border with India, were controlled by a set of interlocking Jinghpaw, Chinese, and Myanmar corporate interests, with oversight from the Myanmar government authorities. Under these circumstances a small number of local tycoons, called *Sutdu* in Jinghpaw, proved most adept at managing their competing loyalties and, in particular, their relationships with the Myanmar government authorities based in Myitkyina. Fortunes were built on the skillful management of logging, mining, agricultural, and transport businesses in a situation wherein collaboration helped to make all sides wealthy. The cease-fire between the Kachin Independence Army and the Myanmar government (agreed in 1993) was the linchpin for these activities. It is telling that in 2010, at a time when this cease-fire agreement looked like it might end, there were dozens of key meetings between Kachin Independence Army commanders, other senior members of Jinghpaw society, including Sutdu, and the Myanmar government leadership. Most of these meetings were held in Myitkyina, the node of control and site for negotiation.

Such ongoing collaboration also required that the government cannot be perceived to be weak, but such preference for dominance can clearly lead to war. In the node of control that was fortified at Myitkyina there was always a recipe for the 'state-repelling' Zomia of old to make a return. Weakness, particularly in a place like Myitkyina, would be fatal, metaphorically, for the Myanmar government. Even before the new civil war the average Myanmar government commander in northern Burma did not need to read *The Art of Not Being Governed* to appreciate the extent to which resistance is embedded in local societies, histories, and cultures. Very crudely, to arrive half-hearted in Myitkyina, without adequate backup or commitment, was always to tempt fate with Zomia's potentially rebellious future reincarnations. In the new conflict the Myanmar government is learning difficult lessons about Zomia and its capacity to test their military and political resolve. Hundreds if not thousands of Myanmar troops have already been killed, most in their efforts to venture far from their nodes of control in clashes in eastern Kachin State and northern Shan State since June 2011.[8] In response, in Myitkyina today there are no half-measures, and security is the only government priority. Nonetheless for the future there must be partners in peace to keep the cogs of business turning; Myitkyina would not survive if the Myanmar government was unwilling to make deals. Future deals will clarify the subtleties that make nodes of control governable.

MIAO

Compared to Myitkyina, the town of Miao is a much smaller government center. A main town in the 'disturbed' (i.e., insurgent) Changlang district of northeast India's Arunachal Pradesh, its population is only a few thousand. Miao is wedged between mountains and the Nao-Dihing River. The strategic location makes it a key site for ambitions that the Indian government is keen to reinforce at any opportunity. As part of Arunachal Pradesh, Miao is almost inevitably caught up in ongoing Sino-Indian border disputes, especially as played out in Tawang, a district of Tibetan culture and history claimed by China, at the other end of the State. It is the ambiguities and multiple allegiances that prevailed in the spaces between state centers that give substance both to Chinese claims and to those who oppose them.

In response to this Zomian history, and to the Chinese claims, the Indian government has sought to dominate and control Arunachal Pradesh. What is striking to any visitor to Miao is that the only people living there are those who have official permission, either through their 'tribal' affiliation and identity documents or, more often, through their government affiliation. Internal permits dictate who has an official right to cross into Miao. Such strict management of access means that the government has a particularly strong role in local society. There are a number of specific areas that are designated as 'colonies' for government employees. There is, for example, an Engineers' Colony and a Teachers' Colony. This system serves to structure the residential pattern of the town by occupational category. It also reinforces the preeminent role played by the government in the life of the town.

Why is Miao such an important node of control? First, as mentioned earlier, by emphasizing its connection to India the authorities hope to neutralize any claim that Arunachal Pradesh could become part of China. Second, and just as important, Miao is integral to an area of Zomia that has seen generations of antigovernment activity. Stretching way back to British colonial efforts to deter local rebellions and to more recent examples of insurgency from the United Liberation Front of Asom and various Naga resistance movements, it

FIGURE 8.3. An Indian government checkpoint on the road to Miao, in Changlang district, Arunachal Pradesh, 2008. Photograph courtesy of N. Farrelly.

has tended to be a flashpoint for conflict. Unsurprisingly this node hosts army, police, and intelligence functions. The Central Bureau of Investigation monitors who enters Miao, but the most high-profile security presence around the town is provided by the Central Reserve Police Force, which was established by the Central Reserve Police Force Act of 1949 and is organized into seventy battalions. The force is lightly armed, at least compared to the army, and is designed to provide support to local police in difficult or unduly dangerous situations. Some of the border districts of Arunachal Pradesh (such as Changlang) that are near Nagaland and have seen incursions from Naga insurgents fall into this category. As the Indian government has made it more difficult for insurgent groups to operate in Assam and in their traditional strongholds, some have sought to exploit the relative ease of movement provided by the mountains of Arunachal Pradesh.

At the same time the senior local civilian officials, such as the additional district commissioner and the extra district commissioner, all have substantial local clout and influence. Some of these officials hail from within Arunachal Pradesh. Others are Assamese or Bengali or from elsewhere in India. They still deal in thick paper files bound with red tape and are direct inheritors of many of the mechanical aspects of the colonial bureaucratic system. One further way that Miao's nodular character is confirmed is through the government-owned guesthouses. The most habitable of these official residences is the Circuit House provided by the Public Works Department. Circuit houses were established in India (and in Burma) during the British colonial period. They have always served as a base for traveling officials who require accommodation in far-flung outposts. They have been retained in the postindependence era, and many new ones have been built, to support the functions of the expanding bureaucracy.

In a context where there is little other economic activity it is the government, almost alone, that structures local practice. The presence of the army and the many other government agencies means that taxes paid elsewhere in India are redistributed to this distant corner (as described by Mishra, in chapter 6, this volume). High-quality roads, often maintained for the benefit of security agencies as much as for any local traffic, are a strong sign of the strategic implications of accessing nodes of control like Miao. When contrasted with Myitkyina, the investment that benefits Miao does not have the same commercial dimension, but it still serves the same basic function in terms of lubricating and reinforcing nodular control. Zomia, under these circumstances, starts to fade away, just as Scott suggests it has over the past sixty years. There may be particular times and places when a Zomian character briefly reemerges, but most of the time there is no such revival of resistance in Miao. Scott's assertions about efforts to repel governments and state-making projects with strategies of illegibility start to look quite different under these conditions. In fact lucrative relationships with the government, particularly with respect to government contracts and concessions, mean that it can be wise to cultivate connections and to endorse the structure of the Miao node of control.

Nodes of Control Today

These examples of Myitkyina and Miao clarify how nodes of control are maintained in the part of the South(east) Asian borderlands where the Myanmar and Indian governments make their claims. For those governments, taking charge of Zomia requires an awareness of the limitations of their own power. With so many other rebellious and potentially rebellious Zomian portions to take care of, the governments have sought to impose themselves as firmly as they can in the places that count.[9] This system of selective dominance is a key way that systems of quasi-colonial rule survive in the areas of the 'geo-bodies' that I discuss in this chapter.

In order to control anarchic Zomia, the full 'geo-body' need not be 'controlled.' Instead of asserting total control everywhere, the Myanmar and Indian governments have taken on roles as the nodular rulers of the key pressure points. For Zomia more generally—and here I am also thinking of certain areas of Thailand and Laos, Nepal and Bangladesh—it is these nodes of government control, some of which are very old, some of which are new, that are defended and maintained at any cost. From strategic but rickety bridges in obscure valleys to the airports and markets of the major towns, it is usually clear where a government sees its interests at stake. In areas where there is a lingering perception that local people detest the government, there is a possibility that without these muscular impositions the ambitions of the central state systems would collapse. Whether any categorically different local form of the state could rise in place of these systems is a point of hypothetical speculation. The system imposed by the Kachin Independence Army in its former cease-fire Special Region suggests that replicating the Myanmar government approach to strategic nodular control would also be their aim.[10] In frontier regions where wealth and power mix carelessly, with much frustration, there is perhaps no other way.

The response of local elites (such as the Kachin Independence Army and the ethnic elite in Miao) to the implementation of nodes of control is, it appears, a key reason why they survive. Even after the breakdown of the cease-fire in northern Burma there has been no aggressive Kachin effort to dislodge the Myanmar authorities from their Myitkyina node of control. There is an acceptance that such a direct confrontation would be imprudent, and so instead symbolic, lightning assaults are preferred. More generally many members of the local elites across these South(east) Asian borderlands have been the most keen (and most able) to explore opportunities for profit and prestige that come from aligning with governments. These alignments are not always robust, and there are many cases where local power-sharing arrangements have moved in and out of official favor. The advantage that members of the local elites often have is access to wealth and social capital that is beyond the scope of figures who do not share their local affiliations. In Arunachal Pradesh, for instance, the central government has sponsored the formation of elected local political elites to defend its own interests in the borderlands.

These comparatively wealthy men are drawn from a range of ethnic groups and can use their connections and influence to direct the largesse of the government to key constituencies.

The maintenance of such ethnic activities at these nodes in the borderlands provides some hope for those whose political aspirations lie with alternative government forms, such as an autonomous Kachin 'substate.' Nonetheless in the borderlands where they share a common border it is difficult to envisage a time when India or Myanmar would give up the lucrative and strategic interests that they have painstakingly defended at their nodes of control. Both governments hope to harvest greater shares of the spoils as better infrastructure combines with more open borders to create a new growth hub in these borderlands. Their local collaborators will, as this chapter has described, be playing their own roles at the margins of national control. It is they, ultimately, who have largely given up dreams of independence to allow the presence of the nodes of government control.

Knowledge of Zomia

It is clear that contemporary Zomia cannot be explained by state-repelling narratives alone. Nor can it be understood through a dialectic of hegemonies and counterhegemonies as sketched by Winichakul in his analysis of polity formation. This region can, however, be illuminated by a middle path that takes Van Schendel's Zomia as a starting point and the 'geo-body' ambition of Winichakul and finds some middle ground. It is in this middle ground that nodular control, exercised by the Myanmar and Indian governments, offers a way forward for the understanding of contemporary politics in northeast India and northern Burma. In this middle ground there is not merely control and authoritarian imposition. In fact the nodes of control that have evolved bring opportunities that are not available outside of the government structure.

Obviously the two nodes described in this chapter are different, and their differences have much to do with the political cultures from which they have evolved and from the scale at which they are implemented. Nonetheless, taken together, they offer a stark rebuttal to purely antistate interpretations of the ways that spatial control is exercised in these borderlands. Giving the appropriate weight to such nodes is arguably the only way that the contemporary social and political dynamics of the borderlands will be fully understood. Each of the different forms of nodes has evolved to serve the interests of its government sponsors and, while they retain favor, the local elites who rely on them for contingent patronage. Such contingency is understandable while these nodes are a strategic intervention in areas where the central governments naturally feel quite ill at ease. Government frustration with intractable political conflicts in these specific borderlands (whether in Assam or Nagaland or the Kachin or Shan States) has forced them to take an approach to local contexts that generally serves their purposes. These state efforts to minimize the chances of future insurrection have been managed through the nodes.

Some would see such resistance to these patterns of power and politics emerging from tradition (i.e., from Zomia). However, the situation that emerged after the collapse of the Kachin Independence Army cease-fire in 2011 suggests a different pattern. The resistance paradigm associated with Zomia now requires different interpretations of economic and political conditions. Any respatialization of these borderlands will be predicated on the accumulation of sufficient capital and resources by ethnic elites to challenge governments with their own proto-governmental forms (as also shown in Joshi's discussion of Nagaland, in chapter 7, this volume).

For now, the borders between India and Burma are in fact real and unreal, demarcated and unmarked, conflicted and uncontested. The borders that scholars determine matter in the study of various parts of Asia are of a similar form. Indeed we may sometimes find that there are *epistemological* nodes of control that have direct relevance to the ways that areas studies specialists govern the knowledge about their specialist areas.[11] There is the intriguing possibility that such nodes of control exist not only on our maps but also in our minds. This epistemic observation about Van Schendel's and Scott's Zomia could serve to make the ambiguous South(east) Asian borderlands worthy of study, argument, and reflection for generations to come.

NOTES TO CHAPTER 8

1. It remains somewhat awkward that there is lingering contention about the nomenclature of the country once known as Burma but now, in the eyes of its government and the United Nations, officially called the Union of Myanmar. In light of such ongoing contention my recent academic practice has been to reserve 'Myanmar' for contemporary (post-1989) references to the government and to retain 'Burma' for the country as a whole. This is one way of clarifying the enduring contest about Myanmar government claims to rule certain parts of the country, especially areas discussed in this chapter.

2. In fact in the parts of South Asia and Southeast Asia discussed in this chapter there are a number of other geopolitical groupings that also require close scrutiny. While some organizations, such as the Greater Mekong Subregion, include involvement from China, there are other groupings, like the Bay of Bengal Initiative for Multisectoral Technical and Economic Cooperation and the Mekong-Ganga Cooperation, which include members from both South Asia and Southeast Asia. It is perhaps relevant that both the latter two groupings have failed, in spanning South Asia and Southeast Asia, to develop the profile or status of ASEAN or SAARC.

3. The same critical impulse that has informed Van Schendel's and Scott's work is now driving new waves of discussion about their ideas. This is perhaps the first time since the publication of Edmund Leach's *Political Systems of Highland Burma* (1954) that the social, historical, and political dimensions of these borderlands between South, East, Southeast, and Central Asia have been a hot scholarly topic. To emphasize the thrust of this new discussion Jonsson (2010: 195) has offered a tough-minded analysis: "As van Schendel suggested, the construction of an area-knowledge runs the risk of creating its own unthinkables. *Zomia* as a field of study is open to various reifications. . . . A one-dimensional sense of the highland area will only replicate previous analytical problems of regional history making."

4. I am not alone in taking on the challenges of responding to Scott's and Van Schendel's work (see, e.g., Giersch 2010; Shneiderman 2010; Michaud 2009, 2010; Jonsson 2010; Lieberman 2010; Sadan 2010). Even some Austrian School economists have now taken up this issue (see, for intriguing examples, Stringham and Miles 2012; Powell and Nair 2010). My former Australian National University colleague Nicholas Tapp (2010), who built his anthropological/'Zomianist' reputation on the study of the Hmong in northern Thailand and southern China, calls *The Art of Not Being Governed* a "glorious romp." In another brief review Scott is attributed "a venerable anarchist perspective" (Clarence-Smith 2010: 185).

5. An etymological quirk is worth noting at this juncture. The Thai word *chaat* (nation) is derived from the South Asian *jati* (for 'species' or 'birth group'). In South Asian languages this commonly refers to caste communal units such as Rajputs, Yadavs, and so on, although it can also mean 'nation' (as it does in Bengali). In Thailand it most commonly means 'nation' and is also a homonym for 'birth' (i.e., incarnation). There are obviously countless such linguistic and cultural connections that tend to be overlooked by scholars habituated to one side or the other of the prevailing area studies boundaries.

6. In 2009 and 2010 the Myanmar government attempted to implement local Border Guard Force agreements in areas where cease-fire armies have continued to operate. While some ethnic armies (such as the New Democratic Army–Kachin) were convinced to become Border Guard Forces subordinate to Myanmar military command, others continued, at the time of writing, to assert their independence. The United

Wa State Army in the Shan State and the Kachin Independence Army were the most significant groups that resisted these new agreements.

7. There is no single or neat way of referring to the peoples who are often called Jinghpaw in Burma and Singpho in India. These are the dominant local populations in both Myitkyina and Miao. One option is to refer to them all as 'Kachin' (which is a Burmese term), but my preference is to use the locally relevant ethnonym whenever possible.

8. The number of combatants killed during the war that commenced on 9 June 2011 remains a matter of some dispute. Discussions of the number of dead are provided by a range of sources, including the Kachin News Group (2012) and Farrelly (2011, 2012). At the time of final revisions, mid-2012, there is no final tally of the dead and injured.

9. Some of those areas include the Shan and Chin States of Burma, not to mention Karen and Karenni areas, that have experienced decades of war. In India, of course, there are low-level conflicts in many parts of the country.

10. In the Kachin State, the former Special Region 2 is controlled by this insurgent army. Its 'capital,' a small border town called Laiza, is the closest the Kachin have to their own independent node of control. It is, however, so beholden to China for access, and to Chinese gamblers for much of its local economic activity, that it has a long way to go before it rivals government nodes like Myitkyina for status or power. After the collapse of the cease-fire it became a destination for Kachin refugees fleeing fighting elsewhere in northern Burma.

11. The concentration, for instance, of knowledge about particular regions in certain well-known institutions is perhaps part of this same story. A discussion of nodes of control, or whatever we want to call them, in the wider realm of area studies projects is one that I hope to return to at some later stage.

Histories of Belonging(s)

Narrating Territory, Possession, and
Dispossession at the India-Bangladesh Border

The date 26 June 2007 marked the fifteenth anniversary of the opening of the
Tin Bigha Corridor, a narrow strip of land running through Indian territory
that connects the Bangladeshi *chhitmahal* of Dahagram with mainland Bangladesh.[1] Dahagram is the largest of a series of chhitmahals, or enclaves—
literally pieces of India inside of Bangladesh and vice versa—scattered along
the northern part of the India-Bangladesh border.[2] These enclaves have
emerged as persistent problems in the relationship between India and East Pakistan and later Bangladesh.[3] Situated at the margins of both state and nation,
they are at once symbols of an incomplete and ongoing Partition (Chatterji
1999) and spaces that complicate easy equations of nation, identity, and territory (Van Schendel 2002b). Within the broad complexity of the chhitmahals,
Dahagram is particularly marked. Its peculiar history, especially the long and
acrimonious debate over the Corridor, has marked it as an exceptionally unstable and sensitive space,[4] one where people continually struggle both for
forms of belonging and to maintain their belongings. The instabilities of life
within Dahagram are contingent on a range of shifting relations: the political
climate between two countries, the vagaries of policing and securing the border, and local communal politics and struggles over territory. The history of
the enclave, seen from the ground level, shapes, articulates with, and differs
from national histories of struggle over space and territory in postcolonial
Bengal. It is this complexity and the local histories of claiming various forms
of belonging that I propose to examine here (see map 9.1).

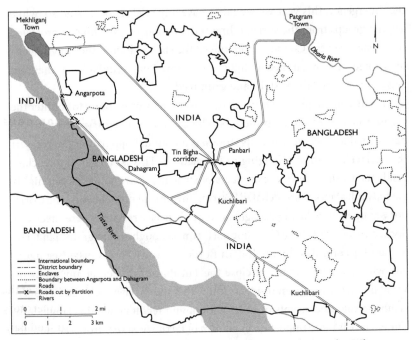

MAP 9.1. Dahagram, Angarpota, and Tin Bigha. Based on a map by Brendan Whyte, 2002. Reproduced with permission.

Usually 26 June is a day of celebration for Dahagram's sixteen thousand residents, commemorating the long political struggle over the opening of the Corridor. Friends had been telling me for months about the festivities that would accompany the Corridor Open Day. *You must come. There will be music, sweets. Indians will parade in the Corridor to protest and we will also protest back, demanding a full opening of the Corridor.*[5] Traveling to the enclave from Patgram, a busy market town in northern Lalmonirhat district in Bangladesh, in a light summer rain, I was looking forward to this spectacle of territorial belonging. As I arrived, there was a crowd of Indian protesters in the Corridor itself, yet there was no corresponding crowd from Dahagram. Curious, I proceeded directly to my friend Tariq's tailoring shop to find out what had happened.[6] As it turned out, the celebrations had fallen victim to the ban on political gatherings put in place by the Emergency Administration, which had come to power after the collapse of Bangladesh's interim government in January 2007.[7] "We spoke to the UNO [*upazila nirbahi* officer],"[8] Tariq sourly told me after whisking me away for a cup of tea, "and decided that because of the Emergency, this year we wouldn't have any celebrations." And so, while activist groups from the surrounding Indian village of Mekhliganj protested the existence of the Corridor, and indeed the enclave itself—shouting slogans of "United we stand, united we fight" and "Leave Bharat [India]!"—Dahagram residents gathered in tea stalls and grumbled.

This discontent marked more than a lost holiday or inability to counter the taunts and jeers of Indian protesters. The 26 June anniversary, even with the paltry media coverage it usually draws, is an annual opportunity to reassert the enclave's claim of belonging to Bangladesh. This is so critical to enclave residents because, despite sixty years of struggle, such claims remain highly partial and, at moments, debated. During the time of my fieldwork, the Corridor was open only during daylight hours and enclave residents were effectively 'locked in' at night.[9] The Corridor itself runs through sovereign Indian territory and is controlled by the Indian Border Security Forces (BSF) (see figure 9.1), who many believe might close the Tin Bigha for good at any moment. What is more, Dahagram residents know that the enclave itself plays a largely symbolic role in concepts of state, nation, and territory within Bangladesh. The enclave is more important as an *idea* of territory 'saved' from the clutches of a 'spatially greedy' Indian state than as a material geographic reality that is complicated, problematic, and economically and socially marginal from the perspective of the central government. Belonging is a question, as such, that is rarely taken for granted within the enclave.

The issue of understanding life in areas such as Dahagram has recently reemerged as central problematic in social science and historical research. The outpouring of literature on borders and frontiers has highlighted the importance and the possibilities of engaging borders as "privileged site[s] for assessing the power and limitations of the nation state" (Aggarwal and Bhan 2009: 521).[10] As many of these studies show, life for borderland residents is often one of tenuous negotiation.[11] At the same time, debates over rights and sovereignty set against the backdrop of the global war on terror have foregrounded the contingency of membership within nations and states, thus reviving Arendtian (1968) concerns about how tenuous rights are for those identified as 'stateless.'[12]

Despite these critical interventions, the methodological and linguistic approaches to understanding and describing life in unstable and sensitive border areas such as Dahagram are often overdetermined by broad and abstract concepts such as citizenship, statelessness, and, in the wake of Agamben's (1998)

FIGURE 9.1. A BSF (Indian) watchtower, viewed from Dahagram, 2007. The buildings at the base of the tower in the grove are a BSF encampment. Photograph courtesy of J. Cons.

influential *Homo Sacer*, exception and 'bare life.' Though such concepts have been productive in thinking through the processes and practices of securing border areas (Basaran 2008; R. Jones 2009a), they often get in the way of understanding how residents of such spaces frame their own struggles, histories, and concerns (a common concern of contributors to this volume). In a recent critique of the paucity of language for exploring such conditions, Butler argues, "I think we must describe destitution . . . but if the language by which we describe [it] presumes, time and again, that the key terms are sovereignty and bare life, we deprive ourselves of the lexicon we need to understand the other networks of power to which it belongs, or how power is recast in that place or even saturated in that place" (Butler and Spivak 2007: 42–43). As Butler suggests, the reliance on such tropes limits our ability to describe complex conditions of statelessness and the ways that people who live in such conditions forge their own claims to rights and resources as well as the ways they frame their own conditions, histories, and political possibilities.

What, then, is the grammar with which we should begin to reconstruct such histories and claims for those who live in places such as Dahagram? My modest response to this question is that a critical starting point is to explore the ways that such issues are framed by those who live in such conditions themselves. To do this, I draw on thirteen months of ethnographic and historical fieldwork conducted in 2006 and 2007. The bulk of my ethnographic work focused on Dahagram, where I collected oral histories; engaged as a participant observer in the day-to-day social reproduction and negotiation of borders and boundaries; and conducted unstructured interviews with residents of the enclave, government officials, and members of both Indian and Bangladeshi border security forces.

In exploring histories of belonging(s) within Dahagram, this chapter sheds light on how people frame particular claims to membership—in communities, in nations, in states—and how they seek to actualize rights. The landscape of Dahagram is historically sedimented with histories of belonging (Moore 2005). Citizenship, displacement, security (both national and personal), and rights are all subsumed within a range of notions of belonging and indeed belongings (material goods). Movement and the ability to hold and dispose of possessions—land, clothing, houses, crops, livestock—are central to my exploration. Yet belonging is more than purely a question of possession. It is also one of community and identity: who has the right to belong and why (compare Joshi, this volume). I explore history from within the enclave, examining the intertwined political economies and cultural politics of belonging(s) in Dahagram largely as its residents told them to me. Rather than establishing the 'facts' of Dahagram's history, I argue that these narrations are both the memories of possessions and dispossessions and the bases for ongoing claims to belonging. These claims in turn structure particular notions of nation and community that govern who is a legitimate member and what such membership means.

My opportunistic adoption of the homonym 'belonging' is intended to draw attention to the ways that the politics of membership within the enclave are inseparable from debates over and claims of ownership. Enclave residents would occasionally use Bengali words and phrases such as *ami oi barir lok*, *gramer lok*, or more often *chhiter lok* (I belong to that household, village, or enclave) to denote belonging as membership, and *jinishta amar* (that is mine) or *dokhol kora niechi* (I [forcefully] took) to denote belonging as possession. The limited usage of these terms per se is not what interests me here. Rather

I am suggesting that broadly exploring ways that membership and property are linked in narrations of Dahagram's history is a more productive way to understand the dilemmas of life in unstable and sensitive spaces than more narrowly defined concepts such as 'statelessness' or 'citizenship.'

Tensions of Belonging

Prior to Partition in 1947, the chhitmahals were discontinuous landholdings dating back to the Mughal incursion north from Dacca (Dhaka in contemporary spelling) into the Kingdom of Koch (Cooch) Behar in the late seventeenth century. According to Whyte (2002), Mughals were unable to dislodge a number of powerful chieftains from the lands around Boda, Patgram, and Purvabhag—areas on the frontier between Koch and Mughal rule—that were granted to them by treaty in 1713. These lands remained officially part of the Kingdom of Koch Behar while becoming enclaves within the Mughal Empire. Similarly Mughal soldiers had occupied lands inside of Koch Behar, lands that became a discontinuous part of Mughal territory. During the colonial period, many of these enclaves were spread along the border between Rangpur district, under direct colonial administration, and Koch Behar, an indirectly ruled princely state. Though the existence of such territorial ambiguities caused confusion for colonial administrators (Glazier 1873; Vas 1911), projects and proposals to 'solve' the chhitmahal issue either ran into administrative complications or simply came to no fruitful end. Roughly two hundred chhitmahals became state enclaves—in the sense of being completely bounded by another sovereign state—at and shortly after Partition in 1947 with the accession of Cooch Behar to India in 1949.[13] Of these, Dahagram was the largest in terms of both land and population. Situated on the banks of the Tista River, it is, at its closest point, roughly 170 meters from what became the official border between India and East Pakistan.

While the Partition boundary in West Bengal, known as the Radcliffe Line, was nominally drawn by separating majority Hindu districts from majority Muslim districts, this process was much more complicated on the ground. As Van Schendel (2005a: ch. 3) argues, very little of the border actually separated majority Muslim and Hindu districts, and in practice the border more frequently ran through areas where there was a majority of the same religious group on both sides. Further, "the clear lines that appeared on the maps used by colonial officials, including the Bengal Boundary (or Radcliffe) Committee, did not correspond with anything visible 'out there.' There was no way un-equivocally to recognize the new border on the ground" (55–56) (see figure 9.2). In practice the border was worked out through lengthy and often contentious legal and political negotiations between India and Pakistan. Many of the ambiguities resulting from this process, including the enclaves themselves, continue to plague border residents and are the source of ongoing conflicts.

Though punctuated by moments of violence and open conflict, the history of Dahagram during the East Pakistan period (1947–70) is perhaps best described as a story of uncomfortable belonging to both India and Pakistan.[14] From Partition, or more specifically from the accession of Cooch Behar to India in 1948, the complicated border configurations in the Patgram-Mekhliganj region meant that residents of Dahagram had to illegally cross one and often two borders simply to take their goods to market. In the years following Partition, and even after the introduction of the official passport system in 1952,[15] movement across the border was not heavily regulated (Chatterji 1999; Murayama 2006; Rahman and Van Schendel 2003). There was regular travel back and forth along the length of the Bengal border, as many border residents had lands and even families bifurcated by the haphazardly drawn Partition boundary. Yet as tension between the two countries grew, the number of border incidents skyrocketed.[16] Regulation and control along the border became more intense and the border itself more formalized with the establishment of boundary commissions to settle territorial controversies and the creation of paramilitary organizations to patrol and secure the border, such as the Ansars in East Pakistan and the Bangiya Jatiya Rakshi Bahini (West Bengal National Volunteer Force) in West Bengal (Van Schendel 2005a).[17]

This gradual formalization ossified an asymmetrical relationship of rights and power inside the enclave drawn along communal lines. Van Schendel (2002b: 127) argues that notions of citizenship in the post-Partition period had a general character of *transterritoriality*: "Both states saw themselves as being in charge of the populations living in their own territory, but also of a [religious] category of people living in the territory of the other state." Dahagram's population was roughly divided between Hindus and Muslims. As movement across the border became more and more legally precarious, the ability of Muslims living within Dahagram to travel freely and safely to market in surrounding areas decreased. Such informal or unstated policies meant that Hindus in Dahagram were residents of India in all but address. At the

FIGURE 9.2. A border post in Dahagram (viewed from India) announces "Bangla," for Bangladesh. The opposite side of the pillar reads "Bharat," for India. "4, 2-s" is the identifying number of the pillar. Photograph courtesy of J. Cons.

same time, Muslims were doubly alienated from membership within Pakistan, legally residing within sovereign East Pakistani territory yet hemmed in by another state and residing side by side with others who effectively held more rights than they. While Hindus in Dahagram were able to live largely as though they were actually residing in India, Muslims had to negotiate the vagaries of paramilitary forces, police, and often hostile neighbors simply to buy and sell goods.

As with Indian enclaves in East Pakistan, daily navigation of such issues posed intermittent problems. When disputes arose over ownership of livestock or crops, Muslim residents had little recourse, as those who could legally represent and protect their rights were situated across an international border. With the 1958 Nehru-Noon Accords that made provisions to exchange the enclaves—provisions that were fiercely challenged and ultimately never implemented—these situations became more precarious. As tensions rose, Dahagram became a zone of contention; monitoring of and hostility toward its residents grew. An Indian border security camp was established near what is now the Tin Bigha Corridor,[18] and both residents of the surrounding Indian Thana of Mekhliganj and border security *jawans* (soldiers) began to patrol its perimeter.

Dahagram residents characterize this period as one of suffering, when the act of going to market was fraught with risk and life within the enclave was one of extreme instability. Residents recall that it was common practice for the BSF to require a payment or bribe for passage in or out of the enclave. As Akkas Ali, a smallholder farmer living in the north of Dahagram, described it, "Whenever we crossed into Indian territory, we had to go through BSF scrutiny.[19] The BSF would note our name, put some mark on our shoulder, as when branding cows. They even compelled us to do work for them, doing such chores as cleaning their lavatories, cutting their lawns, sawing wood for them, et cetera." While residents in the south of the enclave, closest to Bangladesh, frequently dodged security forces to reach the East Pakistani mainland, others residing in the north would more frequently make the trip into India. This trip was more risky as it made one vulnerable longer. Many were arrested in the *haat* (market) in Mekhliganj.[20] Enclave residents frequently reminded me, *There is not a single family in the enclave who has not suffered* [koshto] *while a household member was detained in an Indian jail.* Beyond the problem of moving into and out of the enclave, Muslim residents faced vulnerability from looting by both Indians in Mekhliganj and Hindus living within the enclave.

The Dahagram War

Such tensions of belonging characterized life for (Muslim) Dahagram residents both before and after the Liberation War in 1971. Indeed this situation substantively changed only with the opening of the Tin Bigha Corridor in 1992. However, this is neither to say that the difficulties of life within and movement out of the enclave were unchanging nor that they were purely reflections of local struggles over the status of the enclave and its residents. Certain moments in agricultural cycles—rice harvests, for example—were more violent than others. Conflicts regularly arose over the exact location of the border, and raids were carried out on both sides of the border to carry off the fresh harvest. Moreover the politics of belonging within the enclave were indexed to broader debates and struggles over territory, sovereignty, and space between India and Pakistan. In moments of tension, for example during the debate over the Nehru-Noon Accords, daily practices of regulating movement periodically flared up into moments of crisis and open violence. In such moments, residents of the enclaves, and indeed residents of the border region more broadly, were more likely to experience expropriation, thefts, and various forms of organized communal attacks.

Perhaps the most vividly remembered of these incidents within Dahagram occurred in the spring of 1965 and resulted in the destruction of much of the enclave. This incident, which came to be known as the Dahagram War, continues to resonate in enclave politics today. The war was set against the backdrop of increasing tension between India and Pakistan over Kashmir. As the dispute intensified, there was a marked buildup of Indian and Pakistani troops along border regions in both the East and West.[21] Beginning in January the BSF began to mass troops and dig trenches in the area along the Tin Bigha, by far the closest point of the enclave to the mainland. This effectively cut Dahagram residents off from Patgram Thana in East Pakistan and forced them to make the more risky crossing into Mekhliganj in India to buy and sell goods.[22] Tension in Dahagram reached a dangerous height following India's buildup along the Rann of Kachchh—another space that had been contentious and sensitive in the relationship between India and Pakistan, situated on India's west coast—in early March and a series of incursions along the East Pakistan border.[23] Violence seemed inevitable to residents of Dahagram.

On the morning of 13 March 1965, in the Dangbari neighborhood of Angarpota, a small herd of goats were rustled by a group of Indians from Mekhliganj. Such back-and-forth rustling was a common occurrence, particularly along Dahagram's northern border.[24] Yet in periods of tension, disputes could quickly escalate to overt violence. Bachao Miah, the goats' owner, crossed the border to demand their return and was shot in the leg by a man who was repeatedly described to me as a 'BSF officer.' Miah, assisted by his sons, retreated back into Dahagram. That night Indians surrounded Dahagram on three sides. With the support of the BSF, they began moving from the border in toward the enclave's center, burning Muslim homes as they went.[25]

For most, the memory of the outbreak of the war is one of confusion and chaos. Kolim Hyder, who was a boy of eight in 1965, tried to explain the confusion and rupture of that night:

> It was around eight in the evening. We saw people north of the village crossing the road. Everybody was carrying bundles, gripping their children, and walking fast. . . . People were carrying pillows, quilts. . . .

I remember we hadn't taken our evening meal, though usually we ate ear-lier. My father took the rice pot [*bhater hari*]. A few days earlier, we had harvested *mashkalai dal*.[26] Our yard was filled with *kalais* [seed pods]. Do you know how to collect kalais from [the] field? The roots come out, not just the plant. Kalai bunches were lying scattered in the yard where during the day ten or twelve people labored to husk them.

My father rushed to the cowshed and untied all of the cows, so that they could save their lives and also eat the dal. In those days, we used to grow plenty of kalai. We had vast plots of land [*anek jomi*] near the *char* [siltation island in the riverbed], which have now gone under the river. My father took hold of the rice pot. We kids were walking alongside my mother. We reached Tin Bigha.

When we arrived at the Tin Bigha, the BSF weren't allowing us to pass. . . . The BSF was firing to prevent people from crossing Indian territory, but we were desperate, and by 10 P.M. we passed Tin Bigha and reached the mainland. Not everyone could pass. Others had to wait until the next night. . . . We went to Patgram. We took shelter in a school and we had no food that night. My father threw away the rice pot he carried in the rush across the Tin Bigha, as he had to grip us children. There was a huge crowd. My father threw the rice pot when the BSF fired in Tin Bigha. I walked all the way to Patgram [eleven kilometers away]. My mother took hold of my young sisters while my father looked after the older pair. During the crossing, my father held tight so that I would not be lost in the crowd [*Par howar shamoi, abba amar hat dhore rhakse, jano ami harai najai*].

The themes of chaos in Kolim's vivid remembrances were echoed by almost all who recall the war. Only a few were able to escape through the Tin Bigha on that first night. Most were held there for another twenty-four hours in terror of an attack from the front by the BSF or from behind by the same villagers who had burned their homes.

Perhaps what are most vivid in Kolim's narrative are the loss of means to eat and the trauma of separation from places and belongings. His description highlights the stark contrast between the bounty of the dal harvest and the sudden loss of even a pot to cook rice in. Indeed the story of rescuing a rice pot from a burning house only to lose it in the panic of flight was repeated, in various ways, by many people. Some simply could not carry their cooking pots on the mad dash south. Some report saving their pots only to lose the rice that was in them. Some remember a fortunate and generous few, mostly those with homes situated close to Tin Bigha, who were able to salvage some rice and share it with those huddled together in hunger and fear, waiting for more than a day for clearance to cross into safety. These collective memories seem to symbolize and encapsulate the loss of homes and the flight from the enclave. For Kolim, the forced discarding of the pot seems to mark a stripping away of belongings, reducing the residents of Dahagram to refugees dependent on the hospitality of others. The loss of the pot presaged the difficulties to come.

The large influx of refugees into Patgram dangerously stretched the town's resources. Refugees from Dahagram were billeted in impromptu camps set up in Patgram's schools and railway stations. The day after residents fled, fighting began between the East Pakistan Rifles post in Panbari and the BSF post near the Tin Bigha in Mekhliganj. Heavy fire was exchanged almost continually for the next two weeks.[27] As demands for a withdrawal of aggression were swapped between India and East Pakistan, troop buildups continued in the border regions around Patgram, along the length of the Rangpur Division border (i.e., the whole northwest of Bangladesh), and around other border districts such as Kushtia in the west and Sylhet in the northeast.[28] Meanwhile waves of Muslim refugees living in the Indian district of Cooch Behar began moving across the border amid reports that they were being forcibly expelled by the BSF.[29]

On 1 April a cease-fire arrangement was reached and Dahagram residents began to return to their homes from Patgram.[30] As part of the arrangement, the Indian government agreed to provide basic compensation for victims of the attack. These included essentials such as a small amount of rice and cooking oil and a cow for every family that had lost their home so that they could retill their fields. These meager supplies were inadequate to carry most residents through the next harvest cycle. Many had lost not only their homes and possessions but also the stores of rice and dal necessary for both income and household self-sufficiency. What is more, many of the fields planted with rice for the *boro* [rice] harvest in midsummer had been burned or damaged.

Tensions along the border remained high. The declaration of war between India and Pakistan in June caused further military buildup along all of East Pakistan's borders. Though there was no further direct military action against Dahagram, residents of the surrounding Mekhliganj Thana enacted a blockade of the enclave, preventing Muslim residents from traveling either to Mekhliganj or to Patgram markets. As one resident bitterly recalled, "We used to wait for rain or darkness so that we could rush through [the Tin Bigha] to Patgram to buy essentials. Life was very hard in those days. There was nothing human in that vast India." Others remember sifting through the dirt and remains of their burned homes to recover even tiny amounts of rice. Many families were forced to slaughter the cows provided as compensation for food. Most supplemented insufficient diets by fishing the Tista River.

The loss proved to be one that many families were unable to recover from. Jasmine Begum, now an elderly woman living in a rundown home built on the site of her family's original property, bitterly recalls the war as the beginning of her family's long descent into poverty. They had been moderately wealthy, with livestock, enough rice to run a self-sufficient home, and jute to sell in the Mekhliganj and Patgram markets. "During the fire, we were unable to take anything away with us. We survived on whatever relief we got. We have never recovered from the fire. We learned fear then. Fear has been part of our life since."

The Dahagram War marked a moment of trauma that laid bare the vagaries of life for enclave residents in the years before the Liberation War. In memories of this moment, the stakes in imagining forms of belonging within nation and state as linked to possession are clarified. The inability of the East Pakistani state to protect residents in their own homes, the loss of the very means to cook food, and the meager recompense for loss of homes, crops, and livestock all speak to memories and experiences of instability, uncertainty, and anxiety that were part of daily life within the enclave. Yet it also marked the way that questions of territorial belonging resonated both within and in relation to Dahagram. Not only were the stakes of national belonging high for enclave residents, but the space of the enclave itself was imbricated in broader questions of territory. While it may be an exaggeration to claim, as many enclave residents do, that the 1965 India-Pakistan War broke out first in Dahagram, it is certainly true that the fate of enclave residents and their ability to live within and move into and out of the space of Dahagram was intimately linked to broader conceptions of national space. Such conceptions were to form the basis of future claims for inclusion and membership.

Belonging to Bangladesh

If the East Pakistan period was characterized by periodic violence and territorial uncertainty, the period after Bangladesh's independence in 1971 leading up to the opening of the Corridor in 1992 was the most unstable and contentious period in Dahagram's postcolonial history. During this time the lines of belonging and exclusion were starkly drawn, and the complications that shaped the lives of residents during the East Pakistan period more frequently became open conflicts. Though not far from areas that saw intense fighting during the Liberation War, Dahagram escaped direct involvement. In any case, the Liberation War, at least initially, led to significantly more relaxed conditions for Dahagram residents. Following India's military and humanitarian interventions in the Liberation War, a climate of cooperation emerged between India and Bangladesh. During this period residents moved more freely both across the border to trade in Indian markets in Mekhliganj and to the Bangladeshi mainland to trade in Patgram.

This relaxing of tensions began to end with the controversies surrounding the Indira-Mujib Pact in 1974. The Pact, also known as the Land Boundary Agreement, conceived of a range of long-standing territorial disagreements between the two countries as fundamentally linked to animosity between India and Pakistan. In the wake of the Liberation War—when the border had been effectively, if temporarily, erased—the Pact sought to address these issues. Among the range of agreements reached in the Pact were provisions to resolve outstanding disputes over demarcating the border and the exchange of all the enclaves with the exception of Dahagram and Berubari Union, a disputed area along the border with Jalpaiguri. To address these two contentious spaces, the Pact proposed to cede the disputed area of Berubari to India in exchange for the leasing of the Tin Bigha Corridor to Bangladesh into perpetuity.

The Pact transformed Dahagram into a focal point and symbol of territorial tension and political dispute between Bangladesh and India. In Bangladesh the Mujib administration fell under immediate criticism for failing to address the question of the Farakka Barage and water sharing on the Ganges—a long-standing dispute and issue of pressing concern for Bangladesh residents living downstream of India.[31] Moreover, opposition parties cited the decision to hand over Berubari as a "serious attack on the national interest of the country [that] chopped Bangladesh's interest with an axe."[32] A writ to block the Berubari handover was turned down by the Supreme Court, and the disputed territory was handed over to India shortly thereafter.[33] In India a similar dispute emerged over the legality of leasing land to Bangladesh. As the representative of Cooch Behar argued in the Lok Sabha, "This type of gift of Tinbigha to Bangladesh must be stopped at all costs. Certainly, we want friendship with Bangladesh, but not at the cost of our motherland. No more appeasement. No more surrenders. No more cessation of our motherland."[34] While the Berubari issue was resolved by constitutional amendment within Bangladesh that allowed for the acceptance of the conditions of the Pact, the leasing of the Corridor remained both politically and legally problematic and unresolved in India.[35]

As legal disputes over the Corridor began to grow, movement again became complicated for Dahagram's Muslim residents. The BSF imposed a five-kilogram limit on goods moving into and out of the enclave. This effectively meant that residents could not sell enough crops to purchase household essentials. Residents describe being forced into positions of compromise as it became harder to access markets without negotiating with border security forces. Yet for many residents, memories from this period are also framed as claims of stoic resistance to territorial aggression. As Bashar, who grew up during this period as a member of a politically influential, though comparatively less wealthy family in the enclave, put it:

> The BSF would come, demand mangos, wood, or timber, and take anything away they wanted. Anything. A goat, a hen. We had no way to say no. They would bring in their laborers with them. If we said no, the next day they would punish [shasti] us on our way to Mekhliganj. Believe me, we were just like prisoners [ashami]. Worse than prisoners. A prisoner is not in want of food or medicine. We had want of everything. Moreover we had no freedom to move. The period from 1982 to 1992, we were in a condition that is not describable in any language [bhashai bola jai na]. For example, if you take Ethiopia, though they are in want of food or medicine, they at least have the freedom to roam around. We had nothing. No freedom, no essentials. Children died of diarrhea. They were buried without clothes [kafoner kapor chara]. . . . But, brother, still Dahagram people did not give their allegiance to India [India ke kono chhar die ni]. They didn't surrender. Even after such severe torture and blockades.

The equation of life inside Dahagram to a prison was a frequent analogy I heard during my research. Here this metaphor is extended to suggest that Dahagram was worse off than a country beset by war and famine. Though hyperbolic—male residents did regularly leave Dahagram to access both Mekhliganj and Patgram—the narrative's ultimate claim to belonging is clear: despite deprivation and suffering, Muslim residents persevered and refused to surrender their land and allegiance to India. The communal claim to belonging repeatedly positioned residents as stoic sufferers holding their land in the name of a Muslim Bengali state.

The challenges posed by these regulations of movement led to increased 'illegal' border crossings by often desperate residents. Many tell stories of men waiting for dark, rain, or fog to cross the Tin Bigha to reach Bangladesh. Others tried their luck in the Mekhliganj markets. Both these activities had a risk of arrest, for which the standard penalty was a fine and one month in jail, though many were detained longer. During this period detainees had no way to communicate with their families to inform them of their arrest, leaving their households in a state of anxiety until their release. But if the position for men was complicated, women were in an even more vulnerable and compromised position. Movement into and out of the enclave was markedly gendered. While men would periodically risk crossing to India or Bangladesh—frequently returning with boastful tales about near misses and bold evasive ploys—women rarely left Dahagram. Their movements were confined not only by religious prohibitions on their leaving the home but by the added belief, much repeated by men, in their inability to flee from pursuers. During this period many women died of complications related to childbirth, as access to medical facilities was impractical if not impossible. The threat of violence from hostile neighbors and security forces created further arguments for the cloistering of women within the enclave.

Yet there were more complications and dangers of living in the enclave than just the restriction of movement. Kidnapping and rape were common features of life in Dahagram during this period. Women from within the enclave were periodically taken by villagers from surrounding areas and tortured for days before being allowed to return. Men within the enclave also engaged in the kidnapping of women from Mekhliganj. Indeed these kidnappings were occasionally remembered as celebrations of resistance by Muslim men who had been regularly humiliated by BSF tolls on movement, insults in Mekhliganj haats, and Hindu neighbors who accentuated such insults through the very freedom of their own movement. The gendered violence involved in territory making in the post-Independence and pre-Corridor years marked women's bodies as both belongings (objects within the political and spatial economy of territory) and belonging (symbols of nation and community in need of protection, preservation, and purity).[36] Women in Dahagram were thus regularly caught up in the multiple and violent politics of possession and inclusion.

The Dahagram Movement Committee

If the Bangladesh period saw an increase in projects seeking forcibly to exclude Muslim residents within Dahagram, it also saw a renewed interest in claiming Dahagram as part of Bangladesh. This movement was intimately linked to the political shift away from secularism in the wake of the assassination of Mujib in 1975 and the assumption of the presidency by Ziaur Rahman in 1977.[37] This period saw an extension of the communal politicization of territory signaled in the debate over the Indira-Mujib Pact in 1974. In 1977 the Zia administration issued sixteen 'civil guns' to Dahagram. These guns, nominally for use in defense, were given to the enclave's unofficial Union Parishad governing body and seem to have been distributed to wealthy and politically influential Muslim families within the enclave. This endorsement of violent defense marked, for many, the first concrete step in Bangladesh securing the enclave as a part of its national territory. If, from the perspective of the administration, the distribution of these guns marked territorial sovereignty over Dahagram, for residents, they signified a political acknowledgment that Dahagram belonged to Bangladesh and could be defended as such. While it is not clear how or if the weapons were used (many residents told me stories wherein the guns played significant roles in intimidating Indians, though none shared stories of their being fired), the guns are spoken of almost reverentially as critical symbols of belonging. While representatives of the state could not directly 'administer' the enclave, they could encourage residents to claim and defend their own territory.

Zia's awarding of the 'civil guns' presaged a series of events in the early 1980s that would bring the question of belonging and the issues around the Corridor to a head. In July 1981 the Bangladesh Bureau of Statistics attempted to conduct a census in the enclave as a first step in negotiating the terms of the Tin Bigha Corridor's lease. For Bashar Hassan, this census was a catalyst for galvanizing political elites in the enclave into broader advocacy and protest for realization of the Indira-Mujib Pact. At the time, he was one of the privileged few within the enclave whose families could afford to send them to school in Patgram. Bashar's memories position the census as a focal moment of both suffering and of resistance.

Dahagram's first census happened in 1981. If you hear the stories, you will simply tremble. Bangladesh decided to conduct a census to show the world that "Dahagram is ours and we are controlling it [*Dahagram amader neontrone*]." We who were studying here [in Patgram], were trained as enumerators. . . . However, we were blocked on the way in. Indians came with bows and arrows. . . . Indians were saying that though the enclave belongs to Bangladesh on paper, they would not allow the possession of it. Then the two DCs [district commissioners] of the neighboring districts sat again. Indian politicians suggested that "if you have to do a census, then go through Changrabhanda [far to the north of the Tin Bigha]."

Three census officials entered Dahagram by that round-about way. We, however, were instructed by the Bangladesh authorities to do our fieldwork earlier, going through the Tin Bigha in the night as we used to when going to and coming from Patgram. However, after the census, Indians [who were maintaining the blockade] only allowed the officials to return. We fieldworkers had no way to come back. They were on guard on all corners of Dahagram with bows and arrows. They imposed a total blockade which lasted for a long twenty-two days. These days were the most sad and helpless days of my life. None was able to get out of Dahagram. During these twenty-two days, twenty-six of our people died from a scarcity of medicines and other essentials. We had to bury them without any cloth or with old clothes.[38]

As Foucault (1991) has argued, modernity is characterized by a political paradigm primarily concerned with the management of populations through technologies of governance. The census is one strategy by which governments make populations "legible" and "manageable" (Scott 1998). As such, it is both a technology of governance and a tool of inclusion and incorporation (Markowitz 2007). In Dahagram, the very process of conducting the census became a battleground of belonging. To mark residents of Dahagram as members of Bangladesh through enumeration would be to solidify their claims of national inclusion. Bashar's narrative emphasizes this. The purpose of the census was to officially claim, "Dahagram is ours, and we are controlling it." In this same sense, the protests and attempts to block the census offered a counternarrative. An article in the *Bangladesh Observer* reported at the time, "What happened on July 6 when Bangladesh officials in their third bid went to conduct [the] census inside these enclaves was a naked attempt by India to foil the census and show the world that people of these enclaves no more want to remain with Bangladesh" (quoted in Whyte 2002: 134).

Following the census, the group of students who were trained as enumerators decided that direct political action was needed if the enclaves were to be claimed for Bangladesh. To this end, they formed what came to be known as the Dahagram Shangram Shomiti (Dahagram Movement Committee, or DSS). All of these students were from elite and powerful families within Dahagram, families that had been involved in the enclave's politics for a long time. The link between the census and the Movement Committee is striking. Cohn (1987) points out that the census in British India was perhaps most significant for politicizing its enumerators. Though the politics were different in Dahagram than they were in nineteenth-century colonial India, the stakes in classification and inclusion and the political significance of the census were no less apparent to the enumerators who formed the DSS. Indeed for this group of students, the census and the blockade following it offered a clear message that spurred them to find other ways to forcefully assert their inclusion in Bangladesh. Bashar recalls, "We proceeded with the demand that we should be given back our territory, the territory which belonged to us according to the '74 treaty. After the formation of the Committee, Bangladeshi administration began to evaluate us. Prior to that, we were just like dogs and foxes." In other words, through the actions of the Committee, residents of Dahagram would not only reclaim their territory but also achieve the status of belonging within Bangladesh, and its residents would be recognized as rights-bearing citizens as opposed to marginal people beyond the bounds of the state.

The DSS began to raise public awareness of the situation in Dahagram. Mohammad Yusuf, another member of the DSS, described their activities as claims not just for membership in Bangladesh but also for the dignity of the residents of Dahagram. The DSS, as such, argued not simply for implementing the Indira-Mujib Pact, but also that residents were deserving members of the nation. In Yusuf's words:

> We didn't take any subscription or monetary help from anybody outside the Committee. We did it on our own [ja korsi, nijera korci]. One day, three of us were on our way to Ishwardi Junction to stick handbills over a train there that was headed to Chittagong. We only had three *taka* [rupees] with us and no tickets. It was our decision that we wouldn't extend our hand, as no movement can be run with money earned by begging. What a movement needs is self-confidence. While we were returning, the ticket collector found me. I began showing our handbills

and saying, "You see, we are from Dahagram, we are running our movement." He was convinced. He fed us *pao rutti* [toast]. I realized that whoever fights for his country gets respect. Those were good days. A kid like me, who was just in his tenth grade, would go before the DC [district commissioner] and say, "Sir, I am from Dahagram Shangram Shamiti. We are fighting to realize the '74 Treaty." And the DC would pay attention to me, extend his hand to shake with me, and say, "Sit down, my son."

Yusuf tells a story of both inclusion through struggle and the recognition by other Bangladeshis of the righteousness of their cause. Moreover he narrates a decidedly local negotiation with institutions of local government. As this local history illustrates, renderings of populations and territory engendered dynamics within Dahagram that would prove integral to the shaping of belonging and life within it and, more broadly, within the nation-state. As Chatterjee (2004: 57, emphasis in original) argues, a central strategy in the negotiation between populations who are, at best, contextually members of the nation-state and the institutions that seek to govern them is to "*give to the empirical form of a population group the moral attributes of a community.*" Yusuf's emphasis on the dignity of the movement's activities, made through earnest appeal as opposed to begging, stakes out this territory both for movement members and for the residents they represented. He describes Dahagram residents not as downtrodden burdens on the state but rather as active political citizens, ready to struggle for their territory and their belonging. In other words, he asserts their belonging in the nation as a means of making a claim for administrative inclusion in the state.

The DSS began to draw the notice of authorities in both Bangladesh and India. In Mekhliganj the police mounted an effort to locate and arrest members of the Committee, while the already existing Kuchlibari Shangram Shamiti [Kuchlibari Movement Committee; KSS] in India, which opposed the opening of Corridor, and its companion organization, the Tin Bigha Shangram Shamiti [Tin Bigha Movement Committee; TBSS], began to increase their own protests and activities.[39] Tensions rose and blockades and arrests became more frequent. As the DSS's activities became more and more visible, their Indian counterparts in the KSS expanded their campaign by reaching out to the Hindu nationalist Bharatiya Janata Party (BJP) to help renationalize the question of the Corridor. In response, the DSS contacted the Jatiya Ganotantri Party (JAGPA) in Bangladesh, an ardently nationalist party led by Shaiful Alam Prodhan.[40]

In 1984, with JAGPA's support, the DSS organized its most dramatic and visible protest, which they called the Long March. Riaz, another member of the Movement Committee, described the march: "Twenty-two youths from Dahagram joined JAGPA members in a procession wearing funeral robes [*kafoner kapor*]. First, we performed a *Janozah* [funeral rites] prayer in Dhaka. Then we began the Long March. We said that by any means necessary we would march through the Tin Bigha, as it should have been Bangladeshi land according to the treaty. Our march got huge attention because of JAGPA's participation. At Lalmonirhat, more than 100,000 people came out of their homes to join us.[41] It was a huge procession, looking like it was just waiting to explode."

Riaz's description highlights the symbolic import of the march. Cut off from the Bangladeshi mainland, Dahagram residents were slowly dying. By formally conducting funeral rites and marching with the intent to pass through the Tin Bigha, DSS members were intent on forcing an international event that would highlight the debate over the Corridor and emphasize their willingness to confront death in defense of territory, rather than a slow starvation at the hands of the BSF and residents of Mekhliganj. In other words, the Long March drew attention to Dahagram not simply as a moral community in Chatterjee's sense of the term, but also as a moral obligation to the Bangladeshi state and nation.

Opening the Corridor

The DSS's activities coincided with the rise to power in Bangladesh of General Hossain Mohammad Ershad following the assassination of Zia in 1981. Ershad, whose controversial tenure as head of the Bangladesh government lasted from 1982 to 1991, radically curbed democratic liberties and persistently blocked efforts to overturn military rule and restore parliamentary democracy within Bangladesh. Further, his regime continued the move initiated by Zia away from secular Bengali nationalism and toward a more overtly Islamist Bangladeshi state. Against this backdrop the political relationship between India and Bangladesh remained strained. This relationship was further stressed by the increasingly virulent rhetoric of the BJP in India against the threat of illegal immigration from Muslim Bangladesh and pressuring of the Congress Party to take action against it. This pressure led, among other things, to the 1986 Indo-Bangladesh Border Roads and Fences Project (Van Schendel 2005a: 212–13).[42]

In 1982, in a conference to resolve border issues, technical experts and security forces from India and Bangladesh reached an agreement on lease terms for the Tin Bigha. Contrary to the terms of the Indira-Mujib Pact, this new agreement stated that sovereign control over the Corridor would remain in the hands of Indian officials. Despite this clarification, no direct action to open the Corridor was taken, though an active debate reemerged in India over the legality of the creation of Tin Bigha.[43] This debate was deployed in different ways by different parties. The Left Front in West Bengal, and notably Amar Roy Prodhan, pressed for the full exchange of all the enclaves, as opposed to the partial solution of addressing just Dahagram.[44] The BJP enthusiastically adopted the cause of opposing the opening of the Corridor on nationalist grounds. Claiming to defend a country marred by Partition and betrayed by its political leaders, the BJP began to use the Tin Bigha issue as a whip to beat both Congress and West Bengal's left-front government.[45] A pamphlet published in 1992 mirrored much of the rhetoric deployed in public and in the Lok Sabha: "BJP [was] not there in 1947 to resist that evil design, but today, in 1992, things have changed. Today we, the general people, refuse to be a mute party to the sinister design of transferring Tinbigha Corridor to Bangladesh by Rao Govt.-Jyoti Basu combine."[46]

Nationalist claims to territory and territorial defense were no less prevalent in the Ershad government. Ershad, originally from Rangpur himself and a supporter of all causes linked to the betterment of north Bengal, championed the cause of Dahagram and the Tin Bigha Corridor as a nationalist issue, using the 1982 lease as a basis to pressure the Indian administration over Dahagram. As the DSS's activities gained attention, Ershad began to bring the debate over the Corridor to a head. In 1986 and again in 1988 he made personal visits to the enclave. These visits remain among the most celebrated and fondly remembered moments in Dahagram's history. Sharif Udin Talukdar, who was a member of the DSS, a prominent political player in the enclave, and a future Union Parishad chairman, remembers the visit as a moment of extreme emotions: "He was the first high-profile leader to step into Dahagram. He came here by helicopter. After Ershad's arrival, we were quite speechless. It was as though we helpless folks got our father. We began weeping before him."

Ershad's visit did indeed mark a turning point in enclave politics. During his visit he distributed over 25,000Tk-worth of goods to needy households. He also made Angarpota and Dahagram into an official Union Parishad within

Patgram Upazilla, giving it formal political standing within the Bangladesh administrative system, despite its territorial dislocation from the Bangladeshi mainland. He further allocated funds for the development of schools and medical facilities in Dahagram. What is more, Ershad began actively advocating for a solution to the Corridor problem, proposing, among other things, the construction of a fly-over for the Tin Bigha, so that residents could effectively pass from Dahagram to Panbari without ever having to touch Indian soil. Yet his visits also increased the tensions over belonging within the enclave. As Riaz explained it to me, "Seeing the emotional outburst on our part at Ershad's visit, Indians understood our true desires and where our commitments lay. After realizing that we were truly Bangladeshi, Indians escalated their tortures. Earlier, they believed that some day we may be India-minded. They hoped that there would be a new generation in Dahagram that was pro-India. After Ershad came, those hopes were gone."

Thus while Ershad's visit brought renewed hope to residents, it also marked an increase in tensions with Mekhliganj. Residents spoke of numerous blockades from the mid-1980s on. Many echoed Bashar's comment on the impossibility of even acquiring *kafan* cloth to shroud dead bodies in accordance with Islamic funerary rights. *We had nothing to bury our dead in and were forced to cover them in banana leaves.* Along with an increase in violence between Muslim residents and surrounding areas, Hindus living within the enclave began an active campaign to demonstrate that Dahagram residents 'desired' to be part of India. Muslim residents recall that they were often forced or extorted to sign petitions and documents claiming allegiance to India by Hindus living within the enclave, themselves formulating their own claims of belonging to India.

Tensions between the DSS and the KSS, as well as the regular blockades and increases in arrests, continued throughout Ershad's presidency. Yet in 1991 the relationship between India and Bangladesh again briefly thawed with the collapse of the Ershad regime under joint pressure and activism from a coalition of parties and public protests within Bangladesh.[47] As the Bangladesh National Party (BNP) assumed power and a series of court cases blocking the Corridor in India were resolved, the possibility of opening the Corridor became real. On 26 June 1992, amid protest by the KSS and the BJP, the Corridor finally opened.[48] While this was seen almost uniformly within the enclave as a major and important victory, the Corridor has also created new and complicated configurations of sovereignty, sensitivity, and belonging within the enclave. Further, the opening of the Corridor has served to ossify the borders of Dahagram. Traveling to Mekhliganj in India is now unambiguously illegal, and to get there one must negotiate frequent border patrols and the panoptic BSF watchtowers that now surround the enclave. Access to Bangladesh is now similarly restricted except through the Tin Bigha Corridor, which, until 2011, remained open only during daylight.[49]

Many members of the DSS feel that the partial and contingent fulfillment of the Indira-Mujib Pact is a betrayal to those who fought and struggled for the Corridor. Riaz told me, "The government that was in power then, the Khalida Zia government, did it wrong to receive the Indian suggestion [that the BSF would control the Corridor]. What could we people of Dahagram do? We had no options. We were helpless. We have no political representation at the national level. We have no strong lobby. We have no strong voice to raise the issue at some international level. In 1982 President Ershad said to India, "Give me my territory." What Khalida Zia did in 1992 was cheap politics [shasta rajniti]."[50] Riaz's claim marks frustration at the partial fulfillment of the Indira-Mujib Pact but also another statement of inclusion within Bangladesh. Riaz speaks of heads of state claiming "their" territory. A failure to defend the rights of enclave residents is a lack of commitment to "national" interest. At the same time, the "cheap politics" of the BNP administration highlight that despite long struggle, belonging in Dahagram remains partial, contingent, and contested.

Understanding the Politics of Belonging

The opening of the Corridor transformed the landscape of politics in Dahagram in many ways. Yet the enclave remains an unstable place where the stakes of various forms of uncertain belonging remain high. When it opened in 1992, the Corridor was open for only one hour a day. Since then the amount of time has increased, and during my fieldwork the Corridor remained open during daylight hours, a reality that posed a range of uncertainties and anxieties for residents—among them, complications accessing urgent medical care at night. Inside the enclave the political fault lines have shifted. Following the opening of the Corridor, the majority of the Hindu families within Dahagram left, leaving a glut of land that residents had little money to purchase. Much of this land was snapped up by new migrants moving from elsewhere in Bangladesh. If the pre-Corridor history is remembered largely along communal lines, many of the contemporary political struggles in the enclave are between long-term residents and these newer migrants, many of whom were able to purchase large amounts of land and have become prosperous smallholder farmers. The opening of the Corridor has allowed for the Bangladesh Rifles (Bangladesh's border security force) to establish several camps within the enclave. It has also led to the establishment of a range of BSF camps around Dahagram's perimeter and the construction of ten panoptic watchtowers staffed by armed BSF soldiers. Despite and in part because of such changes, the question of belonging remains acute for residents.

It is no surprise, then, that the enclave's history is remembered and narrated as a claim both to membership and to the right and ability to hold and possess belongings. The manner in which Dahagram's pre-Corridor past is remembered and talked about constitutes stories of possession and dispossession and at the same time advances ongoing claims—claims that the partial belonging afforded by the Corridor is inadequate and insufficient for those who have struggled, persevered, and suffered for Bangladeshi territory. This is not to claim that such narratives are uniform or that they constitute and encompass all of Dahagram's fragmentary narratives and pasts. Rather it is to say that the history of Dahagram as told by its residents is an ongoing and unfinished project of transforming and redefining Dahagram's ambiguous and liminal position within the Bengali state and nation—of asserting Dahagram as a moral community worthy and deserving of inclusion within Bangladesh. Chhitmahal residents are frequently referred to as 'stateless,'[51] yet their history has also been an ongoing negotiation with what such a term might mean. If residents are stateless, their lives are also overdetermined by the Indian and East Pakistani/Bangladeshi state and the tension between symbolic and more grounded forms of belonging within and to them. The histories that I have recounted are both narrations of Dahagram's past and projects to claim a national belonging as a means to actualize political membership within the Bangladeshi state. These claims and negotiation go beyond, as they partially encompass, liberal normative notions of rights and citizenship. At the same time, they cannot be understood solely from the perspective of statelessness or bare life. Such terms fail to capture the ways that enclave residents have actively resisted attempts to limit their rights and struggled to frame their own notions of belonging at both national and local scales.

In sensitive, unstable, and contentious zones such as border regions, upland areas, and enclaves, such histories of belonging(s) are more than simple narrations of the past. They also form the basis of ongoing struggles over how such spaces and their residents fit or do not fit into constructions of nation and state. Attending to such histories and taking seriously the ways that residents of these zones frame them can provide critical insights into the terrain of negotiation between states and groups and spaces that only imperfectly fit into categories of 'citizen' and 'national territory.' Gellner (introduction, this volume) suggests that ethnographic encounters with the state must grapple with both sides of Abrams's (1988) problematic of the 'state-system' and 'state-idea.' I would suggest that the histories of belonging I engage in this chapter are crucial sites to begin unraveling this problematic. These emic understandings of the past are thus critical in rethinking the politics of inclusion and exclusion that frame the ideas of nation and state, as well as the broad networks of power within which they are inscribed.

Seen in this light, discontent over the inability to celebrate such anniversaries as Corridor Open Day in Dahagram acquires a different meaning. Residents rarely have the opportunity to publicly articulate their histories of suffering for territory (Moore 2005) or their ongoing demands for full inclusion in Bangladesh. Belonging, for residents of Dahagram, determines their ability to move into and out of the enclave and the ability to go to market to sell and purchase essentials; belonging confronts the constant specter of violence and fear that haunts those who lived through the long struggle to gain substantive as well as formal membership within the territory of Bangladesh. The stakes of articulating claims to belonging are thus more than symbolic. They are about the ongoing negotiation of life in a sensitive, contingent, and unstable space.

NOTES TO CHAPTER 9

Support for this research was generously provided by a Social Science Research Council International Dissertation Research Fellowship. Generous feedback, direction, and assistance were provided by Jaideep Chatterjee, Dia Da Costa, Shelley Feldman, David Gellner, Sayeed Hassan, Reece Jones, Erin Lentz, Xulhaz Mannan, Nayanika Mathur, Philip McMichael, Yasmin Saikia, Eric Tagliacozzo, Brendan Whyte, and especially Townsend Middleton. Thanks especially to Brendan Whyte for permission to use his excellent maps. This chapter appeared originally in *Modern Asian Studies* and is republished with permission and slightly adapted.

1. The official name of the enclave is Angarpota-Dahagram, denoting two separate but conjoined enclaves. By shortening the name to Dahagram, I am following the convention adhered to by residents.

2. This paper deals primarily with the history of Dahagram. The literature on the chhitmahals is limited, but for more on enclaves beyond Dahagram see Van Schendel 2002b; Whyte 2002; Butalia 2003; R. Jones 2009b, 2010; Sen 2002.

3. See, for example, Ahmed (2006, 2007), who identifies the enclaves as one of the seven persistent barriers to amicable relations between India and Bangladesh.

4. By 'sensitive,' I mean a political process that both regulates knowledge about sensitive spaces and structures actions, behaviors, and possibilities within them. The 'sensitivity' of the enclaves has tangible effects not just for residents of these fraught areas but also for government officials, security forces, and researchers seeking to understand them. See Cons (2014).

5. I use the convention of italicizing quotations and discussions from my field notes. Verbatim quotations from recorded interviews are not italicized.

6. I have changed the names of my informants to protect their identity.

7. The Emergency was declared after months of political chaos leading up to the general elections. On the Emergency Administration's goals, see Lt. Gen. Moeen U. Ahmed, "The Challenging Interface of Democracy and Security," *Daily Star* (Dhaka), 4 April 2007. On the suspension of democratic liberties during the Emergency, see Odhikar Report, *Due Process of Law Must Be Followed,* 12 March 2008, www .odhikar.org/documents/14monthsofstateofemergency.pdf; Freedom House, *Freedom of the Press 2008—Bangladesh,* 29 April 2008, http://www.unhcr.org/refworld/docid /4871f5ee2.html, both accessed 24 May 2013.

8. *Upazilas* are Bangladesh's second-smallest administrative unit in Bangladesh above the union parishads (councils) and below districts. In this case, Patgram upazila is a subdistrict in Lalmonirhat district. The UNO is the upazila's chief executive officer.

9. On 8 September 2011 the governments of Bangladesh and India signed a protocol to keep the Corridor open twenty-four hours a day. On 19 October 2011 this protocol was put in place to great fanfare within the enclave. See "Dahagram Celebrates While Other Enclaves Unhappy," *Daily Star* (Dhaka), 8 September 2011; H. Habib, "Freedom from Virtual Captivity," *Hindu* (Delhi), 2 November 2011.

10. I draw from concerns within this exhaustive literature on ways to understand the relational production of state, society, security, and identity in borderlands (Gellner, this volume). See also Baud and Van Schendel (1997) and the collections of essays in Wilson and Donnan 1998a; Donnan and Wilson 1999; Rajaram and Grundy-Warr 2007; Diener and Hagen 2010a; Zartman 2010.

11. And not one that need necessarily always be cast in the negative. See Walker 1999.

12. See, for example, essays in Hansen and Stepputat 2005.

13. Numerous other enclaves, particularly those falling between the districts of

Jalpaiguri and Cooch Behar—both districts within West Bengal, India—posed few administrative problems and were eventually simply absorbed into their bounding district. Princely states were nominally given a choice as to which state, India or Pakistan, they wished to join at independence. In practice this choice often boiled down to territorial contiguity. After a brief period of hesitation, Cooch Behar opted for India. On the accession of Cooch Behar, see Ghosh (1993).

14. In other words, in the period following Partition, in which Bengal was split into West Bengal (in India) and East Pakistan and before the Liberation War in 1971, in which East Pakistan gained independence from West Pakistan and became Bangladesh.

15. Indeed the passport agreement made specific provisions for enclave residents, though in practice this freedom was short-lived (see Whyte 2002: appendix 1–22).

16. See numerous accounts in the Home Political Confidential Records from 1948–60, Bangladesh National Archives (BNA: Home CR List 119, bundles 1–52).

17. These paramilitary groups were the predecessors of and were eventually superseded by the East Pakistan (later Bangladesh) Rifles in East Pakistan and the Indian Border Security Forces (BSF).

18. Though I have not been able to verify the exact date that this camp was put in place, residents agree that it was before 1965 and after 1958. This suggests that the camp was initially established by the West Bengal Rifles, before they became incorporated into the new, national BSF in 1965.

19. No residents of Dahagram that I spoke with made any distinction between the BSF and the various paramilitary groups that preceded their formation.

20. As Whyte (2002) notes, residents of the enclave could frequently get a better price for agricultural products in East Pakistan as prices in India were fixed. As such, there was a double incentive to make the crossing to Patgram Thana.

21. For a detailed exploration of the 1965 war, see Gupta 1967.

22. "India Deploys Dogras, Jats, Rajputs along Ranpur [sic] Border," *Pakistan Observer*, 20 March 1965.

23. There is a marked link between the Rann of Kachchh and the enclaves on the other side of the subcontinent. Both were areas of political and geographical ambiguity that emerged out of the post-Partition reshuffling of the princely states. Both are areas of continuing ambiguity and intrigue that have led to frequent violence between border security forces and within communities living on either side of the border. Indeed on 20 March, six days after the outbreak of the Dahagram War, fighting broke out in the Rann between India and Pakistan. The two regions are further similar in that they have both been the focus of intense negotiations over the meaning of space, identity, and nation and are critical sites in the construction of contested borders. For more on the Kachchhi frontier, see Ibrahim 2009. See "Pakistan Warns India Vacate Aggression in Dahagram," *Pakistan Observer*, 18 March 1965.

24. For a classic study of communal social conflict in Bangladesh around livestock, see Roy 1994.

25. It is worth noting that there is some controversy over what exactly happened during the Dahagram War. Indian papers reported that Muslim residents burned Hindu residents' homes, forcing them to flee the enclave. These reports claimed that the BSF entered the enclave in defense of or retaliation for this attack (Whyte 2002).

26. A type of lentil grown widely in North Bengal.

27. None of the newspaper coverage of the war that I was able to locate reported any casualties.

28. "India Sternly Told: No Talks without Restoration of Status Quo," *Pakistani Observer,* 28 March 1965; "Pakistan Warns India Vacate Aggression in Dahagram"; "India Deploys Dogras, Jats, Rajputs along Rangpur Border"; "Intruders at Kalirhat Driven Out," *Pakistani Observer,* 19 March 1965; "Indian Forces Fire on Sylhet Border," *Pakistani Observer,* 18 March 1965; "India Deploys More Troops along East Pakistan Border," *Pakistani Observer,* 25 March 1965; "Indian Troops Deployed along Kushtia Border," *Pakistani Observer,* 28 March 1965; "In Patgram-Baura Sector: Indiscriminant Firing by Indian Troops," *Pakistani Observer,* 29 March 1965.

29. "Fresh Influx of Refugees: Evictions from Cooch Behar," *Pakistani Observer,* 25 March 1965.

30. "Cease Fire at Dahagram," *Pakistani Observer,* 1 April 1965.

31. "Ae Porajoyer Glani Dhakben Keamon Korey [How Will You Cover Up the Shame of Such Defeat?]," *Ganokantha* (Dhaka), 18 May 1974; "Jukto Ghoshonay Vashanir Protikriya [Vashani's Reaction to Joint Decision]," *Ittefaq* (Dhaka), 18 May 1974.

32. "Shimanto Chukti o Jukto Ghoshona Proshongay JSD-er Oveemot: Desh ke Noya Uponibeshe Porinoto Korar Padokkhep [JSD–Jatiyo Samajtantrik Dal/National Socialist Party–on Border Treaty and Joint Declaration: Attempts to Turn the Country into a New Colony]," *Ganokantha* (Dhaka), 19 May 1974.

33. "Berubari Shongkranto Reet Aebondon Nakoch: Apeeler Onumoti Daan [Writ Petition on Berubari Dismissed: Appeal Approved]," *Ittefaq* (Dhaka), 21 May 1974; "Berubari Shomporke Injunction Aabedon Supreme Court-ey Utthapito [Berubari Injunction Appeal Placed before Supreme Court]," *Shangbad* (Dhaka), 21 May 1975; "Berubari Mamlar Churanto Shunanir Din 14-ey June [The Final Hearing Date of the Berubari Case is on the 14th of June]," *Ganokantha* (Dhaka), 30 May 1974.

34. Quoted in Jacques (2000: 45). Of particular concern to the representative was that the leasing of the Corridor to Bangladesh would potentially create an enclave of the village of Kuchlibari cut off from the rest of Mekhliganj Thana. See note 44 below.

35. "Constitution (Third Amendment) Act, 1974, 27 November 1974," appendix 1–42 in Whyte (2002: 381). For a full description of the legal battle in India over the Corridor, see Whyte 2002.

36. On the violent and gendered politics of nation making and territory, see Saikia (2004), Mookherjee (2006), essays in Chatterjee and Jeganathan (2000), Menon and Bhasin (1998), and Butalia (1998).

37. In 1977, after a period as chief martial law administrator, Ziaur Rahman became president. On 22 April he pushed through a martial law ordinance to amend the official principles of the Bangladesh state by removing "socialism" and "secularism" from the constitution and inserting "economic and social justice" and "trust and faith in Almighty Allah" (Anisuzzaman 2001).

38. This assertion was echoed in a *Bangladesh Observer* report that claimed that people in Dahagram had died due to blockades which prevented medical assistance and food from moving into the Corridor. As the report claimed, "Equipped with guns, arrows, *lathis* [clubs] and hand bombs, the Indian nationals are patrolling around these enclaves preventing helpless Bangladeshi nationals of Dahagram and Angarpota to come out and enter Bangladesh main soil to purchase essential commodities" (quoted in Bhasin 1996: 808).

39. The KSS was not simply opposed to the opening of the Corridor on ideological or communal grounds. The Corridor, if leased to Bangladesh, would have effectively enclaved Kuchlibari, a district of Mekhliganj. Kuchlibari is bordered on the east by Bangladesh and on the west by the Tista River. Residents feared that if the narrow strip of land connecting them to the rest of Mekhliganj was closed, they would be in the same territorially dislocated situation as Dahagram. Though the terms of the Tin Bigha Lease proposed in 1982 (see below) and the eventual agreement to open the Corridor made it clear that sovereign control over the Corridor would remain with India, the KSS and TBSS, with the support of the BJP and the break-off Forward Bloc in West Bengal, aggressively opposed the opening of the Corridor.

40. JAGPA regularly participated in and organized protests in relation to a range of border controversies throughout the 1980s. See documentation in Bhasin (1996).

41. Such numbers are likely exaggerated.

42. On BJP rhetoric over 'infiltration' from Bangladesh, see Gillan (2002) and Ramachandran (1999). For details of the debate over fencing beginning in 1983 between India and Bangladesh, see Bhasin (1996).

43. For details of this lease, see Whyte (2002: appendix 1–42).

44. "Tin Bigha Corridor Hostantore Forward Blocker Tibro Apotti [Strong Objection by Forward Block in Handing over the Tin Bigha Corridor]," *Ittefaq* (Dhaka), 28 September 1991.

45. For a discussion of the ways the BJP deployed rhetoric over the sundering of national territory throughout the 1980s and early 1990s, see Krishna 1996.

46. Pamphlet reprinted in Whyte (2002: 384–85). The political reference here is to the Narasima Rao–led Congress Party government and the Jyoti Basu–led CPI(M) government in West Bengal.

47. Though this represented a return to democratic rule, it did not necessarily mean a move back to a secular pan-Bengali political stance. For more on the opening of the Corridor, see Whyte (2002). For more on Bangladesh's emergence from Ershad's rule, see Van Schendel (2009).

48. A report collected in Bhasin (1996) claims that more than three thousand anti-Corridor activists were arrested in Cooch Behar and adjoining districts and that at least one death resulted from skirmishes between Indian activists marching to stop the opening of the Corridor and members of the local police and the BSF.

49. For more on the current state of Dahagram and the Tin Bigha Corridor, see Cons 2007.

50. Zia was the BNP prime minister of Bangladesh at the time.

51. For example, Van Schendel 2002b; Sen 2002; R. Jones 2009b.

Geographies and Identities

Subaltern Partition Stories along Bengal's Southern Frontier

Because a bottle of oil broke
You get angry with the young girl
All you fat guys
You break and divide India
Regions are broken, districts are broken,
Fields, houses and homes,
Roads, storehouses, granaries,
Factories and railways.

Subaltern Narratives of Partition

Haripada read this poem aloud one evening from his diary.[1] A fisherman by day, he often wrote poems by night. We kept meeting each other in two very different settings. The first was in the informal surroundings of fishing or walking through the village; the second was in the highly formalized locale of literary seminars. Haripada, about fifty-five years old, was a keen participant in these gatherings. He never sought me out in the first locale, when silent and taciturn; he would keep a steely glance on his net, chain-smoke *bidis*, dressed in only a loincloth, while his thin, dark body was speckled white by the dried squirts from walking in the cloying grayish mud of the river bank. The other times, the times he sought my companionship, was when we were both at an 'up' island, participants of literary seminars organized on certain special weekends or auspicious days, both with notebook and pen, groomed and well-dressed, he in his white terry-cotton kurta pyjama and me in a starched saree.

He'd call me over: "*Khuki* [young girl], come and sit here next to me." The others were mostly schoolteachers, although, like the two of us, there were a few oddballs, such as Rakhal, more popularly known as Rakhal-dadu (Rakhal grandfather), the blind elderly poet who made a living by also composing poems on the great and the good, which sometimes included the NGO leaders and socialites visiting the area, and Binod Bera, famous for persisting in writing poetry even though he was a small cultivator and cursed, in the eyes of the islanders, with five daughters and no sons. There was also, from time to time, Sudharani Mridha, the wife of one of the schoolteachers, who was a keen politician. She shared with her husband not simply a love for lyrical words but also an interest in the workings of the state and was eager to join these meetings to further her literary leanings, buff her contacts, and gain greater political mileage.

I'd go, like many of the others, to relieve the boredom of everyday life on the islands. It was an opportunity that allowed one to travel to an 'up' island, which meant a more 'developed' one, usually Rangabelia (next to Gosaba) or Basanti, and once the seminar was over, visit shops, sit under a fan, make phone calls. Haripada was an avid partaker of these meetings, but I rarely saw him share space with the schoolteachers when they assembled in small groups to smoke or drink tea either at the seminar or during the weekly bazaar day. His dark skin, oiled for the event, was so taut on his face that below his cheekbones two grooves caved in and one could make out the contours of his skull every time he took a drag. He stuck out in a room where people were generally lighter skinned and fatter. I suppose he sought me out because we were both oddities and we knew each other 'from the village,' where I was conducting anthropological fieldwork for my PhD; the others could sense we both had other lives, that he was a fisher with practically no formal education and I a PhD student with a foreign background who was nonetheless unmarried and far from home.

Later, when we would all be sitting in rows on benches in front of our platefuls of rice, he'd focus on his food and keep very quiet. Sometimes he would smile and nod at what the schoolteacher sitting next to him had said. Yet when it was his turn to read his piece, he strove to adhere to the canons of respectability. Mouthing the words, he declaimed carefully so that they did

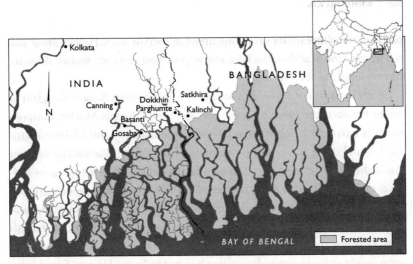

MAP 10.1. The Sundarbans in West Bengal and Bangladesh.

not come out garbled and rustic. His subjects were always popular rehashed topics like 'the beauty of the forest,' 'the plight of the Sundarbans islander,' 'the Partition of Bengal.' He did not live very far from where I had set up house and, sometimes, when we came across each other at the marketplace or on the roadside, he'd whisper, "Come over this evening, I've written a new one." I'd usually buy time before heading to his place, as his readings, one poem after another, would often stretch in an unstoppable flow for a couple of hours. On my last visit to the Sundarbans, I decided to pay him a visit to tell him I was now working in Bangladesh, where his family was from. He just replied, "Khuki, listen to this," and he read out the famous poem by Annadashankar Roy that opens this chapter.

Once he had ended, he lit a bidi. He asked me to write it down—"It will be important for your work on Bangladesh"—and while I was doing so he muttered, as if to no one in particular, "And yet, when one small bottle of oil breaks, it's the poor young girl that gets beaten up. They play dice, we get pawned." I knew Haripada had firsthand experience with dice being cast, regions being broken, and people being pawned. His family was from "the other side of the river," and he and his parents and eight siblings had to leave their East Bengali homestead as *udbastu* (literally, 'uprooted from one's homestead,' a common term for refugees) sometime in the 1960s, "after the riots." Haripada never told me that the Muslim inhabitants of the village he now lived in had been chased away. Neither had anyone else spoken about it in the first few months I was there in late 1999. This time I asked, "What happened here? Tell me, whose land was this, the land where your house stands today? Why are they no longer here?" Silence.

On my more recent fieldwork, conducted along the West Bengal–Bangladesh border between 2007 and 2009, for a project on the Bengal Muslim diaspora which is currently being written up with Joya Chatterji and Claire Alexander, I would come across similar blaming of the ruling elite for the division that had ensued between eastern and western Bengal and an analogous reticence to talk about what really happened in their neck of the woods (compare Gupta's observations on the silence around Partition in the Kargil region, chapter 2, this volume). I was traveling in Bangladesh's Dinajpur in the north when I came across a nonagenarian, Abdul Rahman Biswas, who had wielded some power in his younger days, when he lived in India. He now found himself a refugee in Bangladesh, having had to flee West Bengal after riots against Muslims in his village. I repeat what he said:

> When Lord Mountbatten was the big *lat* [corrupt form of 'lord'] of this place, the oppression started, so people rebelled against him. He complained to Churchill about this when he traveled to London. So Churchill called an Indian, Gandhi, and told him "Okay, I'll return you your country and you can stop complaining." But inwardly he thought, "I'll divide the place so that they're forever consumed in fire." People started to fight because of this curse of Churchill's, and the fire that was lit then has since never been extinguished. Nehru and Jinnah started to fight, three *annas* [sixteenth parts] for Pakistan and thirteen *annas* for India.
>
> Radcliffe was summoned to divide the country. He started cutting up regions. He split Punjab into two and then Bengal, and five *thanas* [districts] of Malda ended up in Pakistan: Bholahat, Shibganj, Chapai-Nowabganj, Nachol, and Gomosthapur. My land was divided into two. I had some in Pakistan but most of it was in India. So I initially stayed in India.

As I came to know later, if the loss was a personal one, speakers on both sides of the border consistently blamed the elite for what had befallen the 'common people' after Partition. When I mentioned riots, for example, people would talk about the national riots, rarely mentioning the violence that had taken place in their own backyard or village. It was as if Partition and its bloody aftermath was willed and its divisive politics perpetrated by the ruling elite—first by the

British ruling elite and later, after Independence, by the Indian—and they, the rural folk, were simply the pawns in the divisive designs of this elite. When I pressed victims of Partition who lived along the border to give me details, they usually talked of the "hordes of migrants" who had come "from the other side, invited by the politicians" and had taken over their land, cattle, homesteads. It was never the neighbors themselves who were blamed or introduced in the narrative. And the chapter had to be quickly closed—"Those were so many years ago." Nobody wanted to dwell on those memories. Whether Hindu or Muslim, whether from this side or that, the official story was that they were all *desher lok*, here meaning from the same region as well as stressing one's rural identity. In Malda they called themselves Maldoiyas (usually referring to people who practice shifting cultivation on *chars* [suddenly appearing river-beds]); when from the south, they referred to themselves as 'tide people' (*bhatir lok*), united in their primary identity as the people of the godforsaken, and usually state-forsaken, islands of the Sundarbans.

And yet, below the veneer, just as Nayanika Mathur, following Li (2001: 58), argues in this volume, the way the rural people judge each other is ordained by a set of standards derived from and centered on, in this case, the urban. Much like the mountains of Uttarakhand, in the Sundarbans too the farther away from the plains the islanders live, the more backward they are considered to be. Here too a denigration of one's 'backwardness,' particularly when living in the dangerous borderlands of the state, makes one aspire to greater respect-ability, and unfortunately that means giving up on certain shared practices such as *qawali* singing during the Urs of a Sufi saint or the veneration of the forest deity Bonbibi. These practices, lying at the interstices, make one look 'uneducated' because these are not shared by the urban elite. Similarly the messy stories of Partition, when there weren't necessarily heroes and villains, did not fit the grand nationalist narratives of Partition and were therefore seen as unfit to be told. Besides, for many, it wasn't an event in the past; it was something they were still living.

As Cons (chapter 9, this volume) shows in relation to enclave dwellers, "be-longing is a question, as such, that is rarely taken for granted." Indeed belong-ing is never taken for granted and is always an ongoing and unfinished pro-cess. The Muslim minority in the rural areas are still made to feel the brunt of this separation between a 'Hindu' India and a 'Muslim' Bangladesh, especially by the Hindu immigrants who are still making inroads into West Bengal's hinterland. This caginess or reserve in relation to talking about one's history is totally linked to one's identity and status in relation to the majority community of the village. Even today the chief minister of West Bengal/Paschimbanga has few qualms about conflating West Bengal's Muslims with an Urdu-based identity, thus making them feel even more as if they are the epitome of the 'other' in West Bengal. The Trinamool Congress's "Vision Document," published in 2011, prior to the State Assembly elections that brought the ruling party to power, announced in its "Action Agenda" that the chief minister would create Muslim universities and colleges, more madrasas, and Urdu schools for West Bengal's Muslims.[2] At this point, it is important to remember that most Muslims of Pashchimbanga have no connection to Urdu whatsoever: "To create this association willy-nilly is a high-stakes game for this game has a flip-side. The people of the majority faith are also being fed this rubbish that implies some intrinsic connection between Muslims in Pashchimbanga and Urdu. For right-wing bigots in the majority community of Pashchimbanga, this only helps consolidate their long-standing charge of Muslims of Bengal being less Bengalee than their Hindu counterparts" (Chatterjee 2012). And the same is true on the Bangladeshi side of the border, where to be Bengali is conflated with being Muslim, and Hindus are considered secret India-loving 'traitors' to the Bangladeshi nation.

This reticence toward narrating one's Partition story in the Bengali hinterland is very different from the outpouring of stories of shock and loss I grew up hearing from the families of my better-off friends in West Bengal's Kolkata. The theme of Partition, especially among Hindu West Bengalis, was always exclusively about the Hindus who had had to leave their homes in East Bengal to come to West Bengal, more specifically to Kolkata, and live in relatives' homes or in camps. Besides, it was always seen as a deed in the past, one that was sealed off, dealt with, and from which one had moved on. As Rahman and Van Schendel (2003: 555) point out, the literature focuses on two aspects of Partition; the first is the relationship "between the refugees and the state, both in terms of state policies toward the newcomers and in terms of the effects that refugees had on politics in Calcutta and the rest of West Bengal."[3] The second theme, which I would argue is more dominant in popular urban consciousness, is formed by "the voices and identities of a particular group of refugees to West Bengal, the Bengali *bhodrolok* (the educated upper and middle class), with their often traumatic and nostalgic memories of a lost homeland in East Bengal" (556).[4] Rahman and Van Schendel rightly argue that "concentrating on refugees within these specific parameters, scholars have presented us with a partial picture of post-Partition population movements" and that we need "additional research" (556). Baud and Van Schendel (1997: 212) have urged students of borders and borderlands to go beyond legal, geographical, and geopolitical questions and to look at "the historical effects of borders," especially on people "from the periphery."

As highlighted by Nilanjana Chatterjee (1990), the left's master narrative for Hindu-Muslim conflict lay in explaining away the violence by highlighting the economic disparities between the two communities, the exploitation of one by the other. The expropriation and attack on the Bengali Muslim by the Bengali Hindu is understood by the left as an aberration that can be corrected by 'consciousness raising.' "The fact that the Congress and the CPM [Communist Party of India (Marxist)] insist on a small figure for Muslim out-migration to Pakistan (relative to east Bengali Hindus) and take pride in the state's apparent restitution of property to Muslim 'returnees,' posits secularism as normative in India as a policy and an objective condition" (Chatterjee 1990: 22)— a story fitting into bhadralok narratives of Partition. In his work with Rahman, Van Schendel goes beyond these bhadralok narratives by presenting us with stories of people who migrated from India into Rajshahi, a town that lies today in Bangladesh. Rahman and Van Schendel (2003) identify four groups of migrants: (1) "the Optees," those who were employees of the colonial state and who migrated within days of Partition in August 1947; (2) "the displaced by education," people who opted for East Pakistan as the labor market for university graduates was much better there; (3) "the Riot refugees," those who were violently expelled or fled, especially during the bloody riots of 1950 and 1962; and (4) "the displaced by exchange," people who moved only after they could exchange their immovable property with that of others from the other side.

In this chapter, in a bid to look at the historical effects of the Bangladesh-India border on those who were 'peripheral' to the whole process and the product of "condescension and erasure" (Chatterjee 1990: 22), I present Partition stories narrated by those who were 'riot refugees.' Those mentioned here were not from the urban elite or the middle classes but from a poorer background and from the rural areas, especially those areas along the West Bengal–Bangladesh border. There is a huge disparity between the way they remember, narrate, or silence Partition and its aftermath and those stories that have been passed down by the states' ruling elites. I also look at how Partition stories still very much color relations between communities living along the border. What we can learn from these more rural and 'peripheral' narratives is that they are, finally, not just about Partition and its aftermath; they are also a reflection of the ways people have to live their social and religious identities along the Bengal borderland today.

Silencing Everyday Indignities and Marking Religious Geographies

At the beginning of my fieldwork in Kalinchi, Satkhira, Bangladesh, I visited eighty-five-year old Jalal Gazi. I had been given the usual generic story about elites dividing Bengal among themselves, Partition, the loss of land and honor, and the experience of being dropped into second-class citizenry. After a few visits the old man began to share more about his personal experience of Partition:

> We are originally from Kalitola. The East Bengalis kicked us away from there so we came to Dokkhin Parghumte, where we had family. Our whole place in Kalitola used to be Muslim. Then one day, sometime during the early '50s, some refugees who had come from the other side announced that Muslims wouldn't be allowed to live here, that they would have to leave. Our zamindar, Krishnapada Chattopadhyay, was on our side and said he'd take our defense. But then the police started aligning themselves with the refugees, and slowly the locals sided with them as well, and they all started pressuring us.
>
> They went from house to house, sometimes raped and looted, at other times burned down our homes and our granaries. They made things very difficult for the zamindar, and so he called us to him and said, "All these years I've been protecting you, but now I can't any more," and he left for Kolkata the next day. When the zamindar left we felt we wouldn't be able to keep our honor, so some of us left for Pakistan. At that time all the Muslims of Jogeshganj, Parghumte, Kalitola, Samshernagar, Gobindokati left together. But before leaving for Pakistan we went to Dokkhin Parghumte, where we had family and where we were a Muslim-majority village.
>
> But the refugees from the other side of the river started to come in hordes to Dokkhin Parghumte too. Our maternal house was set on fire; poison was mixed with the straw used to feed our buffaloes; only four of

our seventeen buffaloes survived. Our family's land used to stretch all the way to the river; now, the last time I visited about fifteen years ago, it ended with the small field that surrounds my nephew Fakhruddin's homestead. Gradually the physical threats were growing, houses were burned, women defiled, lives threatened. When nothing more worked, we stole away in the dead of night on our boats to Pakistan to save our skins and in hope of a more equal future. Little by little we all left except my eldest brother, Shahid Gazi, who stayed back "to look after the mosque and the graves of our ancestors."

My elder brother Shahid and his immediate family stayed on to protect the graves because Hindus have no respect for graves. They just dig out our bones and chuck them into the river and start tilling our graveyards as if they were crop fields. You know, Fakhruddin's paddy stack was burned down. It burned for four or five days nonstop. We kept dowsing the fire with water but it wouldn't subside and die out. But Fakhruddin said, "I'm ready to give up my life, but I can't give up the graves of my father and mother." And so he stayed back with Shahid.

Later, on the other side of the border, in India, I tracked down Jalal's brother's family and paid them a visit. Ninety-three-year-old Shahid Gazi, Jalal's brother, still lived in West Bengal's Dokkhin Parghumte. Everybody told me the old man had gone mad. I was also introduced to his relatives, who were now reduced to a mere fifty people. Originally the village had been mainly Muslim. I asked Jalal and Shahid's sixty-year-old nephew Fakhruddin to tell me more, but he was reluctant as "it was so many years ago." I realized there were neighbors squatting or standing around us. A teenager blurted that the local mosque had been destroyed five years earlier, and Fakhruddin nodded in acquiescence but said nothing. A young man in his mid-twenties came forward and said, "Those were many years ago, we all get along fine now, there is no use to dwell on old memories. We have nothing to report to journalists from this village."

I remonstrated, saying I was not a journalist, but did not press the matter. In a place where the hierarchy of age usually supersedes that of level of formal education, this young Hindu man felt he could talk in the name of the little group that had by now assembled in Fakhruddin's courtyard. I started feeling what Jalal had said when he had talked of the daily indignities they had had to live with before leaving for East Pakistan. I later asked if the young man had politically important relatives, but I was told it was not so. I did not want

FIGURE 10.1. Jalal Gazi showing his grandchildren a picture of his brother on the author's laptop, 2009. Photograph courtesy of A. Jalais.

Fakhruddin or his family to face new affronts, whether verbal and physical, so I let it be. When later I went to the village next door in Gobindokati and started to ask questions about a mosque that had recently been destroyed, another group of young men came and told me to stop asking "Hindu-Muslim questions." "Everyone is fine now," they said, "all living happily together."

Both times, the people I had been speaking with went completely quiet. I realized the young men wanted me to leave, to stop me from asking questions by their presence. I said, "These people are from the older generation, they know what happened. How would you know these stories? You're too young." They answered, "We know all there is to know, nobody else needs to know." Annoyed at such blatant intimidation and maybe to get back at them, I remarked out loud, "You're from the other side, aren't you? When did you guys come over?" "Yes, but we're Hindu, and we're in Hindustan," they shot back, chillingly unfazed. Their majoritarian religious identity now allowed them to take on a position they saw as superior to the usual Bengali hierarchies of age and education.

From a conversation I serendipitously had with Fakhruddin, when we found ourselves traveling together a few days later, he mentioned the loss of his thirteen buffalo and his land. He explained that Shahid had refused to follow the rest of the five brothers because he deemed himself "too old to call a new place 'home.'" His village, where he had settled as a young man to tend his childless maternal uncle's land, was his "homeland," he said, and it was because he continued to live there that Fakhruddin, who had then been a young man, had risked staying on. But staying had become increasingly difficult with every new departure:

> When even the Union Board president, Dr. Sofed Ali, went missing, many of us had felt that they had nobody who could protect us any more. A few more families then left, and our village, from being a Muslim-majority one, became a Hindu-majority one. Geographies became religious—you were either in 'Hindustan' or 'Pakistan,' and depending on your religion you were either in the 'right' or the 'wrong' country, whatever the majority of your village.
>
> Becoming a 'minority' is about losing the link to power and status. With community leaders replaced by leaders of the majority religion, posts started to disappear, mosques started to be attacked. More than our lives we feared losing our dignity. I was young and headstrong and I loved my uncle Shahid so I stayed, but the others, my uncles, they were respectable and established people, and when they started losing their jobs to young upstarts who had half their degrees and qualifications, they left.

Jalal and Shahid's family had counted a doctor, a school headmaster, and a couple of teachers. Shahid and Fakhruddin's children and grandchildren had left the area to try to make a living as, despite their education and qualifications, they had been passed over for jobs and opportunities. On the other side of the border, in Bangladesh, Jalal's children were rich but barely educated; they had amassed a different kind of social capital. Jalal had spent his money not so much on education as on buying land and fisheries, going on the haj, and building a mosque. This was also what many East Bengali refugees to West Bengal's borderlands had done—they were the most ardent Hindus of the village, the ones to build and take care of temples, organize Vaishnavite *kirtans* (hymn-singing), and travel to the various sites of pilgrimage across India.

Borders, as Baud and Van Schendel (1997: 214) argue, become markers in two ways: First, they reveal "the territorial consolidation of states. Most states

try to curb regional autonomy and [are] no longer content with 'rough edges.'
. . . By taking possession of disputed or unclaimed areas, state elites tried to
resolve the problem of loosely defined border regions to which two or even
more states might lay claim. In this way, they drew sharper lines between citizens, invested with certain rights and duties, and 'aliens' or 'foreigners.'" New
migrants have to prove their 'allegiances' to their chosen state, and it seems
that in the border areas the best way one can do that is by laying claim to the
religious symbols of the majority.

What was indeed surprising to note was how the most important aspect of
one's identity when acquiring a homestead in the new 'homeland' was to mark
it with the more important indicators of the majority religion. With this went
a necessary silencing of the minority—a minority now perceived as not fitting
into this new 'religious geography.' If those who migrated into the new country were seen as 'sons and daughters of the nation coming home,' those who
were leaving were seen as the deserters of the nation (Van Schendel 2005a:
192). The minorities who were left behind were the "citizens by proxy" (Van
Schendel 2002b). Loss and trauma are shared by all of those who have been
marked by Partition. But the historical repercussions and the narratives are
not shared equally. Speaking of loss is easy among the more urban, middle-
class, or elite Bengalis of both Bangladesh and West Bengal, but Partition
remains an area of silence and of fear for those living in the more rural and
border zones of the two Bengals.

Deltaic South Bengal: Religion and Class

This separation by religion is a new departure. Socioculturally, the people living in the Sundarbans region north of the forest and on either side of the border share not only the same language, culture, and ethnicity but also certain
forms of worship. In pre-Partition Bengal the Sundarbans region was shared
equally by both Hindus and Muslims. After Partition the western side became
predominantly Hindu and the eastern side Muslim. Historically the region is
probably the principal borderland for the encounter of Islam and Hinduism in
Bengal. Richard Eaton (1993: 310) has described how, from 1200 onward, Sufi
holy men and their converts cleared the forests of the northern parts of the
Sundarbans and how agriculture came to be intimately linked to the spread of
Islam in Bengal. The local religious practice of venerating Bonbibi, the lady of
the forest, was undertaken both by Hindus and by Muslims who work in the

FIGURE 10.2. Teashop posters on the West Bengal–Bangladesh border, 2009. A poster of the Jamuna bridge (a well-known landmark in Bangladesh) happily coexists with pictures of Hindu deities and a film poster advertising *Abbajaan's Hindu Daughter* ('Abba' being the term of address used by most Bengali Muslims for their father). Photograph courtesy of A. Jalais.

forest. Similarly both Hindus and Muslims venerate the tombs of certain *pirs* (Muslim saints). People often spoke of how they felt they were at the margins of mainstream Bengali society, with their rustic-sounding names and rural occupations, sharing more in common with each other than with those who, on either side of the border, at the regional or national level, represented what it meant to be Bengali.

Let me take the example of the region I know best: the Sundarbans. Like many parts of rural West Bengal or rural Bangladesh, it is a 'forgotten' region. Not much happens there. It used to be, and in many places it still is, one of the poorest regions of South Asia, and people often talk of how they used to go hungry in the olden days. Not only is the economic scene bleak, but there is also very little opportunity for social mobility. People who have 'respectable jobs' such as teaching are rarely from the area originally and often leave for the suburbs of Kolkata or Dhaka or small towns north of the region as soon as they retire. There is very modest scope here for the fishers or those working in the forest to gain social status. With few radios and even fewer TVs (there is no electricity) there is very little opportunity to learn to become a 'respectable'

Bengali by mastering the ability to speak or write proper Bangla, sing Tagore's songs, know English, and get a 'pen-and-paper' job. There are no libraries and therefore no access to the icons of Bengali literature. Often authors are just names most islanders have heard of but never actually read. Schools are few and far between, and not many offer secondary education.

It was therefore strange to see Haripada, a fisherman, participate in these literary meetings. He was eager to share his poetry and be given a chance to belong to that rarefied category of learned Bengalis, but it was evident that he was, in some ways, considered an impostor. He remained uncomfortable around schoolteachers, who never allowed him to gain social capital. He would constantly be made to feel 'small.' This was something I often heard the islanders talking about: how the 'better-offs' who had connections to towns or were from the city mocked their rural ways and treated them as inferior. Haripada's brother Krishnapada, who had done well in life and was now the proud owner of a boat, told me one day about their early days, after they had newly arrived from East Pakistan.

After they had come from 'the other side' they were so poor that they often went hungry. Two of Haripada's siblings died of hunger; after much searching, their father found someone who could place two of his sons as servants in the city. Haripada, being older, had been kept at home to help his father and work as a fisherman, but Krishnapada and Shyamapada were sent off to Kolkata. Krishnapada told me:

> I worked with our brother Shyamapada for the Kolkata bhadraloks as a child servant, working my bones in a master's house. My brother and I were in different places. But we both had to finish our household chores before we got any food. This would often be late afternoon. But, you know, I didn't mind that, nor the fact that after six months my father was only given eighty rupees for my work, no. What I really resent is the humiliation I was made to feel.
>
> This was through small things, you know, like having to eat from an aluminum plate when everyone else ate from steel ones, being given the ration shop rice while the others ate fine rice, being given the smallest piece of fish; sometimes that too was cut in two so that I had half a tiny piece for lunch, the other half for the next day. The sweets brought as gifts would rarely be shared with me, or they gave them to me when they had turned sour. Every day I was made to drink a pot of rice water [*phan*]

before meals under the supervision of my mistress, who said, "Drinking rice water will make you strong," but it was just to make me feel full so that I ate less rice.

But still these were nothing; after all, when we had arrived in this village we too begged to be able to drink the phan of those more fortunate who had been able to cook rice. And so what if my masters thought that phan was actually fit only to be drunk by cows and servants, this was nothing compared to the mortifying shame I was made to feel when my father came to visit me one day to take me back to attend my sister's wedding.

My master did not serve any food to my father, he just gave him my salary of a few rupees and sent me off with him on an empty stomach. We then went to my brother's place of work to pick him up. There we were coldly received and given a small half-pound bread as dinner to share between the two of us. My father had left home at daybreak without eating and had not even been served rice after traveling the whole day. It was as if we are some kind of 'subhumans' for the *babus*. Thinking of this still burns my insides.

The term *babu* in West Bengal, akin to *shaheb* in Bangladesh, is a term of respect for social superiors. The English-language use of the term is tinged with negativity; however, in Bangla, 'babu' is commonly used to address Hindu schoolteachers and other social superiors, considered to be part of the bhadralok in West Bengal. 'Bhadralok' is often also understood as synonymous with people living in Kolkata, the capital of West Bengal. It is difficult to find an equivalent for the Bangladeshi side; people use 'shaheb' for the equivalent of 'babu' and talked about the *opor moholer lok* (people of higher status). The rural hinterland is exoticized by this urban elite, who use *desher lok* (people from the hinterland) or *gramer lok* (village people) with slight condescension when referring to rural people. The use of 'desher' or 'gramer lok,' sometimes even by those who were village dwellers themselves, indicated both one's superior learning or education and one's distance from those involved in 'rural occupations' such as fishing or cultivating. It is very difficult to gain social status when one comes from the backwaters of rural West Bengal or Bangladesh. Stories abound of being made to feel inferior by the urbanites from Dhaka and Kolkata or by those who have 'pen-and-paper' jobs.

Partition History of the Rural Subaltern Delta-Living Bengali

The main theme of 'Bengali identity' for West Bengalis is arguably the 1947 Partition and its bitter legacy, whereas for Bangladeshis it is the birth of Bangladesh in 1971. If, in West Bengal, there is an extensive literature on the reasons for Partition and the trauma it caused, there is practically nothing on the trauma caused by 1971; it is exactly the opposite in Bangladesh. As Rahman and Van Schendel (2003) point out, the literature on personal histories of Partition has mainly focused on the wealthier Hindus who had to leave East Bengal to come to West Bengal's Kolkata, as well as on those Hindus who found themselves unwanted minorities in East Pakistan. There is little place in writings on Partition for people like Haripada or Jalal, people who lost their leaders and had to leave their homes for a new homeland. Similarly there is little place in the history of 1971 for those who were not from an educated and socially superior background.

The upper-caste landed elite started migrating from East Bengal to what would become West Bengal already in the 1930s and 1940s. In the 1951 census of India it was recorded that 27 percent of Kolkata's population was composed of East Bengali refugees, and subsequent migrants (mainly rural middle-class cultivators and artisans, and later the landless) came after Partition. Some found a niche with relatives and friends in Kolkata, while the poorest squatted on public and private land and tried to resist eviction. Migration continued in large numbers right up to the liberation of Bangladesh in 1971; it increased during periods of particular communal unrest such as the 1964 riots and the 1965 India-Pakistan War, when it is believed that 600,000 refugees left East Pakistan for India. Estimates of the total number of refugees up to 1970 are over five million (about one-fourth left for East Pakistan and the rest for West Bengal).

Another 10 million East Bengalis entered India during the early months of the Bangladesh War of Independence (1971), and two million of them stayed back after Bangladesh became independent. Unlike their richer counterparts, who were backed by family and caste connections, many of the poorer fishing and cultivating migrants did not find shelter or ways of making a living in Kolkata. Some managed to stay and lived in abject poverty along railway lines or under bridges, but many were sent to various camps far from West Bengal in inhospitable and infertile areas, the most famous being those of Umerkote,

Malkangiri, Paralkote, and Kondagoan in the Koraput and Kalahandi districts of Orissa and Bastar district of Madhya Pradesh. Termed the Dandakaranya Project, these camps for East Bengali refugees were situated in the semi-arid and rocky place between Orissa and Chhattisgarh and were entirely removed, both culturally and physically, from the refugees' known world.

Partition is understandably a common subject among the urban intelligentsia of Kolkata because more than a third of the people who are settled in that city, the fount of bhadralok identity, are from East Bengal. But the historical moment that defined those I worked with in the West Bengal Sundarbans was Morichjhanpi. Morichjhanpi is part of the Sundarbans forested islands which had been reclaimed from its wilderness for tamarisk and coconut plantation by the government of West Bengal. After December 1977, when the Left Front government came to power, about thirty thousand of the refugees who had been put in the Dandakaranya Project camps returned to West Bengal and settled there. They built schools, dug ponds and tube-wells, and organized themselves into communes.

To cut a long story short, a year and a half later, in May 1979, Morichjhanpi island was encircled by government forces; the refugees were fired at, their houses burned down, and they were packed into trucks and forcibly taken back to their camps in central India. The argument for chasing them away was that the Sundarbans forest and tigers had to be protected. The Sundarbans islanders, witness to this brutal eviction, often referred to this episode as 'the massacre of Morichjhanpi'; for some of them, it marked the beginning of a politics of betrayal by what they saw as a government run by the urban elite. That the communist government, which came to power especially with the backing of refugees, had put greater importance on the protection of wildlife and had used force against impoverished refugees (resulting in at least two hundred deaths), was seen as a total betrayal of the poor and the marginalized.

I was given a firsthand account of the Morichjhanpi story by Jayanta, one of Haripada's brothers. He had settled there when the refugees came. The islanders had bonded with the refugees not only because they shared a common place of origin (eastern Bengal) but also because they could identify with the terrible hardships the refugees had gone through. Stressing his affinity with the refugees, Jayanta recounted that during the time they had settled in Morichjhanpi they had "all become one big family," as they had "the same hopes, went through the same ordeal, fought on the same side." That was until the moment "Kolkata let us down." After that, he said, "we each went back to the islands or camps we had come from with broken hearts and bloody hands, a broken, disunited, and utterly weakened group."

The chapter was quickly closed. A few journalists questioned the capacity of the upper classes, whether they called themselves communists or something else, to represent the poorest strata of Bengali society. A journalist in the Bengali paper *Jugantar* wrote, "The refugees of Dandakaranya are men of the lowest stratum of society. . . . They are mainly cultivators, fishermen, day-labourers, artisans, the exploited mass of the society. . . . So long as the state machinery will remain in the hands of the upper class elite, the poor, the help-less, the beggar, the refugees will continue to be victimized."[5] "Why have our dead remained unaccounted for and unmourned, forced to hover as spirits in the forest?" Jayanta asked rhetorically and with bitterness.[6] It was while work-ing on Morichjhanpi in the early 2000s that I was confronted by the question "What does it mean to be a Bengali but not a *bhadralok*?" (Jalais 2005).

Bengali, but Not Bhadralok

Haripada's poetry and writing was a way for him to gain, as much as possible, not just social capital but also an entry into the body politic of 'the nation.' The messiness of his Partition story was something he refused to share as, in a way, it did not fit the grander Partition narrative of the Bengali elite. His story of Partition had links to Morichjhanpi, and yet he never mentioned Morichjhanpi in his poems. As discussed earlier, for the urban elite, Partition is a story of betrayal. Growing up in West Bengal I learned in school that Par-tition occurred because "the Muslims preferred to separate and have their own homelands." For individual school friends whose parents were 'Bangal'—a term used for those from eastern Bengal—the stories were mainly about loss and about the 'disloyalty of Muslims,' but it was rarely about the specific Mus-lim cultivators who had worked for generations on their lands.

For the islanders of the Sundarbans on either side of the border and of the religious divide, with little access to formal education, Partition referred to very distinct events they had lived through: Morichjhanpi, or the time the East Bengali refugees were sent to Dandakaranya, or when their buffalo had been killed or their field set ablaze or their mosque torn down. It wasn't a grand overarching narrative; it was what had struck an individual family, a village, or an island 'lot.' (Sundarbans villages were often given 'lot' numbers.) But these little stories had difficulty fitting into the nationalist narrative that is constitutive of Bengali elite identity (and here I include both East and West Bengalis). When one's small story does not fit the national narrative, then what are the historical stories that hold together a nonelite, and necessarily fragmented, Bengali identity?

It was during both of these historical moments (1947 for West Bengalis and 1971 for East Bengalis) that people on either side of the border were faced with what it means to be a Bengali. As those I met in Dandakaranya asked, "Was it because we were lesser Bengalis that we were dumped in Dandakaranya and allowed to rot here, far from our Bengali roots and brethren?" That question took on new meaning with my more recent work (2007–9) in the Bangladesh side of deltaic Bengal, where I heard many disgruntled peasants who had joined the liberation army but had never been celebrated for the role they had played. The bravery awards, medals, prize money, and medical care for the 1971 war veterans had gone to those from the cities or those from the villages who had been better connected. I conducted fieldwork in Bangladesh during the 'caretaker government.' This was after many years of infighting between the two major parties, during which no social redistributive measures had been undertaken. The divide between the rich and the poor is immense. As an old and sickly war veteran in Satkhira said bitterly, "We fought as Bengalis. But have our leaders ever respected our *jat* [race, nation]?"

While working along border areas in Bangladesh more recently, I was curious to find out what constituted the idea of (a) particular Bengali identity(ies) vis-à-vis the celebrated nationalist Bengali identity steeped in the rhetoric of 1971. As Joya Chatterji (1996: 16) has argued, "The Bengali Muslim has long been regarded as a living oxymoron, his Muslimness vitiated to the extent that he is a Bengali." After India was partitioned in 1947 and eastern Bengal became East Pakistan, the West Pakistani administrative elite pushed for greater 'Islamization' of east Bengal. They forced Urdu to be the national language and banned Tagore songs because they felt these were 'too Hindu.' Rabindranath Tagore is the writer and philosopher most revered by Bengalis on both sides of the border and, as such, one of the most important symbols of Bangladeshi nationalism. Bangladesh's national anthem, "Amar Shonar Bangla" (My Golden Bengal), was composed by Tagore.

The rallying call for the creation of independent Bangladesh was the Bengali language. Jibanananda Das's sonnets, published posthumously in *Bengal the Beautiful*, "came to symbolize for many within the ranks of the Mukti Bahini, the Bangladeshi freedom fighters, the very essence of what they were fighting for. The book was reissued more than once during the eight-and-a-half-month span of the liberation war in 1971" (Seely 2008: 248). International Mother Language Day, 21 February, originated in recognition of the Language Movement Day, which has been celebrated in Bangladesh since 1952, when a number of university students in Dhaka were killed by the Pakistani armed forces. What meaning did these icons have for the illiterate working classes of both sides of the Bengali border?

Scholars such as Rafiuddin Ahmed have worked extensively on how Bengali Muslims define their linguistic and regional identity and what it means to be both Muslim and Bengali. However, as Chatterji shows, this relationship has remained an uneasy one. Over the past fifty years, more mainstream and orthodox strands of both Hinduism and Islam have slowly become the primary markers of identity along both sides of the Bengali border. This started with Partition and has gained importance with the ever-increasing numbers of Bangladeshi migrants to the Gulf States and of West Bengali Hindus to other parts of India. Now ideas of religion and what it means to be a 'proper Muslim' or a 'proper Hindu' have become not just more widespread but also more rigid.

Why the Bangladesh-Paschimbanga borderlands? Why look with particular attention today, more than six decades after Partition, and four decades after the birth of Bangladesh? The historical moment defining 'Bengali identity' for most Bengalis living in Paschimbanga is, as noted, the 1947 Partition and its bitter legacy; for Bangladeshis, the moment that defines their identity is the birth of Bangladesh in 1971, the result of the language movement that started in 1952. If in West Bengal there is a considerable amount of literature on the reasons for Partition and the trauma it caused among the elite, there is very little literature on Partition by subalterns or on the trauma caused by 1971. In contrast, in Bangladesh one often hears about 1971 but rarely about 1947. Most Bangladeshis see the period after 1947 as a time when they continued remaining under colonial rule. True freedom, Bangladeshis argue, came in 1971. Along with the growing importance of a more orthodox form of religion for the working classes of both Bangladesh and West Bengal, there has been a generational shift in the way social capital is now accumulated. It is less through Haripada's way of reading and writing poetry and the perfecting of a Bengali diction coming from Kolkata or Dhaka and more through the adoption of religious piety. The terms of entry into a superior social status have changed. It is now, on both sides of the border, more dependent on how well one practices one's near 'nationalized' form of religion rather than on how well one can read or sing Tagore songs.

NOTES FOR CHAPTER 10

1. I have changed the names of people and field sites to protect their anonymity.

2. For the "Vision Document," see All India Trinamool Congress, "West Bengal: A Change for a Better and Brighter Tomorrow," 2011, accessed 11 November 2011, aitmc .org/vision_document_english_2011.pdf.

3. For example, Chakrabarti 1999; Dasgupta 2001; Kudaisya 1998; Mallick 1999; Pakrasi 1971.

4. For examples of this kind of writing, see Chakrabarty 1996; Ghosh 1998; Ray 2001. For the beginnings of similar research on refugee memories and identities in East Pakistan/Bangladesh, see Zaman 1999; Murshid 2001; Guhathakurta 2001. *Bhadralok* is Bengali for 'gentle-folk,' from *bhadra*, translatable as a mix of 'polite,' 'civil,' and 'cultured,' that is, bearing resonances of middle-class sensitivity to culture and refinement, and *lok*, meaning 'group' or 'people.' 'Bhadralok' carries connotations not only of landed wealth but also of education, culture, and Anglicization and of upper-caste exclusiveness (Chatterji 1994: 5). It refers to the rentier class, called *zamindar*, who enjoyed tenurial rights to rents from land appropriated by the Permanent Settlement introduced by the British in 1793. The Permanent Settlement set up a system of parasitic landlordism that led to the sub-infeudation of the peasantry. Shunning manual labor, the bhadralok maintain their status by keeping a careful social distance between themselves and those they consider their social inferiors, the *nimnoborno*, literally meaning 'inferior color' and denoting those who were leather workers, liquor dealers, boatmen, or fishermen, that is, those who were classified as Untouchables in British Bengal (5).

5. Sikar (1982: 2), quoting *Jugantar*, 29 May 1979.

6. The events around Morichjhanpi have been developed at greater length in my book, *Forest of Tigers* (Jalais 2010).

Making the Most of 'Sensitive' Borders

It is past midnight. The village is quiet, except for frogs croaking in the rice fields. But listen! Do you hear the faint clinking of metal? That's the smugglers on their way to the border. Their bicycles are laden with huge bundles and they try to be as unobtrusive as they can. Listening nervously for the sound of patrolling boots, they slowly approach an invisible line in the landscape and slip across. Then they spot a flash of light in the darkness and heave a sigh of relief. Their partners are waiting for them. Mission accomplished.

The modern world is webbed with international borders, and scenes like this can be observed in many places. The ubiquity of borders makes them key sites for comparative social research because it is not just smugglers but all of us who feel the effects of borders on our lives and our thoughts. Modern borders share many characteristics, and yet they defy easy categorization. If there is one thing that the contributions to this book demonstrate, it is that borders vary locally in terms of regulatory regimes, symbolic significance, permeability, social advantage, and change over time.

So what could be the rationale for bringing together these particular border case studies in one volume? As David Gellner argues in the introduction, it is their relative proximity to each other. All of them are located in what he calls 'Northern South Asia.' In addition, each deals with the state of India. Jointly they explore connections across India's international borders with China, Burma/Myanmar, Bangladesh, Nepal, Bhutan, and Pakistan/Kashmir, as well as provincial ('State') borders within India. They show that it makes little sense to think of a border as an unambiguous entity encasing a country's territory. It is always compound, if only because each country may maintain several regional border regimes concurrently. Today, on the Indian side alone, different stretches of the border are the domain of different bodies of border guards, contrasting regulations and practices regarding the treatment of foreigners (e.g., Pakistanis and Nepalis), unequal levels of control, and divergent narratives. It is this variation that makes the study of the Northern South Asian borderlands so valuable. Until recently, however, social scientists showed very little interest in studying them—let alone in studying them comparatively. As this book shows, that neglect is now a thing of the past.

Why have borderland studies been so slow to develop in South Asia compared to other regions in the world? There are two principal reasons. On the one hand, social researchers had a firmly national mind-set; on the other, politicians and bureaucrats created an overarching security discourse. The former is largely a result of the partitioning of scholarship following the political breakup of the region in 1947. The latter is the outcome of an official way of thinking in which the region's postcolonial borders were defined as 'sensitive.' As a result, state officials made it very difficult for social scientists to collect data. In the name of national security they restricted access to border zones, even for their own nationals (as Vibha Joshi describes in chapter 7) and declared basic knowledge to be classified information. Such attitudes persist. Even today the Indian Ministry of Defense sees itself as the owner of Indian geographic data and enforces severe restrictions on their public use.

What causes this feeling of sensitivity about borders in South Asia? Undeniably, in one way or another, every modern state considers its borders to be problematic, vulnerable, and in need of special policy measures. This is simply a result of the centrality of territory in state self-definition. Control of space, or rather the practice of territoriality, is at the core of the modern state. Territoriality, a strategy to control resources and people by controlling area, becomes problematic at the edges of that area, where it is challenged by the neighboring state's territoriality. In this sense national borders are always a central state concern.

But states in Northern South Asia stand out from the crowd. Their territoriality is acutely apprehensive; they have been described as "fearful states" (Ali 1993) that suffer from "cartographic anxiety" (Krishna 1996). This shows up in many forms. South Asian states continue to hang on to rigorous visa regimes toward each other, unlike their neighbors in Southeast Asia. Whereas nationals of ASEAN countries can visit each other's countries without visas, members of SAARC countries do not have that luxury. And for some, notably Pakistanis wishing to visit India and vice versa, visa rules continue to be draconian. In South Asia the only exception is the relationship between India and Nepal, based on a bilateral agreement dating back to 1950.

Apprehensive territoriality is the result of many different factors in South Asia. Some are linked to a long history of uncertain border making. The chapters in this book indicate that decisions that were taken decades or centuries ago continue to shape life in today's borderlands, and well beyond. South Asian border issues can be categorized by the period in which they first appeared. Jason Cons (chapter 9) describes the enclaves dotting the northern India-Bangladesh borderland. These represent the oldest issues; they are remnants of precolonial border making. The border between India and China, as discussed by Nayanika Mathur (chapter 3) and Deepak Mishra (chapter 6), is a colonial relic; it is the contested result of failed negotiations between British India, Tibet, and China in the early twentieth century.[1] The India-Bangladesh border, discussed by Jason Cons (chapter 9) and Annu Jalais (chapter 10), came into being when British India was partitioned in 1947.[2] And the border between India and Pakistan in Kashmir, discussed by Radhika Gupta (chapter 2), did not materialize till after decolonization.[3] These four historical layers are not separate but may interact, as in the case of the enclaves. Here almost forgotten precolonial borders were 'reactivated' by cross-cutting Partition borders.[4]

It is not the layering of border issues as such but the contested nature of their legitimacy that leads to sensitivity. Contested borders lead to opacity regarding the territorial dimensions of the state. Such opacity translates into confusion about the limits of sovereignty as well as about the distinction between what is domestic and what foreign. Where does 'my' society end and 'yours' begin? From a state point of view, such confusion must be avoided at all cost and, if it crops up, needs to be resolved by bilateral talks, capture, or international mediation.

Northern South Asia is a world region where this confusion has been allowed to continue for so long that many now consider it almost intractable. This is a region especially rich in border contestation between neighboring states, or, put differently, a region in which states have remarkably frayed edges. Strangely the case that seems to stand out as the most bizarre—the two-hundred-odd minuscule enclaves shared by Bangladesh and India—is not one of contested borders at all. Both states actually agree on the legitimacy of enclave borders. The long-standing and considerable diplomatic tension between them revolves around access to and future exchange of enclaves, not with the 'correctness' of their borders. At the other end of the spectrum are two cases in which disagreement between states is so intense that the very term 'border' cannot be used. The best-known case is the India-Pakistan border in Kashmir. To all intents and purposes this has been acting as an international border for over six decades, and yet in official parlance it is not. It started out as a United Nations brokered 'Cease-fire Line' in 1949, and in 1972 Pakistan and India agreed on changing its name to 'Line of Control.' Similarly the India-China border is referred to as the 'McMahon Line' and (in Kashmir) as the 'Line of Actual Control.' These international borders are in permanent legal and diplomatic limbo, and military confrontations may occur there at any time. This is also the case for stretches of the long Bangladesh-India border, which is dotted with 'flash points' of uncertain possession that experience recurrent cross-border violence.

Uncertain sovereignty and apprehensive territoriality lead to sensitive borders. Since sensitive borders tend to be patrolled by armed men in state uniforms, the result is volatile borderlands. Volatile borderlands are fearful places; here a standoff is never far removed from a showdown. In South Asia such volatility is generally understood in terms of state security or foreign policy. It can also be understood in local terms, however, and it is this perspective that this book's chapters focus on. The result is a new way of approaching Northern South Asia's borders, more concerned with the anthropology of frayed edges than with the geography of lines. Such studies of the human relations that create, maintain, undermine, and evade borders challenge the idea of a national homeland "viewed as a divinely sanctioned stage upon which a national drama" plays out (Diener and Hagen 2010b: 192).[5] Instead they conceive of the borderland as a place of interaction, meeting, struggle, exchange, belonging, and transition, sometimes despite vigorous attempts at state interdiction. They look across the borderline (contested or not) to take in both sides of the borderland (e.g., Rosalind Evans, chapter 5). They convey the lifeworlds of borderlanders, their ideas about the border, and the technologies available to various borderlanders to give shape to their life (for example, Annu Jalais, chapter 10). They show that the state as it manifests itself at the local level may not fit the models that inspire social science theorizing. Here the state can be seen habitually flaunting its own regulations. Its democratic institutions may stand by as other state personnel intimidate and kill fellow citizens who happen to be border residents or unauthorized traders. Or its sentinels may temper the state claim to monopolize the legitimate 'means of movement' by relegating some border checks to a nongovernment organization (Hausner and Sharma, chapter 4).[6] This is what links all chapters of this book: each explores how people make the most of the sensitive borders and the local state practices they interact with.

The sensitivity of borders fluctuates, in space and time. In Northern South Asia it has been high for decades.[7] High sensitivity makes the study of borderlands difficult yet urgent and revealing because the effects of borders are in no way restricted to border zones. On the contrary, borders fashion societies and states. As Radhika Gupta (chapter 2) reminds us, a borderland can be seen as "a territorial margin that takes us to the center of the state, revealing the contradictions that underlie its discourse." This has been a central point in the recent emergence of borderland studies worldwide: to provide a fresh and important vantage point for the study of societies, offer a corrective to the many nation- and state-centered approaches that drive social science research, and force us to confront what Nicholas Farrelly (chapter 8) calls our "epistemological nodes of control"—for example, the container model of state-society-individual.

The study of international borders in Northern South Asia demonstrates how border sensitivity reverberates throughout state territories and translates into a host of social processes that at first appear to have little to do with borders: state evasion (chapter 1), developmentalism (chapter 6), protracted nonresolution of secessionism (chapter 7), nodal forms of political control (chapter 8), claims to national belonging and citizenship (chapter 9), and struggles over local and national narratives of the past (chapters 9 and 10). The very sensitivity of most of Northern South Asia's borders creates opportunities for a better understanding of how these social processes connect with strategies of territoriality and border making.

Jointly these chapters constitute the beginning of an important conversation that was impossible just a few years ago, essentially because of a lack of relevant empirical research. As this conversation develops, it will need to address certain concerns, for example Anastasia Piliavsky's (chapter 1) fear that privileging international borders may make us lose sight of their similarity with borders within national territories. This is especially relevant in the context of India, where provincial borders can be highly 'sensitive,' as Vibha Joshi (chapter 7) explains. Another concern is the development of an adequate language with which to do justice to the complexities that face social scientists studying borderlands in Northern South Asia. We are still groping for narrative perspectives and analytical notions to capture those complexities. There are various suggestions in these chapters, for example, state-people-border configuration, sensorial border, liminality, transborder identities, nodes of control, and histories of belonging(s). There are also new developments in sociospatial theory that may be helpful.[8] As more research becomes available and enriches the conversation, we can expect the testing of such concepts regarding borderlands—in Northern South Asia and well beyond.

NOTES TO AFTERWORD

1. The Nepal-India and Bhutan-India borders (chapters 4 and 5) are other examples of this category, created earlier in the colonial period. Another—now defunct—example was the Sikkim-India border. It was an international border from 1947 to 1975, when India annexed Sikkim. These international borders, formalized during British rule in India, sometimes partly coincided with older, precolonial boundary formations.

2. The border that separates Burma/Myanmar from India and Bangladesh falls between these colonial and Partition categories. A provincial border within British India until 1937, it became a border between two colonies, British Burma and British India, that year. A decade later the Partition of Pakistan and India (1947) and Burma's independence (1948) turned this border into an international one.

3. Elsewhere I have tried to elucidate South Asian border issues by categorizing them as McMahonian, Radcliffian, and Kashmirian (Van Schendel 2007).

4. For another example of interaction, see Ludden 2003.

5. See also Nayanika Mathur's analysis of the 'sensorial border' and the 'traditionally sacred border' in chapter 3.

6. On state monopolization of the legitimate means of movement, see Torpey 2007.

7. Even the apparently most relaxed, the Nepal-India border, has been embroiled in conflict after 1962, when India occupied the Kalapani region, which Nepal claims as its own.

8. See, for example, the suggestion by Jessop et al. (2008: 389) that territories, places, scales, and networks be viewed as "mutually constitutive and relationally intertwined dimensions of sociospatial relations." They present a framework to study these more systematically.

CONTRIBUTORS

JASON CONS is an assistant professor in the Department of International Relations at Bucknell University. His PhD is from Cornell University's Department of Development Sociology. He has published in a number of venues, including *Modern Asian Studies* and *Third World Quarterly*.

ROSALIND EVANS completed her doctoral research on the experience of young Bhutanese refugees in 2009 within Oxford's Department of International Development, following an MSc in forced migration. She is the cofounder and chair of trustees of a small volunteer-led charity, Refugee Youth Project, which supports young refugees in the United Kingdom, Lebanon, and Nepal. Since finishing her doctorate she has been working with young refugees and asylum seekers in London and Manchester.

NICHOLAS FARRELLY is a research fellow in the Australian National University's College of Asia and the Pacific. He completed master's and doctoral degrees at the University of Oxford and has undertaken field research in northeast India, northern Burma, and southwest China.

DAVID N. GELLNER is a professor of social anthropology at the University of Oxford and a fellow of All Souls. He has worked on Nepal and the Himalayas since 1981. His most recent edited volumes are *Varieties of Activist Experience: Civil Society in South Asia* (2010) and *Ethnic Activism and Civil Society in South Asia* (2009). His most recent monograph (with Sarah LeVine) is *Rebuilding Buddhism: The Theravada Movement in Twentieth-Century Nepal* (2005).

RADHIKA GUPTA obtained her DPhil in social anthropology from the University of Oxford in 2011, following which she took up a postdoctoral research fellowship at the Max Planck Institute for the Study of Religious and Ethnic Diversity in Göttingen. As part of this fellowship she initiated a new project in Mumbai on urban religiosity and political subjectivity among Shi'a Muslims in the city. Her research interests include the anthropology of religion (especially Islam), nationalism, urbanization, postcolonial public cultures and politics in South Asia, and the Himalayas.

SONDRA L. HAUSNER is a university lecturer in the study of religion, University of Oxford, and a research associate at the Centre on Migration, Policy and Society. Her monograph, *Wandering with Sadhus: Ascetics in the Hindu Himalayas* (2007), won the Joseph W. Elder Prize from the American Institute of Indian Studies. She has also published on migration, border towns, and religious practice. Her research focuses on Himalayan and South Asian religions in the region and globally; current work is on ritual, migration, and diaspora religion.

ANNU JALAIS is an assistant professor in South Asian studies at the National University of Singapore. She obtained her PhD from the London School of Economics in 2004 and has since continued working on Bangladesh and West Bengal, India. She is the author of *Forest of Tigers: People, Politics and Environment in the Sundarbans* (2010) and the coauthor (with Joya Chatterji and Claire Alexander) of *The Bengal Muslim Diaspora* (2013).

VIBHA JOSHI is visiting professor and research leader at Tuebingen University, Germany, and research associate at the Institute of Social and Cultural Anthropology, University of Oxford. She was formerly research fellow at the Max Planck Institute for the Study of Religious and Ethnic Diversity, Goettingen, Germany. She was cocurator of the exhibition and coeditor of the accompanying publication titled, *Naga: A Forgotten Mountain Region Rediscovered* at the Museum der Kulturen, Basel in 2008–9. She is the author of *The Land of the Nagas* (2004) and the monograph, *A Matter of Belief: Christian Conversion and Healing in North-East India* (2012).

NAYANIKA MATHUR is a research fellow at Centre for the Arts, Social Sciences and Humanities at the University of Cambridge. She obtained her PhD in social anthropology from the University of Cambridge in 2010, and her revised thesis is to be published as a monograph entitled *Paper Tiger: Bureaucracy and the Developmental State in Himalayan India*. Her work is centered on the anthropology of the state, bureaucracy, law, development, big cat conservationism, and capitalism. Currently she is exploring the effects of new technologies on statecraft in India and is coediting a volume entitled *The New Public Good*.

DEEPAK K. MISHRA is an associate professor at the Centre for the Study of Regional Development, School of Social Sciences, Jawaharlal Nehru University, New Delhi. He has worked in the areas of agrarian relations, gender, migration, and livelihood diversification in mountain economies. He is the coauthor of *The Unfolding Crisis in Assam's Tea Plantations: Employment and Occupational Mobility* (2012).

ANASTASIA PILIAVSKY is a Zukerman Research Fellow at King's College, Cambridge. She holds a doctorate in social anthropology from Oxford and has written on secrecy, India's Criminal Tribes, and contemporary vernacular politics in South Asia. She is currently leading a team research project on the cultures of democracy in South Asia and editing a volume on *Patronage in South Asia* (forthcoming).

JEEVAN R. SHARMA is a lecturer in South Asia and international development at the University of Edinburgh. His research interests include labor migration, social change, livelihoods, the state, political violence, and humanitarian and development issues in South Asia.

WILLEM VAN SCHENDEL is a professor of modern Asian history at the University of Amsterdam. He also heads the South Asia Department of the International Institute of Social History. Among his books are *The Bengal Borderland* (2005); *Illicit Flows and Criminal Things* (2005, coedited with I. Abraham); *A History of Bangladesh* (2009); and *The Bangladesh Reader* (Duke University Press, 2013, coedited with M. Guhathakurta). He invented the now much-used concept of Zomia in his paper "Geographies of Knowing, Geographies of Ignorance: Jumping Scale in Southeast Asia," *Environment and Planning D: Society and Space* 20 (2002): 647–68.

BIBLIOGRAPHY

Abraham, I., and W. van Schendel. 2005. "Introduction: The Making of Illicitness."
In W. van Schendel and I. Abraham, eds., *Illicit Flows and Criminal Things*, 1–37.
Bloomington: Indiana University Press.

Abrams, P. 1988. "Some Notes on the Difficulty of Studying the State." *Journal of
Historical Sociology* 1: 58–89.

Adelman, J., and S. Aron. 1999. "From Borderlands to Borders: Empires, Nation-
States, and the Peoples in between American History." *American Historical Review* 104, no. 3: 814–41.

Adhikari, D. 2007. "Red Army in the Dragon Kingdom." Naxal Resistance, July–
September 2009. Accessed 1 August 2012. naxalresistance.wordpress.com. Originally published in *Kantipur*.

Agamben, G. 1998. *Homo Sacer: Sovereign Power and Bare Life*. Translated by
D. Heller-Roazen. Palo Alto, CA: Stanford University Press.

———. 2005. *State of Exception*. Translated by K. Attell. Chicago: University of
Chicago Press.

Aggarwal, R. 2004. *Beyond Lines of Control: Performing Borders in Ladakh, India*.
Durham, NC: Duke University Press.

Aggarwal, R., and M. Bhan 2009. "'Disarming Violence': Development, Democracy
and Security on the Borders of India." *Journal of Asian Studies* 68, no. 2: 519–42.

Ahmed, I. 2006. "Bangladesh-India Relations: The Context of SAARC and the
Emerging Global Scenario." *Asian Affairs* 28, no. 2: 46–62.

———. 2007. "The Indo-Bangla SAARC Puzzle." *Himal Southasian*, March,
himalmag.com.

AHURA. *See* Association of Human Rights Activists.

Ali, S. M. 1993. *The Fearful State: Power, People and Internal War in South Asia*.
London: Zed Books.

Ammelina, A., D. D. Nergiz, T. Faist, and N. Glick Schiller, eds. 2012. *Beyond Methodological Nationalism: Research Methodologies for Cross-Border Studies*. New
York: Routledge.

Amnesty International. 1992. *Bhutan: Human Rights Violations against the Nepali-
speaking Population in the South*. London: Amnesty International.

Anderson, B. 1991. *Imagined Communities: Reflections on the Origin and Spread of Nationalism.* London: Verso.

Anisuzzaman, A. 2001. "The Identity Question and Politics." In R. Jahan, ed., *Bangladesh: Promise and Performance*, 45–56. Dhaka: Dhaka University Press.

Ao, A. M. 1970. *A Brief Historical Account of Nagaland.* Kohima, Nagaland: Naga Institute of Culture.

Ao, T. 2000. *These Hills Called Home: Stories from a War Zone.* New Delhi: Zubaan.

Appadurai, A., ed. 1986. *The Social Life of Things: Commodities in Cultural Perspective.* Cambridge: Cambridge University Press.

Arendt, H. 1968. *The Origins of Totalitarianism.* New York: Harcourt Brace.

Aretxaga, B. 1998. "What the Border Hides: Partition and the Gender Politics of Irish Nationalism." *Social Analysis* 42, no. 1: 16–32. Reprinted in J. Zulaika, ed., *States of Terror: Begona Aretxaga's Essays.* Reno, NV: University of Nevada, Center for Basque Studies.

Arnold, D. 1986. *Police Power and Colonial Rule: Madras, 1859–1947.* Delhi: Oxford University Press.

Asiwaju, A. I., and P. O. Adenyi, eds. 1989. *Borderlands in Africa.* Lagos: University of Lagos Press.

Association of Human Rights Activists (AHURA). 2000. *Bhutan: A Shangri-La without Human Rights.* Jhapa, Nepal: Association of Human Rights Activists, Bhutan.

Atkinson, E. T. 1881. *Gazetteer of the Himalayan Districts of the North Western Provinces of India.* Vol. 2. Allahabad: Oudh Press. Reprinted as *The Himalayan Gazetteer* (New Delhi: COSMO, 1973).

Bandopadhyaya, M. 1973. *Padma River Boatman.* Translated by B. Painter and Y. Lovelock. St. Lucia, Queensland: University of Queensland Press. Originally published as *Padma Nadir Majhi* (Calcutta: Granthalaya, 1934).

Banerjee, P. 2001. "Between Two Armed Patriarchies: Women in Assam and Nagaland." In R. Manchanda, ed., *Women, War and Peace in South Asia: Beyond Victimhood to Agency*, 131–76. Delhi: Sage.

Banerjee, P., and A. Basu Ray Chaudhury, eds. 2011. *Women in Indian Borderlands.* London: Sage.

Barpujari, H. K. 1992. *The Comprehensive History of Assam.* Vol. 2. Guwahati: Assam Publication Board.

Barth, F., ed. 1969. Introduction to *Ethnic Groups and Boundaries*, 1–38. Boston: Little, Brown.

Baruah, S. 1999. *India against Itself: Assam and the Politics of Nationality.* Philadelphia: University of Pennsylvania Press.

———. 2003a. "Nationalizing Space: Cosmetic Federalism and the Politics of Development in Northeast India." *Development and Change* 34, no. 5: 915–39.

———. 2003b. "Protective Discrimination and Crisis of Citizenship in North-East India." *Economic and Political Weekly* 38, no. 17: 1624–26.

——. 2004a. *Between South and Southeast Asia: Northeast India and the Look East Policy*. CENISEAS Papers 4. Guwahati: Centre for Northeast India, South and Southeast Asia Studies.

——. 2004b. "Citizens and Denizens: Ethnicity, Homelands and Crisis of Displacement in North East India." *Social Change and Development* 2, no. 1: 105–30.

——. 2005. *Durable Disorder: Understanding the Politics of Northeast India*. Delhi: Oxford University Press.

——, ed. 2009. *Beyond Counter-Insurgency: Breaking the Impasse in Northeast India*. Delhi: Oxford University Press.

Basaran, T. 2008. "Security, Law, Borders: Spaces of Exclusion." *International Political Sociology* 2: 339–54.

Bates, R. H. 1998. "Comment on 'Structure and Strategy in Ethnic Conflict' by Donald L. Horowitz." In B. Bleskovic and J. E. Stiglitz, eds., *Annual World Bank Conference on Development Economics*, 371–76. Washington, DC: World Bank.

Baud, M., and W. van Schendel. 1997. "Toward a Comparative History of Borderlands." *Journal of World History* 8, no. 2: 211–42.

Baylen, J. O. 1969. "W. T. Stead's 'Borderland: A Quarterly Review and Index of Psychic Phenomena,' 1893–97." *Victorian Periodicals Newsletter* 2, no. 1: 30–35.

Behera, N. 2000. *State, Identity and Violence: Jammu, Kashmir and Ladakh*. New Delhi: Manohar.

Bénéi, V. 2000. "Teaching Nationalism in Maharashtra Schools." In C. J. Fuller and V. Bénéi, eds., *The Everyday State and Society in Modern India*, 194–221. New Delhi: Social Science Press.

Bennett, L. 2006. *Unequal Citizens: Gender, Caste, and Ethnic Exclusion in Nepal*. Kathmandu: World Bank and DFID.

Berdahl, D. 1999. *Where the World Ended: Re-unification and Identity in the German Borderland*. Berkeley: University of California Press.

Berenschot, W. 2008. "Moneypower and Musclepower in a Gujarati Locality: On the Usefulness of *Goondas* in Indian Politics." *Amsterdam School for Social Science Research Working Paper* 8, no. 4: 1–16.

Berti, D., and G. Tarabout, eds. 2009. *Territory, Soil and Society in South Asia*. Delhi: Manohar.

Bhasin, A. S., ed. 1996. *India-Bangladesh Relations 1971–1994: Documents*. Vol. 2. Delhi: Siba Exim.

Bhattacharjee, J. B. 1997. "The Eastern Himalayan Trade of Assam in the Colonial Period." In S. Dutta, ed., *Studies in the History, Economy and Culture of Arunachal Pradesh*, 269–85. Itanagar, India: Himalayan.

——. 2002. "Cross-Country Trade of Arunachal Pradesh in Retrospect." In S. Dutta, ed., *Cross-Border Trade of North-East India*, 33–41. Gurgaon: Hope India.

Bhuyan, S. K. 1974. *Anglo-Assamese Relations, 1771–1826*. Gauhati, India: Lawyer's Book Stall.

Blackburn, S. 2007. "Oral Stories and Culture Areas: From Northeast India to South-west China." In E. de Maaker and V. Joshi, eds., "Northeast and Beyond: Region and Change." Special issue. *South Asia: Journal of South Asian Studies* 30, no. 3: 419–37.

Blaikie, P., J. Cameron, and D. Seddon. 1980. *Nepal in Crisis: Growth and Stagnation at the Periphery*. Delhi: Oxford University Press.

Bolton, H. E. [1921]. 1996. *The Spanish Borderlands: A Chronicle of Old Florida and the Southwest*. Albuquerque: University of New Mexico Press.

Borneman, M. 1997. "State, Territory and National Identity Formation in the Two Berlins, 1945–1995." In A. Gupta and J. Ferguson, eds., *Culture, Power, Place: Explorations in Critical Anthropology*, 93–117. Durham, NC: Duke University Press.

Bose, M. L. 1979. *Historical and Constitutional Documents of North-Eastern India: 1824–1973*. Delhi: Concept.

Boyd, T. P. 1922. *Borderland Experiences; Or, Do the Dead Return? A Study of Spirit States and Activities*. San Francisco: T. P. Boyd.

Brass, P. 1984. "National Power and Local Politics in India: A Twenty-Year Perspective." *Modern Asian Studies* 18, no. 1: 89–118.

———. 1997. *Theft of an Idol: Text and Context in the Representation of Collective Violence*. Princeton, NJ: Princeton University Press.

Bray, J., ed. 2005. *Ladakhi Histories: Local and Regional Perspectives*. Leiden: Brill.

Bruslé, T. 2010. "Who's in a Labour Camp? A Socio-economic Analysis of Nepalese Migrants in Qatar." *European Bulletin of Himalayan Research*, nos. 35–36: 154–170.

Burling, R. 2007. "Language Ethnicity and Migration in Northeast India." In E. de Maaker and V. Joshi, eds., "Northeast and Beyond: Region and Change." Special issue. *South Asia: Journal of South Asian Studies* 30, no. 3: 391–403.

Butalia, U. 1998. *The Other Side of Silence: Voices from the Partition of India*. New Delhi: Penguin.

———. 2003. "The Nowhere People." In J. Bagchi and S. Dasgupta, eds., *The Trauma and the Triumph: Gender and Partition in East India*, 113–22. Kolkata: Stree.

Butler, J., and G. C. Spivak. 2007. *Who Sings the Nation-State?* Kolkata: Seagull Books.

Campbell, B. 1997. "The Heavy Loads of Tamang Identity." In D. N. Gellner, J. Pfaff-Czarnecka, and J. Whelpton, eds., *Nationalism and Ethnicity in a Hindu Kingdom: The Politics of Culture in Contemporary Nepal*, 205–35. Amsterdam: Harwood.

CBS. 2007. *Rastriya Janganana, 2058: Jat/jatiko Jansankhya* [National Census 2001: Caste/Ethnic Breakdown]. Thapathali, Kathmandu: Central Bureau of Statistics. Accessed 16 May 2013. http://cbs.gov.np/.

Census Commissioner of India. 2011. *Census of India*. www.ecnsusindia.gov.in.

Chakrabarti, P. K. 1999. *The Marginal Men: The Refugees and the Left Political Syndrome in West Bengal*. Calcutta: Naya Udyog.

Chakrabarty, D. 1996. "Remembered Villages: Representation of Hindu-Bengali

Memories in the Aftermath of the Partition." *Economic and Political Weekly* 31, no. 32: 2143–51.

Chakravarti, P. C. 1971. *The Evolution of India's Northern Borders*. London: Asia Publishing House for the Indian Council of World Affairs.

Chasie, C. 1999. *Naga Imbroglio: A Personal Perspective*. Kohima, Nagaland: Standard.

Chatterjee, G. 2012. "How Not to Love Thy Minority in Pashchimbanga." *Daily Star* (Dhaka), 13 February. Accessed 13 February 2012. www.thedailystar.net/newDesign /news-details.php?nid=222132.

Chatterjee, N. 1990. "Interrogating Victimhood: East Bengali Refugee Narratives of Communal Violence." Department of Anthropology, University of North Carolina-Chapel Hill. Accessed 1 May 2012. http://www.swadhinata.org.uk/document /chatterjeeEastBengal%20Refugee.pdf.

Chatterjee, P. 2004. *The Politics of the Governed: Reflections on Popular Politics in Most of the World*. Delhi: Permanent Black.

Chatterjee, P., and P. Jeganathan, eds. 2000. *Subaltern Studies XI: Community, Gender, and Violence*. Delhi: Permanent Black.

Chatterji, B. 1981. "The Darogah and the Countryside: The Imposition of Police Control in Bengal and Its Impact (1793–1837)." *Indian Economic and Social History Review* 18, no. 1: 19–42.

Chatterji, J. 1994. *Bengal Divided: Hindu Communalism and Partition 1932–1947*. Cambridge: Cambridge University Press.

———. 1996. "The Bengali Muslim: A Contradiction in Terms? An Overview of the Debate on Bengali Muslim Identity." *Comparative Studies of South Asia, Africa, and the Middle East* 16, no. 2: 16–24.

———. 1999. "The Fashioning of a Frontier: The Radcliffe Line and Bengal's Border Landscape, 1947–52." *Modern Asian Studies* 33, no. 1: 185–242.

Chatterji, S. K. 1955. *The Place of Assam in the History and Civilization of India*. Gauhati, India: Gauhati University Press.

Chattopadhyay, B. 2000. *Crime and Control in Early Colonial Bengal, 1770–1860*. Calcutta: K. P. Bagchi.

Chaube, S. K. 1999. *Hill Politics in North East India*. Hyderabad: Orient Longman.

Clarence-Smith, W. G. 2010. "Editorial note—Zomia and Beyond." *Journal of Global History* 5: 185–86.

Coedès, G. 1968. *The Indianized States of Southeast Asia*. Edited by W. F. Vella. Translated by S. B. Cowing. Honolulu: East-West Center Press.

Cohn, B. 1987. "The Census, Social Structure, and Objectification in South Asia." In B. Cohn, ed., *An Anthropologist among the Historians and Other Essays*, 224–54. Delhi: Oxford University Press.

Collier, P. 1998. "The Political Economy of Ethnicity." In B. Bleskovic and J. E. Stiglitz, eds., *Annual World Bank Conference on Development Economics*, 387–99. Washington, DC: World Bank.

Cons, J. 2007. "The Tin Bigha Corridor 15 Years On: Official and Unofficial Views." *Forum: A Monthly Publication of the Daily Star,* October.

————. 2014. "The Fragments and Their Nation(s): Sensitive Space at the Indian-Bangladesh Border." Unpublished manuscript.

Corbridge, S., G. Williams, M. Srivastava, and R. Véron. 2005. *Seeing the State: Governance and Governmentality in India.* Cambridge: Cambridge University Press.

Curzon, G. 1907. *Frontiers.* The Romanes Lecture, delivered on 2 November 1907 at the Sheldonian Theatre, Oxford. en.wikisource.org/wiki/Frontiers.

Das, G. 1995. *Tribes of Arunachal Pradesh in Transition.* New Delhi: Vikas.

Das, S. K. 2007. "Conflict and Peace in India's Northeast: The Role of Civil Society." *Policy Studies* 42. Washington, DC: East-West Center.

Das, V. 2004. "The Signature of the State: The Paradox of Illegibility." In V. Das and D. Poole, eds., *Anthropology in the Margins of the State,* 225–52. Santa Fe: School of American Research Press.

Das, V., and D. Poole, eds. 2004. *Anthropology in the Margins of the State.* Santa Fe: School of American Research Press.

Das Gupta, J. 1988. "Ethnicity, Democracy and Development in India: Assam in a General Perspective." In A. Kohli, ed., *India's Democracy: An Analysis of Changing State-Society Relations,* 144–68. Princeton, NJ: Princeton University Press.

Dasgupta, A. 2001. "The Politics of Agitation and Confession: Displaced Bengalis in West Bengal." In S. K. Roy, ed., *Refugees and Human Rights,* 95–129. New Delhi: Rawat.

Desai, K. 2006. *The Inheritance of Loss.* London: Hamish Hamilton, Penguin.

Des Chene, M. K. 1991. "Relics of Empire: A Cultural History of the Gurkhas 1815–1987." PhD diss., Stanford University.

de Wilde, R. 2009. "Opium Poppy Husk Traders in Rajasthan: The Lives and Work of Businessmen in the Contemporary Indian Opium Industry." PhD diss., London School of Economics and Political Science.

Dhakal, D. N. S., and C. Strawn. 1994. *Bhutan: A Movement in Exile.* Jaipur: Nirala.

Diener, A., and J. Hagen, eds. 2010a. *Borderlines and Borderlands: Political Oddities at the Edge of the Nation-State.* New York: Rowman and Littlefield.

Diener, A., and J. Hagen. 2010b. "Conclusion: Borders in a Changing Global Context." In A. Diener and J. Hagen, eds., *Borderlines and Borderlands: Political Oddities at the Edge of the Nation-State,* 189–94. New York: Rowman and Littlefield.

Dixit, K. M. 2003. "The Myth-Making of Greater Nepal." In A. C. Sinha and T. B. Subba, eds., *The Nepalis in Northeast India: A Community in Search of Indian Identity,* 321–38. New Delhi: Indus.

Dolfuss, P., M. Lecomte-Tilouine, and O. Aubriot. 2001. "Un araire dans la tête: Réflexions sur la répartition géographique de l'outil en Himalaya." *Techniques and Culture* 37: 3–50.

Donnan, H., and T. M. Wilson. 1999. *Borders: Frontiers of Identity, Nation and State.* Oxford: Berg.

——. 2010. "Ethnography, Security and the 'Frontier Effect' in Borderlands." In H. Donnan and T. M. Wilson, eds., *Borderlands: Ethnographic Approaches to Security, Power, and Identity*, 1–20. Lanham, MD: University Press of America.

D'Souza, A. 2001. *Traditional Systems of Forest Conservation in North-East India: The Angami Tribe of Nagaland*. Guwahati, India: North-Eastern Social Research Centre.

Dube, S., ed. 2004. *Postcolonial Passages: Contemporary History Writing in India*. Delhi: Oxford University Press.

Dutta, P. C. 2003. *Tribal Chieftainship*. Itanagar, India: Himalayan.

Dutta, S., and B. N. Jha. 2002. "Historical Perspectives of the Cross-Country Trade through Tawang Route." In S. Dutta, ed., *Cross-Border Trade of North-East India*, 61–71. Gurgaon: Hope India.

Eaton, R. M. 1993. *The Rise of Islam and the Bengal Frontier, 1204–1760*. Berkeley: University of California Press.

——. 1997. "Comparative History as World History: Religious Conversion in Modern India." *Journal of World History* 8, no. 2: 243–71.

Eck, D. L. 1998. *Darsan: Seeing the Divine Image in India*. New York: Columbia University Press.

Elwin, V. [1957]. 1999. *A Philosophy for NEFA (Arunachal Pradesh)*. Itanagar, India: Directorate of Research, Government of Arunachal Pradesh.

——. 1961. *Nagaland*. Shillong, India: Research Department, Advisor's Secretariat.

Ethnographical Survey of India. 1909. *Anthropometric Data from the N.W. Borderland*. Calcutta.

Farrelly, N. 2010. "Spatial Control and Symbolic Politics at the Intersection of China, India and Burma." DPhil thesis, University of Oxford.

——. 2011. "One Observation, Ten Questions and Much to Ponder about the New Kachin War." *New Mandala*, 6 October. Accessed 28 May 2013. asiapacific.anu .edu.au/newmandala.

——. 2012. "3,000 Dead Burmese Soldiers?" *New Mandala*, 11 April. Accessed 28 May 2013. Asiapacific.anu.edu.au/newmandala.

Fernandes, W., and M. Pereira. 2005. *Changing Land Relations and Ethnic Conflicts: The Case of North-Eastern India*. Guwahati, India: North-Eastern Social Research Centre.

Foucault, M. 1991. "Governmentality." In G. Burchell, C. Gordon, and P. Miller, eds., *The Foucault Effect: Studies in Governmentality*, 87–105. Chicago: University of Chicago Press.

Franke, M. 2009. *War and Nationalism in South Asia: The Indian State and the Nagas*. Abingdon, UK: Routledge.

Freitag, S. B. 1991. "Crime in the Social Order of Colonial North India." *Modern Asian Studies* 25, no. 2: 227–61.

Friedman, L. 2005. *A Simplified Account of the Conflict in Nepal to December 2004*. Kathmandu: Shtrii Shakti.

Fuller, C., and V. Bénéï, eds. 2001. *The Everyday State in India.* London: Hurst.

Fürer-Haimendorf, C. von. 1982. *Highlanders of Arunachal Pradesh.* Delhi: Vikas.

Gaige, F. H. [1975]. 2009. *Regionalism and National Unity in Nepal.* Kathmandu: Social Science Baha.

Gait, E. A. [1905]. 1926. *A History of Assam.* Calcutta: Thacker, Spink.

Gangopadhyay, D. K. 1990. *Revenue Administration in Assam.* Dispur, Assam: Government of Assam.

Geertz, C. 1980. *Negara: The Theatre State in Nineteenth-Century Bali.* Princeton, NJ: Princeton University Press.

Gellner, D. N. 1991. "Hinduism, Tribalism, and the Position of Women: The Problem of Newar Identity." *Man,* n.s., 26, no. 1: 105–25. Reprinted in D. N. Gellner, *The Anthropology of Buddhism and Hinduism* (Delhi: Oxford University Press, 2001).

———. 2012. "Uncomfortable Antinomies: Going beyond Methodological Nationalism in Social and Cultural Anthropology." In A. Ammelina, D. D. Nergiz, T. Faist, and N. Glick Schiller, eds., *Beyond Methodological Nationalism: Research Methodologies for Cross-Border Studies,* 111–28. New York: Routledge.

———. 2013. "Warriors, Workers, Traders, and Peasants: The Nepali/Gorkhali Diaspora since the Nineteenth Century." In D. Washbrook and J. Chatterjee, eds., *Routledge Handbook of South Asian Diasporas,* 134–48. London: Routledge.

Ghosh, A. G. 1993. "Problem of the Integration of Coochbehar State with Indian Union." In N. R. Ray, ed., *Dimensions of National Integration: The Experiences and Lessons of Indian History,* 407–19. Calcutta: Punthi Pustak.

Ghosh, B. B. 1982. *History of Nagaland.* New Delhi: S. Chand.

Ghosh, G. 1998. "'God Is a Refugee': Nationalism, Morality and History in the 1947 Partition of India." *Social Analysis* 42, no. 1: 33–62.

Ghosh, P., D. K. Mishra, and V. Upadhyay. 2005. *Electoral Politics in Arunachal Pradesh: An Analysis of the 14th Loksabha Election.* Guwahati, India: Omeo Kumar Das Institute of Development Studies Project Report.

Gibson, L. J., and A. C. Renteria. 1985. *The U.S. and Mexico: Borderland Development and the National Economies.* Boulder, CO: Westview.

Giersch, C. P. 2006. *Asian Borderlands: The Transformation of Qing China's Yunnan Frontier.* Cambridge: Harvard University Press.

———. 2010. "Across Zomia with Merchants, Monks, and Musk: Process Geographies, Trade Networks, and the Inner-East–Southeast Asian Borderlands." *Journal of Global History* 5: 215–39.

Gillan, M. 2002. "Refugees or Infiltrators? The Bharatiya Janata Party and 'Illegal' Migration from Bangladesh." *Asian Studies Review* 26, no. 1: 73–95.

Glazier, E. G. 1873. *A Report of the District of Runpore.* Calcutta: Central Press.

Gordon, S. 1994. *Marathas, Marauders, and State Formation in Eighteenth-Century India.* Delhi: Oxford University Press.

Goswami, A. 2002. Introduction to A. Goswami, ed., *Traditional Self-governing Institutions among the Hill Tribes of North-east India,* 1–19. New Delhi: Akansha.

Goswami, M. 2004. *Producing India: From Colonial Economy to National Space.* Chicago: Chicago University Press.

Goswami, N. 2007. "The Naga Narrative of Conflict: Envisioning a Resolution Roadmap." *Strategic Analysis* 31, no. 2: 287–313.

———. 2008. "The Naga Rebel Groups: Narratives of Dissent." In P. Das and N. Goswami, eds., *India's Northeast: New Vistas for Peace*, 117–33. Delhi: Manas Publication and Institute for Defence Studies and Analysis.

Government of Arunachal Pradesh. 2006. *Arunachal Pradesh Human Development Report 2005.* Itanagar, India: Government of Arunachal Pradesh.

———. 2009. *Arunachal Pradesh Development Report.* Delhi: Academic.

Gravers, M. 2007. "Conversion and Identity: Religion and the Formation of Karen Ethnic Identity in Burma." In M. Gravers, ed., *Exploring Ethnic Diversity in Burma*, 227–58. Copenhagen: Nias Press.

Grist, N. 1998. "Local Politics in the Suru Valley of Northern India." PhD diss., Goldsmith's College, University of London.

Guha, A. 1991. *Medieval and Early Colonial Assam: Society, Polity, Economy.* Calcutta: K. P. Bagchi.

Guha, S. 1999. *Environment and Ethnicity in India, 1200–1991.* Cambridge: Cambridge University Press.

Guhathakurta, M. 2001. "Families, Displacement." *Transeuropéennes* 19, no. 20: 131–42.

Gundevia, Y. D. 1975. *War and Peace in Nagaland.* Dehradun, India: Palit and Palit.

Gupta, A. 1995. "Blurred Boundaries: The Discourse of Corruption, the Culture of Politics, and the Imagined State." *American Ethnologist* 22, no. 2: 375–402.

Gupta, H. 1967. *India-Pakistan War 1965.* Vols. 1 and 2. Delhi: Hariyana Prakashan.

Gupta, R. 2011. "Piety, Politics and Patriotism in Kargil, India." DPhil diss., University of Oxford.

Gutiérrez-Witt, L. 1990. "United States–Mexico Border Studies and *Borderline.*" *Mexican Studies/Estudios Mexicanos* 6, no. 1: 121–31.

Hall, D. G. E. 1955. *A History of Southeast Asia.* London: Macmillan.

Hansen, T. B. 2001. *Wages of Violence: Naming and Identity in Postcolonial Bombay.* Princeton, NJ: Princeton University Press.

Hansen, T. B., and F. Stepputat, eds. 2001. *States of Imagination: Ethnographic Explorations of the Postcolonial State.* Durham, NC: Duke University Press.

———, eds. 2005. *Sovereign Bodies: Citizens, Migrants, and States in the Postcolonial World.* Durham, NC: Duke University Press.

Harriss-White, B., D. K. Mishra, and V. Upadhyay. 2009. "Institutional Diversity and Capitalist Transition: The Political Economy of Agrarian Change in Arunachal Pradesh, India." *Journal of Agrarian Change* 9, no. 4: 512–47.

Harriss-White, B., A. Prakash, and D. Mishra. 2010. "Globalisation, Economic Citizenship and India's Developmentalism." Unpublished manuscript.

Hausner, S. L. 2005. *Migration, Trafficking and Prostitution in the Context of Nepal's Armed Conflict*. Kathmandu: Save the Children-USA.

———. 2007a. "Border Towns in the Tarai: Sites of Migration." In R. B. Chhetri and L. P. Uprety, eds., *Occasional Papers in Sociology and Anthropology 10*, 107–23. Kathmandu: Tribhuvan University, Central Department of Sociology and Anthropology.

———. 2007b. *Wandering with Sadhus: Ascetics in the Hindu Himalayas*. Bloomington: Indiana University Press.

Heine-Geldern, R. 1942. "Conceptions of State and Kingship in Southeast Asia." *Far Eastern Quarterly* 2, no. 1: 15–30.

Herzog, L. A. 1990. *Where North Meets South: Cities, Space, and Politics on the U.S.-Mexico Border*. Austin, TX: Center for Mexican American Studies.

Heyman, J. 1994. "The Mexico–United States Border in Anthropology: A Critique and Reformulation." *Journal of Political Ecology* 1: 43–66.

———. 1995. "Putting Power in the Anthropology of Bureaucracy: The Immigration and Naturalization Service at the Mexico–United States Border." *Current Anthropology* 36, no. 2: 261–87.

Hilaly, S. 2007. *The Railways in Assam, 1885–1947*. Varanasi, India: Pilgrims.

Himal. 2009. "Fresh Paradigms for Peace: Evolving a New Framework for Negotiations in North Southasia (Excerpts from the Eighth Panos-Himal Roundtable, 6–7 Oct 2009, in Salzburg)." *Himal South Asian*, December. Accessed 23 January 2010. www.himalmag.com.

Hinton, R. 1996. "Health in Transition: The Bhutanese Refugees." PhD diss., University of Cambridge.

Hitchcock, J. T. 1961. "A Nepalese Hill Village and Indian Employment." *Asian Survey* 1, no. 9: 15–20.

Hodgson, W. H. 1908. *The House on the Borderland*. London: Sphere.

Hodson, T. C. 1911. *The Naga Tribes of Manipur*. London: Macmillan.

Hoftun, M., W. Raeper, and J. Whelpton. 1999. *People, Politics, and Ideology: Democracy and Social Change in Nepal*. Kathmandu: Mandala Book Point.

Holdich, T. H. 1901. *The Indian Borderland, 1880–1900*. London: Methuen.

Horam, M. 1975. *Naga Polity*. Delhi: B. R. Publishing.

———. 1988. *Naga Insurgency: The Last Thirty Years*. New Delhi: Cosmo.

Horstmann, A. 2004. "Incorporation and Resistance: Borderlands, Transnational Communities and Social Change in Southeast Asia." Accessed 28 May 2013. www.transcomm.ox.ac.uk.

House, J. W. 1982. *Frontier on the Rio Grande: A Political Geography of Development and Social Deprivation*. Oxford: Clarendon.

HRW. 2003. *Trapped by Inequality: Bhutanese Refugee Women in Nepal*. New York: Human Rights Watch.

———. 2007. *Last Hope: The Need for Durable Solutions for Bhutanese Refugees in Nepal and India*. New York: Human Rights Watch.

HUROB. 1992. *Annual Report*. Kathmandu: Human Rights Organisation of Bhutan.

Hussanan, M. 2008. "Memory Is a Collective Ocean." *Himal South Asian*, June. Accessed 28 May 2013. www.himalmag.com.

Hutt, M. 1989. "A Hero or a Traitor? The Gurkha Soldier in Nepali Literature." *South Asia Research* 9, no. 1: 21–32.

———. 1993. "Refugees from Shangri-La." *Index on Censorship* 22, no. 4: 9–14.

———. 1997. "Being Nepali without Nepal: Reflections on a South Asian Diaspora." In D. N. Gellner, J. Pfaff-Czarnecka, and J. Whelpton, eds., *Nationalism and Ethnicity in a Hindu Kingdom*, 101–44. Amsterdam: Harwood.

———. 2003. *Unbecoming Citizens: Culture, Nationhood, and the Flight of Refugees from Bhutan*. Delhi: Oxford University Press.

———. 2005. "The Bhutanese Refugees: Between Verification, Repatriation and Royal Realpolitik." *Peace and Democracy in South Asia* 1: 44–56.

Hutton, J. H. 1921. *The Angami Naga*. London: Macmillan.

———. 1945. "Problems of Reconstruction in the Assam Hills." *Journal of the Royal Anthropological Institute* 65: 1–7.

———. 1965. "The Mixed Culture of the Naga Tribes." *Journal of the Royal Anthropological Institute of Great Britain and Ireland* 95, no. 1: 16–43.

Ibrahim, F. 2009. *Settlers, Saints and Sovereigns: An Ethnography of State Formation in Western India*. Delhi: Routledge.

International Organization for Migration (IOM). 2003. *The International Convention on the Protection of Rights for Migrant Workers and Members of their Families*. Washington, DC: IOM.

Iralu, K. 2000. *Nagaland and India: Blood and Tears*. Kohima, India: Self-published.

Ishii, H., D. N. Gellner, and K. Nawa, eds. 2007a. *Nepalis Inside and Outside Nepal*. Delhi: Manohar.

———. 2007b. *Political and Social Transformations in North India and Nepal*. Delhi: Manohar.

Ispahani, M. 1989. *Roads and Rivals: The Politics of Access in the Borderlands of Asia*. London: Tauris.

IWGIA. 1986. *The Naga Nation and Its Struggle against Genocide*. Document 56. Copenhagen: International Work Group for Indigenous Affairs.

Jacobs, J., A. Macfarlane, S. Harrison, and A. Herle. 1990. *The Nagas: Hill Peoples of Northeast India: Society, Culture and the Colonial Encounter*. London: Thames and Hudson.

Jacques, K. 2000. *Bangladesh, India and Pakistan: International Relations and Regional Tensions in South Asia*. New York: St. Martin's Press.

Jalais, A. 2005. "Dwelling on Morichjhanpi: When Tigers Became 'Citizens,' Refugees 'Tiger-Food.'" *Economic and Political Weekly*, 23 April, 1757–62.

———. 2010. *Forest of Tigers: People, Politics and Environment in the Sundarbans*. New Delhi: Routledge.

Jaleel, M. 1999. "It Was Not Our War." In R. Bedi et al., *Guns and Yellow Roses: Essays on the Kargil War*, 63–94. Delhi: HarperCollins.

Jamir, S. C. 2000. "Bedrock of Naga Society." Kohima: Nagaland Pradesh Congress Committee (I). Accessed 28 May 2013. http://www.nenanews.com/ng10.htm/.

Jamir, T., and D. Vasa. 2008. "Archaeology of Local Cultures: New Findings and Interpretations in Nagaland." In M. Oppitz, T. Kaiser, A. von Stockhausen, and M. Wettstein, eds., *Naga Identities: Changing Local Cultures in the Northeast of India*, 323–39. Gent, Belgium: Snoeck.

Jayal, N. G. 2013. *Citizenship and Its Discontents: An Indian History*. Cambridge, MA: Harvard University Press.

Jessop, B., N. Brenner, and M. Jones. 2008. "Theorizing Sociospatial Relations." *Environment and Planning D: Society and Space* 26: 389–401.

Jha, B. N. 1997. "Politics of Posa: A Case Study of Pre and Post Independence Scenario in Arunachal Pradesh and Assam." In *Proceedings of the Indian History Congress: 57th Session*. Kolkata: Indian History Congress.

Jha, P. 2007. "Open Border, Closed Minds." *Nepali Times*, 369. Accessed 28 May 2013. http://nepalitimes.com/news.php?id=14109#.UaSU_9gQPfo.

Jodha, N. S. 2001. *Life on the Edge: Sustaining Agriculture and Community Resources in Fragile Environments*. Delhi: Oxford University Press.

Jones, D. 2009. "Borderlands: Spiritualism and the Occult in *fin de siècle* and Edwardian Welsh and Irish Horror." *Irish Studies Review* 17, no. 1: 31–44.

Jones, R. 2009a. "Agents of Exception: Border Security and the Marginalization of Muslims in India." *Environment and Planning D: Society and Space* 27, no. 5: 879–97.

———. 2009b. "Sovereignty and Statelessness in the Border Enclaves of India and Bangladesh." *Political Geography* 28: 373–81.

———. 2010. "The Border Enclaves of India and Bangladesh: The Forgotten Lands." In A. Diener and J. Hagen, eds., *Borderlines and Borderlands: Political Oddities at the Edge of the Nation-State*, 15–32. New York: Rowman and Littlefield.

Jonsson, H. 2006. *Mien Relations: Mountain People and State Control in Thailand*. Chiang Mai, Thailand: Silkworm Books.

———. 2010. "Above and Beyond: *Zomia* and the Ethnographic Challenge of/for Regional History." *History and Anthropology* 21, no. 2: 191–212.

Joseph C., M. 1999. *Ethnic Conflict in Bhutan*. New Delhi: Nirala.

Joshi, M. P. 1990. *Uttaranchal Himalaya: An Essay in Historical Anthropology*. Almora, India: Almora Book Depot.

Joshi (as Patel), V. 1994. "Naga and Kuki: Who Is to Blame?" *Economic and Political Weekly* 29 (22–28 May): 1331–32.

Joshi, V. 2007. "The Birth of Christian Enthusiasm among the Angami in Nagaland." In E. de Maaker and V. Joshi, eds., "Northeast and Beyond: Region and Change." Special issue. *South Asia: Journal of South Asian Studies* 30, no. 3: 541–57.

———. 2008a. "The Naga: An Introduction." In R. Kunz and V. Joshi, eds., *Naga: A Forgotten Mountain Region Rediscovered*, 37–47. Basel: Christoph Merian Verlag and Museum der Kulturen Basel.

———. 2008b. "Pluralistic Beliefs: Christianity and Healing among the Angami Naga." In M. Oppitz et al., eds., *Naga Identities*, 393–402. Gent, Belgium: Snoeck.

———. 2012. *A Matter of Belief: Christian Conversion and Healing in Northeast India*. New York: Berghahn Books.

Kabui, G. K. 2004. *The History of the Zeliangrong Naga: From Makhel to Rani Gaidinliu*. Guwahati, India: Spectrum.

Kachin News Group. 2012. "Time for Thein Sein to Come Clean about Burmese Losses in Kachin State." *Kachin News Group*, 22 September. Accessed 28 May 2013. www.kachinnews.com/news/.

Kapila, K. 2008. "The Measure of a Tribe: The Cultural Politics of Constitutional Reclassification in North India." *Journal of the Royal Anthropological Institute* 14: 117–34.

Kearney, M. 1995. "The Local and the Global: The Anthropology of Globalization and Transnationalism." *Annual Review of Anthropology* 24: 547–65.

———. 2004. "The Classifying and Value-filtering Missions of Borders." *Anthropological Theory* 4, no. 2: 131–56.

Keay, J. 1983. *Where Men and Mountains Meet: The Explorers of the Western Himalayas, 1820–1875*. London: Century.

Keay, J. K. 2000. *The Great Arc: The Dramatic Tale of How India Was Mapped and Everest Was Named*. London: HarperCollins.

Khilnani, S. 1997. *The Idea of India*. London: Hamish Hamilton.

Kidd, C. 1993. *Subverting Scotland's Past*. Cambridge: Cambridge University Press.

Kirsch, T. A. 1973. *Feasting and Social Oscillation: Religion and Society in Upland Southeast Asia*. Ithaca, NY: Cornell University Press.

Kolff, D. H. A. 1990. *Naukar, Rajput and Sepoy: The Ethnohistory of the Military Labour Market in Hindustan, 1450–1850*. Cambridge: Cambridge University Press.

Krauskopff, G. 2003. "An 'Indigenous Minority' in a Border Area: Tharu Ethnic Associations, NGOs, and the Nepalese State." In D. N. Gellner, ed., *Resistance and the State: Nepalese Experiences*, 199–243. Delhi: Social Science Press.

Krishna, S. 1996. "Cartographic Anxiety: Mapping the Body Politic in India." In M. J. Shapiro and H. R. Alker, eds., *Challenging Boundaries: Global Flows, Territorial Identities*, 193–214. Minneapolis: University of Minnesota Press.

———. 2004. "Gender, Tribe and Political Participation: Control of Natural Resources in North-Eastern India." In S. Krishna, ed., *Livelihood and Gender: Equity in Community Resource Management*, 375–94. New Delhi: Sage.

Kudaisya, G. 1998. "Divided Landscape, Fragmented Identities: East Bengal Refugees and Their Rehabilitation in India, 1947–1979." In D. A. Low and H. Brasted, eds., *Freedom, Trauma, Continuities: Northern India and Independence*, 105–31. New Delhi: Sage.

Kumar, B. B. 2002. "Border Trade in Arunachal Pradesh: An Historical Perspective." In S. Dutta, ed., *Cross-Border Trade of North-East India*, 50–55. Gurgaon: Hope India.

Kumar, P. 2000. *The Uttarakhand Movement: Construction of a Regional Identity.* New Delhi: Kanishka.

Lamb, A. 1997. *Incomplete Partition: The Genesis of the Kashmir Dispute, 1947–1948.* Hertingfordbury, UK: Roxford Books.

Leach, E. R. 1954. *Political Systems of Highland Burma: A Study of Kachin Social Structure.* Cambridge, MA: Harvard University Press.

Lecomte-Tilouine, M. 2009. "Ruling Social Groups—From Species to Nations: Reflections on Changing Conceptions of Caste and Ethnicity in Nepal." In D. N. Gellner, ed., *Ethnic Activism and Civil Society in South Asia*, 291–336. Delhi: Sage.

Lehman, F. K. 1989. "Internal Inflationary Pressures in the Prestige Economy of the Feast of Merit Complex: The Chin and Kachin Cases from Upper Burma." In S. D. Russell, ed., *Ritual, Power, and Economy: Upland-Lowland Contrasts in Mainland Southeast Asia*, 89–102. DeKalb: Northern Illinois University, Center for Southeast Asian Studies, Monographs Series on Southeast Asia.

Li, T. M. 2001. "Relational Histories and the Production of Difference on Sulawesi's Upland Frontier." *Journal of Asian Studies* 60, no. 1: 41–66.

Lieberman, V. 2010. "A Zone of Refuge in Southeast Asia? Reconceptualizing Interior Spaces." *Journal of Global History* 5: 333–46.

Liechty, M. 2003. *Suitably Modern: Making Middle-Class Culture in a New Consumer Society.* Princeton, NJ: Princeton University Press.

Lintner, B. 1990. *Land of Jade: A Journey through Insurgent Burma.* Edinburgh: Kiscadale.

Longchar, P. 2002. *Historical Development of the Ao Naga in Nagaland.* Dimapur, India: Self-published.

Longkumer, A. 2007. "Religious and Economic Reform: The Gaidinliu Movement and the Heraka in North Cachar Hills." In E. de Maaker and V. Joshi, eds., "Northeast and Beyond: Region and Change." Special issue. *South Asia: Journal of South Asian Studies* 30, no. 3: 499–515.

———. 2009. "Exploring the Diversity of Religion: The Geo-political Dimensions of Fieldwork and Identity in the North East of India." *Fieldwork in Religion* 4, no. 1: 46–66.

———. 2010. *Reform, Identity, and Narratives of Belonging: The Heraka Movement in North East India.* London: Continuum.

Lotha, A. 2008. "Naga Identity: Enduring Heritage." In M. Oppitz et al., eds., *Naga Identities*, 47–56. Gent, Belgium: Snoeck.

Ludden, D. 2003. "The First Boundary of Bangladesh on Sylhet's Northern Frontiers." *Journal of the Asiatic Society of Bangladesh* 48, no. 1: 1–54. Short online version,

"Political Maps and Cultural Territories," in *Himal*, July 2003. www.himalmag .com.

Luen, M. I. 2009. *The Fire of Revival*. Secunderabad, India: Authentic Books, Biblica South Asia.

Luithui, L., and N. Haksar. 1984. *Nagaland File: A Question of Human Rights*. New Delhi: Lancer International.

Luthra, P. N. 1993. *Constitutional and Administrative Growth of the Arunachal Pradesh*. Itanagar, India: Directorate of Research, Government of Arunachal Pradesh.

Mabbett, I. W. 1977. "The 'Indianization' of Southeast Asia: Reflections on the Historical Sources." *Journal of Southeast Asian Studies* 8: 143–61.

MacDonald, K. 2006. "Memories of Tibet: Transnationalism, Transculturation and the Production of Cultural Ideology in Northern Pakistan." *India Review* 5, no. 2: 190–219.

Mackenzie, A. 1884. *A History of the Relations of the Government with the Hill Tribes of the North-East of Bengal*. Calcutta.

Malkki, L. 1997. "National Geographic: The Rooting of Peoples and the Territorialization of National Identity among Scholars and Refugees." In A. Gupta and J. Ferguson, eds., *Culture, Power, Place: Explorations in Critical Anthropology*, 52–74. Durham, NC: Duke University Press. Originally published in *Cultural Anthropology* 7, no. 1, 1992: 24–44.

Mallick, R. 1999. "Refugee Settlement in Forest Reserves: West Bengal Policy Reversal and the Marichjhapi Massacre." *Journal of Asian Studies* 58, no. 1: 104–25.

Mann, M. 1993. *The Sources of Social Power*, vol. 2: *The Rise of Classes and Nation-States, 1760–1914*. Cambridge: Cambridge University Press.

Markowitz, F. 2007. "Census and Sensibilities in Sarajevo." *Comparative Studies in Society and History* 49, no. 1: 40–73.

Martínez, O. J. 1994. *Border People: Life and Society in the U.S.-Mexico Borderlands*. Tucson: University of Arizona Press.

Mathur, N. 2010. "Paper Tiger? The Everyday Life of the State in the Indian Himalaya." PhD diss., University of Cambridge.

Maud, P. 1904. "Exploration in the Southern Borderland of Abyssinia." *Geographical Journal* 23, no. 5: 552–79.

Maxwell, N. 1970. *India's China War*. London: Jonathan Cape.

———. 1979. *India and the Nagas and the North-east*. London: Minority Rights Group Report 17.

Mayaram, S. 2003. *Against History, against State: Counterperspectives from the Margins*. New York: Columbia University Press.

McKinsey, L. S., and V. A. Konrad. 1989. *Borderlands Reflections: The United States and Canada*. Orono, ME: Borderlands Project.

Menon, R., and K. Bhasin. 1998. *Borders and Boundaries: Women in India's Partition*. New Delhi: Kali.

Mibang, T. 2002. "Ethnic Relations and Transborder Trade." In S. Dutta, ed., *Cross-Border Trade of North-East India*, 42–49. Gurgaon: Hope India.

Michael, B. 2007. "Land, Labour, Local Power and the Constitution of Agrarian Territories on the Anglo-Gorkha Frontier, 1700–1815." *International Quarterly for Asian Studies* 38, nos. 3–4: 309–28.

———. 2009. "Spatiality, Power, and Statemaking in Colonial South Asia: The Case of the Anglo-Gorkha Frontier, 1740–1816." In P. W. Kirby, ed., *Boundless Worlds: Social Dynamics of 'Space,' Power, and Movement*, 45–68. New York: Berghahn.

Michaud, J. 2009. "Handling Mountain Minorities in China, Vietnam and Laos: From History to Current Concerns." *Asian Ethnicity* 10, no. 1: 25–49.

———. 2010. "Editorial: Zomia and Beyond." *Journal of Global History* 5: 187–214.

Michelutti, L. 2008. *The Vernacularisation of Democracy: Politics, Caste and Religion in India*. London: Routledge.

Migdal, J. S. 1988. *Strong Societies and Weak States: State-Society Relations and State Capabilities in the Third World*. Princeton, NJ: Princeton University Press.

Ministry of Development of North Eastern Region and North Eastern Council. 2008. *North Eastern Region Vision 2020*. New Delhi: Government of India.

Mishra, A. K., and A. K. Thakur. 2004. "Transition in Arunachal Pradesh: Nocte Villages in Perspective." In T. Mibang and M. C. Behera, eds., *Tribal Villages in Arunachal Pradesh: Changing Human Interface*, 169–90. Delhi: Abhijeet.

Mishra, D. K. 2002. "Agrarian Structure and Labour-Use Patterns in Rural Arunachal Pradesh: A Case Study." *Arunachal University Research Journal* 5, no. 2: 31–56.

———. 2004. "Institutional Sustainability in Natural Resource Management: A Study of Arunachal Pradesh India." *Asian Profile* 32, no. 6: 583–94.

———. 2006. "Institutional Specificities and Agrarian Transformation in Arunachal Pradesh: Changing Realities and Emerging Challenges." *Indian Journal of Agricultural Economics* 61, no. 3: 314–27.

———. 2007. "Gender, Forests and Livelihoods: A Note on the Political Economy of Transition in North-East India." *Social Change* 37, no. 4: 65–90.

Mishra, D. K., and V. Upadhyay. 2007. "In the Name of the Community: Gender, Development and Governance in Arunachal Pradesh." In S. Krishna, ed., *Women's Livelihoods Rights: Recasting Citizenship for Development*, 167–206. New Delhi: Sage.

Mishra, S. N. 1983. "Arunachal's Tribal Economic Formation and Their Dissolution." *Economic and Political Weekly* 18, no. 43: 1837–46.

Mishra, T. P. 2010. "Rise of Red-army in the Last Shangri-La." Bhutan News Service, 23 March 2010. Accessed 14 September 2012. www.bhutannewsservice.com.

Misra, B. P. 1979. "Kirata Karyokinesis: Mode of Production in Tribal Communities of North East India." In A. N. Das and V. Nilakant, eds., *Agrarian Relations in India*, 51–81. Delhi: Manohar.

Mitchell, T. 1991. "The Limits of the State: Beyond Statist Approaches and Their Critics." *American Political Science Review* 85, no. 1: 77–96.

Mookherjee, N. 2006. "'Remembering to Forget': Public Secrecy and Memory of Sexual Violence in the Bangladesh War of 1971." *Journal of the Royal Anthropological Institute* 12, no. 2: 433–50.

Moore, D. 2005. *Suffering for Territory: Race, Place, and Power in Zimbabwe.* Durham, NC: Duke University Press.

Muggah, R. 2005. "Distinguishing Means and Ends: The Counterintuitive Effects of UNHCR's Community Development Approach in Nepal." *Journal of Refugee Studies* 18, no. 2: 151–64.

Murayama, M. 2006. "Borders, Migration and Sub-Regional Cooperation in Eastern South Asia." *Economic and Political Weekly*, April 8, 1351–59.

Murshid, T. M. 2001. "Nations Imagined and Fragmented: Bengal." In W. van Schendel and E. J. Zürcher, eds., *Identity Politics in Central Asia and the Muslim World*, 85–105. London: I. B. Tauris.

Nag, S. 2008. "Funding the Struggle: Political Economy of Insurgency." In P. Das and N. Goswami, eds., *India's North East: New Vistas for Peace*, 37–55. Delhi: Manas.

Nalven, J., ed. 1984. "Border Perspectives on the U.S./Mexico Relationship." Special issue. *New Scholar* 9, nos. 1–2. Santa Barbara: University of California Press.

Newman, D. 2006a. "Borders and Bordering: Towards an Interdisciplinary Dialogue." *European Journal of Social Theory* 9, no. 2: 171–86.

———. 2006b. "The Lines That Continue to Separate Us: Borders in Our 'Borderless' World." *Progress in Human Geography* 30, no. 2: 143–61.

Nibedon, N. [1978]. 1983. *Nagaland: The Night of the Guerillas.* New Delhi: Lancers.

———. 1981. *North East India: The Ethnic Explosion.* New Delhi: Lancers.

Nigam, S. 1990. "Disciplining and Policing the 'Criminals by Birth,' Part 2: The Development of a Disciplinary System, 1871–1900." *Indian Economic and Social History Review* 27, no. 3: 257–87.

Nuh, V. K., and W. Lasuh. 2002. *Naga Chronicle.* New Delhi: Regency, Indian Council of Social Science Research, North Eastern Regional Centre.

Paasi, A. 1999. "Boundaries as Social Processes: Territoriality in the World of Flows." In D. Newman, ed., *Boundaries, Territory and Postmodernity*, 69–88. London: Frank Cass.

———. 2011. "A *Border Theory*: An Unattainable Dream or a Realistic Aim for Border Scholars?" In D. Wastl-Walter, ed., *The Ashgate Research Companion to Border Studies*, 11–31. Farnham, UK: Ashgate.

Pahari, R. 2005. *Aniket: Janpad Chamoli Ank.* Dehradun, India: Valley Offset Press.

Pakrasi, K. B. 1971. *The Uprooted: A Sociological Study of the Refugees of West Bengal, India.* Calcutta: Editions Indian.

Pandey, B. B., D. K. Duarah, and N. Sarkar, eds. 1999. *Tribal Village Councils of*

Arunachal Pradesh. Itanagar, India: Directorate of Research, Government of Arunachal Pradesh.

Parmanand. 1998. *The Politics of Bhutan: Retrospect and Prospect*. Delhi: Pragati.

Parry, J. P. 1979. *Caste and Kinship in Kangra*. London: Routledge.

Peer, B. 2008. *Curfewed Night*. Noida, India: Random House.

Pemberton, B. R. 1835. *Report on the Eastern Frontier of British India*. Calcutta.

Peters, P. E. 1998. "Comment on 'The Political Economy of Ethnicity' by Paul Collier." In B. Bleskovic and J. E. Stiglitz, eds., *Annual World Bank Conference on Development Economics*, 400–405. Washington, DC: World Bank.

Pfaff-Czarnecka, J. 1995. "Migration under Marginality Conditions: The Case of Bajhang." In INFRAS and IDA, eds., *Rural-Urban Interlinkages: A Challenge for Swiss Development Cooperation*, 97–108. Zurich: INFRAS.

Phuntsho, K. 2006. "Bhutanese Reform, Nepalese Criticism." *Open Democracy*, 13 October. Accessed 28 May 2013. www.opendemocracy.net/democracy-protest /bhutan_nepal_3996.jsp.

Piliavsky, A. 2011a. "A Secret in the Oxford Sense: Theft and the Rhetoric of Mystification in Western India." *Comparative Studies in Society and History* 53, no. 2: 290–313.

———. 2011b. "Theft, Patronage and Society in Western India." DPhil diss., University of Oxford.

———. 2013. "The Moghia Menace, or the Watch over Watchmen in British India." *Modern Asian Studies*, 47, no. 3: 751–79.

Pittock, M. G. H. 2001. *Scottish Nationality*. Houndmills, UK: Palgrave.

Platts, J. T. 1884. *Dictionary of Urdu, Classical Hindi, and English*. London: W. H. Allen.

Pommaret, F. 1997a. "The Birth of a Nation." In F. Pommaret and C. Schicklgruber, eds., *Bhutan: Mountain Fortress of the Gods*, 179–207. London: Serindia.

———. 1997b. "Ethnic Mosaic: Peoples of Bhutan." In F. Pommaret and C. Schicklgruber, eds., *Bhutan: Mountain Fortress of the Gods*, 43–59. London: Serindia.

Portes, A. 2008. "Migration and Social Change: Some Conceptual Reflections." International Migration Institute, Oxford University. Accessed 28 May 2013. www.imi.ox.ac.uk/pdfs.

Powell, B., and M. Nair. 2010. "On the Governance of 'Not Being Governed.'" *Review of Austrian Economics* 25: 9–16.

Pradhan, R. 2002. "Ethnicity, Caste and a Pluralist Society." In K. Dixit and S. Ramachandran, eds. *State of Nepal*, 1–21. Patan, Nepal: Himal Books.

Price, P., and A. E. Raud, eds. 2010. *Power and Influence in India: Bosses, Lords and Captains*. Delhi: Routledge.

Radcliffe-Brown, A. R. 1940. Preface to M. Fortes and E. E. Evans-Pritchard, eds., *African Political Systems*, xi–xxiii. London: Oxford University Press.

Radhakrishna, M. 1992. "Surveillance and Settlements under the Criminal Tribes Act in Madras." *Indian Economic and Social History Review* 29, no. 2: 171–98.

———. 2001. *Dishonoured by History: "Criminal Tribes" and British Colonial Policy.* Hyderabad: Orient Longman.

Rahman, M. M., and W. van Schendel. 2003. "'I Am Not a Refugee': Rethinking Partition Migration." *Modern Asian Studies* 37, no. 3: 551–84.

Rajaram, P. K., and C. Grundy-Warr, eds. 2007. *Borderscapes: Hidden Geographies and Politics at Territory's Edge.* Minneapolis: University of Minnesota Press.

Ramachandran, S. 1999. "Of Boundaries and Border Crossings: Undocumented Bangladeshi 'Infiltrators' and the Hegemony of Hindu Nationalism in India." *Interventions* 1, no. 2: 235–53.

Ramble, C. 1997. "Tibetan Pride of Place; Or, Why Nepal's Bhotiyas Are Not an Ethnic Group." In D. Gellner, J. Pfaff-Czarnecka, and J. Whelpton, eds., *Nationalism and Ethnicity in a Hindu Kingdom: The Politics of Culture in Contemporary Nepal,* 379–413. Amsterdam: Harwood Academic.

Ramesh, J. 2005. "Northeast India in a New Asia." In *Gateway to the East: A Symposium on Northeast India and the Look East Policy, India Seminar* 550. Accessed 28 May 2013. www.india-seminar.com/2005/550/550%20jairam%20ramesh.htm.

Rammuny, M. 1988. *The World of the Naga.* New Delhi: Northern Book Centre.

Rangan, H. 2000. *Of Myths and Movements: Rewriting Chipko into Himalayan History.* London: Verso.

Rao, M. G. n.d. "Changing Contours in Federal Fiscal Arrangements in India." Hitotsubashi University Department of Economics. Accessed 28 May 2013. www.econ.hit-u.ac.jp/~kokyo/APPPsymp004/India.pdf.

Rao, M. G., and N. Singh. 2004. "Asymmetric Federalism in India." Working Paper 6. New Delhi: National Institute of Public Finance and Policy. Accessed 28 May 2013. www.nipfp.org.in/working_paper/wp04_nipfp_006.pdf.

Ray, H. 2005. "The Silk Route from Northeastern India to China and the Bay of Bengal: Some New Lights." In A. Barua, ed., *India's North-East: Developmental Issues in Historical Perspective,* 43–70. Delhi: Manohar.

Ray, M. 2001. "Growing Up Refugee: On Memory and Locality." *Hindi: Language, Discourse, Writing* 1, nos. 3–4: 148–98.

Regmi, M. C. 1978. *Thatched Huts and Stucco Palaces: Peasants and Landlords in 19th Century Nepal.* New Delhi: Vikas.

Riddi, A. 2004. "Understanding 'the Village' in Changing Situation: A Case of the Tagin Village." In T. Mibang and M. C. Behera, eds., *Tribal Villages in Arunachal Pradesh: Changing Human Interface,* 45–59. Delhi: Abhijeet.

Rizal, D. P., and Y. Yokota. 2006. *Understanding Development, Conflict and Violence: The Cases of Bhutan, Nepal, North-east India and the Chittagong Hill Tracts of Bangladesh.* New Delhi: Adroit.

Rizvi, J. 1996. *Ladakh: Crossroads of High Asia.* New Delhi: Oxford University Press.

———. 1999. *Trans-Himalayan Caravans: Merchant Princes and Peasant Traders in Ladakh.* New Delhi: Oxford University Press.

Robb, P. 1997. "The Colonial State and Constructions of Indian Identity: An Example on the Northeast Frontier in the 1880s." *Modern Asian Studies* 31, no. 2: 245–83.

Rose, L. 1977. *The Politics of Bhutan*. Ithaca, NY: Cornell University Press.

Rösler, M., and T. Wendl, eds. 1999. *Frontiers and Borderlands: Anthropological Perspectives*. Frankfurt am Main: Peter Lang.

Roy, B. 1994. *Some Trouble with Cows: Making Sense of Social Conflict*. Berkeley: University of California Press.

Roy Burman, B. K. 1968. "Perspective from Nagaland." *Institute for Defence Study and Analyses Journal* 1, nos. 1–2: 110–22.

Royal Government of Bhutan (RGB). 1992. *Anti-national Activities in Southern Bhutan: An Update on the Terrorist Movement*. Thimpu, Bhutan: Department of Information.

———. 1993. *The Southern Bhutan Problem: Threat to a Nation's Survival*. Thimpu, Bhutan: Ministry of Home Affairs.

———. 2007. *Poverty Analysis Report*. Thimpu, Bhutan: National Statistics Bureau. Accessed 28 May 2013. www.undp.org.bt.

Rustomji, N. 1983. *Imperilled Frontiers: India's Northeastern Borderlands*. Delhi: Oxford University Press.

Sachdeva, G. 2000. *Economy of the North-East: Policy, Present Conditions and Future Possibilities*. New Delhi: Centre for Policy Research, Konark.

Sadan, M. 2010. "Review of *The Art of Not Being Governed: An Anarchist History of Upland Southeast Asia*." Review 903. Reviews in History. Accessed 28 May 2013. www.history.ac.uk/reviews/review/903.

Saikia, Y. 2004. "Beyond the Archive of Silence: Narratives of Violence of the 1971 Liberation War of Bangladesh." *History Workshop Journal* 58: 275–87.

Sakhong, L. H. 2007. "Christianity and Chin Identity." In M. Gravers, ed., *Exploring Ethnic Diversity in Burma*, 200–26. Copenhagen: Nias Press.

Salam, M. A. 2007. *Agricultural Transformation in North-East India: With Special Reference to Arunachal Pradesh*. New Delhi: Mittal.

———. 2008. "Money, Market and Trade: Case of Lhou Village in Arunachal Pradesh." in A. K. J. R. Nayak and M. G. Jomon, eds., *India in the Emerging Global Order*, 301–14. New Delhi: Tata McGraw-Hill.

Samaddar, R. 1999. *The Marginal Nation: Transborder Migration from Bangladesh to West Bengal*. New Delhi: Sage.

Sandos, J. A. 1994. "From 'Boltonlands' to 'Weberlands': The Borderlands Enter American History." *American Quarterly* 46: 595–604.

Sanyü, V. 1996. *A History of Naga and Nagaland: Dynamics of Oral Tradition in Village Formation*. New Delhi: Commonwealth.

Sarma, A. 2005. "Why the North-eastern States Continue to Decelerate," *Man and Society* (spring): 1–20.

Sayer, D. 1994. "Everyday Forms of State Formation: Some Dissident Remarks on

'Hegemony.'" In G. M. Joseph and D. Nugent, eds., *Everyday Forms of State Formation: Revolution and the Negotiation of Rule in Modern Mexico*, 367–77. Durham, NC: Duke University Press.

Schicklgruber, C. 1997. Introduction to F. Pommaret and C. Schicklgruber, eds., *Bhutan: Mountain Fortress of the Gods*, 13–27. London: Serindia.

Scott, J. C. 1985. *Weapons of the Weak: Everyday Forms of Peasant Resistance*. New Haven, CT: Yale University Press.

———. 1998. *Seeing Like a State: How Certain Schemes to Improve the Human Condition Have Failed*. New Haven, CT: Yale University Press.

———. 2007. "Peasants, Power, and the Art of Resistance." In R. Snyder and G. L. Munck, eds., *Passion, Craft, and Method in Comparative Politics*, 351–91. Baltimore: Johns Hopkins University Press.

———. 2008. "Stilled to Silence at 500 Metres: Making Sense of Historical Change in Southeast Asia." *IIAS Newsletter* 49 (autumn): 12–13.

———. 2009. *The Art of Not Being Governed: An Anarchist History of Upland Southeast Asia*. New Haven, CT: Yale University Press.

Scott, W. 1998. *Rob Roy*. Edited by I. Duncan. Oxford World's Classics. Oxford: Oxford University Press.

Sebastian, K. O. 2002. "Trade Route of Pangsu Pass: Retrospect and Prospects." In S. Dutta, ed., *Cross-Border Trade of North-East India*, 80–92. Gurgaon: Hope India.

Seddon, D. 2005. "Nepal's Dependence on Exporting Labor." Washington, DC: Migration Policy Institute. Accessed 28 May 2013. www.migrationinformation .org/Profiles/display.cfm?id=277.

Seddon, D., J. Adhikari, and G. Gurung. 2002. "Foreign Labour Migration and the Remittance Economy of Nepal." *Critical Asian Studies* 34, no. 1: 19–40.

Seely, C. B. 2008. *Barisal and Beyond: Essays on Bangla Literature*. New Delhi: Chronicle Books.

Segura, D. A., and P. Zavella, eds. 2007. *Women and Migration in the U.S.-Mexico Borderlands: A Reader*. Durham, NC: Duke University Press.

Sema, H. 1986. *Emergence of Nagaland: Socio-economic and Political Transformation and the Future*. New Delhi: Vikas.

Sentsi, P. 2004. *Memoirs of a Naga Centenarian*. Guwahati, India: Spectrum.

Shah, A. 2010. *In the Shadows of the State: Indigenous Politics, Environmentalism, and Insurgency in Jharkand, India*. Durham, NC: Duke University Press.

Sharma, J. R. 2007. "Mobility, Pathology and Livelihoods: An Ethnography of Forms of Mobility in/from Nepal." PhD diss., University of Edinburgh.

———. 2008. "Practices of Male Labor Migration from the Hills of Nepal to India in Development Discourses: Which Pathology?" *Gender, Technology and Development* 12, no. 3: 303–23.

———. 2010. "On State Reconstruction in Nepal." *Economic and Political Weekly* 45, no. 4: 20–23.

Sharma, P. 2008. *Unravelling the Mosaic: Spatial Aspects of Ethnicity in Nepal.* Kathmandu: Social Science Baha, Himal Books.

Shaw, R., and C. Stewart. 1994. "Introduction: Problematizing Syncretism." In C. Stewart and R. Shaw, eds., *Syncretism/Anti-syncretism: The Politics of Religious Synthesis,* 1–26. London: Routledge.

Shimray, A. S. 2005. *Let Freedom Ring: Story of Naga Nationalism.* New Delhi: Promilla.

Shneiderman, S. 2010. "Are the Himalayas in Zomia? Some Scholarly and Political Considerations across Time." *Journal of Global History* 5: 289–312. Accessed 28 May 2013. http://journals.cambridge.org/repo_A78bnDUP.

Shneiderman, S., and M. Turin. 2006. "Seeking the Tribe: Ethno-politics in Sikkim and Darjeeling." *Himal South Asian* 19, no. 2: 54–58. www.himalmag.com.

Shrestha, B. N. 2011. "Border Fences, Walls and Identity of Nepal." Border Nepal Buddhi, 25 May 2011. Accessed 21 September 2011. bordernepal.wordpress.com /2011/05/25/border-fences-walls-and-identities-of-nepal/.

Sikar, R. K. 1982. "Marichjhapi Massacre." *Oppressed Indian* 4, no. 4: 21–23.

Sikdar, S. 1982. "Tribalism vs. Colonialism: British Capitalistic Intervention and Transformation of Primitive Economy of Arunachal Pradesh in the Nineteenth Century." *Social Scientist* 10, no. 12: 15–31.

———. 1997. "Cross-Country Trade in the Making of British Policy towards Arunachalis in the Nineteenth Century." In S. Dutta, ed., *Studies in the History, Economy and Culture of Arunachal Pradesh,* 313–25. Itanagar, India: Himalayan.

Simmel, G. [1909]. 1994. "Bridge and Door." Translated by M. Ritter. *Theory, Culture and Society* 11: 5–10.

Simpson, J., and E. Weiner, eds. 1989. *The Oxford English Dictionary.* Oxford: Oxford University Press.

Singh, P. [1972]. 1995. *Nagaland.* New Delhi: National Book Trust.

Singh, P. M. 2006. "Remittance Economy: Nepal's Evolution towards Accepting and Incorporating the Labour of Its Overseas Workers." *Himal South Asian* 18, no. 5: 73–77.

Singh, R. 1988. *Land, Power and People: Rural Elite in Transition, 1801–1970.* Delhi: Sage.

Singha, R. 1993. "'Providential Circumstances': The Thuggee Campaign of the 1830s and Legal Innovation." *Modern Asian Studies* 27, no. 1: 83–146.

———. 1998. *A Despotism of Law: Crime and Justice in Early Colonial India.* Delhi: Oxford University Press.

Sinha, A. C. 2001. *Himalayan Kingdom Bhutan: Tradition, Transition and Transformation.* New Delhi: Indus.

Sinha, S. 1962. "State Formation and Rajput Myth in Central India." *Man in India* 42, no. 1: 35–80.

Skaria, A. 1999. *Hybrid Histories: Forests, Frontiers and Wildness in Western India.* Delhi: Oxford University Press.

Smith, A. D. 1984. "National Identity and Myths of Ethnic Descent." *Research in Social Movements, Conflicts and Change* 7: 95–130.

———. [1994]. 1998. "The Politics of Culture: Ethnicity and Nationalism." In T. Ingold, ed., *Companion Encyclopaedia of Anthropology: Humanity, Culture and Social Life*, 706–33. London: Routledge.

Sneath, D., M. Holbraad, and M. A. Pedersen. 2009. "Technologies of the Imagination: An Introduction." *Ethnos* 74, no. 1: 5–30.

Sökefeld, M. 1997. "*Jang azadi*: Perspectives on a Major Theme in Northern Areas' History." In I. Stellrecht, ed., *The Past in the Present: Horizons of Remembering in the Pakistan Himalaya*, 61–82. Köln, Germany: Köppe.

Spencer, J. 2007. *Anthropology, Politics and the State: Democracy and Violence in South Asia*. Cambridge: Cambridge University Press.

Stiller, L. F. 1976. *The Silent Cry: The People of Nepal, 1816–1839*. Kathmandu: Sahayogi.

Stoddard, E. R., R. L. Nostrand, and J. P. West, eds. 1983. *Borderlands Sourcebook: A Guide to the Literature on Northern Mexico and the American Southwest*. Norman: University of Oklahoma Press.

Stokes, E. 1978. *The Peasant and the Raj: Studies in Agrarian Society and Peasant Rebellion*. Cambridge: Cambridge University Press.

Strawn, C. 1994. "The Dissidents." In M. Hutt, ed., *Bhutan: Perspectives on Conflict and Dissent*, 97–128. Gartmore, Scotland: Kiscadale Asia Research Series.

Stringham, E. P., and C. J. Miles. 2012. "Repelling States: Evidence from Upland Southeast Asia." *Review of Austrian Economics* 25, no. 1: 17–33.

Sturgeon, J. C. 1997. "Claiming and Naming Resources on the Border of the State: Akha Strategies in China and Thailand." *Asia Pacific Viewpoint* 38, no. 2: 131–44.

———. 2004. "Border Practices, Boundaries, and the Control of Resource Access: A Case from China, Thailand and Burma." *Development and Change* 35, no. 3: 463–84.

———. 2005. *Border Landscapes: The Politics of Akha Land Use in China and Thailand*. Seattle: University of Washington Press.

Tambiah, S. J. [1977]. 1985. "The Galactic Polity: The Structure of Traditional Kingdoms in Southeast Asia." In S. J. Tambiah, ed., *Culture, Thought, and Social Action*, 252–86. Cambridge: Harvard University Press.

Tapp, N. 2010. "Review of *The Art of Not Being Governed* by James C. Scott." *ASEASUK* 47 (spring): 11–15.

Tarlo, E. 2003. *Unsettling Memories: Narratives of the Emergency in Delhi*. London: Hurst.

Thakur, S. 1999. "Journeys without Maps." In R. Bedi et al., *Guns and Yellow Roses: Essays on the Kargil War*, 1–34. Delhi: HarperCollins.

Thapa, D., ed. 2003. *Understanding the Maoist Movement of Nepal*. Kathmandu: Martin Chautari and Centre for Social Research and Development.

Thinley, J. Y. 1994. "Bhutan: A Kingdom Besieged." In M. Hutt, ed., *Bhutan:*

Perspectives on Conflict and Dissent, 43–76. Gartmore, Scotland: Kiscadale Asia Research Series.

Thomas, D. H., ed. 1989–91. *Columbian Consequences*. 3 vols. Washington, DC: Smithsonian Institution Press.

———. 1991. *Spanish Borderlands Source Books*. 27 vols. New York: Garland.

Torpey, J. C. 2007. *The Invention of the Passport: Surveillance, Citizenship and the State*. Cambridge: Cambridge University Press.

Trouillot, M.-R. 2001. "The Anthropology of the State in the Age of Globalization: Close Encounters of the Deceptive Kind." *Current Anthropology* 42, no. 1: 125–38.

Tsing, A. L. 1993. *In the Realm of the Diamond Queen: Marginality in an Out of the Way Place*. Princeton, NJ: Princeton University Press.

———. 1994. "Further Inflections: Towards Ethnographies of the Future." *Cultural Anthropology* 9, no. 3: 279–97.

Turner, F. J. [1893]. 1920. "The Significance of the Frontier in American History." In *Proceedings of the State Historical Society of Wisconsin 14 December*. New York: H. Holt.

Turner, V. 1995. *The Ritual Process: Structure and Anti-structure*. New York: Aldine de Gruyter.

Uberoi, J. P. S. 1978. "The Structural Concept of the Asian Frontier." In D. Chatto-padhyaya, ed., *History and Society: Essays in Honour of Professor Nilanjan Ray*, 67–76. Calcutta: K. P Bagchi.

Valk, B. G., and A. M. Cobos. 1988. *Borderline: A Bibliography of the United States-Mexico Borderlands*. Los Angeles: UCLA Latin American Center Publications.

Van Beek, M. 1996. "Identity Fetishism and the Art of Representation." PhD diss., Cornell University.

———. 2001. "Public Secrets, Conscious Amnesia, and the Celebration of Autonomy for Ladakh." In T. B. Hansen and F. Stepputat, eds., *States of Imagination: Ethnographic Explorations of the Postcolonial State*, 365–90. Durham, NC: Duke University Press.

Van Driem, G. 1994. "Language Policy in Bhutan." In M. Aris and M. Hutt, eds., *Bhutan: Aspects of Culture and Development*, 87–106. Gartmore, Scotland: Kiscadale.

Van Schendel, W. 1992. "The Invention of the 'Jummas': State Formation and Ethnicity in Southeastern Bangladesh." *Modern Asian Studies* 26, no. 1: 95–128.

———. 1993. "Easy Come, Easy Go: Smugglers on the Ganges." *Journal of Contemporary Asia* 23, no. 2: 189–213.

———. 2001. "Working through Partition: Making a Living in the Bengal Borderlands." *International Review of Social History* 46: 393–421.

———. 2002a. "Geographies of Knowing, Geographies of Ignorance: Jumping Scale in Southeast Asia." *Environment and Planning D: Society and Space* 20: 647–68.

———. 2002b. "Stateless in South Asia: The Making of the India-Bangladesh Enclaves." *Journal of Asian Studies* 61, no. 1: 115–47.

———. 2005a. *The Bengal Borderland: Beyond State and Nation in South Asia.* London: Anthem.

———. 2005b. "Spaces of Engagement: How Borderlands, Illegal Flows, and Territorial States Interlock." In W. van Schendel and I. Abraham, eds., *Illicit Flows and Criminal Things: States, Borders, and the Other Side of Globalization*, 38–68. Bloomington: Indiana University Press.

———. 2007. "The Wagah Syndrome: Territorial Roots of Contemporary Violence in South Asia." In A. Basu and S. Roy, eds., *Violence and Democracy in India*, 36–82. London: Berg.

———. 2009. *A History of Bangladesh.* New York: Cambridge University Press.

Van Schendel, W., and I. Abraham, eds. 2005. *Illicit Flows and Criminal Things: States, Borders, and the Other Side of Globalization.* Bloomington: Indiana University Press.

Vas, J. A. 1911. *Eastern Bengal and Assam District Gazetteers: Rangpur.* Alahabad, India: Pioneer Press.

Vashum, R. 2000. *Nagas' Right to Self-determination.* New Delhi: Mittal.

Walker, A. 1999. *Legend of the Golden Boat: Regulation, Trade and Traders in the Borderlands of Laos, Thailand, China and Burma.* Honolulu: University of Hawai'i Press.

Walton, H. G. [1910]. 1989. *A Gazetteer of the Garhwal Himalaya.* Dehradun, India: Natraj Publishers.

Wastl-Walter, D., ed. 2011. *The Ashgate Research Companion to Border Studies.* Farnham, UK: Ashgate.

Weber, D. J. 1986. "Turner, the Boltonians, and the Borderlands." *American Historical Review* 91, no. 1: 66–81.

Weiner, M. 1985. "Transborder Peoples." In W. Conner, ed., *Mexican Americans in Comparative Perspective*, 130–58. Washington, D.C.: Urban Institute.

West, A. 1999. "The Most Dangerous Legacy: The Development of Identity, Power and Marginality in the British Transfer to India and the Naga." Occasional Paper 34. Hull, UK: University of Hull, Centre for South-East Asian Studies.

WFP and UNHCR. 2008. *Joint Assessment Mission Report: Assistance to the Bhutanese Refugees in Nepal (09-20 June 2008).* Accessed 28 May 2013. documents.wfp.org.

Whelpton, J. 2005. *A History of Nepal.* Cambridge: Cambridge University Press.

Whitecross, R. W. 2009. "Intimacy, Loyalty and State Formation: The Spectre of the 'Anti-National.'" In S. Thiranagama and T. Kelly, eds., *Traitors: Suspicion, Intimacy and the Ethics of State-Building*, 68–88. Philadelphia: University of Pennsylvania Press.

Whyte, B. 2002. *Waiting for the Esquimo: An Historical and Documentary Study of the Cooch Behar Enclaves of India and Bangladesh.* Melbourne: University of Melbourne School of Anthropology, Geography, and Environmental Studies.

Wilson, T., and H. Donnan, eds. 1998a. *Border Identities: Nation and State at International Frontiers.* Cambridge: Cambridge University Press

———. 1998b. "Nation, State and Identity at International Borders." In T. Wilson and H. Donnan, eds., *Border Identities: Nation and State at International Frontiers*, 1–30. Cambridge: Cambridge University Press.

———. 2012a. "Borders and Border Studies." In T. Wilson and H. Donnan, eds., *A Companion to Border Studies*, 1–25. Chichester, UK: Wiley-Blackwell.

———, eds. 2012b. *A Companion to Border Studies*. Chichester, UK: Wiley-Blackwell.

Windling, T., ed. 1986. *Borderland*. New York: New American Library.

Winichakul, T. 1994. *Siam Mapped: A History of the Geo-Body of a Nation*. Honolulu: University of Hawai'i Press.

Wink, A. 1986. *Land and Sovereignty in India: Agrarian Society and Politics under the Eighteenth-century Maratha Svarajya*. Cambridge: Cambridge University Press.

Wood, A. G., ed. 2009. *The Borderlands: An Encyclopedia of Culture and Politics on the U.S.-Mexico Divide*. Westport, CT: Greenwood.

Woodman, D. 1969. *Himalayan Frontiers: A Political Review of British, Chinese, Indian and Russian Rivalries*. London: Barrie and Rockliff, Cresset Press.

Woodward, R. M. 1989. "Economy, Polity and Cosmology in the Ao Naga Mithun Feast." In S. D. Russell, ed., *Ritual, Power, and Economy: Upland-Lowland Contrasts in Mainland Southeast Asia*, 121–42. DeKalb: Northern Illinois University, Center for Southeast Asian Studies, Monographs Series on Southeast Asia.

Wouters, J. 2011. "'Keeping the Hill Tribes at Bay': A Critique from India's Northeast of James C. Scott's Paradigm of State Evasion." *European Bulletin of Himalayan Research* 39: 41–65.

Yonuo, A. 1974. *The Rising Naga: A Historical and Political Study*. Delhi: Vivek.

Zaman, N. 1999. *A Divided Legacy: The Partition in Selected Novels of India, Pakistan and Bangladesh*. Dhaka: Dhaka University Press.

Zartman, I. W., ed. 2010. *Understanding Life in the Borderland: Boundaries in Depth and in Motion*. Athens: University of Georgia Press.

Zeppa, J. 1999. *Beyond the Sky and the Earth: A Journey into Bhutan*. New York: Riverhead Books.

Zurick, D., and P. P. Karan. 1999. *Himalaya: Life on the Edge of the World*. Baltimore: Johns Hopkins University Press.

INDEX

Page numbers followed by f indicate illustrations.